AMBIGUOUS BORDERLANDS

AMBIGUOUS BORDERLANDS

SHADOW IMAGERY IN COLD WAR AMERICAN CULTURE

ERIK MORTENSON

Southern Illinois University Press
Carbondale

Chapter 4 contains portions of a previously published article, "The Ghost of Humanism: Rethinking the Subjective Turn in Postwar American Photography," *History of Photography* 38.4 (2014): 418–34. http://www.tandfonline.com.

Chapter 6 contains portions of a previously published article, "A Journey into the Shadows: *The Twilight Zone*'s Visual Critique of the Cold War," *Science Fiction Film and Television* 7.1 (2014): 55–76.

Printed in the United States of America

19 18 17 16 4 3 2 1

Cover illustration: shadow of a dancer suggesting that even in the arts, the presence of Communist subversives, or Americans with Communist ties, was inescapable. From Communist Blueprint for Conquest (US Department of the Army, 1956), 16-millimeter black-and-white print, Fort Devens Collection, Harvard Film Archive, Harvard Library.

Library of Congress Cataloging-in-Publication Data

Mortenson, Erik, 1970–

Ambiguous borderlands : shadow imagery in Cold War American culture / Erik Mortenson.

pages cm

Summary: "This book examines shadow imagery in postwar literature, television, film, photography, and popular culture"— Provided by publisher.

Includes bibliographical references and index.

ISBN 978-0-8093-3432-2 (paperback) — ISBN 978-0-8093-3433-9 (e-book)

1. American literature—20th century—History and criticism. 2. Metaphor in literature. 3. Cold War in literature. 4. Cold War in motion pictures. 5. Cold War—Social aspects—United States. 6. Politics and culture—United States—History—20th century. 7. Cold War—Influence. 8. United States—Civilization—1945– 9. Popular culture—United States—History—20th century. I. Title.

PS374.C57M67 2016

813'.5093581—dc23 2015025806

Printed on recycled paper. ♻

To Barrett Watten, teacher, mentor, friend

Shadows present, foreshadowing deeper shadows to come.
—Herman Melville, from his novella of a slave
rebellion, "Benito Cereno" (1856)

Freedom is pitted against slavery; lightness against the dark.
—President Dwight D. Eisenhower, discussing America's
fight against Communism in his 1953 inaugural speech

The shadow of a shadow is the ghost of a bomb.
—Recording artist Beck, from the song "Motorcade"
on his album *The Information* (2006)

CONTENTS

FIGURES

ACKNOWLEDGMENTS

The completion of this book would not have been possible without the support of a myriad of people, and I would like to take the time to thank them here.

Parts of this manuscript were published previously. A section of chapter 4 appeared in *History of Photography*, and I thank the editors of that journal for allowing its use here and for supplying the editorial work of Luke Gartlan, who was extremely helpful in providing feedback. A portion of chapter 6 first appeared in the journal *Science Fiction Film and Television*, and I thank its editor, Sherryl Vint, for her willingness to allow me to use it here and for her very useful comments on the work.

Thanks are due to the executor of the Jack Kerouac estate, John Sampas, for his permission to quote from Kerouac's archived materials and to the always helpful Peter Hale at the Ginsberg Trust, who came through again when acquiring Ginsberg's copyrights. Don Marcus gave permission to use Edwin Marcus's cartoons, and Alex Matter gave permission to use Herbert Matter's *Atomic Head.* Sarah Greenough and curatorial assistant Maryanna G. Ramirez were extremely helpful in tracking down rights holders for several of the photographic images in this book, as was William Harris in his assistance in acquiring the rights to Amiri Baraka's poem "In Memory of Radio."

Koç University was kind enough to make available the time and the funding for me to spend two summers at Harvard University and another summer at the Harry Ransom Center at the University of Texas at Austin.

I am grateful to Visual Resources librarian William Connor and to the helpful staff of Harvard University's Fine Arts Library. I would like to acknowledge and thank those at the Harvard Film Archive for capturing several images and providing documentation for them. The staff at the Harry Ransom Center likewise deserve praise for their professionalism and supportive work, especially Jullianne Ballou, who was kind enough to track down material impossible to find in Istanbul. I appreciate my previous dean, Sami Gülgöz, and my present dean, Ahmet Içduygu, for their support of my research and for making such research trips possible.

Without the advice of colleagues, this work could not have been finished. Robert Burgoyne was kind enough to read several chapters at an early stage and offered much-needed support and encouragement, for which I am grateful. I thank Barrett Watten for bringing the work of Ralph Eugene Meatyard to my attention and for his support over the years. John Drabble offered encouragement and the chance to present my work at an early stage. Tom Gunning was generous enough to listen to my description of the project and to offer helpful advice and articles. Mary Sherman helped me to track down various shadow images. Isaac Gewirtz, curator of the Berg Collection at the New York Public Library, was kind enough to share his knowledge of the Kerouac archives and his work with me. The manuscript, especially its third chapter, benefited tremendously by the comments of three great Beat scholars—Tony Trigilio offered invaluable assistance with the Ginsberg section, while Tim Hunt and Matt Theado provided helpful feedback on my discussion of Kerouac. Such colleagues make it a delight to be part of the Beat studies field, and I thank all three of them for their kindness and willingness to engage in meaningful and interesting discussion.

I owe a huge debt of gratitude to my editor, Karl Kageff, who piloted my first book as well as this one through the sometimes stormy seas of academic publishing and continues to be a source of support and advice. Karl is a wonderful editor, and our discussions were always positive and fruitful. The entire Southern Illinois University Press staff were helpful and considerate and made publishing both my books a pleasure, and I thank them for their generous support throughout this project. Kurt Hemmer, an extremely knowledgeable Beat and postwar scholar, and another unknown reader at Southern Illinois University Press offered valuable feedback on the manuscript, and I thank them both heartily.

Last, but certainly not least, this project would not have been possible without the kind support of friends and family. I am grateful for my longtime friends Mark Huston and Christopher Kramer for lending an ear to my sometimes-disconnected ramblings as I discussed this project (and other things) over the years. I owe a debt to two of my Turkish friends, Teoman Türeli and Sinan Ünver, Jungians both. Teoman pointed out at an early stage the similarities between Carl Jung's and Jack Kerouac's dreams of the Shrouded Stranger, which helped shape my thinking on the project. I especially want to thank Sinan, not only for our fruitful discussion of Jungian shadows but also for his willingness to listen to my late-night thoughts as I unburdened myself of the ups and downs that accompany any long-term writing project. Abigail Malin provided feedback on chapter 3, and Gordon Marshall was kind enough to read and respond to my second chapter. I also thank my wife, Lia McCoskey, for her innumerable revisions over the course of the project that were crucial to the success of the book and for her constant love and support. Finally, my thanks go out to my parents, who have always been there for me.

Any errors in the text, of course, remain my own.

AMBIGUOUS BORDERLANDS

INTRODUCTION

Shadows and Their Place in Postwar America

On July 16, 1945, theoretical physicist J. Robert Oppenheimer described the first atomic detonation in terms of light, famously comparing the blast to the "radiance of a thousand suns." His response to the unprecedented intensity of the detonation was not unique—accounts inevitably employed metaphor and hyperbole in a vain attempt to convey the brightness of the event. William Laurence, the sole reporter allowed access to the site, claimed he felt as though he were "present at the moment of creation when God said 'let there be light'" (qtd. in Masco 59–60).[1] Such fascination led to what critics have called the "nuclear sublime." Americans were in awe of the bomb's immense destructive potential, and the power of the detonation reinforced American pride in an unprecedentedly optimistic time in American culture. The atomic bomb and the mushroom cloud thus became symbols of American technological strength and superiority as the United States assumed the role of leader of the free world.

But the initial fixation on the brilliance of the blast gave way to a more disturbed reaction as accounts of the bomb's destruction circulated. Images of piercing light were replaced by a darkness that became linked to an encroaching Soviet threat, and the possible apocalypse that a showdown with America's nemesis could unleash obscured an otherwise bright American future. One source of this anxiety came from the discovery of shadow images of bomb victims "burnt" onto streets and walls. John Hersey's description of these shadow effects first appeared in the *New Yorker* (August 31, 1946) before being widely distributed a year later in the book *Hiroshima*. Such uncanny reminders of the bomb's awesome power quickly became a myth that infiltrated the American unconscious. Ray Bradbury used the image in his short story "There Will Come Soft Rains" (1950), where a child's ball is captured in midflight, along with the silhouettes of a family burned onto the side of their house after a nuclear attack. Darkened shadows, as well as brilliant light, would continue to invoke a nuclear sublime throughout the Cold War. Only three years before the Berlin Wall fell, Alan Moore and Dave Gibbons, in their graphic novel *Watchmen*, used the silhouette of two lovers spray-painted onto the walls of a city to evoke the threat of World War III, with the aptly named Rorschach commenting, "It reminded me of the people disintegrated at Hiroshima, leaving only their indelible shadows" (VI, 16).[2] The symbolic struggle between light and dark, played out in both public rhetoric and popular culture, would come to characterize the Cold War and leave a legacy that continues into today.

The forces of light and dark converged in the figure of the shadow—an image that would become inextricably linked with the period in the minds of Americans. Postwar artists in particular were fascinated by the shadow as an ambiguous borderland, a mutable horizon where the invisible becomes visible, where light and dark battle for supremacy, and where meaning struggles to announce itself. Shadows not only appear in the written works of writers like Sylvia Plath, Jack Kerouac, Allen Ginsberg, and Amiri Baraka but also are manifested visually in the postwar photography of Robert Frank, William Klein, and Ralph Eugene Meatyard; in late film noirs such as *The Night of the Hunter*, *Kiss Me Deadly*, and Orson Welles's masterpiece *Touch of Evil*; and perhaps most dramatically in the television show *The Twilight Zone*. This study examines the figure of the shadow as it appears in these works in order to reveal the anxieties haunting 1950s and 1960s American culture. Postwar artists invoked shadows in an attempt to expose the culturally occluded and, in the process, used this in-between space to offer their own imaginative solutions to the paradoxes the Cold War created.

What is it about shadows that is so intriguing, and why were these artists drawn to them during the late 1950s and early 1960s? This book proposes that the answer is to be found in the notion of ambiguity. As transitory images produced on the border between light and darkness, shadows occupy an in-between space that challenges us to make sense of their vague and shifting outlines. Shadows were useful to postwar artists because they opened up a gap between trace and origin that could be productively exploited. Gesturing to a source that can only be inferred, shadows work to simultaneously produce fear and wonder, anxiety and curiosity. It is precisely this indeterminacy that makes them so attractive and allows them to be laden with a multiplicity of meaning that creates an opening for new modes of thinking to occur. Contradictory, polyvalent, and overburdened, shadows are ciphers—absences that must be read into presence, but without an intrinsic code that tells us how such interpretation must take place. The use of shadows allowed artists of the postwar era to craft works that gestured in several directions simultaneously, complicating reception by burdening the audience with the task of reconciling the disparate connotations shadows invoke. Shadows fold thinking back onto itself, forcing us to question the choices we make and compelling our imaginations to provide "third terms" outside existing binaries.

Their inherent ambiguity made shadows well suited to comment on a postwar culture in the midst of cataclysmic changes. America's heightened responsibility as a dominant player in a nuclear world filled its citizens with a strange admixture of pride, duty, and fear. Although the bomb was initially seen as a necessary evil that saved more lives than it destroyed, as the Cold War wore on such logic became increasingly suspect. Despite the bomb's initial association with light, subsequent events—the development of an even more powerful hydrogen bomb, the emergence of a nuclear-armed Soviet Union, troubling reports about a "Disease X" in Japan—created a growing unease about the possibility of an impending darkness. The irony of a device that protected its citizens through the threat of world annihilation was not lost on Americans. Sublime enough to inspire awe and dread alike, the bomb was an ever-present force during the Cold War.

The economic boom that accompanied the end of World War II further complicated this picture. While the threat of nuclear destruction loomed, Americans were enjoying unprecedented increases in their standard of living. With the country virtually unscathed, an expanding middle class was free to enjoy the fruits of a burgeoning consumer society. Consumer goods, cars, and even new homes were brought within the reach of many. Yet this prosperity was bought at a price. Alan Nadel argues that the rhetoric developed around the idea of containing the Communist threat abroad became internalized domestically as the need to conform. He writes, "It was a period, as many prominent studies have indicated, when 'conformity' became a positive value in and of itself" (4). The pressure to adhere to middle-class social standards undermined the myth of American freedom and individualism, and many wondered if a family, a job, and a home were all there was to life. Americans were placed in a difficult position as they struggled to reconcile their personal desires with the social requirement to "fit in." In addition, these gains were unequally distributed. Minorities, many of whom were veterans themselves, were excluded from the American dream. Life in midcentury America was thus fraught with paradox.

The shadow was one site where these issues were negotiated, where they were allowed to surface in cultural forms that gave Americans a glimpse of the paradoxes inherent in Nadel's "containment culture." The use of shadows cast doubt on the seemingly bright future that Americans were promised. Instead, they offered an alternative space where social assumptions could be reconsidered, questioned, and even challenged. Of course not every use of the shadow in the postwar period led to an attack on American cultural norms; shadows were used to bolster containment culture as well as to question it. But standing behind all of these uses was the possibility for thinking otherwise, whether personally or politically. Shadows' association with a general foreboding and uncertainty captured the unease and tension that permeated postwar America. By crafting a space where doubt and uncertainty reigned, artists used such anxiety to their advantage, invoking shadows as a site for deconstructing the assumptions of postwar culture and offering the possibility for thinking anew. Tracing the motif of the shadow at what many consider to be the height of the Cold War years thus helps us to better understand the functioning of an image that both repels and beckons and the reasons for its hold on the collective unconscious of America.

This project reads a variety of texts from the period through the trope of the shadow to reveal a new problematic: the functioning of a symbol as it occurs across artists, media, and genres in the 1950s and early 1960s. In doing so, it follows a path laid out by previous studies that challenge the view of Cold War culture as monolithic and homogeneous. Daniel Belgrad's *Culture of Spontaneity*, Michael Davidson's *Guys Like Us*, W. T. Lhamon's *Deliberate Speed*, and Maria Damon's *The Dark End of the Street* all demonstrate the broad array of culturally resistant practices that challenged dominant discourse during the period. Belgrad offers spontaneous action as a counterpoint to the culture of containment, Davidson the notion of homosocial masculinity, Lhamon speed, and Damon the marginal and outcast. This study's discussion of the shadow explores the nonnormativity common to all of these approaches while complicating our thinking about the postwar in interesting ways. As with other examples of resistance, shadows pose a challenge to accepted cultural modes. But unlike the rubrics offered by these critics, shadows are much more unstable. Shadows are a Gothic "return of the repressed" whose meanings quickly overflow into excess. There is a politics of resistance here, but one that works not by offering radically new alternatives but through unsettling accepted categories and assumptions. Though they help to give a coherent shape to the intangible, shadows are not so much a counterdiscourse as they are an antidiscourse, an invitation to deconstruct the complex strands of Cold War thinking.

Artists of the shadow use such ambiguity to their advantage. The postwar period was one generally described as subjective. In contradistinction to a collectivist Soviet Union, the United States saw itself as a collection of individuals whose freedom to pursue their own interests was the cornerstone of democracy. Personal acts, however, had political consequences, as those falling outside societal norms quickly discovered. Artists were no exception. Social pressures to conform combined with the generational rejection of earlier, more politically engaged art led many to explore self rather than society. Confessional poetry and street photography were two well-known results. But that did not mean the social was elided. Discussing the use of "spontaneity" as an artistic strategy, Belgrad claims that the "social significance" of this postwar culture "can be appreciated only if this aesthetic practice is understood as a crucial site of cultural work: that is, a set of activities and texts engaged in the struggle over meanings and values" (*Culture* 1). Culture, manifested through immediate personal expression, became the space for challenging social norms, and shadows became a weapon in this struggle. By invoking the unstable trope of the shadow, these postwar artists forced their audiences to struggle with the openness that characterizes this metaphor. This study traces the development of such an aesthetic practice as it winds its way through cultural history. Shadows may speak directly to the personal, but the existential questioning they invoke has significant cultural implications. Belgrad notes that postwar American culture "fostered the internalization and privatization of cultural struggles that a decade before had seemed intensely social in nature" (2). The shadow's ambiguity made it a poor tool for direct political action but a remarkable one for planting the seed of doubt that flowered into a challenge to Cold War rhetoric. While the work discussed here may not be overtly political, it led to a clearing in thought that allowed for the possibility of thinking outside existing conceptions.

The history of shadow use and interpretation does not, of course, begin in the American twentieth century; it has existed since the dawn of civilization. Ambiguity exists in the very definition of the term. The idea of a shadow seems straightforward enough—an object blocking a light source produces a darkened area. The venerable art historian E. H. Gombrich, in his book *Shadows: The Depiction of Cast Shadows in Western Art*, draws on the work of Filippo Baldinucci, a Florentine chronicler of baroque art, to refine this definition. Gombrich claims, "In the language of painters [the shadow] is generally understood to refer to the more or less dark color which serves in painting to give relief to the representation by gradually becoming lighter. It is divided in three degrees called shadow, half-shadow and cast shadow" (n.p.). Strict demarcations between these definitions are impossible, however, since it is difficult to know where a shadow ends and a half-shadow begins. The quality of a shadow's darkness is another issue.[3] The shadow is not quite darkness, at least not in the sense of the complete absence of light. It is an in-between color, darker than light and lighter than dark, depending on the strength of the illuminating source, the opaqueness of the object, and the quality of the surface on which it appears. The cast shadow, by contrast, is more of a silhouette, a "shadow that is caused on the ground or elsewhere by the depicted object" (n.p.). But when exactly does a penumbra (or a half-shadow, for that matter) become a cast shadow? While we use the term "shadow" quite freely, closer inspection reveals that its meaning is not so obvious.

The ambiguities inherent in the shadow have led to a corresponding instability in interpretation. A history of thinking on the shadow produces several contradictory trends. The most famous account of shadows as deceptive comes from Plato. Once light is equated with truth, the darkened shadows become furtive and false, an account very much in keeping with ideological attempts to cast Communists (and, later, terrorists) as shady enemies of freedom. But in the history of painting that begins with the Roman encyclopedist Pliny the Elder, the opposite is true. Shadows are traces that point back to the real objects that cast them. Seeing shadows as markers of reality quickly leads to imbuing them with a mystical quality that helps us to understand the shadow's historic association with the soul. Early civilizations, the Greeks, the Egyptians, romantic artists, and science fiction writers have all employed this connection. The ever-shifting shadow, however, also offers the opportunity to think anew. Contra Plato, there is a nineteenth- and twentieth-century philosophical tradition of viewing shady borderlands as the site for imagination. The ambiguous and uncertain provide the lacuna for thought to emerge, and it is precisely here where many of the artists under consideration chose to locate their use of shadow imagery.

In his famous "Allegory of the Cave" section of *The Republic*, Plato describes a group of prisoners, chained to a wall, who are forced to watch shadows cast by figures they cannot see. Tricked by these false representations, the prisoners construct their world from these apparitions, oblivious to the light of truth outside the cave. Truth, then, becomes the shadow of those artifacts rather than the things themselves. Plato castigates the false representation of reality that shadows represent in the allegory, but for Plato, this is the unfortunate state of most human understanding. The rescued prisoners cannot see the "things themselves" until they have trained their eyes and thus must begin with mere shadows, however false, before they can see their true source in the sun. Later, they will recognize shadows for what they are—mere reflections of the truth. Light equals understanding and the good, shadows their occlusion. For Plato, such a realization is immanent in everyone; individuals just need to learn how to see correctly.

Plato's allegory is important because it inaugurates a perception of shadows as deceptive that has remained influential. Another thinker equally central to the philosophical tradition, René Descartes, continues this critique. In his *Meditations on First Philosophy*, Descartes compares his fear of challenging his long-standing beliefs with that of a sleeper unwilling to wake from a pleasant dream. Descartes worries that should he awaken, he must spend the rest of his time "not in the light but among the inextricable shadows" (17). Light is truth, darkness is falseness, and shadows are those spaces between that lead the philosopher astray. Ironically, this doubt is central to his project, and Descartes will go on to extricate himself from the shadows with his famous "cogito ergo sum." He must exist because he thinks, and Descartes will use this understanding as the foundation of his method and indeed of his philosophy. Plato established a type of thinking about the inadvisability of following shadows that has become a leitmotif in both popular culture and philosophical discourse, creating an industry of shadow critique that has remained compelling. The shadow is philosophy's other, a placeholder for the sort of irrationality and confusion that it defines itself against.

While the insubstantial nature of shadows does give some credence to Plato's and Descartes's accounts, it is also true that shadows can be a sign of presence. The shadows produced at Hiroshima and Nagasaki, for example, highlight a long-standing connection between body and shadow that has been a human inheritance from the beginnings of recorded history. Writing in the first century of the Common Era, Pliny the Elder claimed in his *Natural History* that "there is universal agreement that [painting] began by the outlining of a man's shadow" (325). Nothing pejorative attaches to Pliny's assertion. On the contrary, these captured shadows acted as stand-ins for the more substantial objects they limned. Pliny goes on to claim that sculpture, too, began as a project of capturing the reliefs of people in order that their likenesses could live beyond them. He invokes the story of the Corinthian potter Butades whose daughter wanted a memento of her lover: "She was in love with a young man, and when he was going abroad she drew a silhouette on the wall round the shadow of his face cast by the lamp. Her father pressed clay on this to make a relief and fired it" (336). Here the shadow is seen not as falseness but as a means of re-presenting the human form that made the shadow possible in the first place. Shadows take on an almost magical quality as traces that invoke the presence of their absent origins.[4]

This connection between silhouette, shadow, and presence continues unabated into the present. Consider the art of photography, which, from its beginnings, was linked to an increased demand for the silhouette.[5] A rising commercial class wanted to be memorialized alongside the rich but lacked the financial means or the time required for traditional portraiture. As Michel Frizot explains in his *New History of Photography*, "By the end of the eighteenth century profiling machines had been developed based on the concept of a silhouette produced by the projection of light (sun or lantern), the profile being reduced mechanically" (17). The sitter, illuminated from one side by a light source, would then have his or her profile outlined from the other side by the artist tracing the shadow created on a screen. Yet such machines could produce only a single image at a time. The "physionotrace," invented by Gilles-Louis Chrétien in 1786, was introduced to fill this need (Hirsch 6). Chrétien's device allowed the user to "trace a profile onto glass using a stylus connected to an engraving tool that duplicated the gestures of the stylus onto a copper plate" (6). From this copper plate, multiple images of the subject could be produced. The camera would take these devices a step further, capturing a more detailed tracing with the aid of better lenses and making it permanent with an array of chemical process meant to permanently fix the image onto a material like paper. It should come as no surprise, then, that the word "photography" literally means "light writing," and earlier the medium was also known as "heliography," or "sun writing." The Chinese term for photography, *sheying*, is derived from "*she* meaning 'to absorb; or take in,' and *ying* meaning an image, particularly a projected image such as a reflection or shadow" (Schaefer 130).

Historically, it was a very short jump from seeing shadows as traces of living beings to connecting them with the idea of spirit. Shadows signal the presence of a human form, and such natural representations quickly gave way to artistic attempts to "capture" that silhouette for ritualistic purposes. Discussing the primitive cave drawings at Lascaux, France, which were made roughly 15,000 to 10,000 years before the Common Era, Gombrich remarks,

> The most likely explanation of these finds is still that they are the oldest relics of that universal belief in the power of picture-making; in other words, that these primitive hunters thought that if they only made a picture of their prey—and perhaps belabored it with their spears or stone axes—the real animals would also succumb to their power. (*Story of Art*, 39–40)

While Gombrich admits that it is impossible to know for certain, scholars speculate that these silhouettes carried a magical, invocative quality that was meant to ensure successful events such as a good hunt or a victory over enemies in battle. Cave drawings were thus more than simple representations. These earliest records of humanity demonstrate a belief in the power of a shadow divorced from its source object to influence worldly events. Shadows, far from being misleading, actually lie at the very center of human existence. They are the sign of a mystical truth lying inside everyone, evidence of a transcendent spirit that sets us apart from mere objects. They are the beginnings of the idea of "soul."

This link between shadow and soul can be found throughout the ancient world in a wide variety of contexts. For ancient civilizations like the Egyptians and Greeks, shadows retained a magical quality, becoming a literal second self that needed to be protected and, as such, occasioning much anxiety and ritual. According to Victor Stoichita in *A Short History of the Shadow*, Egyptologists believe that "the relationship between the two variations of the shadow is interchangeable: while the man is alive his black shadow is an externalization of his being. Disappearing the instant he dies, the function of the double is taken over by the *ka* as well as by the statue on the one hand and the mummy on the other" (19). The same sort of logic held for the Greeks as well. Stoichita, drawing on the work of the Hellenist scholar Erwin Rohde, claims that "the Greeks symbolically linked shadow, soul and a person's double" (18). Such a seemingly "heathen" idea of the shadow's importance even finds its way into the New Testament. In the book of Acts, the shadow of Peter could cure the sick: "They even carried out the sick into the streets, and laid them on cots and mats, in order that Peter's shadow might fall on some of them as he came by" (5:15, New Revised Standard Version). Far from being considered false, reproductions such as shadows, statues, and mummies would have signified the presence of a person's soul and were literal stand-ins for the deceased.

Nor is this connection limited to the Mediterranean region. In many cultures and religions around the globe, walking across someone else's shadow or allowing the shadow of one lower in society to be cast across another is still something to be avoided. Discussing his travels to India in the thirteenth century, Marco Polo related that in one area of the country he visited, "when they are about to make a purchase of goods, they immediately observe the shadow cast by their own bodies in the sunshine; and if the shadow be as large as it should be, they make the purchase that day" (235). Once shadows become intimately connected to the soul, they need to be safeguarded and consulted.

If the shadow represents a person's soul, then the loss of one's shadow becomes the loss of an essential element of human existence. This idea has produced numerous works that explore what happens when a shadow is severed from its owner. Perhaps the most famous is the work of Adelbert von Chamisso, whose *Peter Schlemihl* (1814) tells the story of a man who sells his shadow to the devil. Schlemihl, rebuked by a society of millionaires because of his poverty, is approached by a strange man in gray who offers him a magic purse that never runs out of gold. The condition is that Schlemihl must give the man his shadow. Schlemihl accepts, but as everybody he meets becomes suspicious of him because of his lack of a shadow, eventually Schlemihl realizes he had made a poor bargain. The devil appears again and proposes a second exchange—Schlemihl gets his shadow back but the devil gets his soul upon death. This time Schlemihl resists, casts the devil away, and throws the magic purse into an abyss. He then goes on to live in absolute isolation, with only his love of botany to keep him company.[6]

While shadows may presuppose an initial source, they are easily divorced from their origins. Shadows are by their very nature a fleeting and transitory phenomenon, and a shift in light easily displaces them. Moreover, shadows can quickly become engaging in their own right. The idea that an image can simply re-present an original object has come under increased scrutiny in our postmodern world. Following Jacques Derrida, the shadow is just as important an entity in its own right than as a "trace" of something else. Besides, as Derrida has successfully demonstrated, the trace gestures toward an origin that is unattainable. We may want to use it as a clue to a lost beginning, to follow it back to the start, but such a desire for secure origins is a myth. In the case of the shadow, it is easy to make invidious distinctions because shadows are seldom perfect outlines and, even when they are, they lack the depth and contour of three-dimensional images. Shadows are clearly *not* their sources, and their inherent ambiguity lies precisely in this gap. Yet the irony of shadows is that their indeterminate nature is actually their greatest strength.

Illumination kills imagination. Without the room to explore, the mind is left with the mere function of receiving a world already produced. Derrida makes this point explicit in his fascinating study *Specters of Marx*. In a footnote, Derrida quotes Max Stirner's discussion of ghosts as seen by the romantics in *The Ego and His Own* (1845). Stirner, an anarchist whose work equated all social institutions with ghosts haunting the minds of humankind, observed,

> The faithful and the Church Fathers did not realize that by destroying belief in ghosts, they were also taking away the basis of religion. . . . Whoever no longer believes in ghosts has only to pursue his unbelief to its conclusion to realize that there is no being hidden behind things, no ghost or—what comes down to the same thing if one understands the word in its naïve sense—no "spirit." (239n13)

Ghosts are not exactly shadows, of course, but there is certainly an affinity between their spectrality and the fleeting and transient nature of a shadow.[7] Without a sense that there might be something else "behind things," there is little room for imagination, and thus little room for thinking otherwise, be it in the form of God, spirit, or even possibility. The Enlightenment tried to extinguish the shadow world by exposing it to the blinding light of reason, but such an attack on imagination often leads to the foreshortening of the possibilities of thought itself. Shadows, spirits, ghosts, and specters are reminders that other worlds besides this one are indeed thinkable—thus the continued popularity of the romantic and Gothic as genres always willing to challenge rational assumptions in order to stimulate the imagination into a belief in the unknown.

The indeterminate nature of shadows makes them the perfect means of stimulating thought into new directions. They are neither light nor dark and, in that transitional space between, open themselves up to the possibility of thinking anew. As G. W. F. Hegel explains in *The Science of Logic*, a work fundamental to his corpus, "Pure light and pure darkness are two voids which are the same thing . . . and for this reason, . . . it is only darkened light and illuminated darkness which have within themselves the moment of difference" (qtd. in Stoichita 8). Hegel draws attention to the inability of a single term to produce something new. In keeping with his insistence on the dialectic as generator of change, Hegel believes that neither light nor dark, by itself, has any meaning since both terms are "voids" unable to produce the type of synthesis that thought requires. It is only in that in-between space, that space of shadow, where thought can begin to emerge. Hegel thus inverts the classical thinking on shadows inherited from Plato and Descartes. While the purity of light is often contrasted with the negativity of darkness, the strange truth is that meaning emerges only in adulteration. It is only when darkness shades the brightness of light or when the light illuminates a patch of darkness that we truly begin to see.

Shadows lend themselves to the imaginative because of their ambiguous and transient nature. They are neither light nor dark, neither substantial nor pure illusion, and in these in-between spaces the imagination begins to work, filling in openings and positing theories. The Japanese novelist Junichirō Tanizaki explores this ambiguity in his 1933 treatise on aesthetics, *In Praise of Shadows.* Tanizaki laments a Westernization of Japan that brings the desire for illumination in its wake. Instead, Tanizaki praises what he sees as an older, more Japanese aesthetic of the shadow. Discussing the alcoves of traditional Japanese rooms where light had difficulty penetrating, Tanizaki observes, "This was the genius of our ancestors, that by cutting off the light from this empty space they imparted to the world of shadows that formed there a quality of mystery and depth superior to that of any wall painting or ornament" (33). For Tanizaki, it is their "mystery" that lends shadows their particular magic. They create a space for the mind to roam freely, unencumbered by the strict reality that light brings.[8]

Ambiguous Horizons does not attempt to abstract the vast range of usages into a single narrative—the figure of the shadow is much too polyvalent and ubiquitous to make such an attempt plausible or even desirable. But there is a renewed interest in shadows during the postwar period, both in popular culture and in artistic works. This study operates by creating a nexus of readings that gestures toward a way of understanding what shadows signify, why they might be useful to writers and artists of the postwar, and why the public might have found this image to be an apt visual metaphor for the sort of issues that affected them daily. In doing so, it provides a novel lens for viewing a series of texts that have never been grouped together before, extending the horizons of interpretation for each single text through a comparison with its neighbor. Reordering texts along thematic lines also allows us to take a fresh look at an era often revisited nostalgically as one of innocence. Shadows provide a new take on an old paradigm by demonstrating that the binary rhetoric of the postwar world was under constant revision. An analysis of how and why shadows appeared in postwar America helps us to understand how the image of the shadow becomes reworked at particular historical moments, shedding light not only on how social forces influence artistic production (and vice versa) but also on the possible uses of the shadow as an aesthetic strategy. The postwar period bred a type of thinking that shadows captured perfectly, and by reading their ambiguous outlines we can better appreciate the wishes and fears of the age.

In order to understand the reasons shadows were such a potent trope in the period, we must provide a context for their use. The first chapter examines Cold War discourse along with a series of cultural artifacts in order to disclose the ways in which shadow imagery functioned in the early postwar period. An analysis of political cartoons and anti-Communist propaganda films demonstrates that Cold War shadows were a direct legacy of World War II. But the atomic bomb, with its dual emphasis on piercing light and apocalyptic darkness, required the image to be updated. As tension mounted throughout the decade, anti-Communist rhetoric picked up on nuclear anxiety, positing a world of infiltration, contamination, and subversion, captured most notably in the figure of the spy. Shadows became symbols of this instability, placeholders for the permeable borders that seemed to threaten America from both within and without. The final line of defense became the home, as government publications and advertisements attempted to demonstrate. Yet this supposed bastion of security was likewise experiencing the stresses of the postwar era. Many Americans felt trapped in a life of suburban conformity. At the same time, they were menaced by the shadow of the nuclear bomb looming overhead as well as by the specter of racial difference that eventually boiled over into riots in the 1960s. The early Cold War preoccupation with the breakdown of borders made the Gothic particularly suited to address fears of contamination that ran throughout the period, including those of miscegenation. But the most peculiar phenomenon to call into question American prosperity was the bomb shelter. Buried in the dark underground, it formed the shadow to the bright, open ranch-style home sitting above it. Shadows were a volatile image in the postwar period—they signaled both the fear of nuclear holocaust as well as the strange anxieties this new world created.

The shadow is such a powerful trope because it creates a space where multiple, and sometimes even contradictory, meanings can coexist. The second chapter explores such polyvalence through an examination of the reemergence of a popular Depression- and World War II–era crime fighter in the work of Sylvia Plath, Jack Kerouac, and Amiri Baraka. The Shadow was a radio phenomenon and the subject of an immensely successful pulp magazine known to millions during the 1930s and 1940s. In the pulps, he was drawn in the hard-boiled style of the era: a black outline with a signature slouch hat that passed through the shadows to apprehend criminal masterminds and gun-toting mobsters. During radio's "golden age," he was known by his eerie, disembodied laugh and the tagline, "Who knows what evil lurks in the hearts of men? The Shadow knows . . ." This dark mysteriousness, along with his willingness to use vigilante justice in order to punish his adversaries, marks the Shadow as a strange sort of crime fighter. While he is clearly on the side of justice, there remains a hint of darkness in his character, as his name implies. The Shadow is an enigmatic hero who is able to inspire both admiration and unease in his audiences.

It was precisely this uncertainty that compelled Plath, Kerouac, and Baraka to put the Shadow to new uses in their works. All three drew on the figure of the Shadow to comment on the loss of childhood innocence as the seemingly easy binaries that defined it gave way to the complexities of adult life. For these artists, meaning was found in the shadows because life is never simply black and white. None of these writers, however, longed for the past. The Shadow was a figure who presciently anticipated the future, even if the child was unaware of how that future would unfold.

It is important to note that this nostalgic looking-back took place within a postwar present. It is no coincidence that all of these writers published their Shadow-inspired works in 1959, at what many consider to be the height of the Cold War. Plath, in her poems and short fiction, makes the dark spaces of shadows the place where truth resides and imagination reigns. While these pieces appear to be intensely personal in keeping with the confessional nature of her work, reading them against the backdrop of the postwar period demonstrates the multiple meanings that shadows necessarily create. Kerouac, rewriting the crime fighter in his novel *Dr. Sax*, turns shadows into a site of memory. The Shadow represents a childhood trying to become present again, with all the inconsistencies, slippages, and difficulties that such a remembering entails as it emerges within the specifically Cold War moment of the text's production. Baraka reworks the Shadow to investigate the tension inherent in being a black poet in a racist American society. If the Shadow "knows," just how culpable is this "knowing"? Shadows, alas, offer no easy answers. The Shadow comes to stand for a haunting made literal as all three of these writers explore the nostalgic past of childhood innocence and its dissolution. As the Gothic genre has repeatedly demonstrated, such a haunting has as much to do with the present as it does with the past.

Chapter 3 delves deeper into the functioning of the shadow as a trope by drawing on archival accounts of a recurring dream that Kerouac and Ginsberg shared of a "Shrouded Stranger." While the Beats are typically seen as championing spontaneity as an antidote to the 1950s culture of containment, there is a negativity that lies at the heart of their project. Shadows stand as a symbol of this negativity. They represent a hole, a gap, a lacuna that begs for an explanation. Kerouac's and Ginsberg's attempts to (in the words of Jean-Francois Lyotard) "describe the indescribable" demonstrate a move from representation to presentation that was instrumental in the development of their careers, thematically and stylistically. The difficulty Kerouac had in describing this "dark haunted thing" pushed his writing into a more spontaneous realm, challenging him to represent the unrepresentable absence of death itself. Ginsberg's use of this figure helped him to jettison an early, more abstract style in favor of a concrete poetics that he believed better presented the truth of the world. Rather than rendering the Shrouded Stranger as a symbol, Ginsberg opted to make him an object, allowing the reader to draw his or her own conclusions. Both realized that shadows retained the power to unsettle and disturb only when the reader encountered them as a force, not as an abstraction. While the Shrouded Stranger receded as their respective careers developed, the negativity of this figure continues to reverberate in their later works.

Shadows are a poignant symbol for influence, as phrases such as "being overshadowed" or "standing in one's shadow" suggest. The Shrouded Stranger is no exception. This image can be read as the anxiety of influence both young writers faced from established authors they admired. But this pair's desire to capture the figure haunting their dreams must be read against the influence of the grand dream interpreter of the twentieth century: Sigmund Freud. Although they initially became interested in Freud's writings, as time went on Kerouac and Ginsberg began to distance themselves from his theories. The reason for this lies in their belief that dreams were as equally real as waking life. For Freud, dreams were the "royal road" back to the unconscious, a means of identifying a deeper reality buried in the self. Kerouac and Ginsberg were more interested in dreams as a means of inspiration, both for their personal lives and for their nascent writing careers. For both, dreams were visions of a possible future, not symptoms of a recurrent past. Kerouac and Ginsberg used the Shrouded Stranger to write their way out of Freud's shadow by focusing on imaginative composition in place of cure.

If the Beats rejected Freud, they had a more difficult relationship with that other dominant figure of dreams and shadow, Carl Gustav Jung. Although he enjoyed far less popularity than Freud and thus received less critical attention, Jung was an important influence on postwar America. Jung's concept of a "shadow" that represents the repressed aspects of an individual's character that must be confronted and integrated is much closer to Kerouac's and Ginsberg's idea of engaging the Shrouded Stranger as a means of self-discovery. Ultimately, however, Jung was likewise too restrictive. Kerouac did not attempt to recover the Shrouded Stranger in a Jungian sense of integrating the dark parts of himself. The Shrouded Stranger remained enigmatic, pushing Kerouac's writing in ever-new directions as he constantly confronted the negativity that this figure represented. Ginsberg may have read this shade as a symptom of some of his personal struggles (most notably his struggles with homosexuality, which he initially attempted to disavow), but ultimately he was more interested in re-presenting those issues than in solving them. For both, dreams were as "real" as reality and thus did not need to be read as evidence of a problem or a lack. Shadows are meant to inspire, stimulate, provoke—not in order to make whole but to disrupt being in the search for new modes of existence.

Chapter 4 engages the work of postwar photographers Robert Frank, William Klein, and Ralph Eugene Meatyard, who present human figures as disembodied ghosts that haunt their work as an uncanny reminder of the anxieties of the nuclear age. Photography as a medium has long been associated with the capturing of its subjects in a very literal manner. Originally emerging out of the silhouette tradition, where a shadow cast by a light source provided the means to trace the outline of a figure, photography has a claim on the real denied to other mediums. As Roland Barthes argues, the photograph serves an indexical function, pointing directly to an object that was once there in front of the camera. Thus the photograph is itself already a shadow of reality, a trace that speaks to a lost origin. The human figure thus haunts the photograph as an absence that is made present again. These photographers take that haunting to the next level, creating human figures whose disintegration highlights the anxiety not just over the role of photography in representing the world but over the fate of humankind as well.

Through the use of shadow, blur, graininess, and reflection, the work of these photographers defines a style that deemphasizes the naturalness of the human figure. In contrast to the more comforting images of people exhibited in Edward Steichen's immensely popular 1955 show *The Family of Man*, the photographs of Frank, Klein, and Meatyard are meant to challenge viewer expectations by presenting subjects in the act of disintegration. By the mid-1950s, the bomb had become both more powerful and more prevalent, and the threat of annihilation was building. These photographers captured that dread with shadowy images that turn their subjects into ghostly presences. Earlier documentarians like Walker Evans used the dignity of the human face to invoke a sense of humankind's interconnectedness. But the works of these postwar photographers demonstrate the opposite tendency—fascination and unease replace responsibility as humans become less and less recognizable. The term "subjective" has long been used to describe their style, but this term refers to the vision of the photographer as the defining element of 1950s photography. Yet the ambiguity they create has ramifications for the subjectivity of the viewer, who becomes forced to confront such difficult images and try to make sense of them. This challenge to the sanctity of the human figure signaled the beginning of an attack on humanism that would culminate in the later postmodern work of figures like Diane Arbus, Garry Winogrand, and Lee Friedlander.

Film noir, rather than blurring boundaries, used chiaroscuro lighting effects to highlight the differences between black and white in order to bring the binaries of the Cold War out into the open. Drawing mainly on German expressionist cinema, film noir harnessed shadows to capture the undercurrent of postwar despair and to highlight the moral degeneracy of its characters. But by the end of this cycle, film noir was becoming conscious of itself. As a result, we see a more calculated use of shadows during the mid- to late 1950s. Shadows became symbolic of the ambiguities inherent in a Cold War world of suspicion, fear, and threat. Chapter 5 examines their use in three of the most discussed 1950s noirs ever, *The Night of the Hunter*, *Kiss Me Deadly*, and *Touch of Evil*, in order to explore the role shadows played in capturing the underlying fear and uncertainty that was a hallmark of the period. All of these works use shadows to challenge the binaries that we have come to associate with light and dark and in the process make a comment on the cultural conditions of their production.

The Night of the Hunter, with its stark contrast between the evil of the murderous preacher and the goodness of the innocent children he is chasing, sets up a battle that is filmed in terms of light and dark. But such images are malleable, and a film ostensibly set in the Depression quickly resonates in the present tense of its unfolding in the Cold War. While we normally think of good in terms of the visible, *Kiss Me Deadly* sunders this bond to make light the harbinger of annihilation, while the dark spaces of shadow become the place where meaning resides. The explosion of a nuclear device at the film's close is figured as a release of light that is catastrophic, calling into question the ability of rationality in solving problems, narrative or otherwise. Folding film noir back upon itself, *Touch of Evil* is a film aware of its status as perhaps the last film noir ever made. In the process of this doubling, shadows are deconstructed to reveal not just their role in previous film noirs but also their functioning as border spaces where light battles dark in a struggle for control.

The discussion ends with an analysis of the ever-popular television series *The Twilight Zone*, which, in many ways, picked up where film noir left off. This series, which blended film noir effects with a burgeoning science fiction aesthetic, used the space of shadow to question the assumptions that undergirded life in early Cold War America. In order to discuss such delicate matters as nuclear anxiety, racial tension, and suburban conformity, creator Rod Serling asked viewers to journey into what he termed a "land of shadows" where normal rules and expectations broke down. In *The Twilight Zone*, shadows became the site of a cultural critique that utilized these liminal spaces of ambiguity to challenge the dualistic thinking of the times. Serling and his cowriters' scripts offered strange, twisting tales that caught viewers off guard, forcing them to rethink commonly held beliefs. The visual feel of the majority of the episodes, populated by shadow and chiaroscuro, worked in tandem with the show's content to create a world where the common assumptions of the Cold War were interrogated and, oftentimes, overturned. It is perhaps fitting that shadows find their apogee in *The Twilight Zone*. As the black-and-white 1950s and early 1960s gave way to the Day-Glo 1960s, shadows disappeared in a riot of color.

Shadows haunt postwar poetry, prose, television, film, photography, and popular culture. Once glimpsed, their vague outlines give rise to an uncertainty that sends the mind racing for answers. The postwar artists who delved into the world of shadows sought in them the specter of the anxieties of the age, as well as the imaginative space to vanquish such ghosts. But in the overburdened trace of the shadow they found even more: the shadow of the past falling on the present as an anxiety of influence; the shadow of race that haunts America and was very much on the minds of those living through the riots, migrations, and integrations of the 1950s; even the shadow of doubt as they contemplated the possibility that there was no meaning to be found at all. Regardless of outcome, their journeys into this borderland help us to better understand the complex longings and fears that permeated American society at midcentury. Shadows fascinate because they give us back to ourselves, only refracted. In that disjointed gap we can catch a glimpse of other possibilities.

1. A FASCINATING ANXIETY

The Paradoxes of Life in the Shadow of the Bomb

There is something about the Cold War that invokes the figure of the shadow. Even today, books dealing with the Cold War routinely employ the term "shadow" in their titles. A search made in 2012 using the keywords "shadows and cold war" at Harvard University's library system yielded 255 total hits. Out of these, 15 had both "shadow" and "cold war" in their title, while at least another dozen or so employed these terms in combination in either their titles or their tables of contents. Most were histories of the Cold War period or discussions of its politics. Shadow imagery, for reasons this study tries to make clear, captures something essential about the Cold War. That connection, however, is often unexplored. The vast majority of studies that employ the figure of the shadow in their titles do so without giving thought to the rationale behind their choice. This chapter explores a broad range of shadow imagery from the early Cold War period in order to understand the reasons for the shadow's association with the era.

The ambiguous shadow is a fitting image for the uncertainty of the Cold War. The early postwar time was an extremely paradoxical one, best exemplified by the discourse surrounding the atomic bomb. While

 the threat posed by a Communist Soviet Union would probably have existed without it, the bomb upped the ante in America's game of nuclear brinksmanship. But far from being universally maligned, the bomb compelled fascination as well as fear as Americans struggled to understand the new world it created. Anxiety over Soviet nuclear capability led to an equally confusing discussion surrounding the proper American response. At the same time that American democracy and exceptionalism were being touted, calls for conformity of thought in the face of the Soviet threat sent a mixed message to citizens. Such conflicted rhetoric quickly seeped into private lives, creating double standards and confusing discourse surrounding the home, family, race, and sexuality. While the shadow was certainly not the only figure Americans used to understand this complex postwar world, it often manifested these tensions in ways that revealed the paradoxes underlying containment culture.

The very ambiguity of shadows, however, meant that they could be used in numerous ways. Any discussion of shadows therefore runs into the problem of understanding the complex set of possibilities that this image inaugurates. This situation is further exacerbated by the long history of shadow interpretation. Shadows have been seen as false images designed to mislead, talismanic stand-ins for the soul, and catalysts for the imagination. All of these approaches appear in postwar culture, oftentimes in ways that seem piebald or contradictory. The Cold War use of shadows drew on many of the long-established trends in shadow interpretation but updated them for twentieth-century concerns. Uses were never consistent, but neither was Cold War rhetoric—both struggled to understand the vast changes that lent instability and uncertainty to Cold War culture.

Shadows manifested most clearly in Cold War political rhetoric and anti-Communist propaganda, where they were meant to create fear and unease over the Soviet threat. The image, however, was volatile. Shadows pervaded popular culture in ways that both reinforced and undermined the dictates of containment culture. The discussion surrounding bomb shelters provides an excellent example. With the home touted as an important line of defense in stopping the advance of Communism, the bomb shelter sought to placate fears concerning nuclear holocaust. But this dark, buried space became an uneasy reminder of the anxieties buried in the American psyche. Shadows also unwittingly invoked the specter of race that was an ever-present, if latent, American concern. Given the ambiguities of shadows and the paradoxes of the Cold War, such multifarious uses actually make a great deal of sense. Sometimes fearful, sometimes inviting, always compelling—shadows beg for interpretation, and the way in which we respond to them reveals much about who we are and the sort of society in which we live.

THE NUCLEAR SUBLIME

The bomb was the underlying cause of the fear and uncertainty of the postwar era, but it was also an endless source of fascination. Its very existence was fraught with inconsistency. With the Japanese resolved to fight to the finish in World War II, it was believed that more lives would be lost in a ground assault on Japan than in the dropping of the bomb. Thus, paradoxically, the bomb "saved" lives. Others have argued that the bomb could have been avoided if the Allies had softened to Japan's request to surrender but that after all the effort that went into its creation, President Harry S. Truman wanted to test it out. Truman himself had few qualms about its use, at that time or later, responding to the nuclear destruction of Hiroshima by exclaiming, "This is the greatest thing in history" (qtd. in Kuznick and Gilbert 2). Others were less sanguine. The ambiguity of the bomb would continue to haunt America during the Cold War.

The detonation of the atomic bombs on Japan certainly had the added advantage of demonstrating the military superiority of US forces to Joseph Stalin and the Soviet Union. With the end of World War II, America embraced the Truman Doctrine (1947): a commitment to stopping an ambiguously defined threat of Communist expansion across the globe. This doctrine was targeted not just at the Soviet Union as a country but at its ideology as well. The Marshall Plan (1948) was quickly installed to help Europe defend itself against the growth of Communist parties that were on the increase after the devastation of the war. This policy came to be known as "containment." George Kennan, in his famous 1947 article published under the pseudonym Mr. X in the journal *Foreign Affairs*, argued that Communism could not be easily defeated or discouraged by threats but rather must be dealt with through a policy of "long-term, patient but firm and vigilant containment" (Field 2). Along with America's economic power after the war, the possession of an atomic device capable of wreaking massive destruction was a key component in the struggle to thwart Soviet expansion.

But the problem with the postwar nuclear world was that the threat posed by the Soviet Union and its allies was not so easily containable. As the sole possessors of atomic bombs, Americans felt fairly secure in the late 1940s. But such security was short lived. The Soviet Union responded with their own atomic tests in 1949, leading the *Christian Century* to respond in early 1950 that "like a shadow of an eclipse of the sun, atomic darkness is racing across the world" (Boyer 349–50). Further tests by both the United States and the Soviet Union in 1952 and 1953 exacerbated such fears. In 1957 the Soviets launched the first man-made satellite, Sputnik I, and thus demonstrated their technological capability, which quickly put America on the defensive. This advance struck fear into the hearts of many Americans by proving that the Soviet Union was capable of attacking US mainland targets (possibly with nuclear weapons) with an intercontinental ballistic missile (ICBM). Although both major powers had begun negotiations to ban atmospheric nuclear testing in 1958 and Premier Nikita Khrushchev accepted President Dwight D. Eisenhower's invitation to visit American in 1959, the bomb made the late 1950s a particularly tense time in the nation's history. The Cuban missile crisis of October 1962 represented the highest point of tension for what many believe were the Cold War's most dangerous years. As we shall shortly see, what made the atomic bomb so uniquely feared in this period was its ability to permeate borders. It could arrive anywhere, anytime, and when it did the destruction and subsequent radiation it unleashed meant that few could evade its reach.

The irony that the device that proved humankind's supremacy was a weapon capable of destroying its very existence was not lost on those living in the Cold War era. But an even greater irony was that nuclear capabilities were expanded instead of limited. Immediate postwar fears of the bomb quickly gave way to calls for an increased arsenal after the successful Soviet test in 1949. As Paul Boyer maintains, it became a paradoxical strategy: "Rather than generating support for a redoubled diplomatic effort to reduce the atomic threat, these rising war fears had the reverse effect, leading to an increased reliance on the bomb as the best source of security in a threatening world" (335–36). America began stockpiling, and the arms race was on. Numerical superiority, a far less convincing argument, replaced sole ownership of the bomb as a means of security. A policy of "mutually assured destruction" was implemented, the idea being that any nuclear attack would be answered immediately with a retaliatory nuclear strike. As Boyer notes, in a 1950 Gallup poll, "77 percent of Americans said the United States should use the atomic bomb in any future world war. The following January, 66 percent said the U.S. should drop the bomb first" (339). Rather than attempt to limit the production of such weapons, the American public came to increasingly rely on them as a means for security. But it was an unsettling peace. As Joseph Masco observes in *The Nuclear Borderlands*, it was far from reassuring to know that "less than thirty minutes were all that separated the quotidian from annihilation" (27–28). Postwar life existed in this gap.

Due to the omnipresence of the Soviet nuclear threat and US attempts to contain it worldwide, many critics employ the term "the long fifties" when discussing the decade. As the critic Leo P. Ribuffo observes in his contribution to *Rethinking Cold War Culture*, "What is usually called the 'fifties' lasted from 1947–1948, when the anticommunist consensus congealed, to 1965–1966, when opposition to the Vietnam War prompted the reopening of dormant questions about the American way of life" (207). But Ribuffo, along with a handful of other contemporary critics, has questioned the tendency of reducing the decade to the clash of binaries. The contributors to *Rethinking Cold War Culture* argue that the period of the long fifties was not monolithic but rather the reaction of long-term trends with particular Cold War concerns such as the bomb. As Peter Filene expresses it, the Cold War "pervaded and shaped the experience of ordinary Americans far less than historians would have us believe. Although government leaders, social-science experts, and media commentators set the terms of public discourse—and also of public policy—most citizens to a surprising degree defined their world in personal terms" (157). Other critics point out the bias toward viewing postwar American culture as mainly white, middle-class, straight, and most often male. *Containing America*, edited by Nathan Abrams and Julie Hughes, challenges the more homogeneous picture of the American Cold War period presented in works such as Elaine Tyler May's *Homeward Bound* and Alan Nadel's *Containment Culture*. The early Cold War, as much new scholarship informs us, was considerably more heterogeneous than critics previously imagined, and the thinking of its citizens was influenced by more than simply the Soviet threat of nuclear annihilation.

Despite these caveats, it is undeniable that the atomic bomb had a profound effect on Americans. Even when not addressed directly, the bomb formed a backdrop whose images and fears radiated through America's collective unconscious. As Nadel correctly opines, "The crucial factor . . . that gives the cold war its unique qualities is the atomic bomb" (13). The bomb weighed heavily on the minds of Americans, even if responses were varied and sometimes even muted. As Paul Boyer relates in *By the Bomb's Early Light*, it was not a fear of death that unsettled Americans; it was that the bomb offered "death of a new kind, death without warning, death *en masse*" (278). The irrational fear that death could come at any second to annihilate an entire city or even country was what really drove nuclear anxiety. Such wholesale destruction challenged the prevailing American belief in progress, both social and technological. Advances, years in the making, could be swept away by a single detonation. It comes as no surprise, then, that "in 1959, two out of three Americans listed the possibility of nuclear war as the nation's most urgent problem" (May 23).

Another irony of the postwar period was that despite the bomb's importance, it really was not the subject of much literary discussion. Paul Brians claims in *Nuclear Holocausts: Atomic War in Fiction (1895–1984)* that "comparatively little nuclear fiction appeared in print—and . . . when it did, it did not enjoy a huge audience" (xvii).[1] Robert Jay Lifton and Richard Falk, in their work *Indefensible Weapons: The Political and Psychological Case against Nuclearism*, concur: "In the early 1980s something extremely important has happened to nuclear weapons. They have begun to emerge from the shadows. While they have been with us since World War II, it is only now that they have become psychologically and politically visible to the common man and woman" (xvi). But the lack of organized protests and literary depictions does not mean that the bomb went unnoticed. Ignored but not forgotten, the bomb was repressed as a disturbing fact best not thought about. It is just these sorts of latent anxieties existing on the mind's periphery that the shadow best succeeds in capturing. Shadows thus become a sort of Geiger counter, a means of registering this fear and uncertainty without the need of coming out and explicitly naming the bomb.

One possible reason for this seeming acquiescence was the lack of an adequate means of expression to convey the importance of this utterly new device. Boyer explains how the bomb's destructiveness transcended description, and thus "silence may have signaled not a failure of imagination, but intensity of imagination—a recognition of the folly of too quickly trying to assimilate this monstrous novelty" (250). This helps to explain the often-paradoxical responses to its detonation. In his campus novel *Been Down So Long It Looks Like Up to Me*, Richard Fariña's main character, Gnossos Pappadopoulis, witnesses the blast and can only retreat to his motel room to get drunk on martinis. The discussion of the detonation occupies only a few pages, while its anxiety silently permeates the rest of the novel. For Gertrude Stein, it was just another way of killing, and thus uninteresting; for William Faulkner, it was something that numbed, and was thus unwriteable; for

Mary McCarthy, it was an extension of the alienation of modern technology, and thus too banal for words (Boyer 250–51).

The concept of the bomb as both a conscious and unconscious American preoccupation is captured dramatically in Herbert Matter's 1946 cover for the journal *Arts and Architecture*. Titled *Atomic Head*, this photomontage depicts a silhouette of a human head staring at a silhouette of the earth (fig. 1.1). Inside the human's head is the unmistakable image of an atomic bomb's mushroom cloud billowing upward. As Jane Pavitt comments in her contribution to *Cold War Modern*, "the 'bomb in the brain' was a potent representation of the overpowering presence of nuclear anxiety initiated by the USA's atomic bombing of the Japanese cities of Hiroshima and Nagasaki in August 1945" (101). The fact that the rising cloud fills the brain and provides its only contents proves Pavitt's point. The ambiguity of the silhouette form does not allow us to discern whether this is a conscious preoccupation or an anxiety buried deep within the mind. Most probably it is both. The silhouette figure in *Atomic Head* is also without gender, race, country, or class, demonstrating the ubiquity of atomic concern and its relevance for every human on the planet. Matter's depiction of the head is a forceful means of conveying what was on everyone's minds in the aftermath of Hiroshima and Nagasaki in a form that perfectly captured the difficulties of trying to come to terms with the implications of the new device.

To complicate matters further, the head is gazing on the silhouette of the earth. The stark black-and-white imagery of both figures serves to equate them—the mushroom cloud seems to match the cloudlike white continents floating on the earth's dark surface. The artist clearly means to draw a connection between earth and atomic preoccupation, though the exact connection remains undetermined. The human head seems to be contemplating the earth in light of the new revelation of atomic energy, and the initial reaction to the piece was certainly filled with warning and caution. The bomb seems to have replaced the earth as subject of the human's thought. Not only is it what is on the head's mind (literally), but the size of the mushroom cloud dwarfs the earth and seems to have taken on a slightly greater detail than the somewhat blurry outlines of the continents. There is a foreboding here, but also a fascination—humans have created something as monumental as the planet itself (or tapped its secret). *Atomic Head* is undoubtedly a warning, but the ambiguity of the silhouette form and the unequal juxtaposition of the figures leave us more with a statement on the bomb's importance than a distinct comment on its meaning.

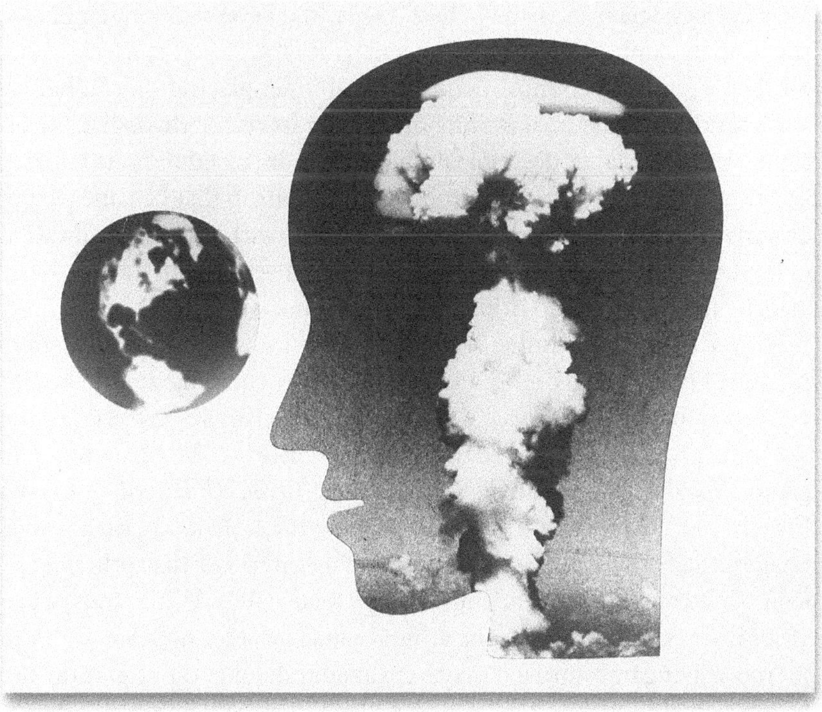

Fig. 1.1. Herbert Matter's 1946 photomontage *Atomic Head* uses the silhouette tradition to demonstrate what exactly was on everyone's mind in the postwar era. M1446, Herbert Matter Papers, Department of Special Collections and University Archives, Stanford University Libraries. Courtesy of the Herbert Matter Estate.

This tension between the bomb as both "magnificent" and "terrifying" played itself out in American popular cultural references as well. In an attempt to control the meaning of the device, the US government opted for the mushroom cloud as the proper symbol for its detonation. The mushroom cloud became a towering tribute to the might and power of the weapon, providing a reassuring image of power that could be used to thwart Soviet aggression. But the mushroom cloud became more than just a symbol of American military superiority: it became a cultural icon. Not only did the image of the mushroom cloud grace numerous magazine and newspaper covers in the postwar years, as A. Costandina Titus explains in "The Mushroom Cloud as Kitsch," it also became a highly potent cultural symbol, appearing on "album covers, postcards, and book jackets; it was featured in comic books and 'price-smashing' sales notices; it lent its shape to hats, cakes, and neon signs; and it graced the shapely contours of beauty queens and Hollywood starlets" (107). Such imagery tapped into the nuclear sublime, playing on the beauty and grandeur of the image while mitigating its terror through association with the banal or desirable.[2] The mushroom cloud became familiar and thus nonthreatening, an almost daily backdrop that became part of everyday life. This potent image dissipated only with the 1963 ratification of the Limited Test Ban Treaty, when nuclear testing went underground and the media turned to other cultural symbols (109).[3]

The Eisenhower administration attempted to sublimate the anxiety produced by its burgeoning nuclear arsenal by equating atomic bombs with technological advance. The atom became "an abstract symbol of scientific progress," an image that became "absorbed into a popular and jaunty visual design vocabulary in the early 1950s" (Pavitt 103). Part of Eisenhower's "Atoms for Peace" campaign in the early 1950s, such atomic imagery had "none of the anxiety-inducing effects of that other visual icon of the nuclear age, the mushroom cloud" (104). While today such 1950s images of electrons flying around a nucleus seem hopelessly kitsch, for those living in the period they were a reminder that the atomic did not have to equal apocalyptic destruction. Such imagery reinforced a meaning of the bomb as technological advance and perhaps even superiority. As Pavitt remarks, the anxiety over nuclear apocalypse was "absorbed into everyday life as the dark consequence to the breezy and optimistic vision of a future world empowered by technology, and made pleasurable and efficient by the influx of new consumer goods" (103). The campaign to assuage fears over nuclear holocaust typically involved shifting attention away from dramatic images of devastation and toward the benign, life-enhancing consequences of a nuclear world. In a burgeoning consumer society, it became easier to focus on the advantages that technological innovation brought in the form of purchasable goods than on the potential for destruction. But shadows remained.

Despite the Eisenhower administration's attempt to concentrate on the positive uses of nuclear technology, the atom remained anything but stable. As the potential consequences of nuclear war began to become apparent, public anxiety escalated. Perhaps the darkest side to the atom's potential was the fear of radioactive fallout. As Boyer maintains, "In the mid-1950s the issue of nuclear weapons again surged dramatically to the forefront. . . . As in 1945–1946, the reason was fear—this time, fear of radioactive fallout" (352). A series of radioactive disasters alerted

Americans to the dangers that the uncontained atom presented. In 1954 a US atomic test in the Pacific caused emergency evacuations and even death to some in the area. Even more startlingly, in 1955 Chicago experienced radioactive rain, and in 1959 strontium 90 appeared in milk. The popular press was quick to pick up on this growing fear. Ralph E. Lapp published his popular study *Radiation: What It Is and How It Affects You* (1957), reminding Americans that radiation knows no political or geographical boundaries. Stephen Spencer's two-part article appeared in the *Saturday Evening Post*, "Fallout: The Silent Killer" (1959), and *Life* ran a special issue in 1961 titled "How to Survive Fallout" (Pavitt 109–10). America could no longer consign the vague threats of the nuclear to their collective unconscious—radiation became a "real" threat.

Reports from Japan only heightened anxiety. In 1955 Michihiko Hachiya's *Hiroshima Diary* was published, which gave an eyewitness account of the atomic bombing of Hiroshima and the horrendous aftermath that followed. The nuclear sublime is rampant in Hachiya's text as well. Many of the witnesses he talked to described the mushroom cloud in awe-inspired terms. One man, Mr. Hashimoto, impressed Hachiya with his detailed description of the billowing cloud: "I saw a huge cloud rise angrily over Hiroshima, and on both sides of the main cloud beautiful smaller clouds spread out like a golden screen. I have never seen anything so magnificent in my life! . . . That beautiful cloud! It was neither red nor yellow. Its beauty defies description" (157–58). Hashimoto was not alone. As Hachiya explains, the Japanese term for the detonation, *pikadon*, was composed shortly after the impact to name this unprecedented event. The term derives from *pika*, or "glitter, sparkle, or bright light," and *don*, a "boom! or loud sound" (223). But for Hachiya, a doctor who treated survivors after the blast, the bombing was more notable for the human tragedy that followed. *Hiroshima Diary* provides an extensive catalog of horror made even more disturbing by the fact that nobody knew exactly what had happened: charred bodies, patients with undiagnosable conditions, and a city strewn with "the shadowy forms of people, some of whom looked like walking ghosts" (16). For an American public encountering such descriptions in the mid-1950s, the reaction must have been not only guilt but also an extreme anxiety over the possibility of such a cataclysmic event occurring in one of their own cities.

In contrast to the billowing mushroom cloud, the human silhouettes etched onto the concrete of Hiroshima and Nagasaki represent an eerie counterpoint to the celebratory rhetoric of nuclear power. The dropping of the hydrogen bomb on these Japanese cities in 1945 produced an incredible heat and light that left both littered with shadows. In *Rain of Ruin*, the authors comment that "a strange phenomenon of shadowing, or ghosting, was an eerie aspect of the bombing. This occurred when certain objects shielded others from heat and radiation. . . . Even human beings vaporized by intense heat left behind shadowy evidence when they briefly masked the pavement beside them" (54). In many cases, shadows made available objects and people that were annihilated by the awesome force of the blast. Ladders, railings, and window frames memorialized themselves as their imprints were left on buildings and sidewalks. Even clothing left its mark. Describing the aftermath of the bombing in his book *Hiroshima*, John Hersey relates that "on some undressed bodies, the burns had made patterns—of undershirt straps and suspenders and, on the skin of some women (since white repelled the heat from the bomb and dark clothes absorbed it and conducted it to the skin), the shapes of flowers they had had on their kimonos" (29). But by far the most horrible and disturbing imprints were left by humans themselves. Hersey describes the uncanny effect produced when a victim stood between the intense illumination produced by the blast and a background capable of recording a shadow: "A few vague human silhouettes were found, and these gave rise to stories that eventually included fancy and precise details. One story told how a painter on a ladder was monumentalized in a kind of bas-relief on the stone façade of a bank building on which he was at work, in the act of dipping his brush into his paint can" (73). In a horrible reversal of the artist's desire to capture life, the bomb unwittingly took a snapshot of death.

What arrests attention in these images is that the traditional relationship between human and shadow breaks down. Rather than death being the evacuation of the shadow, of the soul, from the body, in Hiroshima and Nagasaki it was the body that fled while the shadow remained. The soul became trapped on concrete. What is especially uncanny about these frozen shadows is that they challenge commonplace expectations. Rather than our movements dictating those of our shadows, in Hiroshima and Nagasaki the shadows remain fixed as eerie reminders or traces of a once-living person who is no longer there.[4] Such disturbing shadow images, which inevitably find a place in photographic accounts of the bombings, have continued to reverberate ever since scientists and journalists began to chronicle the effects of the bombs shortly after their detonation.[5] Several of these macabre images are preserved at the

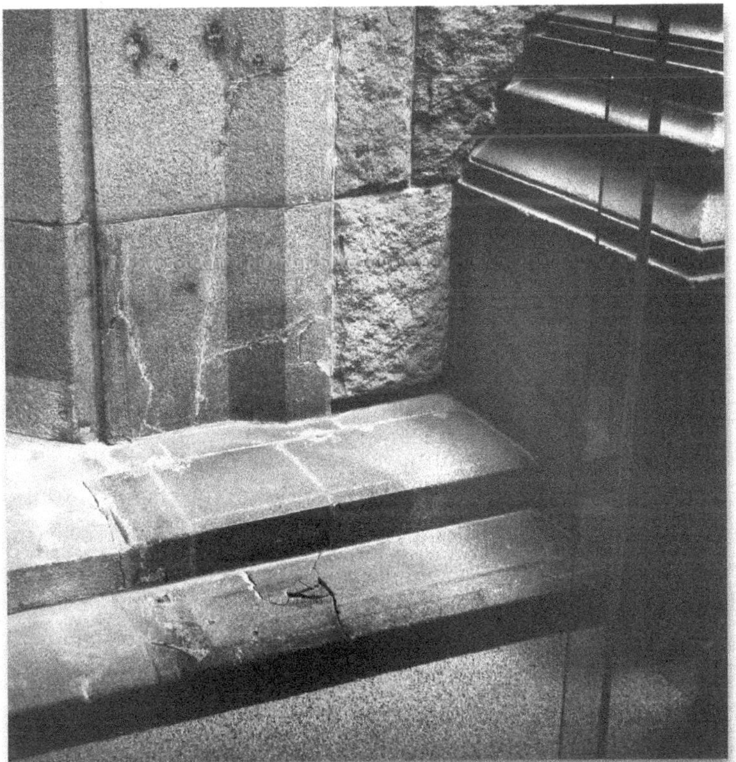

Fig. 1.2. A shadow records the uncanny presence of a victim sitting on the stone steps of Sumitomo Bank in Hiroshima, approximately 250 meters from the bomb's detonation point. The shadow remained clearly visible for ten years, after which the steps were brought inside the Hiroshima Peace Memorial Museum to protect them from wear. Hiromi Tsuchida, *Shadow of Person Sitting on Stone Steps*, 1995, gelatin silver print, Harvard Art Museums / Fogg Museum, gift of the artist and Martha Tepper Takayama, Tepper Takayama Fine Arts, P1999.91; Imaging Department © President and Fellows of Harvard College.

Hiroshima Peace Memorial Museum, including a shadow on the stone steps where a person had been sitting during the explosion (fig. 1.2). The nuclear sublime is located precisely in this dual feeling of fascination and repulsion that characterized the Cold War.

The link between shadow and soul helps to explain the contradictory effects the atomic bomb produced in the American psyche. Even amid this potential destruction, a morbid fascination remained. As Ribuffo remarks of the period, "Fear was neither incessant nor unalloyed with curiosity when, for example, Soviet leader Nikita Khrushchev toured the United States in 1959. Despite Democratic efforts to frame Sputnik as the symbol of a (spurious) 'missile gap,' this Soviet satellite elicited wonderment as well as anxiety" (208). The bomb and the rhetoric it inaugurated were pliant enough to accommodate a wide range of response. Thus while Robert Oppenheimer compared the blast to a "thousand suns," in the same breath he was able to comment, "Now I have become Death, the destroyer of worlds" (Pavitt 103).[6] Although universally feared, and for good reason, the bomb nevertheless created a sense of wonder and awe in the postwar era.

THE DARK THREAT OF COMMUNISM

Shadow imagery was an omnipresent feature of Cold War rhetoric. Politicians sought to harness the ambiguities of the shadow by aligning it with all of the "dark" forces that were threatening an otherwise bright American society. The uncertainty that shadows created were used to full effect, heightening the sense of dread and anxiety but locating that fear squarely in the figure of America's enemies. Shadows became the darkness of Communism made visible, a potent metaphor for the paranoid thinking of the times, and a symbol of all the vaguely defined anxieties that were always lurking in postwar America. As Douglas Field notes in his introduction to *American Cold War Culture*, President Eisenhower set the tone for discussing America's fight against Communism in his 1953 inaugural speech by associating American "freedom" with "light" and then contrasting it to the "slavery" and "darkness" of Communism (4). It was a world of *us* against *them*, and the shadowy Communists were decidedly *them*. Nor did this sort of shadowy imagery end with Eisenhower. The ever-encroaching shadow of the spreading Communist threat proved an irresistible metaphor for numerous US presidents. President Lyndon B. Johnson continued the metaphor into the 1960s, warning America of "the deepening shadow of communist China." Branding America's enemies with the label of "shadow" associated them with dark, evil purposes while hinting at their devious willingness to mislead and misguide. They became those who would block our light, cloud our understanding, and blacken our optimism with their darkened presence.

The idea of a creeping darkness always ready to "overshadow" an America defined through images of light and truth was itself an inheritance from earlier shadow imagery. One obvious antecedent is the "specter of communism" that Karl Marx and Friedrich Engels used to scare an industrializing nineteenth-century Europe in the first sentence of their *Communist Manifesto* (1848). By the 1950s, this ghost had become a reality for an America obsessed with Communist aggression and infiltration. Stephen J. Whitfield, in his classic study *The Culture of the Cold War*, invokes the image in the opening of his work: "The specter that, a century earlier, Marx and Engels had described as stalking the continent of Europe was extending itself to the United States, looming over a nation that had prided itself on its historical immunity to the apocalyptic tragedies of the either/or" (1). The image of a looming specter is the perfect vehicle for invoking anxiety and doubt in its viewers. Like a shadow, we are not sure where it comes from or what it hides, and thus individuals are free to allow their imaginations to run away from them, inventing even more disturbing possibilities to fill in the vague outlines of the image. Shadows provide a more tangible shape for the anxieties swirling just below the surface of society.

An even more direct influence on political rhetoric was the use of shadow imagery in World War II propaganda. Frank Capra's *Prelude to War*, which won a 1943 Academy Award for best documentary, begins with an image of a globe showing the Allied powers. Slowly, out from behind it comes a darker globe that symbolizes the Axis powers. An inevitable contrast ensues—our world, with upbeat music and plenty of light, is challenged by that other darker and somber world. Maps detailing Japan, Germany, and Italy become clouded as an oil-dark blackness spreads across them. War arrives as a shadow across Manchuria from Japan. And as other countries fall, the darkness spreads across them on the map as well. The rhetoric the film employs seems directed at US servicemen, though it was released by the War Department for the public as well in order to propagandize the war effort. Of course, other visual aids like arrows and lines were also employed, but the shadow is the most potent and the most prevalent means of demonstrating the "creep" of the Axis powers. The film ends with the phrase "One world must die; one must live" as the second, shaded world falls in behind ours, with a prominent light on the United States. Although the use of shadows was never entirely consistent in such propaganda, the image of a dark shadow spreading across the globe was a common enough visual image to linger into the postwar world.

The use of shadow imagery for propagandistic purposes is even more apparent in political cartoons. There is a long tradition of using shadows to satirize, ridicule, and mock.[7] Edwin Marcus, an editorial cartoonist for the *New York Times*, employed shadows to masterful effect in work that fully supported the Allied war effort. His work demonstrated the adaptability of the shadow image as he harnessed the aggressive nature of the foreboding shadow (fig. 1.3). In *The Growing Blackout* (1945), a black cloud labeled "Allied successes" begins to cover an image of Japan's rising sun superimposed on the ocean, sending lightning and rain down upon it. Marcus returns to this theme in the aptly titled cartoon *The Eclipse* (1945), where the silhouette of an American soldier, complete with bayonet, is again blotting out the Japanese symbol. Marcus's work demonstrates the pliability of the shadow by reversing the use it typically received in the period. The dark shadow remains a symbol of threat and malice, but one projected onto the enemy. America is the aggressor here, bringing the fight to the Japanese through a metaphoric darkening of their rising sun. Marcus's work runs the risk of casting America as a dark force, but the clearly identifiable silhouettes represent positive figures, saving these cartoons from being critiques of Allied aggression. They are not just blackouts and eclipses but calculated struggles against an oppressor who has wrongly aligned itself with the light.

The threat of instantaneous annihilation arriving without warning from abroad helped to fuel a virulent anti-Communism at home that left an indelible mark on the American psyche. Given the vast ideological differences between the United States and the Soviet Union, as well as Stalin's postwar expansion, confrontation was probably inevitable. But the bomb upped the ante, sending shock waves of fear throughout the American populace. The perceived threat of Communist insurgency took the form of an anxiety over the permeability of borders, both real and imagined. The image of the shadow was well suited to such a climate. Its vague, shifting outline caught the uneasiness of an American public that wanted security but was having a difficult time finding it. Like the threats they came to stand in for, shadows eluded clear understanding and challenged the idea that anything could be known perfectly.

Attempts to thwart Communism were not limited to checking Soviet aggression internationally. America also internalized the Communist threat, creating a culture of suspicion that relentlessly searched for signs of difference at home. Discussing the Cold War containment metaphor in *Pursuing Privacy in Cold War America*, Deborah Nelson observes that

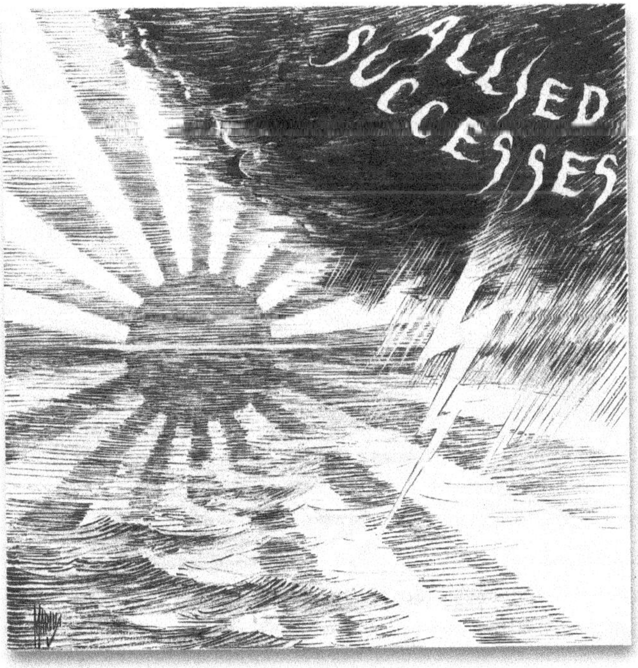

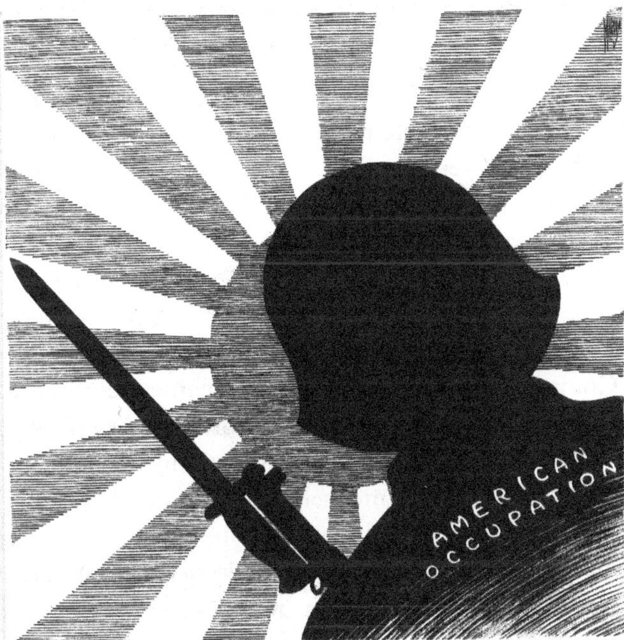

Fig. 1.3. Edwin Marcus turns the dread invoked by shadows into a symbol of the American and Allied determination to blot out Japan's "rising sun." Marcus, *The Growing Blackout* (*left*, 1945) and *The Eclipse* (*right*, 1945); by permission of the Marcus Family.

> the power and mobility of this metaphor of containment were equal only to the power and elasticity of the metaphor of intrusion—the enemy within—which conveyed an uncanny experience of finding one's borders already violated. The impossibility of purity in the internal space meant the perpetual breakdown and failure of the containment project. (xviii)

It was indeed one of the major ironies of the Cold War that despite a Manichaean logic that tried to separate freedom-loving Americans from godless Communists, it became difficult for postwar America to discern the real face of the enemy. American policy makers, in a 1950 report issued by the National Security Council (called NSC-68), argued that unlike previous enemies, the Soviet Union was applying covert methods to infiltrate and corrupt America and its institutions (Field 4). This collapse between "us" and "them" led to a culture of paranoia and anxiety, since the most seemingly "American" citizens could actually be deviant Communists. Shadows made perfect sense in a culture obsessively scrutinizing everyone and everything for traces of otherness.

Although the first Red Scare appeared at the end of World War I as a reaction to the creation of the Soviet state, by the 1950s anti-Communist sentiment became a palpable force in American life.[8] As early as 1947, Truman had signed Executive Order 9835, which demanded loyalty from federal employees and allowed them to be terminated for spying and other "un-American" activities. Federal Bureau of Investigation director J. Edgar Hoover's 1956 clandestine COINTELPRO program illegally targeted Communists through spreading false rumors, unauthorized wiretaps, and forged documents. But it was Senator Joseph McCarthy's hunt for Communist infiltration in the government, military, and Hollywood from 1950 until 1954 that represented the height of the hysteria. McCarthyism and the House Un-American Activities Committee called for all Americans to intensely scrutinize their neighbors in an attempt to weed out the multitudes of Communist spies and saboteurs that McCarthy believed (or at least pretended to believe) were hiding in America. McCarthy was certainly an outspoken advocate against Communism, but he was not the sole voice.[9] This second Red Scare occurred throughout the country and seeped deeper into popular culture. While certainly not every American believed McCarthy's incredible claims that Communists had infiltrated into all areas of American life, the subject of anti-Communism was a real and unavoidable topic during the decade.

Anti-Communist propaganda appeared in a number of forms during the long fifties, including government-sponsored films that warned of the hidden dangers of the Soviet threat. Many of these were produced by the US Department of Defense's Armed Forces Information and Education division. These films, which were meant to alert citizens to the ways in which Communists might infiltrate the country, rely heavily on shadow imagery to emphasize the point that the duplicitousness of Communist agents meant that Americans must remain extremely vigilant at all times and in all places. *Communist Blueprint for Conquest*, for example, is hosted by Boris H. Kiosson, Department of State, and as its title suggests explains the methods and techniques used by the Communist Party to seize power in the United States. The opening of the film sets the tone. The title appears on what seems to be a rather peaceful map with rivers, trees, and mountains, presumably representing America. Shortly into the title, the shadow of a hammer and sickle fall onto the map, as Kiosson, from behind an authoritative desk, explains that power is what Communists want "in all forms—a blacking out of spiritual, political, economic, cultural spheres of human activity" (fig. 1.4). The shadow motif continues throughout the film to denote the underhanded activities of Communist agents as they say one thing but their sinister shadows hint at ulterior motives, as well as to imply their increase as shadows of figures proliferate to indicate the growing presence of Communist subversives. Even the arts are not immune. A figure of a dancer onstage sends the shadow of another hammer and sickle onto the curtain (fig. 1.5). Not only did this implicate the Soviet art world as part of the conspiracy, but it called into question the patriotism of American artists and their supporters. By the end of the film, almost everything is "black," an unsettling reminder of the sort of denial of "human activity" that a Communist America would imply.

Communist Blueprint for Conquest was not alone in its employment of the shadow motif to signal the duplicity of the Communist threat. *The Communist Weapon of Allure*, for example, examines how "Communist persuasion is designed to appeal to the basic human hungers." Warren B. Walsh, professor at Syracuse University, explains in a voice-over that Communism claims that it opposes misery and the exploitation of men, that it is against poverty and injustices, but as this voice-over plays the viewer sees a series of cartoon silhouettes parade across the screen that mock these lofty goals with their base and hidden desires. *Communist Target Youth* continues in this vein by describing Communism's

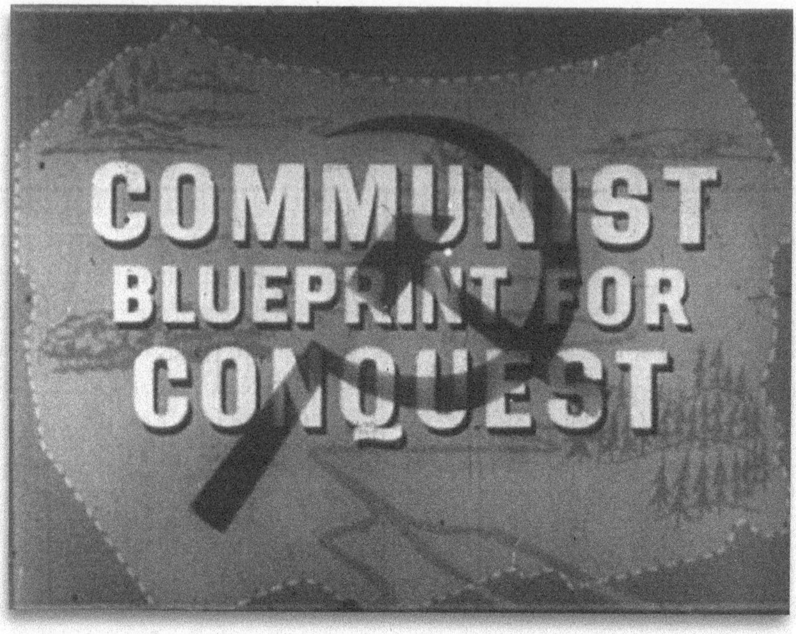

Fig. 1.4. The shadow of a hammer and sickle is used to hint at the underhanded and shady motives of the Soviet Union and its quest to cast influence over America and its freedoms. *Communist Blueprint for Conquest*, US Department of the Army, 1956, 16-millimeter black-and-white print, Fort Devens Collection, Harvard Film Archive, Harvard Library.

emotional appeal to youth while depicting a map of Eastern Europe being slowly blackened by the dark shadow of Communist expansion. To counter this danger, *Our Moral Defenses* encourages moral strength in the face of the Communist threat. As a soldier walks through the forest, four shadows await him—fear, bad ideas, poor values, and wrong principles (fig. 1.6). Here the threat is internalized. The shadows, as silhouettes, have no discernible markings save their red (and thus possibly Russian) eyes. They represent the weaknesses within American citizens that made them susceptible to the Soviet threat. Yet the ambiguity of the shadowy figures is doubled by the vagueness of the terms. What exactly makes an idea "bad," a value "poor," or a principle "wrong"? Given the logic of the film, the answer is simple: anything that does not accord with American ideals. The shadow is a placeholder in these films, a voided silhouette that could stand for almost anything conceived as anti-American, whether an actual Soviet spy, an American working for the party, or simply a confused leftist.

Or perhaps a sexual "deviant." The figure of the homosexual became a frightening specter used to scare the American public in the long fifties. Difficult to spot, corrupting, and seemingly ubiquitous, homosexuality was the dark Other to American "normalcy." This threat, as David K. Johnson makes clear in *The Lavender Scare*, was explicitly linked to the threat of Communism. Johnson notes that "both groups seemed to comprise hidden subcultures, with their own meeting places, literature, cultural codes, and bonds of loyalty. As people feared Communist 'cells' within the federal government, they feared 'nests' of homosexuals" (33). Communists and homosexuals were seen to have formed shadow societies hidden in the very midst of America. Communists posed the more obvious threat, but homosexuals, deficient in vigor and morality, were seen as too weak to support America against the Soviet menace and easily susceptible to blackmail by Russian agents. Perfect examples of holding "poor values" and "wrong principles," homosexuals were perceived, according to John D'Emilio in *Sexual Politics, Sexual Communities*, as "weak-willed,

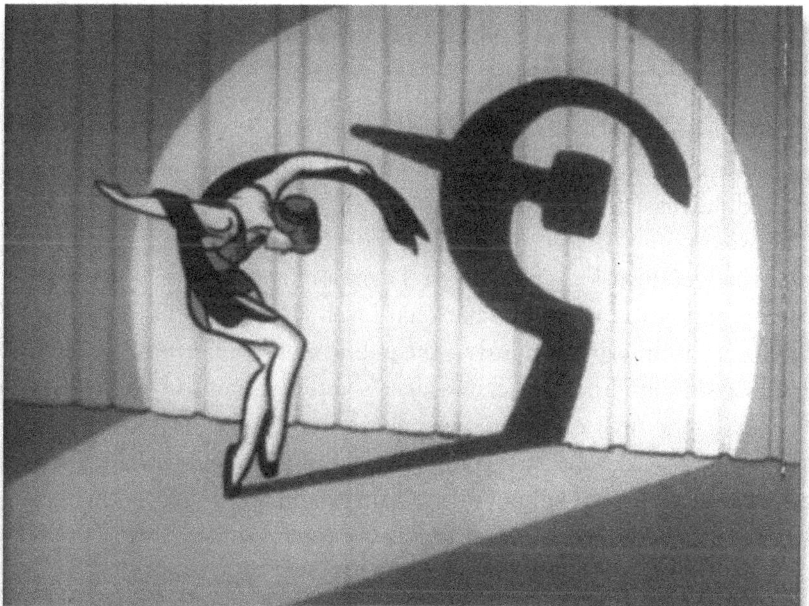

Fig. 1.5. The shadow of a dancer suggests that even in seemingly safe fields such as the arts, the presence of Communist subversives, or Americans with Communist ties, was inescapable. *Communist Blueprint for Conquest*, US Department of the Army, 1956, 16-millimeter black-and-white print, Fort Devens Collection, Harvard Film Archive, Harvard Library.

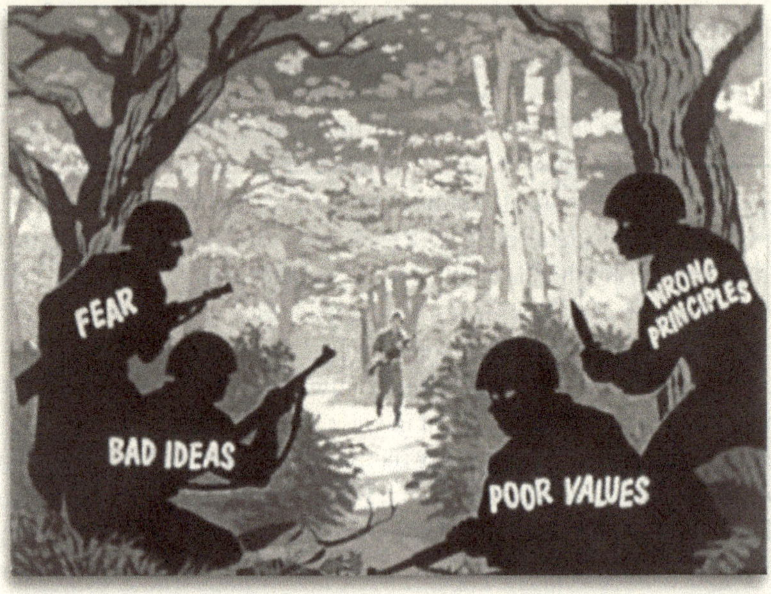

Fig. 1.6. The Communist threat, in the form of dark silhouettes with red eyes, lies waiting for Americans morally weak enough to stray from the path. *Our Moral Defenses*, Armed Forces International Films, ca. 1951, Fort Devens Collection, Harvard Film Archive, Harvard Library.

pleasure-seeking 'half men' [who] feminized everything they touched and sapped the masculine vigor that had tamed a continent" (49). Homosexuality was another threat to the borders of the home, a dangerous disease that could easily infect and weaken the nation from within. This rhetoric of contamination reached a national level, leading to the targeting of homosexuals in private industry, the public sector, and the military. The rhetoric surrounding both homosexuals and Communists was linked to fears of contamination—both were able to "spread" and "pollute" others around them (May 95). In response, Eisenhower stepped up the dismissals from government employment of suspected homosexuals that began with Truman, removing roughly forty per month during the first sixteen months after his 1953 inauguration (D'Emilio 44).

This relentless hunt for those who might undermine American freedom produced hypocrisy and paradox. In the fight to preserve the American way of life against the Communist threat, there were many willing to forgo the very freedoms and liberties that set America apart from the Soviets. According to Whitfield, hypocrisy was rampant: "When it became necessary to explain to the Russians what made American society so praiseworthy, even rabid anti-Communists were compelled to highlight the civil liberties that they themselves have sought to curtail" (25). Privacy in America was seen as a corrective to the authoritarianism of the Soviets—freedom and personal liberty trumped controlled and programmed lives. Yet as Nelson points out, this rhetoric was anything but simple. While privacy was exalted, it was also undermined by a culture of suspicion and surveillance. While the rhetoric of American triumphalism revolved around the idea that the sanctity of American private space set democracy apart from totalitarian regimes, "the very starkness of this choice manufactured the cold war's governing paradox: in the interests of preserving the space of privacy, privacy would have to be penetrated" (xiii). In an attempt to root out possible subversives, Americans were being asked to make their lives available for inspection.

While the country was worried about the specter of Communism infiltrating its borders, at the same time America was casting its own shadow across the globe. As Ralph B. Levering relates in *The Cold War: A Post–Cold War History*, US interventionism was at its height between 1956 and 1965, "with an average of twelve incidents occurring annually during that period. If extensive covert activities, military and economic aid packages, and other types of official and nonofficial actions directed against 'communism' are added in, there can be little doubt that America's Cold War interventionism was reaching its peak" (73). America emerged from the Second World War relatively intact and quickly became the moral and economic leader of the free world. But despite the rhetoric of freedom, America's strategies were fraught with paradox. As the "shadowy" world of espionage and covert operations demonstrated, oftentimes "freedom" required a moral laxity and the instillation of regimes that were anything but free. Covert operations by the nascent Central Intelligence Agency belied the idea that America unequivocally believed in the right of all people to democratically elect their leaders—in 1954, for example, the CIA overthrew the elected governments of Guatemala and Iran. Not that the Soviet Union was blameless. In 1956 the Soviets crushed the Hungarian revolution and created the Warsaw Pact to counter NATO in Europe. But the geographical expansion of the Cold War into the third world that occurred in the 1950s ushered in an era of realpolitik where expediency and the perceived need to check their opponent's aggression at all costs allowed both powers to take refuge in morality's gray areas.

This sublimated battle by proxy that occurred throughout the world has produced one of the most lasting cultural legacies of the Cold War—

the figure of the spy. One of the main reasons that the image of the shadow is indelibly linked to the period is because of its association with the idea of Cold War espionage. Oftentimes, this connection is literal. In *Celluloid Mushroom Clouds*, Joyce A. Evans discusses atomic spy films, tracing them to the shadowy world of film noir (128–29). Communist agents always appear in shadows or in the dark, in keeping with their ambiguous and sinister purposes. But it was the very nature of the spy that placed him or her in an ambiguous position that blurred boundaries. Michael Kackman, in his work *Citizen Spy*, relates that "spies were everywhere in 1950s American media culture. Villains and heroes, they emerged from the shadows just long enough to affirm America's worst fears of Communist infiltration" (1). Although there were real spies, both foreign and domestic, the majority appeared as fictional characters designed to reinforce Cold War values. Many of these shows, in fact, were pitched as semidocumentary and engaged the postwar social world in real ways. Oftentimes, characters directly addressed the camera, breaking the illusion of entertainment in order to admonish audiences to do their civic duty. Discussing the show *I Led 3 Lives*, Kackman observes that "these 1950s programs regularly blurred the distinction between television as entertainment and television as a technologized extension of the public sphere . . . encouraging viewers to participate in neighborhood and city activities as a patriotic local corollary to the national efforts of on-screen spies" (xxxv). In the show, Herb Philbrick is an anti-Communist federal agent but also a suburban patriarch. The television viewer is meant to maintain a vigilant watch for potential subversives and to participate in their local communities in order to fulfill their civic responsibilities.

But the figure of the spy created deeper ambiguities beyond what was real and what was fictive. By their very nature, spies occupy a dangerous middle ground between nations where lying is expected and allegiances are transitory. Exploring FBI informant films where the agent is in an "ambiguous position" as a "potential hero, but nevertheless a person courting the stigma of an informer" (110), Hendershot observes that "the role of the plant is dangerous precisely for this reason: the individual must at the same time be both inside and outside the camp of both the friend and the enemy" (113). The spy raised the issue that was on everyone's minds—how do I know whom to trust? Alliances could quickly shift, turning a pro-American spy into a "double" agent for the Soviets. Films like the Oscar-nominated *I Was a Communist for the FBI* (1951) "illustrate . . . the blurring between fiction and reality that often occurred in anti-Communist propaganda of the early Fifties" (115). This shadowy borderland was precisely the terrain that spies traversed. The figure of the spy challenged clear boundaries by pretending to be one thing when he or she was really another. Standing in the shadows, the spy might claim allegiance, but how could anyone fully trust such a shady figure? Spies were the inverse of proper citizens who were expected to make their allegiances known and to stand behind their claims in the light of day, yet Americans in the postwar period were also being asked to keep a furtive eye on their neighbors, since anyone could harbor Communist sympathies. Early Cold War America forced everyone into the shadows.

TENSIONS ON THE HOME FRONT

It is one of the major ironies of the postwar period that under the shadow of nuclear fear, the majority of Americans nevertheless continued to flourish. Fueled by wartime success, the US economy boomed and the standard of living rose at such a rate that many are still nostalgic for the decade. The symbol of this prosperity was the ranch-style suburban home that became ubiquitous across America. According to Clifford E. Clark Jr. in his contribution to the collection *Recasting America: Culture and Politics in the Age of the Cold War*, due to new construction techniques pioneered by Long Island housing tract developer William Levitt and a liberal home loan policy, housing starts surged, reaching a record 1.65 million in 1955 and remaining at around 1.5 million the rest of the decade (183). The middle class was rapidly expanding. White-collar workers outnumbered blue-collar workers for the first time in America in 1956, 60 percent of the American population had achieved what the government termed a "middle-class" standard of living in 1955 (compared to 31 percent in 1929), and by 1960, 60 percent of US families owned homes and 75 percent owned cars and washing machines (Brinkley 66). Revisionist historians point out that these trends may well have been in place before the Cold War and such opportunities were clearly not open to every American. Nevertheless, it is indisputable that for the majority of Americans, the tense Cold War period was also a time of increased economic opportunity and the beginning of our present-day consumer culture.

Yet the ranch-style suburban home was also the site of ideological struggle. With its connotations of family and private domestic space, the home became the backbone of conceptions of American freedom and democracy. It replaced the public sphere as the site for preserving

American values, a sacrosanct domain that would form a bulwark against the encroaching shadow of the Communist threat. Thus May borrows the metaphor of foreign containment to discuss how domestic policies made the home a battleground, stating, "Containment aptly describes the way in which public policy, personal behavior, and even political values were focused on the home" (14). The most notorious example of such "domestic containment" was Vice President Richard M. Nixon and Soviet premier Nikita Khrushchev's "kitchen debate," where Nixon argued for the supremacy of American capitalism through an appeal to the superiority of its household appliances. Unlike the restrained bungalow of the 1930s, the ranch-style home of the 1950s was designed to foster a more open, relaxed, and healthy environment. As Clark maintains in "Ranch-House Suburbia: Ideals and Realities," "a properly designed modern ranch home would solve the family's needs for work and recreation . . . matching the fun-loving companionate family's needs for a home environment that would be useful, convenient, and enjoyable" (174). If May is correct in arguing that the Cold War offered "private and personal solutions to social problems" and that "the family was the arena in which that adaptation was expected to occur" (14), then the suburban home was seen as instrumental in promoting the happy and healthy families that would lead to a strong and secure America.

The shadow of uncertainty and doubt infected the home from within its borders. America struggled to retain a sense of normalcy in a world that had just emerged from a devastating world war and that threatened nuclear apocalypse at any moment. In order to achieve this, a sense of shared purpose was invoked in order to combat the Communist threat from abroad. The home, as the major site where such cultural ideologies took effect, bore the brunt of such logic. The suburban home was meant to deliver a sense of protection and privacy, blending in peacefully with the natural environment and guarding the family from outside threats. But the idea of the American home was fraught with internal paradox. The irony was that Americans were being asked to be both individualistic and free while yet conforming to social norms that were seen as the foundation for a strong America. According to May, suburbs may have been seen as the bastion of middle-class America, but they also "weakened extended-family ties, promoted homogeneity in the neighborhoods, intensified racial segregation, encouraged conformity, and fostered a style of life based on traditional gender roles in the home" (174). Americans were becoming trapped in their own personal ideals.

The onus of maintaining this domestic space fell mainly on (white) women, but their role as defenders of the American home was problematic.[10] The kitchen debate between Nixon and Khrushchev epitomized the role reserved for women during the period; they were supposed to maintain a bright and cheery household while remaining attractive for their husbands. Such demands meant that the housewife had little time for other pursuits. As Stephanie Coontz notes in *The Way We Never Were*, "The amount of time women spent doing housework actually *increased* during the 1950s, despite the advent of convenience foods and new, labor-saving appliances; child care absorbed more than twice as much time as it had in the 1920s" (27). Coontz traces this increase to a new conception of domesticity as personal service that occurred during the period. Mothers and wives were unable to delegate work to anyone or anything else for fear of losing the "loving touch" that it was her job to provide. Although critics have demonstrated that by no means all women fell into this pattern, a new myth of the American family developed.[11] While the men earned the money for the household, women in turn were expected to keep the home and to provide a safe and comfortable haven for their husbands when they returned home from work.

Women were also made responsible for the maintenance of psychological harmony within the home. Here much of the rhetoric revolved around the issue of sexuality. May ties exaggerated domesticity to anti-Communist domestic containment strategies, arguing that "strong families required two essential ingredients: sexual restraint outside marriage and traditional gender roles in marriage" (99). Women were responsible for both. Rather than turning toward a more repressed image of sex, postwar American discourse encouraged sexual fulfillment, provided it occurred within married households between husband and wife. Male sexual gratification signaled an end to promiscuity and potential homosexuality; female fulfillment meant less infidelity and a happier domestic sphere. A similar logic permeated child rearing. Femininity was both a strength and a potential weakness lurking inside the home: "Mothers who neglected their children bred criminals; mothers who overindulged their sons turned them into passive, weak, and effeminate 'perverts'" (96). Much of this rhetoric concerning domesticity was the result of a troubling image of the housewife as despondent, depressed, and exhausted. As with the unhappiness of their husbands, women shared the problem of conformity and the boredom, despair, and isolation that long hours in the home sometimes fostered. Ironically, the very space meant to be a sanctuary was often the cause of unrest.

The postwar home was conceived as a barrier that protected the family from the dangers lurking without it, but the shadow of the bomb fell over the home as well. As May correctly observes, "The message was ambivalent, however, for the family also seemed particularly vulnerable. It needed heavy protection against the intrusions of forces outside itself" (3). This tension is dramatically captured in an advertisement for asbestos that appeared in the magazine *Newsweek* just one day after the Japanese attack on Pearl Harbor (fig. 1.7). The specter of war in America was represented as a sort of outside threat subject to materialize at any moment. The shadow of the planes in the advertisement, intangible yet clearly representing the potential for destruction, dwarf the new suburban home that was offered to Americans as a symbol of prosperity. Ironically, the viewer cannot be sure whether these are enemy or Allied planes, as the shadows are unable to convey the markings of nationality. But their unmistakable size and the fact that there are three of them clearly demonstrate their importance and threat to the safety of the suburban home. The text of the advertisement states that "peace will return," and when it does the company will be "able to ship you everything you want, when you want it"—normality will return in the form of satisfactory consumer consumption. Though the message sounds reassuring, the shadow of the first plane cuts across a section of the house, reminding readers they still must live under the specter of war.

In the preface to his work *In the Shadow of War*, Michael S. Sherry describes how the figure of the shadow was a fitting metaphor for the anxiety over America's safety. Sherry argues that cultural products such as this *Newsweek* advertisement represent "a metaphor apt for a half-century of anxiety about the nation's safety. . . . War's shadow hung over the nation, but its substance was hard to grasp" (ix). While the advertisement was speaking to a specific threat of attack in World War II, its uneasy message was just as applicable to the Cold War. As William M. Tuttle Jr. observes, "Both the Cold War crusade against an absolutely evil enemy and the nuclear specter—or at least the haunting fear of dying in an air raid—began during the Second World War" (14). In a sense, the advertisement's optimism was not misplaced—the physical damage that the United States suffered during the war was minimal compared to other parts of the world, and after the war the economy did indeed exceed expectations. However, what this advertisement inadvertently conveys is the mental and emotional repercussions that would continue to trouble America into the postwar years. As the hot war turned cold,

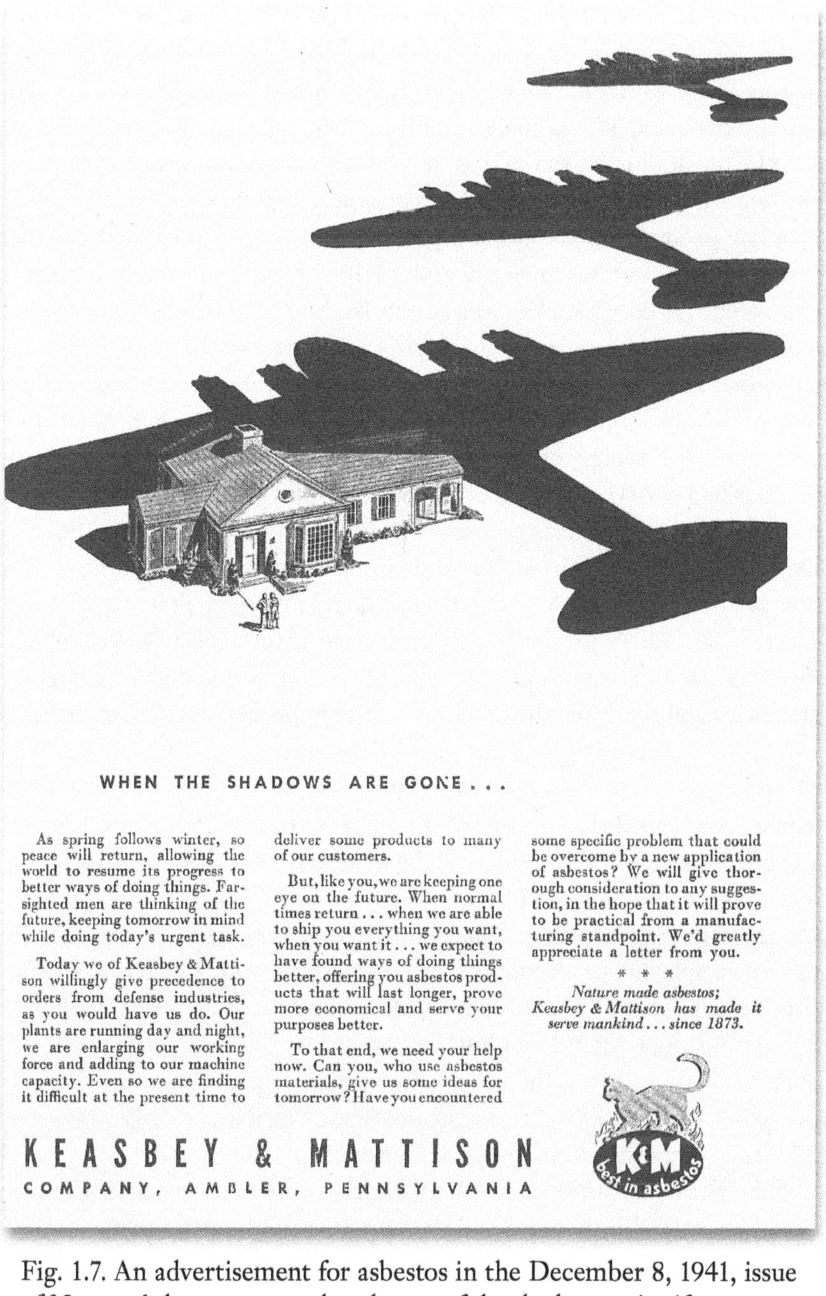

Fig. 1.7. An advertisement for asbestos in the December 8, 1941, issue of *Newsweek* demonstrates that the use of the shadow to signify a vague, unexpected threat against the sanctity of the American home was a strategy that can be traced to World War II.

the shadows that haunted the country changed from rising suns, Nazis, and the "darkness" of the Holocaust into mushroom clouds and radioactive fallout. The fear of nuclear annihilation, total destruction coming instantaneously from somewhere far off in the distance, became the driving concern. The home was a refuge, but not an impermeable one.

The tension between the dark shadows lurking outside and the safety and security of the home was further complicated by one of the most peculiar products of the postwar period—the bomb shelter. With the threat of nuclear attack and radioactive fallout looming, many Americans embraced the bomb shelter as a useful backup plan in the event of the worst. As Janna Jones states in "Living with the Bomb: The Retreat to the Suburban Bomb Shelter," in 1961 President John F. Kennedy called for every house to have a bomb shelter, and *Life* magazine, in the same year, published blueprints for its design. By 1962 over 200,000 American families had one (1). But the idea of a bomb shelter gave the lie to the myth of the suburban home as the space of domestic peace and tranquility. Dark, enclosed, and buried, bomb shelters were the shadow of the ranch homes above ground. As Jones remarks, the fallout shelter, as a buried space, was at odds with the "ranch-style architecture of the period, which idealized the illusion of space" (10). Designers strove to make the shelter attractive and to mimic the openness of the home above it. Since shelters would be useful only in the case of nuclear attack, they "were therefore promoted as attractive additions to the home. Middle-class materialism suppressed, or at least disguised, the purpose of the shelter and the destruction it suggested" (7) (fig. 1.8). Depictions of bomb shelters display a constant tension between purpose and promotion. In an attempt to hide the anxiety of their function, the reality of their subterranean setting had to be downplayed, or alternative uses had to be found. The bomb shelter functioned as a sort of repressed Gothic space. Like Horace Walpole's dungeon, Edgar Allan Poe's burial chamber, or the creepy basements in countless horror films, the bomb shelter was a buried reminder of what everyone wanted to forget—in the postwar case, the cave-like existence awaiting humanity should nuclear war ensue.

The paradoxes that bomb shelters produced were raised at the national level as well. As with the rhetoric surrounding the home, public discussion of the bomb shelter was implicated in larger concerns running throughout the culture. Through a review of civil defense research, Jones demonstrates how the bomb shelter was linked to domestic concerns involving traditional family values, capitalist ideology that equated

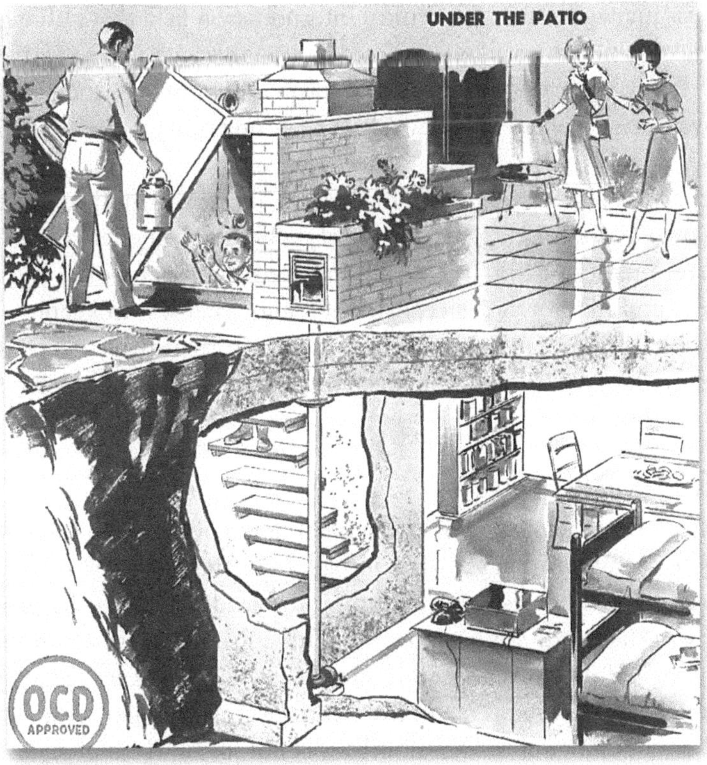

Fig. 1.8. The grim reminder of the possibility of life underground was made palatable by treating the bomb shelter as an extension of the suburban home. In this cutaway plan by the Office of Civil Defense published in the December 1961 issue of *Popular Mechanics*, the reader is shown how to build, underneath the patio, a low-cost shelter that seamlessly meshes with the idealized depiction of family life above.

possessions with freedom and security, and national discourses that buried social problems and anxieties under a veneer of patriarchal safety (3). In order for Americans to accept the containment strategy, they had to be convinced that they could survive a nuclear attack. According to Guy Oakes in his work *The Imaginary War: Civil Defense and American Cold War Culture*, from the standpoint of civil defense administrators, there was both an optimistic and a cynical viewpoint regarding the strategy:

> The optimistic interpretation held that Americans could actually manage their own survival. The purpose of civil defense was to provide them with the information and training necessary for nuclear

> crisis management. The cynical interpretation held that although the state could protect the American people in a nuclear attack and they could not be expected to protect themselves, they could at least be expected to believe that self-protection was possible. (7)

In either case, it was a simple, if disturbing, fact that Americans were on their own in the case of nuclear attack. The bomb shelter represented the irrationality of the dream that inspired the ranch house standing above it and in many ways repeated the logic that was in keeping with the desire of the suburbs in the first place—in their drive for personal accumulation, Americans were becoming more and more isolated from their neighbors.

THE SPECTER OF RACE

For many Americans, racial difference at home became the fearful corollary to Communist aggression abroad. One of the darkest shadows in American life that was only beginning to be addressed in the postwar years was the condition of nonwhite ethnic groups. Here again inconsistencies and paradoxes emerge. According to Coontz in *The Way We Never Were*, the general trend toward marrying younger, establishing families, and moving to the suburbs was not just a white phenomenon (26). More Americans, of every ethnicity, were sharing in the postwar dream of home ownership. But white citizens profited more than most by the upsurge in the economy. As Coontz notes, "Minorities were almost entirely excluded from the gains and privileges accorded white middle-class families," and many faced segregation and even brutality in the face of attempts at integration (30–31). Desegregation in the army occurred in 1948 and in education in 1954, but the decade of the fifties was only the beginning of the civil rights movement. Although there were many racial suburbs, there was still no racial difference *within* suburbs. Recent scholarship on the 1950s reminds us that while the image we have of the decade is overwhelmingly white, the realities of the period were much more diverse. Unfortunately, for many Americans, the Communist threat abroad and the civil rights movements at home were equally troubling in their attempt to break down the barriers between "us" and "them," and the fifties remained a highly segregated society.[12]

Shadows, as racially charged signifiers, haunt the collective American psyche. The figure of the shadow has long been a disturbing metaphor of racial difference. George Lipsitz has remarked that whiteness, as the organizing principle in American culture, "never has to speak its name" (369). It is in the darkened space of the shadow where the occluded forces its appearance. The terms "shade" and "spook" have long been used as derogatory slurs, calling attention to the connection between the darkened shadow and the black body.[13] Shadows invoke the vexed discussion of skin color that is omnipresent (if willingly overlooked) in American society, pointing out racial difference and the hierarchy it creates. The insubstantiality that shadows convey also speak directly to the social, highlighting the existence of marginalized others who, despite their presence, cannot be "seen" by society. Ethnic minorities haunt America in spectral form, reminding mainstream society of those it has pushed to the sidelines. The unstable shadow quickly becomes politicized, a representation of the fear that racial border crossings can create.

The anxiety caused by racial difference is particularly acute in the American Gothic tradition, where the trauma of the past continually returns to haunt the present. As the critic Leslie Fiedler explains in his *Love and Death in the American Novel*, "through these gothic images are projected certain obsessive concerns of our national life: the ambiguity of our relationship with Indian and Negro, the ambiguity of our encounter with nature, the guilt of the revolutionist who feels himself a parricide" (27).[14] Such "ambiguities" between relationships create uneasiness. The Gothic plays on the anxieties generated by the threat of contamination and the destabilization of categories necessary for producing a sense of order. With its images and tropes such as the shadow, this genre revels in instability by rendering it in terms that both call it forth and suppress it simultaneously. In his introduction to *American Gothic: New Interventions in a National Narrative*, Eric Savoy compares this ambiguity as a "'turn' toward compelling but unthematizable narrative" that "might be conceptualized as the emergence of the Lacanian Real" (8). Like Jacques Lacan's *objet petit a*, the shadow is that which struggles to be made manifest but which can never become fully realized, or in the words of Judith Butler, "that which resists and compels symbolization" (qtd. in Savoy 8). Shadows are the Gothic trope par excellence. They are both the real manifestation of our presence and a symbolic other that compels explication. In that intermediary boundary, the Gothic does its unsettling work. In the American context, the Gothic shadow calls to mind the anxiety of race and the fears of miscegenation that it produced in the early Cold War.

Toni Morrison, in her work *Playing in the Dark: Whiteness and the Literary Imagination*, explores how "Africanist" presence informs American thinking, even when African Americans remain unmentioned. In her aptly named section "Romancing the Shadow," she explains,

> Even, and especially, when American texts are not "about" Africanist presences or characters or narrative or idiom, the shadow hovers in implication. . . . Race, in fact, now functions as a metaphor so necessary to the construction of Americanness that it rivals the old pseudo-scientific and class-informed racisms whose dynamics we are more used to deciphering. (46–47)

Morrison points out that figures of darkness, like the shadow, are necessarily overburdened with racial undertones. Especially in the American context, this figure not only is a site for disrupting personal boundaries of subjectivity but likewise calls into question how such identities were founded in the first place. The shadow, as an arbitrary figure standing between black and white, perfectly registers an American unease with the question of race.

This link between shadow and race is made explicit in John Cassavetes's classic postwar film *Shadows* (1959). Cassavetes's film was part of a larger avant-garde trend that used jazz motifs and improvisation to question the assumptions of early Cold War America. While much has been made of the film's experimental style, *Shadows* also registers the uneasy racial dynamics of Eisenhower's America. The short-lived love story of Lelia, an African American passing as white, and Tony, a white man who initiates her sexually but absconds when he realizes she is black, *Shadows* draws attention to the importance of the color line in American cultural life. Interracial friendships and the couple's romance might blur boundaries between the two worlds, but Tony's ultimate betrayal highlights the power of established racial dichotomies. The title itself reflects the multiple levels on which the film operates. "Shadows" represents both the noir-ish aesthetic of the film's cinematography as well as its ambiguous racial politics. Tony is wrong, of course, but in a postwar America defined by black and white binaries, his decision registers a cultural fact. In a postwar world where race mattered immensely, no decision could remain pure and unadulterated but ultimately had to reside in a shadowy world of ambiguities. As its title implies, *Shadows* leaves the viewer guessing.

The rhetoric of the Cold War was based on simple dichotomies. The reality of life in the Cold War, however, was not so simple. Shadows are an important and enduring Cold War image because they captured the unease and tension inherent in an anxious society. Mitigating the line between the supposed truth of light and the evilness of dark, shadows revealed the inconsistencies and paradoxes of the period. Cold War rhetoric, despite its attempt to police boundaries and contain threats, was under constant revision. The American public was indeed anxious about Soviet aggression and the threat of nuclear holocaust, but it was also strangely fascinated by the novelty of the times. Shadows captured that tension. While shadows themselves were too unstable to offer solutions to Cold War problems, they were remarkably adept at unveiling the paradoxes of a culture in which Americans were struggling to understand their strange new world.

The remainder of this study will explore attempts by postwar artists to use shadow imagery as a means to imagine possibilities outside the confines of Cold War logic. Their work demonstrates the usefulness of shadows in challenging the binary thinking that ruled the postwar period. The ways in which shadows were employed were never entirely consistent from one artist or one work to the next, or even within multiple works of a single artist. What does unite the artists and works under consideration is the way in which they all employed shadow imagery to question existing modes of thought. Shadows do not provide a new system to replace the flawed binaries of the Cold War—they are far too ambiguous for that. But they do encourage readers and viewers to rethink their assumptions and to pose questions that otherwise remain unasked. Shadows, by their very nature, unsettle and disturb. For these artists of the postwar period, however, the trouble shadows caused was the starting point for examining the problems of the early Cold War era and what might possibly be done about them.

2. WHAT THE SHADOWS KNOW

The Return of the Crime-Fighting Hero the Shadow in Late-1950s Literature

During the Depression era of the 1930s and the war years of the 1940s, millions of Americans sought escape from the tumultuous times in pulp magazines, comic books, and radio programs. In the face of mob violence, joblessness, war, and social upheaval, masked crusaders provided a much-needed source of security where good triumphed over evil and wrongs were made right. Heroes such as Doc Savage, the Flash, Wonder Woman, Green Lantern, Captain America, and, of course, Superman were always there to save the day, making the world seem fair and in order. This imaginative world not only was an escape from less cheery realities but also ended up providing nostalgic memories of childhood for many of the writers of the early Cold War years. This chapter explores the role that one crime fighting hero from this era, the Shadow, plays in the work of Sylvia Plath, Jack Kerouac, and LeRoi Jones/Amiri Baraka. While clearly on the side of good, the Shadow, as his name suggests, had a dark side that proved irresistible to these writers.

At first glance, this seems an odd assortment of writers to bring together. Though Plath, Kerouac, and Baraka shared an interest in confessional writing that gained momentum in the 1950s, their differences are more striking than their similarities. Plath, who married the British poet Ted Hughes and had two children, spent a good deal of time in England writing highly controlled verse. Kerouac, a peripatetic loner who celebrated America, insisted on spontaneous, free-flowing production. Baraka, an African American writer struggling with a racist America, eventually took the uptown train to Harlem in order to produce more politicized work meant to directly impact his community. What unites these very different writers, however, is their mutual interest in the Shadow. All three penned tributes to this crime fighter, using him to examine the loss of childhood innocence and the entry into the adult world. What attracted Plath, Kerouac, and Baraka was the undercurrent of ambiguity that permeated this character. The Shadow was useful for these writers not only because he embodied a transitional figure between the child's world of caped superheroes and the adult world of harsh realities but also because the ambiguity he represented provided a way of critiquing the binary dichotomies that helped define the postwar world.

In the uncertain world of the Depression and World War II, superheroes like Superman and Captain America emerged as characters meant to provide stability and the sense of a moral order, but the Shadow was a highly ambiguous figure. Called "the Shadow" because he moved undetected in these dark spaces, his name provided a hint to his divided character. Although he was clearly on the side of good, he battled his adversaries in the darkness, fighting the villains and criminals of the 1930s and 1940s on their own terms. The Shadow became an icon of the dualities of the period, when a seemingly orderly world could easily give way to ruin and catastrophe. Though his importance would wane by the mid-1940s, replaced by more ideologically sound wartime superheroes, the imaginative world the Shadow evoked would linger in the minds of Plath, Kerouac, and Baraka. The Shadow, tinged as he was with darkness and uncertainty, became the perfect image of ambiguity when these authors began to explore the dualities of the Cold War.

For these three writers, the Shadow was a liminal figure standing on the shifting borders of memory. Plath, Kerouac, and Baraka all used the Shadow as a means to decode their relationship to their pasts. But the past has little meaning without a present in which to actualize, and thus these authors' explorations of memory necessarily involved them in a comment on the conditions of their writing. Their discussions of the Shadow elicited not just nostalgia for an earlier time but also a foreboding. The Shadow's mysterious and paradoxical nature was an enticement into the world of imagination for their younger selves and ultimately an introduction into the complexities of adulthood. But the Shadow, like his alter ego Lamont Cranston, had a dual role to fill: he also served as a fitting metaphor for the doubts these authors had about the binaries the Cold War fostered. All three authors used the ambiguities the Shadow presented to challenge postwar American society. The Shadow, a slippery character that is difficult to pin down, became a useful gateway into the past that quickly came to reverberate with the anxieties of the Cold War present.

The most obvious payoff for an examination of the Shadow's revival in the work of Plath, Kerouac, and Baraka is that it reveals how each of these writers used a popular culture phenomenon to nostalgically re-create that liminal space between adolescence and adulthood. Childhood is a construct, and these writers re-created a past that had firm roots in the present. Although they professed to be creating accounts of earlier experiences, these three authors were, unconsciously or not, simultaneously writing accounts of the Cold War. While the Shadow might have been a product of the Depression and the Second World War, the ambiguity he represented was surprisingly amenable to the needs of the Cold War era. Finally, the uses of the Shadow in these works also tell us something about shadows themselves—how their ambiguous nature works to create understanding, as well as fear, as we struggle to fill in the vague edges of their outline.

THE SHADOW KNOWS

The importance of the Shadow in American popular culture should not be underestimated. The character started out on the radio, reaching "more than 15 million listeners at home," and the show bearing his name became "the highest rated dramatic program on the air" during its peak years (Cox 224). The 1930s and 1940s were radio's "golden age," and *The Shadow* was one of its most popular shows. Originally, however, the Shadow was merely a spokesperson, an eerie phantom voice that introduced listeners in 1930 with the lines "Conscience is a taskmaster no crook can escape. It is a jeering shadow even in the blackest lives. The Shadow knows . . . and you too shall know if you listen [to] Street & Smith's *Detective Story Magazine*" (Tollin 4). Listeners enjoyed the character so much that they would ask for "that Shadow detective magazine" rather than *Detective Story Magazine*, and thus the circulation manager decided to hire Walter Gibson in 1931 to pen *The Shadow Magazine* to fill the demand (4). Gibson's character was a huge success, with sales so large that the magazine began to come out twice a month, despite the Depression. It was this success that, ironically, led to the Shadow receiving his own radio show, hosted by Orson Welles, in 1937 (5). Both the pulp magazines and the radio show continued into the 1950s, with the character crossing over into television and comic books and even making occasional appearances in film. It is difficult to imagine anyone during the immediate postwar era not being aware of the Shadow, and even today his voice can still be found on the odd late-night radio program.

Although the pulps and the radio both shared the Shadow, the character manifested himself differently in each. An obvious reason for this was the constraints and possibilities of medium—radio can do things print cannot, and vice versa. In the pulps, the Shadow is part hard-boiled detective and part mysterious avenger, in equal turns. Lamont Cranston, his alter ego, is the same "man about town" as in the radio programs and resorts to the same type of deduction to solve his cases. But here the Shadow draws heavily on the detective novels of the period. He is tough and streetwise and lives by his own code of vigilante justice outside the law. The Shadow also has a stable of helpers (along with several alter egos) to do his bidding. With his gang, they battle villains in streets and alleyways until the Shadow ends victorious, the evildoers either dead or behind bars. The illustrations for the pulps likewise point to the influence of the hard-boiled genre on Gibson's writing (fig. 2.1). The stark contrasts of light and darkness are reminiscent of film noir (more about this in chapter 5), a genre that borrowed extensively from the novels of Dashiell Hammett, James M. Cain, and Raymond Chandler. The pulp Shadow, then, fits nicely into a type of fiction that flourished in the 1930s and 1940s—the antihero who is beholden to his own code of ethics.

The Shadow's appeal was due in large part to the specter of crime. The character was born in the Depression, when mob violence and charismatic criminals were very much in the minds of Americans. The Shadow was a tour guide to the underworld, giving his fans a taste of the shady, clandestine lives of the criminals he pursued. The idea that the Shadow was providing the valuable services of not only fighting crime but also informing the public was a conceit that ran throughout both formats but was more pronounced in the pulps. In one of the earlier magazine editions, the Shadow signs a statement on the inside of the front cover certifying that he finds the contents "a true account of my activities" and that "Mr. Grant [Gibson's pen name] and the publishers

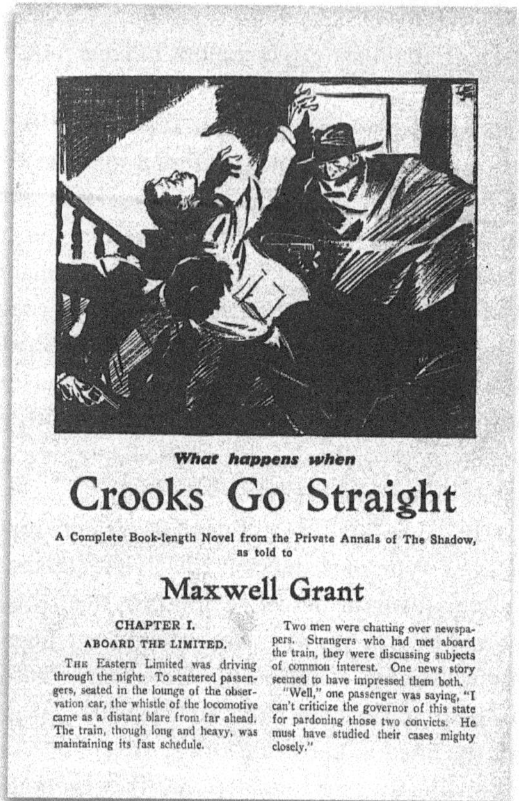

What happens when

Crooks Go Straight

A Complete Book-length Novel from the Private Annals of The Shadow, as told to

Maxwell Grant

CHAPTER I.

ABOARD THE LIMITED.

THE Eastern Limited was driving through the night. To scattered passengers, seated in the lounge of the observation car, the whistle of the locomotive came as a distant blare from far ahead. The train, though long and heavy, was maintaining its fast schedule.

Two men were chatting over newspapers. Strangers who had met aboard the train, they were discussing subjects of common interest. One news story seemed to have impressed them both.

"Well," one passenger was saying, "I can't criticize the governor of this state for pardoning those two convicts. He must have studied their cases mighty closely."

Fig. 2.1. *The Shadow Magazine* depicts the crime fighter, covering his identity with a hat and a cloak as he casts his dark shadow on the wall, in action scenes reminiscent of the hard-boiled and film noir genres.

have been awarded exclusive privilege to such of my future exploits as may be considered of interest to the American public" (*The Shadow: A Detective Magazine*, n.p.). While such a disclaimer surely did not fool adult audiences into believing in the real-life existence of the Shadow, and many adolescents probably understood the ruse as well, the emergence of the Shadow during an intense period of mob violence was no coincidence. Blurring the lines between fiction and reality, the Shadow was both popular entertainment and effective propaganda against the criminal element.[1]

What set the pulp Shadow apart from his hard-boiled counterparts is what the writer Walter Gibson called his "mysterioso" side. In an interview with Ann Charters, Gibson remarked that he "didn't want to go into fantasy or science fiction" with his character but rather wanted to create a "mysterious man who comes out of the dark" ("'True-Story' Novels" 98). This "mysterious" aspect occurs repeatedly in the pulp magazines and is ultimately responsible for creating a character that exists on the border between tough vigilante and superhuman crime fighter. The Shadow's strangeness could be heard in his laugh, which unsettled criminal as well as fan. In "The Red Blot," the narrator declares that "a whispering laugh—an uncanny announcement of a sinister presence—this betokened the arrival of The Shadow" (Gibson 62). In another story, his laugh is described as "mocking," "merciless," and filled with "hollow mirth" (Gibson, "Chinese Disks," 65, 30, 33). Terms like "uncanny presence" and the name "the Shadow" itself reinforce the sort of "mysterioso" atmosphere that Gibson created in his work.

The Shadow is important for our purposes because he becomes a shadow within a shadow. Wearing a black coat and a slouch hat, the Shadow is adept at hiding in the shadows, moving "as a streak of darkness which terminates in perfect silhouette" (Gibson, "Red Blot" 7). What makes the Shadow so mysterious is that he is able to cloak himself by moving in shadows. In the end, the Shadow's secret is his ability to think and act quicker than others—he is not superhuman, just a better human (Gibson, "Voodoo Master" 89). He hides in the shadow, doubling it with a second presence, presiding within absence and trace. Thus he is a double agent, but one aligned with the forces of light and truth even as he uses their "clouding" to affect his deeds.[2] Like a shadow, he must always remain slightly ambiguous—he can never be present in full illumination (unless he assumes one of his alter egos, which works by the light of day) lest he lose the power that gives him the advantage over his foes. It is almost as if a life lived in darkness has cast its own shadow upon him, branding him with a bit of the animosity that remains in his vengeance and his laughter. As we will see, it is this "mysterioso" side that Plath, Kerouac, and Baraka found so appealing about him.

Although they cross-fertilized each other (the magazines listed times and radio stations for each city), the pulp Shadow and his radio cousin were separate phenomena, each with his own historical trajectories. *The Shadow* radio programs hinged on the conceit that the Shadow, through a skill learned "years ago in the Orient," has the ability to "cloud men's minds" so that he can move through the show undetected by the villains (*The Shadow: Radio's Greatest Man of Mystery*, "Murder with Music" episode).[3] Most episodes relied on this power to place the Shadow in private dialogue with the villain in order to extract a confession. The

Shadow becomes the "conscience" of the character, and through threats and cajolery the criminal eventually either confesses or helps the Shadow to apprehend the guilty party. Though the radio program was a bit less violent than the pulps, the Shadow is more than willing to employ vigilante justice in both to achieve his ends. For example, in "The Three Ghosts" episode, the Shadow tricks one villain into running over his partner with a car. The Shadow always prevails—even when someone will not go quietly, the Shadow is able to maneuver him (his adversaries were always male) into the hands of the waiting police.

The Shadow's signature trademark, his diabolical laugh, bookended the show and allowed him to startle his victims, lending an eerie quality to the radio program and striking fear into the hearts of his opponents. Thus his famous line, "Who knows what evil lurks in the hearts of men? The Shadow knows," is both a statement of fact and a threat. The radio show retained a bit more ambiguity than the pulps, since it is not always clear whether "the Shadow knows" before the evildoer confesses or after. Yet like his pulp counterpart, the Shadow, a "student of science" and "man of wealth," can usually deduce what that criminal is plotting ("Death Stalks the Shadow" episode). In the end, however, Lamont Cranston yields to the Shadow in order to extricate an airtight confession and wrap up the facts of the case for the listeners.

The radio show was also a bit more Gothic than the pulps. Creaking doors, organ music, and the presence of ghosts (though always unveiled as fake) created a spooky atmosphere and were undoubtedly part of the show's popularity. As one reviewer comments, "The hiss and crackle of 1930s radio, coupled with the ghostly glow from the radio dial, undoubtedly magnified the gothic mood of the music" (Roach 105). Although the Shadow himself scoffed at the idea of ghosts, his ability to become invisible to his enemies bordered on the supernatural. Of course this ruse made sense given the medium—there had to be a way to have the Shadow be "in the shadows" but at the same time to hear his voice. Making him invisible allowed the listener to appreciate the villain's frustration at a disembodied voice and lent another level of eeriness to the show. Although this device sometimes slipped into incredibility, it nevertheless provided the strange feeling that perhaps there was no Shadow at all, just villains talking with their own vengeful consciences. The radio Shadow might not have resided in actual shadows, but his ability to move through men's minds to extract confessions, coupled with his spiteful laughter at the beginning and end of each show, propelled the character beyond the realms of a normal crime-fighting hero. While he may have declared at the end of the program that "the weed of crime bears bitter fruit . . . crime does not pay," the methods he used to arrive at that conclusion sent a mixed message.

The Shadow, in both his pulp and radio forms, was an ambiguous sort of hero. On the surface, he was clearly defending the interests of the average citizen and, by extension, the average reader or listener. His villains, whether they were the heads of organized crime or the evil masterminds of murderous plots, deserved to be beaten. The Shadow satisfied the demand for a vigilante justice, getting to the root of the problem immediately and making sure that it did not reappear.[4] Yet as a character, the Shadow went beyond the simple exploits of a crime fighter like Superman, and even those he saved were not sure whether they would like to come across him on a dark night in a strange alley. His diabolical laughter was perhaps the best sign of his ambiguity. One would assume that it was directed at his adversaries, but its vengeful and spiteful nature, its uncanniness, struck fear into victims as well as victimizers. Ultimately, it was his secrecy that set the Shadow apart. The Shadow confounds easy dichotomies, proving that the darkness, or better yet, the space between light and darkness, likewise holds the possibility for something positive to emerge. But in the case of the Shadow, it is a good always tinged with an undercurrent of fear, always ready to disappear back into mocking laughter.

PLATH'S DARK UNDERSTANDING

We normally think of understanding in terms of the visible. Phrases such as "seeing is believing" and "shedding light on the subject" highlight this assumption. Truth is illumination, like lightbulbs going on over a cartoon character's head or sunbeams streaming down from the heavens. But for Sylvia Plath, it is the shadows that figure as the source of understanding in her work. In keeping with the ambiguities of shadows themselves, Plath's use of the trope is never entirely consistent. Sometimes figures of insubstantiality, sometimes of inspiration, shadows are always a gateway into knowledge, even if that knowledge is troubled and undesired. Plath relies heavily on shadow imagery in her poetry, but it is in her prose works where her thinking on shadows achieves full expression. The 1955 short story "Superman and Paula Brown's New Snowsuit" as well as her 1963 novel *The Bell Jar* both address the theme of lost innocence while simultaneously commenting on the postwar conditions of their writing.

But it is in her story "The Shadow" (1959) where Plath fully explores her childhood relationship to the crime fighter. The Shadow, with his ability to "know what evil lurks in the hearts of men," reveals the duplicity and hypocrisy that Plath's work repeatedly struggles to announce.

In order to understand Plath's relationship to the Shadow, it is helpful to first examine her use of shadow imagery in her other works. Shadows appear throughout Plath's poetry. Richard M. Matovich's *Concordance to the Collected Poems of Sylvia Plath* reveals that references to "shade" and "shadow" occur sixty-four times in Plath's *Collected Poems* (434–35), often in her more famous works. Plath is obsessed by the role influence plays as both a hindrance and a spur to creative endeavor. In the poem that gives her first collection its title, "The Colossus" (1959), the poet stands within the shadow of her father's bones, her "hours married to shadow" (130). The speaker's "marriage" to a "shadow" that is merely the spatialization of her father's influence lends the poem a melancholy feel. Steven Gould Axelrod, in his study *Sylvia Plath: The Wound and the Cure of Words*, reads "The Colossus" as a poem lamenting creative frustration. He notes that in her journals and letters, as well as in her poems, "the 'I' does not possess her own shadow, her own creative identity, but is possessed by that of another" (214). The shadow of the past thwarts creativity, making the speaker a slave to influence. The sense of insubstantiality captured by the image of the shadow runs throughout Plath's corpus. Shadows represent a space of occlusion, a site where a speaker can easily become lost in the presence of people and forces more powerful. As Axelrod suggests, for Plath "shadow betokens the imaginative self that might have been but was forbidden to be, the self that has been defeated and destroyed" (213). Axelrod is indicative of a trend in scholarship that has tended to view Plath's battle with the past as one of defeat. The use of shadows in the majority of her poems, her subsequent institutionalization for depression, and, of course, her eventual suicide all bolster the conviction that Plath became lost in a world of shadows.

But Plath also uses shadows in her poetry to signal the acceptance of creative inspiration, troubling though it may be. In "The Disquieting Muses" (1957), the speaker takes issue with her mother for allowing some "illbred aunt" or an "unsightly Cousin" (*Collected Poems* 74) to send three "mouthless, eyeless" ladies "with stitched bald head[s]" to attend her christening. These figures, derived from Giorgio de Chirico's painting of the same name, become the "disquieting muses" of the reluctant speaker. The speaker describes these ladies as troublesome, the "hurricane" making "study windows bell[y] in / Like bubbles about to break" (75) and generally acting as the bane of the speaker's childhood. While other girls are dancing and "blinking flashlights like fireflies," the speaker can only stand aside and watch, "in the shadow cast by my dismal-headed / Godmothers" (75). While her mother cries, the speaker summarizes her feelings through an image that Plath will return to in "The Shadow": "And the shadow stretched, the lights went out" (75). Despite the speaker's chastisement of her mother, she remains ultimately reconciled to her fate, and even welcomes it. In the last stanza, the muses are described standing with

Faces blank as the day I was born,
Their shadows long in the setting sun
That never brightens or goes down.

The speaker comes to prefer this static, timeless realm of ancient inspiration, claiming in the last two lines that though it was her mother who bore her to this kingdom, "no frown of mine / Will betray the company I keep" (75–76). Better to reside in the shadows cast by these muses than with her mother, "on a green balloon bright with a million / Flowers and bluebirds that never were" (76).

In discussing her inspiration for the poem, Plath repeatedly refers to the shadows that populate many of de Chirico's artworks. Christina Britzolakis notes in "Conversation amongst the Ruins" that in a BBC radio program interview, Plath stated that "all through the poem I have in mind the enigmatic figures in this painting . . . standing in a weird, clear light that casts the long strong shadows characteristic of Chirico's early work" (176). What drew Plath to the painting was not just the "enigmatically" strange mannequins but the "long strong shadows" that they cast. Plath also discusses her engagement with the painting in her journals, commenting on "the statue, recumbent, of Ariadne, deserted, asleep, in the center of empty, mysteriously shadowed squares. And the long shadows cast by unseen figures—human or stone it is impossible to tell" (*Journals* 211). The "mysterious" indecipherability of the shadows proved compelling to Plath. Discussing de Chirico's style, Britzolakis observes that "though seemingly undertaken in the name of a neoclassical revival of the Renaissance heritage of architectural perspective, [it] is a potent source of estrangement effects" (169). Although seeming to mimic classical proportion and stability, de Chirico's paintings create an eerie, uncanny space that dislocates the viewer. The use of strange shadows is integral to that effect, and Plath appropriates it brilliantly.

Examining how shadows function in Plath's verse is useful, but it is in her prose work where the figure of the shadow receives its most articulated expression and is most closely linked with the influence of the Cold War. Upon her return to Smith College in 1954 after being released from the hospital, Plath produced the short story "Superman and Paula Brown's New Snowsuit" for Alfred Kazin's class (Ferretter 4–5, 112). This story begins with the invocation of blissful childhood innocence, as the narrator watches the rising planes of Boston's airport as the sun sets and lights begin to appear. According to the narrator, "This was the best time of the day, when I could lie in the vague twilight, drifting off to sleep, making up dreams inside my head the way they should go" (Plath, *Johnny Panic* 270). Twilight, that indeterminate zone between day and night, is the space of dream and desire where anything is possible. The narrator relates that "these nightly adventures in space began when Superman started invading my dreams and teaching me how to fly." The planes across the water become translated, through the magic of imagination and her radio hero, into a world of "Technicolor dreams" (270). Unfortunately, this blissful innocence will become lost, a casualty of the "threat of war that was seeping in everywhere" (271) and the all-too-real lessons of prejudice and hypocrisy that the narrator is forced to endure. The twilight world of dream is too precarious to survive into adulthood.

The narrator's problems begin with a film. At her friend Paula Brown's birthday party, the children are taken to see *Snow White*. But the double feature also includes a "movie about prisoners of the Japanese who were being tortured by having no food or water" (272). During an escape attempt, "the Japanese began shooting the prisoners dead, and stamping on them, and laughing," a scene so horrific and disturbing that the narrator has to run "out to the girls' room where I knelt over a toilet bowl and vomited" (272). The juxtaposition of the purity of Snow White and the atrocities of the war film is the beginning of the narrator's loss of innocence. Not only does the film undermine the make-believe world of the fairy tale, it also brings into sharp contrast the artificiality of the innocent war games the narrator had played earlier with her friends. Her twilight dreams of flying with Superman are replaced by darker images of conflict: "No matter how hard I thought of Superman before I went to sleep, no crusading blue figure came roaring down in heavenly anger to smash the yellow men who invaded my dreams" (272). As disturbing as this violent intrusion into her peaceful childhood is, it is only the prelude to a full understanding of the world's horrors.

The true moment of dark understanding occurs when Paula slips in an oil slick and besmirches her new snowsuit. While the slip is accidental, Paula immediately singles out the narrator with an accusatory "You pushed me" (273). The other children pick up the chant, and the narrator walks away. Unfortunately for her, this act of betrayal and hypocrisy is exacerbated by her parents' subsequent actions. She arrives home, where bright images of light appear to support the idea that all is well: "Candles were set on the white linen tablecloth, and miniature flames flickered in the silver and the glasses. I could see another room reflected beyond the dark dining-room window where the people laughed and talked in a secure web of light, held together by its indestructible brilliance" (274). But the arrival of an unexpected visitor breaks the illusion. As her mother learns the rumor from a neighbor, she asks her daughter why she didn't tell her about what happened. When the narrator denies the accusation, her mother claims, "Of course we'll believe you." But this claim of parental support is ambiguous, undermined as it is by the phrase "Of course," which could either signal unwavering support or familial obligation.

The change of mood is reinforced by images of ever-encroaching shadows. The narrator retreats up a darkened staircase and down a hall "without turning on the light switch" to her room (274). Uncle Frank, whom the narrator has earlier associated with Superman, comes to the distraught girl to offer consolation and discover the truth. But his role as male protector is challenged. While the narrator can see his "strong shoulders bulk against the moonlight," nevertheless she claims that "in the shadows his face was featureless" (274). Uncle Frank is equally noncommittal when the narrator repeats her innocence, claiming, "'Okay, but we'll pay for another snowsuit anyway just to make everybody happy'" (275). Good does not triumph here, and it is unclear whether Uncle Frank even believes her. The paying for another snowsuit covers the act in a further layer of hypocrisy, as her family tacitly admits to an act they either believe she did or know she did not do but feel they must nevertheless placate society with a lie. Motives and meanings, like Uncle Frank's shadowed face, have become obscured.

Superman might save the day in the world of children, but in the world of adults, expediency rules. Uncle Frank tries to mitigate the damage with the claim that "ten years from now no one will ever know the difference" (275), but he obviously misses the point—it matters to his niece.

The narrator is left by herself, with a sinking feeling of acceptance: "I lay there alone in bed, feeling the black shadow creeping up the underside of the world like a flood tide" (275). Here the shadow represents the true knowledge of the world. Clear, illuminating light, which made everything *seem* so safe and secure, is replaced by a darkness that, while disturbing, nevertheless stands for a new understanding of how the world operates. In the adult world, darkness remains darkness, with all of its myriad associations—indeterminacy, danger, and the possibility for things to appear other than what they are. The last line provides the story with its moral: "That was the year the war began, and the real world, and the difference" (275). This "difference" is the shadow of doubt that has crept up to overtake the narrator. The world is neither fair nor just. Bad things happen, and nobody is going to be there to stop them.

Plath revisited the theme of lost innocence four years later in a piece titled "The Shadow."[5] The overall structure and theme of this piece is identical to "Superman and Paula Brown's New Snowsuit." The young narrator, who now has the name Sadie, discovers the truth about the world when an innocent game of tickling results in her biting the leg of her friend Leroy. This time the narrator is indeed guilty but claims the incident was a case of justified self-defense. The present narrator, like her earlier counterpart, also attends a birthday party and watches a disturbing film about a Japanese prison camp that haunts her subsequent dreams, though this time the narrator purposefully deceives her mother so that she may be allowed to see the film. The story also includes a Paula Brown stand-in, Maureen Kelly, who is even more manipulative. In keeping with the "Superman" tale, the hypocrisy of the world extends beyond that of deceptive children and all the way into the adult world. But despite these similarities, the differences between "Superman and Paula Brown's New Snowsuit" and "The Shadow" are telling. More ambiguous and in many ways darker, this updated version brings the cultural context of the story into starker contrast.

The title is the first clue to Plath's new emphasis. The figure of Superman dominates the first tale, standing for truth and good and the imagination of flight. Replacing Superman with the Shadow immediately sends a darker message to the reader. The narrator actually likes Leroy, a boy who builds railroads, reads science fiction magazines, and constructs a radio set that "tuned in on regular programs like 'The Shadow'" (Plath, *Johnny Panic* 144). While the narrator's world is filled with the Green Hornet, Wonder Woman, Superman, and Mickey Mouse (146–47), it is the Shadow, with his "nasal, sardonic voice" rhetorically asking, "'Who knows what Evil lurks in the hearts of men? . . . The Shadow knows, heh, heh, heh, heh'" (147) that provides the children with their "accumulating evidence of the warped, brutish emotions current in the world beyond Washington Street and the precincts of the Hunnewell School" (147). Most of the radio programs and comic strips present a brighter picture of the world and lead to Sadie "seeing the picture so small, and in such elementary colors" (147). It is the Shadow who adds ambiguity to this picture, teaching the narrator "how mean people can be" (147).

The uncertainty of the narrator begins with the radio program. Doubt grows slowly until it eventually affects the adult world and leads to the story's climax. As Sadie relates, "Each week Leroy and I studied our lesson: somewhere innocent victims were being turned into rats by a vicious, experimental drug, burned on their bare feet with candles, fed to an indoor pool of piranha fish" (147). But such stylized torture gives way to the real thing, as Leroy learns through hearsay of Japanese bamboo torture methods, which in turn are made real by a wartime film that depicts American POWs dying of thirst while sadistic Japanese guards look on. This "weed" of doubt indeed "bears bitter fruit." Still, the Shadow is a world of make-believe as well, reinstituting, at the end of every half hour, a world of order and stability: "We had no cause to wonder: *Will* the good people win? Only: *How*?" (148).

But the real horror of the world quickly enters the narrator's life in the form of history. Air raids and dark cellars begin to alert the narrator to a new threat that points to both the Second World War and the Cold War. "In spite of my assiduous study of the world," she drily comments, "there was something I had not been told" (149). She finds her answer soon enough in the actions of her friends and neighbors. Although the narrator has made peace with Leroy and his sister, Maureen, the incident of the bite is still circulating throughout the neighborhood. Maureen informs her of this fact on the way to school: "'My mother says it's not your fault for biting Leroy,' she called out in clear, saccharine tones. 'My mother says it's because your father's German'" (149). The narrator tries to make sense of this senseless assertion but cannot. She reasons that although her father does teach German at the city college and does not go to church regularly, "that didn't make him any less American" (150). The racism of the charge along with the hypocrisy of churchgoers groundlessly claiming that a man of German descent might be a "spy" (149) sends the narrator running home to her mother. In a scene reminiscent of "Superman," Sadie enters a house with only "wan light"

(150) and proceeds to question her mother about the accusations. Her mother explains that "'in wartime people often become frightened and forget what they know,'" adding that Sadie's father might have to "go away from us" (150) for a little while to a camp for German citizens. Adult hypocrisy has clearly escalated here to levels dangerous not just to a family or a neighborhood but to a nation.

Plath again closes the story with the image of the shadow figured as understanding: "I understood, then, that she was trying to give me the piece to the puzzle I had not possessed. The shadow in my mind lengthened with the night blotting out our half of the world, and beyond it; the whole globe seemed sunk in darkness" (151). The "lengthening" of the shadow in Sadie's mind dramatizes the slippery slope that such insights inaugurate. Once the dualistic notion of good versus bad, right versus wrong is dispensed with, everything becomes subject to review—friends, neighbors, Superman, America, God, "the whole globe." Sadie's "our half of the world," a reference that points simultaneously to America, the Allied forces, and the free world as opposed to the Communist world, suddenly comes under shadow. Even the Shadow comes under review. In the make-believe world of radio, the darkness is protected by a lurking presence bent on the punishment of the wicked and the support of the praiseworthy. Now darkness has been evacuated, plunging the narrator into a world she never thought possible. The title of the piece takes on a double resonance, standing for both the radio hero who inaugurates Sadie's interest in knowing the world and the lengthening shadow that stands for full realization. Thus Sadie's revelation that "'I don't think there is any God then'" is answered by her mother's terse response, "'Some people think that'" (151). Sadie is denied even the consolation of atheism—whether or not there is still a God is itself an undecidable question, one of many that a newly aware Sadie will be left by herself to ponder. True understanding is the realization that nothing can truly be known.

Given the history of Plath's battle with depression, it is tempting to read these stories as attempts to discover the precise moment when she began her descent into the darkness. The emphasis on hypocrisy as the underlying cause of Plath's frustrations is a theme running throughout her prose. In her novel *The Bell Jar*, Plath chronicles the breakdown and institutionalization of the narrator, Esther Greenwood. Throughout the novel, the one thing that most bothers the narrator is the hypocrisy of the world, especially that of her love interest, Buddy Willard. When Esther discovers that Buddy has had sex, she becomes upset, but not simply because she could not abide the idea of him with another woman. According to the narrator, "What I couldn't stand was Buddy's pretending I was so sexy and he was so pure, when all the time he'd been having an affair with that tarty waitress and must have felt like laughing in my face" (67). Like that other angst-ridden novel of the era, J. D. Salinger's *Catcher in the Rye* (1951), what Esther cannot tolerate is the phoniness of the world, the practiced deception that hides reality behind pretense and artifice.

Yet the irony of *The Bell Jar* (and indeed of Plath's own life, which provided material for the novel) is that Esther is extremely concerned with fitting in and doing the correct thing, even if it annoys her to have to do so. In the first half of the novel, Esther is in New York City on a scholarship but is beginning to have doubts about her life, musing, "All my life I'd told myself studying and reading and writing and working like mad was what I wanted to do, and it actually seemed to be true, I did everything well enough and got all A's, and by the time I made it to college nobody could stop me" (29). Esther, a woman caught between social expectation and personal desire, struggles to make the "right" choice. Despite her chastisement of Buddy's hypocrisy, Esther also engages in lying and deceit in order to hide her true feelings from a world that demands conformity to its standards. In her work *The Haunting of Sylvia Plath*, Jacqueline Rose points out that Plath was highly critical of gender roles, McCarthyism, nuclear expansion policies, and the Korean War but also sought approval in a popular culture that helped to make all of those things possible. Like a double agent, Plath "plays both sides" to arrive at what Rose calls a space not in-between but "at the point of tension" (10).

Shadows are the space of both withdrawal and realization. Later in *The Bell Jar*, as Esther becomes institutionalized in a psychiatric hospital and begins to undergo shock therapy, she starts to meditate on the figure of the shadow. She claims,

> I thought the most beautiful thing in the world must be shadow, the million moving shapes and cul-de-sacs of shadow. There was shadow in bureau drawers and closets and suitcases, and shadow under houses and trees and stones, and shadow at the back of people's eyes and smiles, and shadow, miles and miles and miles of it, on the night side of the earth. (141)

There is certainly an element of melancholy at play here. Esther is becoming withdrawn, and even though she describes them as "the most beautiful thing in the world," shadows are a place to hide. The examples she gives indicate as much; shadows are under, in back of, and behind the objects that cast them, cul-de-sacs that are outside the major thoroughfares. Esther's fascination with the world of shadows (like Plath's), while speaking to a growing melancholy, is nevertheless a first step toward the realization of the nature of her difficulties. In a world of hypocrisy, shadows are at least true to themselves, substantial in a way that the falsely seeming is not. They are the beginning of a means to negotiate, or at least sidestep, the hypocrisy of the world.

The personal difficulties Plath had with the world are intimately intertwined with the paradoxes of the Cold War. Her use of shadow imagery traces a burgeoning understanding not just of the way the world works but of the way that the postwar mentality of fear and suspicion works as well. Plath was drawn to shadows during the 1950s and early 1960s because they were where truth was forced to reside. Robin Peel, in *Writing Back: Sylvia Plath and Cold War Politics*, notes that "the fact that, in both her prose and poetry, Plath generally avoids direct reference to the issues, concerns and debates of the early 1960s should not be taken as evidence that she remained unaffected by them" (30). Cold war discourse was omnipresent, and Plath could not help but be affected. Peel cites John Hersey's *Hiroshima* as one such influence:

> A much read 1946 book, *Hiroshima*, by John Hersey, originally published in a single edition of *The New Yorker*, describes the immediate aftereffects of World War II nuclear explosion on the civilian population of Hiroshima. This text also contains images that are echoed in Plath's writing in England in the 1960s. . . . There seems to be no way of knowing if Plath read Hersey's book, but it is clear that the discourse into which it fed haunted her. . . . In writing about her present world, Plath is drawing on the iconography, imagery, and discourses of her childhood and writing back to her past. (29–30)

Shadows, while not explicitly linked to the postwar in Plath's writing, are one such cultural image that resonates with the anxieties of the Cold War. Hersey's discussion of the brightness of the bomb as well as of the ghostly shadows the blast left on the remaining buildings and roads of Hiroshima find an echo in the sort of shadowy images Plath employs. As we have seen, shadows are pervasive in the era, and Plath's use of shadows resonates in both personal and political registers.

Not that Plath's writing always eschews the political. Plath begins *The Bell Jar* by invoking the Rosenbergs and opens chapter 9 with a character's chilling statement, "I'm so glad they are going to die" (95). Julius and Ethel Rosenberg were arrested and charged in 1950 with having conspired to provide the Soviet Union with details on the Los Alamos atomic bomb project during World War II. Although the trial demonstrated that the details they passed on had little to no significance to the Soviets' construction of a bomb, they were both sentenced to death in a sensational trial. Esther is appalled at the statement, seeing it as a comment on the general inhuman reactions of the majority of Americans at the time. Through the quote Plath highlights the effects of McCarthyism, which provided fuel for the intense hatred for the couple and their act. Although Plath was by no means an antinuclear activist, she became more and more politicized as her career developed. The seeds of her beliefs, however, can be found in isolated, earlier responses to the Cold War situation. Peel discusses a Christmas Eve letter Plath sent to a pen pal in 1950: "I don't see how anyone can believe that the A-bomb would cure us of evils. Surely democracy and freedom would mean little in a world of rubble and radioactive rays" (94). Evidence also suggests that "during her time in England, Plath watched and was impressed by Alain Resnais's film *Hiroshima Mon Amour* (1959)," a film that is set among the nuclear ruin of the Japanese city (Peel 34). Plath's beliefs are indicative of her time and speak to the general anxiety and unease that a nuclear world created for everybody.

Even when not referenced directly, Cold War events stand behind much of Plath's work. This is especially true when Plath discusses World War II and the Holocaust. Peel, along with Al Strangeways in his book *Sylvia Plath: The Shaping of Shadows*, links the discourse surrounding Nazism and the Holocaust with the burgeoning Cold War concern over nuclear war as evidenced by Hiroshima and Nagasaki. The hypocrisy and self-serving ideological rhetoric of the Nazi regime can easily be mapped onto the rampant McCarthyism in the mid-fifties as well as onto the discourse surrounding the postwar nuclear world. Luke Ferretter observes that Plath's references to Japanese concentration camps in both "Superman" and "The Shadow" have a double meaning, since the FBI "arrested over 6,000 German aliens during the war, and detained them in some fifty camps," and that "Plath knew about these camps" (112). Given her German and Austrian ancestry, Plath saw these events as contributing to her sense of the loss of childhood belief in justice. America may claim to be a country of freedom where individuals and their rights are respected, but historical events cast their shadow over such assertions. As a postwar culture of conformity aptly proved, American freedoms were oftentimes paradoxical.

The demand for sharp binaries that failed to fit the facts of the world produced hypocrisy in the postwar period. Facing such stark options, those who disagreed found themselves forced to move behind or between theses polarities, hiding in the shadows that they created. Plath's work certainly demonstrates this tendency. Inverting the tropes of light and darkness, Plath finds meanings in the shadows. Darkness, not light, becomes the bearer of truth. Poetic forebears might block the rays of the sun, but rather than simply accept their shadows, Plath uses them as a refuge, a place to discover herself as a poet. Truth as self-discovery can happen only behind someone's back, so to speak, in the space of one's influence, a space that figure has probably failed to notice. And that space receives heightened political import in Plath's prose. In a hypocritical world where adults lie and superheroes fail, it is the darkened space of shadow that tells the truth. The overt moral order that seems to underpin society is built on negation.

What the Shadow teaches is that, ironically, the space of darkness is where the reality of the world "comes to light." Visibility does not equal understanding because truth is never so clear. The Shadow was still a hero in the Cold War not because he was fighting the obvious criminals of the Depression or the ridiculous master-villains of radio but because he was a symbol of the destruction of a hypocrisy that formed the backbone of McCarthyism, nuclear brinksmanship, and fervent patriotism. A great part of the appeal of this character for Plath (and for Kerouac and Baraka, as we will see) was the fact that he contained both good and evil. Although he was on the side of justice, he nevertheless knew "what evil lurks in the hearts of men." Privy to both the overt world of morals and order and the covert underworld of crime, the Shadow had the sort of knowledge few possess.

DR. SAX AND WRITING DONE IN THE SHADOWS

Jack Kerouac, in his coming-of-age novel *Dr. Sax* (1959, written 1952), utilizes the figure of the Shadow as a portal back into his childhood. Through his recently discovered spontaneous prose style, Kerouac is able to resurrect memory in the act of narration. But this reclamation is anything but stable. Kerouac uses the Shadow, as well as shadow imagery, as a space where the penumbras of adolescence become more and more distinct as the knowledge of the adult world grows. But in the present-tense telling of the past, these shadows also provide Kerouac the space to comment on that loss, as well as to simultaneously critique the postwar social conditions of his novel. Writing about his childhood during the Depression from the vantage point of the Cold War, shadows become fitting metaphors for the permeable gap between past and present. The ostensible theme of lost childhood innocence and entry into the adult world becomes a comment on America's loss of political innocence as postwar patriotism gave way to paranoia and fear. Thus the Shadow becomes re-presented as a critique of the "us versus them" thinking that pitted capitalist American interests against Communist insurgency.

The character of Doctor Sax is clearly modeled on the Shadow. Kerouac was an avid fan of the crime fighter, collecting issues of *The Shadow Magazine* and spending hours perusing them in his room. Many of young Jackie Duluoz's friends are also fans, and there is much reading and trading of the magazines throughout the novel. When it came time for Kerouac to write a novel depicting his childhood, the Shadow was an obvious choice for inclusion. Kerouac even considered titling his work after his favorite boyhood character. In a May 1952 letter to Allen Ginsberg written while he worked on the novel at William S. Burroughs's apartment in Mexico City, Kerouac states, "I have 'Doctor Sax' ready to go now . . . or 'The Shadow of Doctor Sax,' I'll simply blow on the vision of the Shadow in my 13th and 14th years on Sarah Ave. Lowell" (*Selected Letters 1940–1956* 355). The crime fighter provides both a potential title and the theme that Kerouac plans to "blow" upon, using his spontaneous method of composition to resurrect the past from his unconscious. The character of Doctor Sax is an amalgam in the novel, an "embodiment of a recurrent nightmare Kerouac has as a child of a shrouded stranger . . . who represented death, and . . . partly a reflection of the mordant, brooding, and restless presence of Burroughs himself whom Kerouac was observing closely" (Tytell 187). Kerouac places the Shadow, however, squarely at the center of the novel.

Kerouac loved the Shadow so much that he emulated the exploits of this crime fighter. In *Dr. Sax*, Ti Jean takes on the alter ego of the "Black Thief," running around the neighborhood at night stealing small items and mimicking the Shadow's sepulchral laugh. Gerald Nicosia, in his *Memory Babe: A Critical Biography of Jack Kerouac*, claims that in his boyhood Kerouac repeatedly took on a shadowy persona in emulation of this beloved character. With his sister's cloak for a cape, Kerouac "began prowling the neighborhood at night as the 'Silver Tin Can.' Tossing a tin can through someone's open window, he would laugh like the Shadow; or else he would quietly steal things just as an experiment" (35). Though in *Dr. Sax*, *The Shadow Magazine* is the primary focus, Kerouac was also a fan of the radio program. Describing her trip with Kerouac and Neal Cassady recorded in *On the Road*, Luanne Henderson recalls one night in the car when Kerouac told her the story of a friend's death using the style and tone of the Shadow: "That's just how Jack related it. Speaking in a low, mysterious voice, and picturing the whole thing of the river, the darkened streets" (qtd. in Maher 184). Kerouac's love of the Shadow is understandable given the immense popularity of the character in the 1930s. But the mysteriousness of this figure would haunt Kerouac into adulthood, providing the perfect metaphor for the loss of childhood innocence and entry into the adult world.

Dr. Sax is an eclectic book. Its nominal aim is to describe the coming-of-age Kerouac experienced as an adolescent growing up in a French-Canadian household in Lowell, Massachusetts, during the Depression, but its presentation is anything but straightforward. Kerouac interweaves three narrative strands in an interesting, if sometimes disorienting, manner. The first, and by far the most prevalent, is the various childhood remembrances of the narrator. Spending time with his mother, goofing around with his friends, hanging out at his father's club, and other such moments are brought to life in the rich detail and subconscious wordplay characteristic of Kerouac's spontaneous prose at its best. A Gothic plot forms a counterpoint to this childhood world. Interspersed with such remembrances are descriptions of the vampire leader Count Condu and the Wizard. These figures, along with a band of eccentrics, occupy a haunted castle on the hill overlooking the town. They are all part of a plot to expedite the arrival of an evil Snake that is slowly inching its way through the earth. Finally, there is Doctor Sax himself, who makes sporadic appearances throughout the novel, usually hiding in the shadows and emitting his strange, maniacal laugh that associates him with the figure of the Shadow.

Doctor Sax initially represents childhood fears of the dark, but as the novel progresses, he increasingly comes to be seen as a teacher of worldly knowledge. Toward the end of the novel young Jackie Duluoz finally meets the man he has only glimpsed slipping through the shadows.

The novel's climax involves nothing less than a battle between good and evil for the fate of humankind. A showdown ensues between Doctor Sax, with his magical herbs concocted to stop the Snake, and the evil Wizard, who wants to lead the Snake through the world, reveling in its destruction. This final struggle is witnessed by Jackie Duluoz, brought to see the apocalyptic showdown by Doctor Sax. Though Doctor Sax's potions prove ineffectual, the world is saved by a "huge black bird" (242) who grabs the Snake with its beak as it breaks the surface and carries it off into heaven.

The fantastic plot is mirrored by the equally strange shifts in genre. The Gothic is the most obvious candidate for classificatory rubric. Matt Theado, in *Understanding Kerouac*, calls *Dr. Sax* Kerouac's "only sustained foray into a distinct literary genre: Gothic horror" (92), while John Tytell in *Naked Angels* claims it is a "Gothic fairy tale" (187). Kerouac himself refers to it as his "Gothic" story numerous times in his letters. Populated as it is with vampires, ghosts, gnomes, gigantic Mayan spiders, haunted castles, and even "Blook the Monster," a "huge bald fat giant" (220), the Gothic seems the obvious label to assign to Kerouac's book. An earlier version of the novel appears even more Gothic, beginning as it does with a "vampire, in the form of a bat, flying from Rumania to Lowell in a soft nighttime rain" (Nicosia 245). Kerouac is obviously aware of the genre. *Dr. Sax* gestures to the beginning of the Gothic novel with an oblique reference to Horace Walpole's *The Castle of Otranto* (1764), which opens with the discovery of an Italian manuscript that forms the basis for the text. Kerouac's work also employs such a plot device. Amadeus Baroque, "witty, gay ambassador for the Black Cardinal" (106), finds Doctor Sax's hidden manuscript and reads it with laughter. The idea of a snake working its way through the earth has echoes of Bram Stoker's novella *The Lair of the White Worm* (1911), where a giant snake-like creature with green, glowing eyes dwells in a pit. Kerouac was certainly aware of Stoker's *Dracula*, reviewing F. W. Murnau's film version *Nosferatu* (1922) for the New Yorker Film Society in 1960 (*Good Blonde* 132–35). While it is impossible to know if Kerouac read these texts, he was undoubtedly familiar with the Gothic genre and uses it to superb effect in the novel.

To further complicate generic matters, Kerouac undercuts Gothic horror through his recourse to camp. Given Kerouac's love of the cinema and his interest in B films, this comes as no surprise. As the various vampires arrive at the castle, their chatter touches on the mundane details of vampire existence:

> I have some B right now.
> Where'd you get it?
> A young girl in Boston when I got off the ship at dusk, around 7, snow swirls on Milk Street, but then the rain started, all Boston was slushy, I pushed her in an alley and got her just below the ear lobe and sucked up a good pint half of which I saved in my gold jar for nightcap at dawn. (*Dr. Sax* 25)

The ridiculousness of the banter and the idea of vampires discussing weather conditions and the saving of "B" (slang for blood) for a "nightcap at dawn" demonstrate Kerouac's willingness to have fun with the Gothic genre. Kerouac considers *Dr. Sax* an integral part of his "Duluoz Legend," a series of texts that he saw as a chronicle of his life. But as Warren French points out, Kerouac's recourse to the name "Duluoz," which means "louse" in his native Quebecois, "indicates a principal problem that plagued his attempts to shape an epic from his own experiences—a frequent whimsical undercutting of his heroic intentions by devices verging on self-parody" (61). Such juxtapositions between high and low are repeated throughout the text, undermining any attempt at a single reading and challenging the reader to make sense of a text that refuses to remain consistent. Kerouac's work shifts from wistful to parodic with alarming alacrity.[6]

The novel offers a wealth of stylistic innovations as well. The most notable of these is the spontaneous style that Kerouac had been developing just a year or so earlier, as he completed *On the Road* and *Visions of Cody*. As he makes clear in his "Essentials of Spontaneous Prose," Kerouac's method sought to convey the deeper truths of the individual beyond rational, constructed thought. He advises, "Write without consciousnesses in semi-trance (as Yeats' later 'trance writing') allowing subconscious to admit in own uninhibited interesting necessary and so 'modern' language what conscious art would censor" (*Good Blonde* 70). Only by tapping into the subconscious could that be achieved. Despite Kerouac's belief in his new mode of writing, he still employs a plethora of narrative strategies in *Dr. Sax*. In "A Gloomy Bookmovie," Kerouac describes moments from his childhood in cinematic form, dividing the text into "scenes." Dramatic dialogue, as well as one section where Kerouac divides his description of an event into "Sound," "Smell," "Temperature," "Month," and "Supposition" (11), gives the text a heterogeneous, postmodern feel. He even includes a collection of verse, "The Poems of the Night," in the middle of book 5. Narratorial intrusions and slippages in point of view are likewise rife. Kerouac's "I" is polyvalent. The novel is told through a narrator clearly looking back on his childhood with nostalgia. But little Jackie Duluoz can also speak for himself, and does so at many points in the text. Furthermore, according to Nicosia, "Kerouac doesn't distinguish between the mysteries that children invent—such as the secret lives of imaginary beings—and real events and conditions they are too young to comprehend, like birth, sexual attraction, old age and death" (394). Kerouac's spontaneous prose style typically involves a confessional outpouring by a narrator closely associated with the author himself. *Dr. Sax*, with its competing narratives, characters, and structures, makes such a first-person telling more complicated. Kerouac even draws on the style of *The Shadow Magazine* itself, "echoing its constant use of certain words like 'ink' and 'shroud'" (Paton, "Reconceiving" 136). Such features still challenge today's reader; in the 1950s, the novel's reception was even more troubled.[7]

The challenge *Dr. Sax* poses to thematic, generic, and stylistic boundaries is precisely the point. The Shadow represents an unsettling that prompts the narrator to begin his quest into the shadows that will ultimately lead to a reexamination of how he views the world. Describing his fear of "a black coat on a hook on a white door," the narrator goes on to explain what makes shadows so frightening by comparing the coat to the murder mystery *Murder by the Clock* (1931): "You never saw her, just the woeful shadow coming up the davenport tap-tap-tap as her daughters and sisters screech all over the house" (44). Shadows frighten because their indeterminacy gets filled with more fear than the actual image could convey. *Dr. Sax* owes its very existence to the shadows. Without them, there would be no space for imagination to work, no ambiguity to be peopled with the myriad Gothic ghosts and goblins that Kerouac conjures into being. As the narrator claims, "Tragedies of darkness hid in the shadows all around Textile—the waving hedges hid a ghost, a past, a future, a shuddering spirit specter" (57). It is these shadowy spaces that permeate Kerouac's Lowell and make it so haunted. And for Kerouac, Doctor Sax comes to stand as the vague, shadowy image of this haunting, of a past recoverable in the black-and-white print of a text's unfolding. For the described Kerouac of the book, shadows are the space of imagination, even if they terrify and unsettle. In a way, this unsettling is exactly what Jackie wants; it represents a sort of internal, ancestral knowledge that something is out there that goads him into discovering. For the adult

Kerouac, the Shadow and the dark spaces he traverses represent the space of memory, vague enough to allow reentry into a childhood world now gone. But it is likewise a space that is never fully controllable, and thus Kerouac enters it with the burden of the present's personal and social history. Doctor Sax is the door between boyhood's fear and wonder and adulthood's longing and fretfulness.

The narrator undergoes a transformation, a coming into fruition, and Doctor Sax is a central figure in that changeover. When Doctor Sax enters a party, his sinister laugh communicates "his private knowledge of the world . . . publishing to all who were aware the secret wisdom, the huge malevolent humor, the undreamed information that crouched concealed in that unholy head" (142). Kerouac has turned the Shadow's uncanny ability to know "what evil lurks in the hearts of men" into a general understanding of the world and how it works. Yet what makes the novel so compelling is that Kerouac complicates easy dichotomies. Doctor Sax might appear to be evil, but as the narrator later realizes, Doctor Sax is actually his "protector" (151). Doctor Sax comes to represent the search for something vague and indefinable that the narrator was after all along. The figure of the Shadow provides an ambiguous space. As Nancy M. Grace states, "The character of Sax exists more convincingly as a sign that binaries, whether explicit or masked scriptions, are ultimately illusion" (116). While he does create anxiety and "terror," he also allows new thoughts and experiences to emerge. The figure of the Shadow (and shadow imagery in general) becomes a symbol for the unknown that is nevertheless desirable, an undefined possibility that both attracts and disturbs the narrator.

At first glance, the ending of the novel appears to offer a solution to this instability. In "Book Six: The Castle," a novel of adolescence revisited becomes a fairy tale. Doctor Sax takes the narrator to "the pit," where the "Great World Snake" (226) is about to emerge. Here the motivations of the various characters finally become manifest. Count Condu, along with his disciples, is in league with the Wizard, the archenemy of Doctor Sax, who is trying to hasten the evil Snake's arrival. An obvious binary is produced. The Wizard is clearly a malevolent figure, and although his "white eyes" have "snowstorms" in them, "his neck was twisted and strung and streaked with horror" (223). Doctor Sax, by contrast, appears to the narrator in "snow white raiment" looking "like an angel saint" (223). The Snake is Satan embodied, and as the narrator peers into the "horror," "void," and "Dark" of its eyes, he realizes, "*The Snake was coming for me!!*" (238). Thus a classic battle is set—the Wizard wants to lead the Snake into the world, to glory in its destruction of humanity, while Doctor Sax plans on destroying it with his herbs and potions.

Ambiguity, however, returns. Although Doctor Sax fights the Snake with his potions, they are ineffectual. His powers do not work, and the next time the narrator sees him it is without his signature slouch hat and black robe. In the end, a "Great Black Bird came down and picked it up"; as both Doctor Sax and the narrator look on, the bird carries the Snake "into the bedazzling blue hole of heaven" (244). In keeping with the book's theme of resurrection, it is God, or perhaps the Universe, which prevails here, not the earthly wisdom of Doctor Sax. Jackie's revelation is equally enigmatic. Looking into the pit, he exclaims, "I looked down to face my horror, my tormentor, my mad-face mirror of myself" (238). With his knowledge of evil, the narrator has entered into an adult world of self-searching.[8] Doctor Sax is still around, though now he "only deals in glee" (245). Doctor Sax introduced the narrator to evil, and Christian eschatology has tamed this fear, made it bearable, at least until the Snake's reemergence.

What gives *Dr. Sax* its power is not the rather simplistic tale of good triumphing over evil but the complicated and intriguing manner in which Kerouac inscribes himself into the text. At the beginning of the novel, Kerouac admonishes himself to not lose sight of his childhood impressions when writing, "When you do stop, just stop to think of the picture better" (3). Nostalgic memory often occurs in the vague space of shadow, as when Kerouac describes his father and mother as "shadows on a menu card sitting by a shadow-grill window" (7). Memory is not the event but a trace of the event left on Kerouac's mind, a trace that he must pause to "see better" as he pens his spontaneous prose.

As an in-between space, the shadow comes to stand for the writing process of *Dr. Sax* itself. In "Book Six: The Castle," the narrator finally makes contact with Doctor Sax (who he initially thinks is "the Shadow" [193]) and "shadows" him throughout the town. In one section, the narrator literally follows in Doctor Sax's shadows, trailing his "long, hollow, sepulchral laughter" (199). Sax and the narrator take a midnight inventory of the narrator's daytime world. They both become privy to "everything about Lowell" (199), from his mother and sister's banter in the street to Bert Desjardins's brother's sexual escapades with his girlfriend in a shack in the woods. Like his boyhood narrator, Kerouac stands outside the experience, looking in. The shadow affords protection from the past, a distance from which to view the events as they unfold to memory. The cloak of Doctor Sax is used by Kerouac the writer as much as by Kerouac the narrator—Sax's young protégé comments on "actual" scenes taking place, but the clandestine nature of their activity is a fitting metaphor for the process of recording memory. The space of the shadow thus becomes a metaphor for the writing of memory. Cloaked by darkness, the author peers back into a past that remains undisturbed, describing the scenes of his youth from a voyeur's perspective.

Commenting on the act of recording memory has the uncanny result of doubling the author, by projecting his own shadow upon the text in the act of writing. Although Kerouac attempts to recapture the present tense of adolescence in his novel, there is actually a plurality of voices that challenge such a presentation. In the section titled "A Gloomy Bookmovie," Kerouac explicitly addresses his use of parenthesis, writing "in these parentheses sections, so (-), the air is free, do what you will" (88). The "free air" of the parenthesis allows the present-tense writer of the piece to be heard. Doctor Sax is seen through young Jackie's eyes but also again through the older eyes of the author. Does the Kerouac in the story, the Lowell boy of thirteen, know that Doctor Sax is inaugurating a new period in his life? Of course not; that is why the narrator has to make various claims, insertions, and comments about Doctor Sax and what he "means," like when the narrator comments that "Doctor Sax had knowledge of death . . . but he was a mad fool of power, a Faustian man, no true Faustian is afraid of the dark" (43). Like other Duluoz Legend accounts, there is another narrative laid over the spontaneous reclamation of memory.[9] Doctor Sax was undoubtedly not a "Faustian man" who battles evil in the end during Kerouac's adolescence. It is an older Kerouac who recalls his childhood in such terms. Kerouac conceived of *Dr. Sax* as part of his "Duluoz Legend," a chronicling of the past events of his life on paper. But the present is always seeping through.

Given the numerous authorial intrusions by the 1952 Kerouac, it becomes clear even before the ending that matters will not be resolved so simply. Ironically, the postwar world sends its own specter back into the past to haunt Kerouac's Depression-era remembrance. Thus when an older author comments on a cartoon about storing coal in the winter in a parenthesis, "(Depression Themes, now it's atom-bomb bins in the cellar communist dope ring)" (76), we are immediately abstracted out of the time of the narrative and into the time of history. The Cold War fifties replaces the Depression thirties as the historical condition of the text's making. The postwar period is characterized by unseen forces, by "communists" who are everywhere but who must nevertheless be rooted out by investigatory committees from their hiding places, by "dope rings" that threaten even the most quiet and secluded communities, and by an "atomic bomb" in a hidden silo that is pointed directly at us. History intrudes again in the next chapter. Kerouac describes playing a self-made horse-racing game with marbles, describing the loss of one of these as "turning my world upside down like the atombomb" (91). This reference jars the reader out of the Depression setting and into the time of the novel's writing, the early 1950s. Kerouac is writing about the shadows of his childhood from underneath the Cold War's penumbra. *Dr. Sax* is a Cold War book.

Authorial intrusion is rife in the text, and it is within these narratorial asides that the political most clearly manifests itself. Thus, when Doctor Sax enumerates the future to his young charge, it feels as though we have caught up to the act of writing the novel, to the current Kerouac in Mexico in 1952:

> You'll roll your feet together in the tense befuddles of ten thousand evenings in company in the parlor, in the pad—that is known as, ah, socializing. You'll grow numb all over from inner paralytic thoughts, and bad chairs,—that is known as Solitude. You'll inch along the ground on the day of your death and be pursued by the Editorial Cartoon Russian Bear with a knife, and in his bear hug he will poignard you in the reddy blood back to gleam in the pale Siberian sun—that is known as nightmares. (202)

Here Kerouac is parodying Jacques's speech in Shakespeare's *As You Like It* in which he discusses the seven ages of man. Despite the seeming timelessness of the presentation, Kerouac's version leans heavily on the political. One can easily imagine this "Editorial Cartoon Russian Bear" with his arms embraced around postwar America while the knife stabs Uncle Sam in the "reddy blood back." But Kerouac does not label this "reality" or "politics" but "nightmares." In fact, both the Shadow and shadows in general are the perfect figures for the sort of politics Kerouac embraced. Kerouac's political leanings were very complicated. While he might have started his career as something of a Marxist, by the end of his life he supported the Vietnam War and leaned heavily to the right, much to the dismay of his colleagues. But such simple dichotomies do not adequately describe Kerouac. What he really fought against were such easy binaries as left or right. Shadows, as ambiguous spaces that confound notions of "dark" and "light," fit nicely into Kerouac's political rhetoric. Kerouac leaves the question open as to whether the "Russian Bear" is really harmful. What is important for Doctor Sax's friend to realize is that such possibilities will be used for political gain, to create "nightmares" that can then be manipulated.

The ambiguity that shadowy figures like Doctor Sax foster makes them useful in challenging the simple binaries of the Cold War. The showdown at the end of the novel between Doctor Sax and the Wizard, for instance, is as much about postwar politics as it is about adolescent awakening. The arrival of the Snake heralds the second coming of Christ, a fact made explicit to the narrator when Doctor Sax declares, "My son, this is judgment day" (236). But Kerouac shifts registers, and what seems to be a religious battle quickly becomes a political one: "Liberals and reactionaries will be washed down the rivers of his drink, the Left and the Right will form a single silent tapeworm in his indestructible tube" (228). Kerouac avoids taking sides in the political arena of his day. Party lines blur as everyone becomes a candidate for annihilation. In fact, those under the Wizard's leadership are involved in the same sort of intrigues and infighting that characterizes the politics of the postwar adult world. Boaz Jr., for instance, becomes a McCarthy figure in his attempt to scapegoat a key member of a rival sect and to "make blood illegal so the Vampires could be jailed" (232) in order to court favor with the Wizard. Good versus evil is still the point here, but assigning these values to each of the characters becomes a bit more complicated. One of the Wizard's sects, "The Dovists," are the "idealistic left of the Satanic movement," believing that the Snake would not destroy the world at all but "merely be a great skin of doves on coming-out day" (230). Kerouac challenges the polarizing binaries that the Cold War fostered, opting instead for a more transcendent solution. Doctor Sax makes it clear that there is some higher power that supersedes such petty distinctions.

Kerouac's ending also gestures to the atomic bomb. Doctor Sax having proven ineffectual, all the pair can do is watch as the Snake emerges in a fashion reminiscent of the billowing mushroom clouds that held such a fascination for the postwar public:

> Showers of black dust made a shroud of wings and droop-drape bierlike background in the clear sky like a thundercloud without

> sense, in the center of its darkness darkly and more high rose the Mysterious Head twirling and squirming with a dragon's felicity, the hook and curl was sure alive. I could hear girls of eternity as if screaming on rollercoasters; over the water came the hysterical symphony honks of some sad excited commotion in the bustling bosom earth. Into the beautiful glary pale of giant massclouds that had come to cover the sun, leaving a snow White hole, rose the mighty venom headed Serpent of Eternity. (241)

This "thundercloud without sense" provides a feeling much akin to the nuclear sublime. The destruction is rendered as "girls of eternity" scream and the "hysterical symphony" honks. The mushroom cloud becomes the "massclouds," seen as "beautiful glary" and blocking out the sun itself. All this leaves Doctor Sax and his charge gaping in awe, speechless. Drawing on Kerouac's interest in the theories of Oswald Spengler, Fiona Paton theorizes that Kerouac's "Atomic Faustus may hint at the prospect of such political imperialism: with the hydrogen bomb, the idea of ruling the world was not outside the bounds of contemporary political thought" ("Reconceiving" 147). Reading this passage as evidence of an "Atomic Faustus" is compelling, since it combines the Faust legend with direct political concerns in a way that exposes the hidden motivations of knowledge as power. The connection between the Snake and the bomb invokes religious apocalypse, updated for a nuclear-anxious society.

The invocation of the shadowy world of Doctor Sax as a site for ambiguity and the breaking down of boundaries, whether thematic, generic, or stylistic, results in a politicized text that questions the binary assumptions of Kerouac's Cold War milieu. Discussing Kerouac's disruption of mythic and generic assumptions in her essay "Beyond Bakhtin: Towards a Cultural Stylistics," Paton concludes that "this fusing of different mythological systems in a prose style that constantly dialogizes different registers and genres challenges the reductive perspectives engendered by the Cold War" (189). The political nature of *Dr. Sax* was noticed by Kerouac's friend Allen Ginsberg as early as 1952. Discussing the myth part of the book in a letter to Kerouac, Ginsberg explains, "It is the real caviar of the whole book—so intelligent, so apt as metaphysical and *social* commentary, so *hip* and yet so public in reference. I don't see why you can't do more of that" (*Jack Kerouac* 182). Calling into question reader expectation on a literary level opens up the possibility to think otherwise in the political realm as well. In true Gothic fashion, boundaries do not hold up. Readings can indeed be made, but they are always being undercut by other possibilities, and by the author's own comments and intrusions. The shadow-filled *Dr. Sax,* an account of a childhood written fifteen years after the fact by an American author of French-Canadian descent living in Mexico City during the Cold War, demonstrates the fallacy of trying to make binaries hold up in an instable postwar world.

"IN MEMORY OF RADIO" AND THE SHADOW OF RACE

The ambiguity that shadows create allows for multiple readings of this gap between light and darkness. For Kerouac and Plath, such liminality opens a space to critique the assumptions of postwar America. Amiri Baraka, in his early collection of poems titled *Preface to a Twenty Volume Suicide Note* (1961), likewise draws on the shadowy presence of the crime fighter to question American racial conditions. Written before he left Greenwich Village for Harlem in order to write more politically inspired work, *Preface* is oftentimes given short shrift by critics.[10] The African American poet wrote the book while living in New York's Greenwich Village during the 1950s. Thus it has come to be seen as exemplifying Baraka's "Beat period," a time when, writing under his given name, LeRoi Jones, the young poet worked through the vexed connection between poetic form and existential commitment that occupied so many writers after World War II. More forgiving critics view this period as a time when Baraka championed the imagination as an escape from burgeoning doubts about race in America. Here imagination is celebrated as the space where Baraka explores possibilities as a poet. Other critics read this volume from beyond the divide in Baraka's career, looking back at his Greenwich Village days from the vantage point of a later move to Harlem in order to critique *Preface* as an escape from social reality. Imagination, for these critics, becomes a symptom of the apolitical Beat network that Baraka was caught up in at the time. In either case, as success or failure, Baraka's first book of poetry is seen as anticipating the later poet whose movement into the political eclipsed his earlier work.

While these two critical tendencies are broadly accurate, they tend to miss the subtlety at play in Baraka's *Preface.* The shadows that appear throughout this volume of poetry are more than just idle symbols. The ambiguity that shadows connote serves to reinforce the hesitant, searching tenor of many of these poems. Baraka's use of shadow imagery, including his several allusions to the figure of the Shadow himself, and his tribute to the crime fighter in perhaps his best-known poem from the collection, "In Memory of Radio," highlight the uncertainty that characterizes the transitional, "Beat" period of his career. Baraka was an avid fan of the Shadow, claiming in an interview that "what television is probably to little kids now—radio was to us then" (*Conversations* 183). Yet several of the poems that make extensive use of shadow imagery drop out of later collections such as *Transbluesency* and his *Reader*.[11] The fact that Baraka omitted several of these "shadow" poems from his later collections is a clue to the relevancy of this image particularly during the postwar period.

Baraka uses shadow imagery to comment on the difficulty in discovering unadulterated truth. For Baraka, the interesting question is located not at the extremes but in the middle. By rehearsing the binaries that the Cold War fostered, Baraka highlights the difficulties inherent in choosing sides and creating meanings. In the end, *Preface* is about process, and shadows provide Baraka with a metaphor for this space between. This is precisely the reason for the continual anthologization of "In Memory of Radio"—it uses the ambiguity of the Shadow to capture the tensions inherent in the process of producing meaning that occupied Baraka during his Village days.

"In Memory of Radio" works by producing a series of binary divisions that the poem goes on to undermine. The figure of the Shadow is the driving motif that provides consistency to the poem. The first line asks simply enough, "Who has ever stopped to think of the divinity of Lamont Cranston?" (12). Baraka invokes not the Shadow himself but his quotidian alter ego and then proceeds to compare the "divinity" of this character to more ideologically suspect radio figures such as "Oral Roberts," a fundamentalist faith healer; "F. J. Sheen," a Catholic evangelist; and "Goody Knight," a California governor from 1953 to 1959 whom Baraka equates with "Hitler." Thus poets like "Jack Kerouac" and the speaker himself enjoy the "divinity" of the Shadow while "the rest of you" listened to "Kate Smith," a popular singer who immortalized the song "God Bless America" or, as the speaker claims, "something equally unattractive" (12).[12]

Had Baraka stopped here, we would be left with a rather simplistic poem that contrasts the hipness of Beat poets like him and Kerouac with a "square" society concerned only with putting "linoleum in [their] living rooms" (12). But Baraka goes on to problematize this adoration by drawing on the Shadow's famous tagline, "Who knows what evil lurks in the hearts of men? The Shadow knows" (13). Baraka asks his audience,

"& Love is an evil word. / Turn it backwards/see, see what I mean?" (12). Toward the end of the poem, the speaker emphatically repeats, "O, yes he does" (13) to let the reader know that the Shadow, too, is aware of Baraka's discovery. The Shadow now knows more than he claims—besides "evil," he is privy to the "love" embedded within it. But what kind of "love" is this, and how does the Shadow "know" it?

To answer these questions, we must turn to the last line of the poem. "In Memory of Radio" hinges on these final lines—"An evil word it is, / This Love" (13). The demonstrative creates uncertainty here as we ponder to what exactly "This" refers. What makes this poem so complicated is that Baraka's own relationship to his position as a poet is precisely what is under investigation. "This Love" might be referring to the act of poetry, or at least to a sort of imaginative play that goes beyond the worldly concerns that Baraka attacks in the poem. Thus when Baraka exclaims

> *Saturday mornings we listened to Red*
> *Lantern & his undersea folk.*
> *At 11, Let's Pretend/& we did/*
> *& I, the poet, still do, Thank God!*

the reader realizes that it is the ability to "pretend" that sets Baraka and Kerouac apart (12). The Shadow is "divine" in the sense that he transcends the material to arrive at the spiritual—his rewards are not profit but the moral superiority of having done what is right and correct. This "divinity" is possible because the Shadow has abilities that supersede the worldly and thus offer the listener the opportunity to imagine a new solution to the world's ills. But this "divinity" is conferred on him by his listeners—after all, he is an "imaginative" character whose power extends only so far as listeners are willing to "pretend" it exists.

Despite Baraka's faith in "pretending," this insistency on the power of imagination is itself undermined by the hesitant tone of the poem. Baraka may contrast the "divinity of Lamont Cranston" with "the rest of you," but the speaker comes under self-critique as well. "What can I say?" the speaker asks. "Am I a sage or something?" (12). Such doubt casts suspicion on the speaker's pronouncements and comes off sounding a bit defensive and defeatist. After all, the speaker himself admits that when it comes to "love," "I certainly wouldn't like to go out on that kind of limb" (12). It is precisely this hesitancy to embrace life, to engage the social world around him, that a later Baraka will deplore when looking back on his "Beat" period in the Village. The Shadow may "know," but in the end he remains helpless to "do" anything, except in the contained world of the radio airwaves.

The subtle irony of the speaker's own stance is an important point often overlooked by critics. Henry C. Lacey, for example, endorses Denise Levertov's 1961 review that argued Baraka uses figures like the Shadow to create a space for the imagination. But Lacey goes a step further, claiming "the poem ends by returning to the point of departure. Again we are reminded of 'the divinity of Lamont Cranston,' a supernaturally gifted force for goodness and law in a spiritually impoverished world" (10–12). But such solutions are far too easy. We may have "returned to the point of departure" by the end of the poem, but that does not mean that this point is any clearer. The reading rests entirely on the unexamined claim of Lamont Cranston's "divinity."[13] The Shadow, however, is compromised. He can no longer be a "force for goodness" because he has been tainted by the "evil" that "love" brings. Baraka leaves us guessing as to why this has to be, but the somber ending of "In Memory" suggests that the Shadow is a spent force. The imagination is lauded, but not without an uncanny awareness that it, too, is suspicious.

The final line could also be referring to the love that Baraka has for the Shadow. In the rest of the volume, Baraka continually looks back on his youth with a wistful sense of regret. Might not "this Love" be the love for the past itself? The title "In Memory" sounds like a eulogy, a lament for the loss of something sacred and dear. An examination of the rest of Baraka's volume reveals that the theme of nostalgia runs through many of his other poems. Shadows figure as a sign of loss; they are traces that can only gesture to an earlier completeness. In his poem "Turncoat," Baraka uses the figure of the shadow to highlight the gap between the speaker's present and past self. Employing the character of the Shadow, the speaker declares,

> *I move slowly. My cape spread stiff & pressing cautiously*
> *in the first night wind off the Hudson. I glide down*
> *onto my own roof, peering in at the pitiful shadow of myself.*
> (Preface 26)

Shadows are a fitting metaphor for the return to the past because, like nostalgia itself, one must imagine that past again to make it real. The speaker is a "turncoat," a double agent who sells out his present self in order to love his former one in an act of imagination—"I dream long bays & towers . . . & soft steps on moist sand. / I become them, sometimes. Pure flight. Pure fantasy" (26). Here the Shadow's "divinity" consists in the exalted place he occupies in the younger generation's minds. His eerie voice coupled with his pulp and radio exploits made him a symbol of growing up in Depression-era America in the 1930s and 1940s.

But if "this Love" refers to the nostalgia for the past, why does Baraka label it "evol"? Perhaps one reason that this "Love" is "evol" is that it represents a misplaced love for the oppressor. In "Hymn for Lanie Poo," shadows take on social connotations as Baraka deploys the racist term "shade" when describing his sister—she "hates loud shades" (*Preface* 11). Here the shadow becomes a metaphor for an undesirable darkness associated with African Americans. As Baraka mockingly admonishes in the beginning of the poem and will later repeat, "Beware the evil sun . . . / turn you black" (6). Black has yet to become beautiful; rather, it is something to be avoided. If we read "In Memory of Radio" in the context of this poem, an interesting tension emerges. Like a white hipster going uptown for an evening in Harlem, Lamont Cranston, the rich man-about-town, transforms himself into a "shade" called the Shadow as nighttime approaches. If we assume that "this Love" might be referring to Baraka's boyhood love for the Shadow, it could very well signify a burgeoning awareness of the cultural terms through which Baraka has been forced to view race in America. As racial consciousness grows and Jones becomes Baraka, he realizes that much of what he has come to "love" has been shaped by a white world. In the end, Baraka trades the white hipsters infatuated with African American jazz culture for his fellow African Americans. His "love" for the Shadow is "evol" because it too is backwards—a love for a savior coming from the very world that is excluding him.

This is certainly the view of critic Lloyd W. Brown. In his work *Amiri Baraka*, Brown reads *Preface* as an attack on the T. S. Eliot–like "wasteland" that Baraka experiences in postwar America. Discussing the comic heroes that people Baraka's collection, Brown states, "Baraka's comic-strip heroes embody the real corruptions . . . that are endemic to America as wasteland" (111). Brown traces such negative characteristics back to the issue of race in America. Looking specifically at Superman and the Lone Ranger, Brown argues convincingly that these characters are embroiled in a racial politics that seeks to champion white supremacy at the cost of racial integration and tolerance.

While Brown is certainly correct in implicating such figures of seeming "goodness" in the long history of American racial intolerance, he does not always make a convincing argument that Baraka's treatment of these comic heroes is offered in the same critical vein. When Baraka deplores the loss of his "Captain Midnight Decoder" in the poem "Look for You Yesterday, Here You Come Today" (*Preface* 17), for example, is this a rejection of the dominant world such characters represent, or simply a nostalgic look back at lost youth? Baraka's is an ambiguous message. Brown himself says as much—"Generally when Baraka examines the 'all-American' innocence connoted by comic-strip heroes he concludes that here too the image of innocence might be ambiguous, even deceptive" (109). It is the uncertainty of how to respond to such popular culture figures that is itself under consideration in Baraka's *Preface*. And when it comes to an ambiguous figure like the Shadow, things become even more complicated.

Instead of taking sides on this debate, it is best to remain where Baraka leaves us: in the middle. What poems like "In Memory" highlight is that uncertainty itself, the moment when we see both sides and are propelled toward making a decision. Rebecca Meacham, in "'The Sun's Children': Shadow Work in the Poetry of LeRoi Jones/Imamu Amiri Baraka," reads Baraka through a Jungian register. Though she does not discuss "In Memory of Radio," Meacham concludes that "throughout these poems of the early 1960s occur images of reversal, of movement, of flight . . . as if Jones is illuminating his identity conflicts" (210). Baraka's early poetry is not racially blind but is very much engaged with social questions. The ambiguous shadow provides the space for exploring options and responses. The imagination that is required to recognize the "divinity" of radio heroes is endorsed by Baraka throughout the poem. Thus "this Love" of "Lamont Cranston," while coming under scrutiny as being "evil," is not wholly discarded either. While one could argue that the end of the poem rejects the love Baraka has for the Shadow by labeling it "evil," Baraka's final line is more a reconsideration than a reversal.

What ultimately redeems the Shadow is that he too seems to "know" this "evil." The question we need to ask is whether Baraka is directing this attack on his love for the Shadow, or for "Radio" as a whole, as the title suggests. Thus there seems to be a difference. The Shadow "knows" the "evil" lurking in the airwaves, but is he aware of his own complicity in the medium? That question is unanswerable, given the parameters of the poem. Thus, we do not finally know if Baraka is castigating "Radio" or just certain figures in it. There is something evil about the Shadow, and his motives and methods are open to criticism. Yet there is also something alluring about him as well. Baraka cannot reject him, since he is already a part of his identity, as a poem like "Turncoat" makes clear. But Baraka cannot embrace him, either. His burgeoning racial consciousness makes it impossible—the Shadow, despite his heroism, is the product of an American popular culture that, by the early 1960s, Baraka was distancing himself from daily. The Shadow thus remains an enigma, a cipher through which to read his own existential, and hence racial, condition.

The Shadow's real contribution, his "divinity," is his ability to unsettle his listeners and keep them guessing. This is precisely what Baraka learned from his radio hero, and thus the ambiguous ending to "In Memory" is indeed a fitting tribute to the ambiguous character that inspired it. Baraka's poem is not simply a celebration of the powers of imagination. The critique of such naive beliefs in "pretending" that Baraka offers undermines any such straightforward notion. But neither is the poem a wholesale attack on the middle-class white culture that produced the Shadow. Jack Kerouac might be part of the Beat problem of political inaction, but he is also a friend who shares similar inclinations developed from a similar milieu—and thus acceptance or rejection is not so easy for Baraka. The power of the poem, its constant anthologization, rests on its ability to balance itself between these two tendencies, which is precisely what makes it emblematic of the *Preface* as a whole. "In Memory" represents a working through of positions, a pause at the midway point between imagination and action that places the reader in the same difficult position as the poet—forced to make a choice.

The Shadow is aptly named. Like the dark spaces he inhabits, this crime fighter exists on that thin line between fascination and fear. Plath, Kerouac, and Baraka all found this shifting border a useful metaphor for that moment of epiphany when childhood innocence gives way to adult understanding. But given that all of these accounts were penned under another shadow—the shadow of the Cold War—they necessarily disclose the social as well as the personal. The uncertainty that shadows present are unstable, which is precisely what makes them so attractive. They can contain both past and present, both imagination and anxiety. In an era that posited truth as a binary choice between light and darkness, the Shadow was a useful site for deconstructing the Manichaean rhetoric of the Cold War.

3. TAKING BACK THE SHADOWS

Allen Ginsberg's and Jack Kerouac's Struggles to Reclaim the American Unconscious

In the early years of the Cold War, American consciousness was split. America's emergence as a world superpower provided unprecedented opportunities and the potential for a bright future, but within this optimism lurked the seeds of doubt. The threat of nuclear annihilation and foreign subversion created an anxiety that was hidden below a pleasant facade. In order to police the boundary between optimism and dread, containment culture harnessed scientific rationalism and the authority of the expert to seal off the unpleasant possibilities of the Cold War from public consciousness. As Elaine Tyler May claims in *Homeward Bound*, the 1950s saw "the near deification of the post-war professional" (187). The figure of the expert, capable of ensuring the safety and health of American citizens, sought to allay their fears in order for Americans to enjoy the fruits of postwar society. Madison Avenue advertising executives, Washington bureaucrats, and psychologists and psychiatrists all purported to have the answers to everything, from which cigarette to smoke to how best to survive a nuclear attack. For intellectuals like C. Wright Mills or William Whyte, such reliance on the expert ran the risk of embracing a conformism that could quickly lead to totalitarianism, but given the anxieties and uncertainties that the Cold War fostered, for many the expert provided much-needed assurance and advice.

Not all of America's citizens, however, were content with the uneasy truce that the Cold War promoted. In 1948 a journal appeared that attempted to investigate the anxieties of the postwar age independent of the psychologist and psychiatrist. Seeking to reclaim the space between psychoanalytic text and psychoanalyzed patient that had been dominated by the therapist, the journal *Neurotica* (1948–51) set itself the task of delivering a broader, more accessible account of a culture mired in anxiety. In tones both playful and scholarly, the journal took on issues of contemporary importance, asking itself and its readers how America had arrived at this poor state of collective mental health and seeking possible solutions to the rampant neuroticism that postwar culture had inflicted on its citizens. According to contributors, psychoanalytic theory was not the problem; it was the "experts" who needlessly obfuscated the work of their forebears that produced dependent and helpless patients. True healing could come only from within, and the arts were seen as instrumental for a full recovery: "We are interested in exploring the creativeness of this man who has been forced to live underground, and yet lights an utter darkness with his music, poetry, painting, and writing" (Landesman 3). A battle for the American unconscious was underway, pitting those who would seek to normalize the patient by placating their fears against those intrepid souls willing to explore this "neurotic" space in the hopes of discovering a new way out of the impasse.

Beat writers like Allen Ginsberg and Jack Kerouac took this second path. While their forays into America's social underbelly of crime and vice are perhaps better known, Ginsberg and Kerouac likewise sought to map the occluded spaces of the American unconscious through an appeal to a world of dream, ghosts, and shadows. In the process, these writers opened up a space to challenge the binary thinking of their times that relegated doubt to a dark and buried world. Like their Gothic forebears, these writers explored the obverse side of rationality in order to disclose the latent fears and anxieties that a Cold War world of technological progress and scientific authority tried to mask. One of the vehicles for this critique was a dream each had about being pursued by a ghostly apparition that they came to call the "Shrouded Stranger."[1] Each author claimed the Shrouded Stranger for his own and offered competing explanations of his presence. In journals, letters, poems, and prose, Kerouac and Ginsberg discussed the meaning of this figure and tried to understand and represent the unsettling feeling he produced. The Shrouded Stranger helped both writers to work through many of the existential issues plaguing postwar America on a personal level. At the same time, this figure also allowed them to develop a new style of writing. Rather than present their thoughts to the reader in the form of crafted metaphor that was meant to be deciphered in specific ways, Kerouac and Ginsberg sought to convey the enigma of the Shrouded Stranger so that their readers could likewise experience the unsettling effects that held the potential for reexamining both self and society.

Kerouac's and Ginsberg's relationship with the father of psychoanalysis, Sigmund Freud, highlighted their novel attempts to reclaim the unconscious. Freud epitomized the role of the expert, and by the 1950s his method had taken firm root in America. Freud dominated discussions of the unconscious at midcentury, and his concepts permeated both clinical and popular discourse. Given the air of authority Freudian ideas enjoyed, it is unsurprising that both writers began thinking about the Shrouded Stranger in psychoanalytic terms. But they soon grew tired of such explanations, as Freud represented the sort of highly rationalized and constraining thought that Kerouac and Ginsberg hoped to avoid. Instead, these writers turned to a more confessional style that sought to disclose the workings of their inner minds, not in order to read them as symptoms of a problem but rather to re-present images such as the Shrouded Stranger to the reader in order to challenge them to come to terms with such enigmas. Kerouac's and Ginsberg's confessional style, while owing a debt to Freud and his "talking cure," made the analyst redundant since the material content of the telling was less important than the feelings it conveyed. Of course, such writing could itself be read into a psychoanalytic register; Kerouac and Ginsberg were undoubtedly laboring under an "anxiety of influence." Freud was the father who must be challenged, along with literary predecessors and older critics arguing for a more controlled style of writing. Through their engagement with the Shrouded Stranger, however, Kerouac and Ginsberg discovered a style that not only better captured the workings of their minds and the numinous quality of their thoughts but also allowed their readers a mirror into which they could glimpse their own unexamined preoccupations.

Kerouac and Ginsberg used the Shrouded Stranger to explore their own individual unconscious and its possibilities, but in the process they resurrected a specter with cultural resonance in the postwar era. As the work of Carl Gustav Jung has demonstrated, shadowy figures touch a universal chord. This is because they represent the hidden fears and desires in every individual. But for Jung, they also gestured toward the social. The shadow is a figure that stands for all the things that cannot be openly acknowledged in a culture. While by no means Jungian, Kerouac's and Ginsberg's explanation of the Shrouded Stranger highlighted the fears and anxieties not only of their own psyches but also of a Cold War world under the shadow of the bomb. Just as the Soviet Union formed an ideological corollary to American discourse, the world of dream, spirit, and shadow represented an interior corollary to the supposed optimism of waking life in America. In developing poetic strategies that better captured the Shrouded Stranger's uncanniness, these writers simultaneously developed a means of communication that would form the basis of a nascent Beat politics that turned self-examination into social critique.

GINSBERG: RECONCILING SELF AND SOCIETY

In the immediate postwar years, Allen Ginsberg struggled to reconcile the demands of society with his burgeoning understanding of himself as a writer. Though marginalized by his homosexuality, his sense of isolation, and his desire to make his mark as a poet, Ginsberg nevertheless initially tried to fit into an unwelcoming postwar world. It was in these early years that Ginsberg worked through both his existential issues and questions of poetic technique that would lead to his mature style. Standing at the center of this struggle was the figure of the Shrouded Stranger. In notebooks, letters, drafts, and early poems, the dream of a Shrouded Stranger lurking in the shadows became the site where Ginsberg explored not just his own repressed preoccupations but also how to bridge the gap between the world inside his own head and the "real" world without. What Ginsberg discovered was that by writing in a more concrete style that rejected poetic abstraction in favor of presentation, he was better able to convey the unsettling effect of the Shrouded Stranger to his readers.

The Shrouded Stranger appears throughout Ginsberg's early writing, but the publication history of this material in his early poems is complicated. Ginsberg produced the rhymed poems "Please Open the Window and Let Me In" and "The Shrouded Stranger" (both dated 1949) that were published in *The Gates of Wrath: Rhymed Poems, 1948–52* in 1972. Another version, again called "The Shrouded Stranger" but this time undated, stands as the last poem of *Empty Mirror*, a collection of verse written between 1946 and 1951 but published in 1961 after *Howl and Other Poems* (1956) had made Ginsberg a countercultural star. Ginsberg biographer Michael Schumacher points out that while the period of composition for both of these volumes overlaps,

> the works in *Empty Mirror*, of course, are "accidental" poems—prose lines that were taken from journals and broken into poetry lines in an effort to please [William Carlos] Williams. The works in *Gates of Wrath*, on the other hand, find the poet working painstakingly in rhyme and meter schemes, the works displaying technical mastery but very little of the poet's own signature. (552)

Ginsberg was struggling to find his own voice in this period, exploring various stylistic as well as thematic possibilities, and the figure of the Shrouded Stranger was important to this development. Indeed, this overlooked figure stands at the very heart of Ginsberg's attempt not only to come to terms with the fears, anxieties, and desires of his early period but to find a poetic form capable of adequately portraying this enigmatic figure and the postwar concerns he represented.

Though the Shrouded Stranger would appear in subsequent versions, standing as the last poem in *Empty Mirror* and providing the collection with its title, "The Shrouded Stranger" appears to be Ginsberg's final word on this enigmatic presence. This version starts off abstractly, declaring

> *The Shroudy Stranger's reft of realms.*
> *Abhorred he sits upon the city dump.*
> *His broken heart's a bag of shit.*
> *The vast rainfall, an empty mirror.*
>
> (46)

"Abhorred" and "reft of realms," the Shroudy Stranger can only stare at the rain, an "empty mirror" that, given his own forlorn state, gives nothing back. Here, the Shrouded Stranger has become a helpless figure and mirrors Ginsberg's own confusion and disappointment. The poet is still seeking both an identity and a voice with which to announce it, even at the end of the volume. The *Empty Mirror* version likewise mirrors Ginsberg's personal state in the epigraph to the volume. Untitled and undated, this text comes immediately after William Carlos Williams's introduction and begins the volume with the words "I feel as if I am at a dead / end and so I am finished" (7). While this is not necessarily Ginsberg's voice and the reader is given no clue as to when these lines were written or why they appear, the epigraph is nevertheless an apt introduction to a confessional book filled with uncertainty and doubt.

The rest of the poem picks up on this theme of despair, chronicling the Stranger's sense of isolation as well as the inability of the poet to fully record this experience. The second section describes a dream of the Shrouded Stranger as shattered and alone, "trembling / in the naked flowers" (46), hardly the disturbing phantasm that Ginsberg chronicles in other versions. In the next section, the speaker decides to go looking for the Shroudy Stranger "down the years" (46), only to find him "hiding under the springs / crouched in the corner" (47). Ginsberg seems to be tracing an encounter with his own buried self cowering under the bed, but the meeting lacks closure. Rather than offer wisdom, the Shrouded Stranger throws the question of meaning back to Ginsberg, saying "'I'll bet you didn't think / it was me after all'" (47). Here the Shrouded Stranger remains enigmatic. The poem does not go on to solve this problem in its final stanza, instead opting for a meta-critique of its own failure. Subheaded "Fragmenta Monumenti" or "fragments of a monument" (the Latin *monumentum* could also mean a funerary monument), the stanza explains what Ginsberg had *wanted* to accomplish but could not:

> *It was to have a structure, it*
> *was going to tell a story;*
> *it was to be a mass of images*
> *moving on a page, with*
> *a hollow voice at the center.*
> (47)

The *Empty Mirror* version of "The Shrouded Stranger" succeeds only at chronicling its own failure. Ginsberg had wanted to go from the metaphysical to the concrete—from "rainfall's hood and moon" to

> *the street light*
> *of the world's bare physical*
> *appearance*

—but instead ends with a title to a poem he had wanted to write but does not exist: "The Vision of the Shrouded Stranger of the Night" (47).

A major factor in the Shrouded Stranger's current obscurity in Ginsberg's corpus is that Ginsberg was repeatedly dissatisfied with his ability to capture this figure for his readers. The Shrouded Stranger often appeared in Ginsberg's notes as he struggled to develop aesthetic and thematic approaches to his work. In a March 1950 entry, Ginsberg instructs himself to "write a long poem about a man whose pride is swallowed by oblivion. Impulses reverse of normalcy—mine the dregs" (*Martyrdom* 328). While the Shrouded Stranger typically appears as an outcast figure, *The Book of Martyrdom and Artifice* presents a litany of possible approaches to limning the Stranger. Later in the same entry, Ginsberg contemplates a "Lincoln theme" with the Shrouded Stranger as an "angel of responsibility" making a variety of speeches before he breaks down to reveal "freakish and repulsive supernaturally shocking strangerishness" (330) à la Robert Louis Stevenson's *Dr. Jekyll and Mr. Hyde*. Ginsberg will continue with this Gothic stranger. In yet another undated manuscript version, the Shrouded Stranger is described as "gazing red in eye and mouldering in his mouth; / Green his brow has grown, a warehouse for the worm" (500). Continuing in his "Notebook for the poem 'Shroudy Stranger of the Night,'" Ginsberg asks himself in September 1950, "Railroad poem? Dream poem? / A poem-like 'Ode to Judgment' and 'Epilogue'?" (334). As we will see with Kerouac, Ginsberg appeals to other literary classics (invoking Melville and Shakespeare in other entries) when thinking through the Stranger. Ginsberg laments his frustration in a May 1950 entry, explaining,

> The attempt to keep going month after month continuing to shift a set of abstractions about literarily defined problems—languages of dreams and hallucinations—rather than things—compulsive thoughts that I turn from when I really think as others think—attempt to sustain structure which threatens itself with extinction hourly and collapses daily. (330)

The Shrouded Stranger is elusive. Although Ginsberg cannot help returning to him in his bid to craft poetry, he has come no closer to finding an appropriate vehicle for his expression.

The one thing that Ginsberg is sure of is that he wants his work to move from vague abstractions like "dreams" and "hallucinations" to more concrete realities. In another undated entry, Ginsberg explains that he had hoped to go "'from classical mystical shroudy psalmlike stanzas and rhymes, through the history of poetic language, to bare statement of fact objectivist speech. Begin with symbols and end with things'" (Schumacher 128). It seems clear through such entries that Ginsberg considered "shroudy" and "things" to be antonyms—the Shroudy Stranger would go from enigma to an "old beat out decayed Bum of America" (128), a progression that would turn the mystical into the factual and personal uncertainty into a nascent social critique of American consumerism. In a 1949 letter (included in *The Gates of Wrath*) to Ginsberg's mentor, the poet William Carlos Williams, Ginsberg clearly downplays the importance of his Shrouded Stranger work. Speaking of the poem "Please Open the Window and Let Me In," Ginsberg claims that it is "less interesting as a poem (or less sincere) but it connects observations of *things* with an old dream of the void" (n.p.). Ginsberg goes on to explicitly connect the dream, as well as the poem "The Shrouded Stranger," with "my own abyss," telling Williams that he had "contemplated a long work on the shroudy stranger, his wanderings" (n.p.). The fact that Ginsberg chose to include this early letter at the beginning of his volume *The Gates of Wrath*, which was published in 1972, demonstrates both his lingering fascination and frustration with the figure. Ginsberg is trying to employ Williams's attention to concrete particulars to capture a figure he considers important at this stage in his life, but the Shrouded Stranger's vague, shadowy nature resists such a representation.[2]

Despite the sense that the Shrouded Stranger is a failure, this figure helps Ginsberg to hone what would become his mature style. Ginsberg's first manuscript version of "The Shrouded Stranger," collected in the appendix of *The Book of Martyrdom and Artifice* (493–94, undated), is almost a word-for-word transcription of a prose journal entry from November 1949. While Kerouac relates his experience of the Shrouded Stranger, the content of Ginsberg's dream is never directly disclosed. Instead, the Shrouded Stranger appears only in artistic attempts to portray him. In both the journal entry and the first manuscript version, the Stranger sounds much like Kerouac's Doctor Sax, wandering along the streets of "the outer night shadowed areas" (*Martyrdom* 327 [November 1949 entry], 493). This should come as no surprise, since Ginsberg had read Kerouac's *Dr. Sax* and influenced its writing. This first manuscript version still relies heavily on airy and metaphysical language. The poem ends with a very abstract image that is difficult to pin down—what would a "palmy oasis of light" really look like, and how does a "barren firmament plain" help us to understand the Stranger's own particular "eternity," whatever that might be (*Martyrdom* 494, undated)? But Ginsberg does begin to omit pronouns and condense phrases from the journal entry in his revision and is willing to jettison terms like "moodily" and "meditating" in order to present a more "active" poem that better accords with the advice of his mentor, William Carlos Williams. This is the beginning of a sparer style that will characterize his later work.

Such a desire to abandon this sort of abstraction in favor of detail and precision can be seen in a further revision. Ginsberg produced another draft, titled "The Song of the Shroudy Stranger of the Night," that is similar to the final version of the poem published in *The Gates of Wrath*. But differences do appear, and they are significant. For example, in the sixth stanza of the draft version, the speaker discusses his meager existence, claiming, "I sip my soup from old tin cans." The last two lines of the stanza read "But meats and dreaming least me feed / Hunger has another greed" (*Martyrdom* 499). Besides the difficult grammatical inversion "least me feed," these lines have another problem—they rely on one abstraction to explain another. "Hunger" here is meant to be metaphysical, a need that goes beyond acquiring another bowl of "soup." But what other "greed" does it have? One assumes the sexual, and the poem goes on to demonstrate that this is the case. In the next stanza the speaker says, "Love lies beneath the shroudy sky, / Who'll lay down under my darkened thigh?" (499). This final line's use of "darkened thigh" highlights the Shroudy Stranger's connection to the sexual by employing concrete imagery in place of abstract metaphors of love. Ginsberg confronts his readers with an unsettling image of a homeless and hopeless Stranger who gestures directly to sexual desire.

Ginsberg's changes to the final *Gates of Wrath* version of this poem push it further into the realm of the concrete. The title, trimmed down to simply "The Shrouded Stranger," is the first clue to Ginsberg's new approach. The line "But meats and dreaming least me feed / Hunger has another greed" becomes "In Tiger Alley near the jail / I steal away from the garbage pail" (23). This retains the immediacy of the food metaphor, keeping the Shrouded Stranger's need in a more physical, rather than abstract, realm. Ginsberg also removed two entire stanzas from the previous version that included vague descriptions of despair. In the first omitted stanza, the Shrouded Stranger wants someone to "walk down the waterfront with me" in order to "call the dark shaggy things of the sea / Out of the dungeon under the dock" (*Martyrdom* 498). In the next, the Shrouded Stranger had previously ended the stanza with the exclamation, "O tears out of my Hebrew face!" (498). Neither of these laments have the simple power of an image of actual hunger, of taking one's dinner from a "garbage pail." Ginsberg shifts focus from the desire to capture the emotional content of the speaker to a presentation of the uncanny effect of the Shrouded Stranger.

This desire to make the reader complicit in the unsettling effect of the poem is captured perfectly in the changes Ginsberg makes to its penultimate line. Ginsberg alters the original line from the vague claim that "love lies beneath the shroudy sky" (*Martyrdom* 499) in the "Song of the Shroudy Stranger of the Night" draft to the more direct and disturbing query, "Who'll look into my hooded eye[?]" (*Gates of Wrath* 23). While Ginsberg initially tries to convey the Shrouded Stranger by having "shroud" modify "sky," this does not adequately capture the uncanniness of the figure. It is one thing to talk about the vagaries of love in the abstract, quite another to offer oneself to the "hooded eye" of a phantasm sifting through society's debris. This revised image, though concrete, has multiple possible interpretations. Not only does this image of the Shrouded Stranger work to reproduce the physical appearance of the figure in the reader's mind, but it also has the added advantage of subtly connoting the homosexual through an appeal to the phallic. While postwar society might have viewed homosexuality as an aberration from the norm, Ginsberg uses the Shrouded Stranger to suggest homosexuality's connection to a "love" and desire that must reside in the shadows. By making the images of the poem more concrete, Ginsberg produces a more direct poem that is better able to present the very real social difficulties that the speaker encounters.[3]

Ginsberg actively searches for the Shrouded Stranger because the figure represents a submerged aspect of his own unconscious struggling to find vent. The Shrouded Stranger exemplifies Ginsberg's internalization of Cold War demands to fit into prescribed sexual roles. Thus in a November 1951 entry, Ginsberg reads himself back into the Shrouded Stranger: "Form should be life work of A.G. entitled 'Journal of the Shroudy Stranger' telling my most secret ambitions and vagaries" (*Martyrdom* 344). Ginsberg's struggle with his homosexual feelings during this period makes a comparison between the Shrouded Stranger and homosexual desire compelling. The same night he dreams about the Shrouded Stranger, Ginsberg has yet another dream about trying to hold in his ejaculation and observes, "I thought it was like homosexuality—which I can't simply give up by holding my cock tight" (*Martyrdom*, December

1949, 327). Ginsberg might try to repress desire, but it finds voice through this enigmatic figure—the Shrouded Stranger as a recurrent symbol of all the shadowy, submerged desires that Ginsberg is struggling to control during the early postwar years. In still another version, "The Shrouded Stranger of the Night to the Child of the Rainbow," Ginsberg casts the Stranger as an old man wooing a younger one (*Martyrdom*, 497–98, undated). As we saw in the first chapter, the Cold War demanded sexual as well as political conformity; in fact, both were intertwined. Ginsberg struggled to reconcile personal sexual desire with the very social need for inclusion and community in a conformist postwar culture.

For Ginsberg, finding an appropriate poetic form becomes tantamount to bridging the gap between self and society. What is "real" and what is a "dream"? The shadowy stranger is a cipher that forces Ginsberg to confront this question, and his poems are, besides evidence of his growth as a writer, answers to this query. In his poem "The Terms in Which I Think Reality," likewise collected in *Empty Mirror*, Ginsberg describes his belief:

> *Reality is a question*
> *of realizing how real*
> *the world is already.*
> (28)

According to Ginsberg, we are already in "Eternity" even if our world is constantly "changing." The problem is that we cannot see the perfection that exists around us, instead insisting on "gratifying new changes" that are difficult to enact and cause us frustration at every turn (29). Ginsberg had originally included a section in the typescript that castigates those who succumb to this false dichotomy:

> *It's a good thing men are*
> *interested in mysteries*
> *of reality. It's a bad*
>
> *thing they think it's a*
> *dream. The mystery is that*
> *it's not a dream at all:*
>
> *The Mystery itself!*
> (Typescript)

Ginsberg may have cut this section because it sets up an invidious comparison between reality and dream. Ginsberg is trying to point out that the "mysteries of reality" are not beyond our ken. In fact, it is the "Mystery itself" that is real, and claiming that these "mysteries" are "not a dream at all" denudes dreams of their status in the work as equal partners of "reality." That is, Ginsberg wants to erase the distinction between the dream world and the "real" world so that both enjoy the same status as phenomenon. We experience both, and thus both are just as equally "real." In a 1956 letter to Richard Eberhart, Ginsberg claims, "I am paying homage to mystical mysteries in the forms in which they actually occur here in the U.S. in our environment" (*Letters* 131). The scientific rationalism of the postwar period tried to occlude the metaphysical world of shadow, but Ginsberg makes it clear that such "mysteries" are themselves an integral part of life in America.

Concomitant with this idea that there is no difference between "mystery" and "reality" is Ginsberg's insistence on the role of dreams in everyday life. Ginsberg's notebooks, *The Gates of Wrath*, and *Empty Mirror* are all filled with records of his dreams. Explaining the significance of these dream records, Ginsberg states, "The attempt in yoga is to enlarge consciousness, to be conscious that one's own consciousness will include everything which occurs within the body and the mind" (*Spontaneous Mind* 240). Dreams, as part of the mind, are as real to Ginsberg as physical phenomena and thus form an integral part of reality. In an April 1952 entry, Ginsberg declares that *Empty Mirror* was "made up of thoughts that came to me, occurred in my mind, rather than things I tried to think up, in that sense they are objective. They are really the substance of my thought" (*Martyrdom* 375). Mental constructs are abstractions, attempts to simply rearrange thoughts and feelings. Discussing his exploration of the unconscious in a June 1949 letter to his friend and fellow Beat writer John Clellon Holmes, Ginsberg writes, "I abandoned making up systems and set about attempting to seek into myself for the springs of that energy, or life force, or reality, or supernaturality, that had been momentarily released" (*Letters* 47). Ginsberg levels the distinction between "dream" and "reality." Dreams like the Shrouded Stranger are just as real as worldly phenomena because they are the "substance" of the mind. Writing them down provides access to another level of reality, but it is a level that Ginsberg does not invidiously set against everyday, physical phenomena. The world of shadow is just as important as the world of light when trying to achieve understanding.

Ginsberg's decision to erase the difference between dream and reality represents an answer to the crisis of identity he was experiencing at the time. In an October 1950 journal entry, Ginsberg explains that

> I realized that all along when I was fighting off recognition of the reality of the world of appearances that my poetry was an escape from it. . . . And now for them the world is solid and endless, except for death, which they understand as the total apocalypse and end of the world for each of them; while I cling still in various ways to figments of immortality, solitude, onanism, shady thought, spite and shallowness against truly innocent fellow creatures.
>
> (My doctor now calls me psychopathic and bids me choose between ego and world). (*Martyrdom* 335)

Refusing to accept the "reality of the world," Ginsberg initially takes refuge in poetic abstraction. Unfortunately, this cuts him off from his "fellow creatures" who have already accepted the world as "solid and endless." Rather than see poetry as a means to capture this world in order to present it to another, Ginsberg uses it as an "escape" into his own self-creations. The doctor, exemplifying his role as an expert, admonishes Ginsberg in the form of a binary choice: choose between the world you have created for yourself ("ego") and the real world that lies outside. Ginsberg's solution, however, eschews such dichotomies. The "real" world is not figured as false and base, a fall from the lofty heights of poetry, but rather as the salvation of Ginsberg's aesthetic. Choosing the "world" over "ego" does not force Ginsberg to abandon poetry. On the contrary, it produces a more vibrant writing that uses the materiality of Ginsberg's inner world of dreams to forge a connection to the world of others.

Cold war culture sought to build community through a set of shared values. Ginsberg's versions of the Shrouded Stranger, by contrast, offered a competing narrative that sought to disclose what could not be said in American culture. But Ginsberg did not want to simply shock his audience; he wanted a poetry that could communicate directly to others. In his letter to Holmes, Ginsberg declares that

> this has been the burden of all my poems, an attempt
> to use language which is pure fact, not airy poetry, to
> suggest to the mind of the reader that substantial actuality

> of Being or reality or fact, etc. that he dreams of, and to affirm it, though it may seem like madness to him (for truly our world considers it madness; and people are afraid of reality). (*Letters* 49)

Instead of trying to represent the dream through use of symbol, Ginsberg realizes that only by showing readers can they fully grasp its significance. Once such communication takes place, poetry enters into the social realm with force. By getting back to the concrete details of his own mind, Ginsberg is better able to deliver the sort of loneliness that the Shrouded Stranger evokes in him to his readers. Not only does this build a community of those outside the norms of postwar society, but it also challenges the binaries of Cold War thinking by presenting the reader with images such as the Shrouded Stranger that raise issues that cannot be contained by containment culture.

What Ginsberg's use of his Shrouded Stranger dream demonstrates is the beginning of a new method of writing that uses the concrete images of experience (both conscious and unconscious) to craft a poetry that is meant to viscerally impact the reader. Of course at this stage, Ginsberg's method was still rudimentary. It would acquire added force with his realization in *Howl* that by "juxtaposing" two of these images, he could create a gap capable of jolting the reader into realization. At this nascent stage, Ginsberg had only the single image to work with. He himself was aware of this, commenting in a May 1956 letter to Eberhart that "*Howl* is the first discovery as far as *communication* of feeling and truth, that I made" (*Letters* 132). Nevertheless, the Shrouded Stranger discussion that Ginsberg carried on with Kerouac was an important, if often neglected, moment in Ginsberg's development. By providing Ginsberg with an intractable image that was difficult to both present and interpret, the Shrouded Stranger gave Ginsberg an image ambiguous enough to work through some of the important life decisions he was addressing at this stage, such as his relationship to homosexuality and feelings of being outside mainstream society. Just as important, it forced Ginsberg to find novel ways of expressing these unconscious fears and concerns. Ginsberg makes the reader complicit in the process of making meaning by not providing a symbol to be deciphered but rather by presenting an idea meant to deconstruct the binary thinking of the Cold War. Ginsberg used the enigma of the Shrouded Stranger to question and confront the rational assumptions of American culture at midcentury.

KEROUAC'S "DARK HAUNTED THING"

The Shrouded Stranger's ability to unsettle and disturb was equally important to Jack Kerouac's early development as a writer. Having finished his first novel, *The Town and the City* (written 1945–48, published 1950), Kerouac was looking to write something different, something "like a dream; and with that strange continuity of purpose that all our dreams and all our days have . . . such a 'moodwork' as I once called it, or soulwork—or Shrouded Tale" (*Windblown*, October 1949, 243). In order to adequately convey the enigmatic feeling that the Shrouded Stranger represented, Kerouac needed a method that would allow him to stage his dream as an ever-interpretable event rather than as a site for complete and final understanding. Although Kerouac's attempts to present the Shrouded Stranger occurred before his celebrated discovery of his "spontaneous prose" method, the lessons learned from discussing and writing this figure were an important stepping stone to this discovery. Ultimately, as Kerouac struggled to interpret and represent the Shrouded Stranger, he came to realize that the process of making meaning was more important than arriving at a final understanding of this shadowy figure.

For Kerouac, the road beyond the crafted, straightforward narrative style of his first book and into a realm of "dream" ran directly through the Shrouded Stranger. In his journals, Kerouac drew two related diagrams in an attempt to explain the enigma that the Shrouded Stranger represented. Both diagrams depict a circle composed of arrows, with tangential lines shooting off at various points. Lying at the center of the second diagram is what Kerouac calls "the dark haunted thing," defining it thusly: "To me, 'this thing' is that Shrouded Stranger I dreamt once. It is ever-present and ever-pursuing. One may swirl nearer and nearer to that shroud, *and it may only be* our haunted sense of the *thing*, which is ever unnamable and is really our chiefest plaint" (December 1949, 249). Kerouac placed his finger squarely on a defining aspect of human consciousness—a negativity within oneself that demands and defies explication. Although "unnamable," Kerouac would nevertheless spend his career trying to name it and in the process push his writing in ever-new directions.

But what exactly does Kerouac mean by the "Shrouded Stranger"? Kerouac is referring to an earlier dream he had about being chased by a shrouded figure across the desert.[4] In an April 1949 journal entry, Kerouac explains:

> Traveling by dusty road in the white desert, from Arabia to the Protective City, I saw that I was inexorably pursued by a Hooded Wayfarer with a staff, who slowly occupied and traversed the plain behind me, sending up a shroud of dust slowly. I know not how I knew he followed me, but if I could make the Protective City before he caught up with me, I knew I would be safe. But this was out of the question. I waited to waylay him in a house on the side of the road, with a rifle: yet I knew no gun would save me. (*Windblown* 319)

Kerouac begins to make sense of the apparition by reading the dream symbolically. In response to Ginsberg's demand to know what this dream means, Kerouac replies that it was "one's own self merely wearing a shroud" (320). The repeated use of the word "shroud" in their descriptions links the Shrouded Stranger with the figure of death. While Kerouac and Ginsberg use "shroud" as a synonym for "ghost" in general, the literal meaning of the word is a garment that wraps a dead person in burial. Figuratively, the term has come to mean anything that obscures, as in the phrases "shroud of mist" or "shroud of secrecy." The idea that one's own self would wear a shroud seems to indicate that Kerouac reads the dream as an encounter with a dead, or better, buried self whose veiled knowledge would mean annihilation. The "Hooded Wayfarer" becomes that part of the unconscious that cannot be announced. Pursuing Kerouac's conscious across the "white desert" of the mind, this Shrouded Stranger cannot be destroyed, simply because he is an integral part of Kerouac's himself. This "dark haunted thing," then, is an encounter with the mystery of one's self.

But Kerouac, unsurprisingly, is not content with this more psychoanalytic explanation of his Shrouded Stranger dream. A few pages later in his journals, Kerouac provides a more nuanced explanation to Ginsberg.

> Being born in the darkness a Shrouded Infant, we come, ambiguous & secret, to the actual world, with a mission, a personal holy mission, which outs one way or the other. The dream is our reminder of darkness, the Shrouded Stranger pursuing us on to heaven which is great life on earth; and if we lag, he may catch us and cast us down in the darkness again. (323)

Here the Shrouded Stranger acts as a sort of watchdog, reminding us to cherish our time in the light. Perhaps our "mission" is to discover what exactly is "pursuing" us and make peace with it, before it overtakes us to "cast us down . . . again." This movement from reading the dream in a more psychological vein to reading it through an almost Christian eschatology can be seen throughout Kerouac's corpus. As his career progressed, Kerouac came to rely ever more heavily on the Catholicism that saw him through his childhood years, supplemented with his interest in Buddhism. Nevertheless, the "dark haunted thing" at the center of existence remains enigmatic. As Kerouac was working on his Buddhist-inspired *Some of the Dharma* (written 1953–56), he became convinced that the Shrouded Stranger was as important as ever, admonishing Ginsberg in May 1954, "Don't you forget our liquid ghosts oogling behind buildings, and the eternity radar machines in the sky, and dead eyes see, because, boy, I've now found that it was all instinct pure and true, and I must say, we weren't so dumb" (qtd. in Schumacher 175). Although he remains important, the Shrouded Stranger also remains obscure: Is he the devil tempting us, God reminding us, or just our own innate understanding that life is precious and thus should not be wasted? The power of the Shrouded Stranger is that he does not answer such questions but forces the act of interpretation onto the reader.

Kerouac's "dark haunted thing" pushes him to explore the occluded space within himself. But such shrouds and shadows also produce the material for great writing because everyone has them, yet nobody knows what they mean. This oscillation between the dream as self-revelatory and the dream as transcendental reminder defines Kerouac's relationship to this "Shrouded Existence" (*Windblown* 324) that he finds so productive as a writer. In a letter to his friend Ed White, Kerouac extracts these Shrouded Stranger portions of his notebook to convey his goal as a writer: "What I want to do is explain it all someday, and get that mad cark out of my heart (and the reader's heart) thereby . . . so that we can proceed to greater things somehow" ("Letters," May 1949, 129). As Kerouac declares to White, he wants "to go off, like Shakespeare and like the good ones, and dance on the edges of relative knowledge, dance to all the plaints" (130). In the end, it is these "edges" that make for good writing, these in-between spaces where mystery can unfold into creation. According to Kerouac, God himself is responsible for this ambiguity, since he is "playing the game with us undoubtedly, the game concerning light and darkness" (*Windblown*, April 1949, 325). The dream world's "Shrouded Existence" purposefully leaves us in a space of shadows where nothing is certain. Kerouac's writing attempts to remain in this space between light and darkness, to struggle to decipher this "Celestial Tongue" (325) that hints at both.

Continually invoking "the good ones" like Shakespeare reveals another anxiety lying at the heart of the Shrouded Stranger: the anxiety of influence. Kerouac feels overshadowed by the great writers preceding him, and his engagement with the Shrouded Stranger is a means of propelling himself to their heights. Like Ginsberg, Kerouac repeatedly invokes his literary masters when discussing this figure. In his journals, Kerouac compares this "thing" that is haunting him to "Melville's 'inscrutable thing,'" William Blake's "gate of Wrath," Emily Dickinson's "third event," and Shakespeare's 'Nature,'" among others (*Windblown*, December 1949, 249). In his book *The Anxiety of Influence*, Harold Bloom discusses what he terms "poetic misprision" (xxiii). According to Bloom, "poetic history" is a succession of "strong poets . . . misreading one another, so as to clear imaginative space for themselves" (5). Although Bloom would not consider Kerouac (or any Beat author, probably) as a "strong poet," the sort of anxiety that he discusses appears applicable to both Kerouac and Ginsberg.[5] Both writers struggle to use the Shrouded Stranger to rethink Bloom's own exemplar, Shakespeare, and references to other such luminaries appear repeatedly in Kerouac's journal entries. The Shrouded Stranger can thus be read as a sort of ghost of "the good ones" haunting his nascent career, a shroud that would need to be exorcised before the Shrouded Stranger could become *On the Road* and *Dr. Sax*, two books (along with *Visions of Cody*) that Kerouac saw as defining his mature style. Bloom claims that "every poet begins (however 'unconsciously') by rebelling more strongly against the consciousness of death's necessity than all other men and women do" (10). Nothing could be truer of Kerouac. The Shrouded Stranger is an attempt to understand death, to confront it, and then to fold that encounter into a writing capable of transmitting such transcendent moments.

The message the Shrouded Stranger delivers changes again when he finds his way into Kerouac's celebrated novel. *On the Road* chronicles the evolving relationship between the aspiring writer and narrator Sal Paradise and an energetic young muse named Dean Moriarty. *On the Road* is very much a roman à clef, with Paradise representing Kerouac himself and Moriarty a stand-in for his friend and inspiration Neal Cassady. While the Shrouded Stranger remains enigmatic in journals and letters, here he is given a more definitive interpretation. After Sal relates the dream (though this time the Shrouded Traveler "overtook me," he claims), he proposes that the "Shrouded Traveler" was simply himself "wearing a shroud" (124). This reading, however, is quickly dismissed in favor of death as an explanation: "The one thing that we yearn for in our living days . . . is the remembrance of some lost bliss that was probably experienced in the womb and can only be reproduced (though we hate to admit it) in death" (124). This explanation, which hints at the Freudian notion of Thanatos or the "death drive," reverses the one given in the journal. Rather than the "womb" being a place of darkness, a "hell" from which we escape, it now becomes formulated in terms of desire. We want to return in order to experience the unrecoverable pleasure that "can only be reproduced . . . in death."

Dean, however, disagrees. As the narrator comments, Dean "instantly recognized it as the mere simple longing for pure death; and because we're all of us never in life again, he, rightly, would have nothing to do with it" (124). Dean's reading is consistent with his role in the novel. As an energetic force that compels the narrator Sal forward into new experiences, Dean comes to represent a world devoid of social constraint that is defined chiefly by exuberance. Dean's rejection of Sal's more pessimistic interpretation is therefore apt. In a 1955 letter to Dean's real-life inspiration, Neal Cassady, Kerouac tells him that he is "looking at you waiting for whatever you got to say next . . . my name Shadow—I be your shadow" (letter to Neal Cassady). Kerouac is drawn to Neal's energy and verve, "shadowing" his movements in much the same manner as the Shrouded Stranger shadows his own dreams and writings.

Kerouac personifies the Shrouded Stranger throughout *On the Road* in ways that make him a placeholder for the obverse of mainstream American culture. As Isaac Gewirtz notes in *Beatific Soul: Jack Kerouac on the Road*, in a 1949 outline titled "NIGHT NOTES and Diagrams for *ON THE ROAD*," Kerouac lists the "definite 'unities' (As yet un-named)" for the book, which begins with an allusion to "Kerouac's brief encounter with an old, bearded hobo, the 'Ghost of the Susquehanna'" (83). In Harrisburg, Kerouac encounters this ghost, an old man who was "headed for Canady" (*On the Road* 105). Though in the end Sal realizes he was a "semi-respectable walking hobo of some kind," nevertheless this ghost is associated with an "Eastern Wilderness" (104) that Sal did not know still existed. James T. Jones, in "Sharing a Shadow," chronicles several other emendations throughout the novel, including Hyman Solomon, a "modern wandering Jew"; a Negro traveler; an old white-haired man, "Zacatecan Jack"; and an apparition of a white horse in Mexico.

As Jones rightly concludes, "The Shrouded Stranger pervades *On the Road*" (227–28). Perhaps the most important Shrouded Stranger figure is Dean's alcoholic father, who haunts the novel as a melancholic reminder of an earlier America that is the antithesis of *On the Road*'s Cold War setting. This figure comes to stand for a vanishing hobo America that was quickly succumbing to a postwar world of affluence and the loss of communal feeling that accompanied it. Tim Hunt, in *The Textuality of Soulwork*, argues that *On the Road* is built from "recursiveness" rather than on plot: "Each repetition deepens the central conflicts rather than progressing toward some final resolution" (74).[6] The various iterations of the Shrouded Stranger help emphasize the countercultural nature of its plot. The Shrouded Stranger represents those marginalized in postwar society, ghosts and phantoms reduced to wandering back and forth across the American continent in much the same way as Sal and Dean.

This attempt to communicate the "dark haunted thing" that is the driving force behind Kerouac's life and work will ultimately form an uncanny counterpoint to a novel that is generally considered a classic of countercultural enthusiasm. *On the Road* is a book that, when read while young, seems full of hope and promise but, after repeated readings, comes to nostalgically represent the search for meaning that must always lead to failure. Dean's father, for example, is never found. Like the Shrouded Stranger, he remains something of an enigma, a riddle, and as such is inextricably bound with the nostalgic search for lost origins. But such pessimism also represents an existential struggle between Sal's lust for life and his fascination with death. In *Kerouac's Crooked Road*, Hunt discusses the dream of the Shrouded Stranger, pointing out that "Sal and Dean do want to die just as they want to live and Sal's interpretation avoids recognizing this conflict" (31). In the original 1951 edition of the novel, after Sal relates Dean's rejection of the dream as a "longing for pure death," the narrator ends the discussion by stating, "And I agree with him now" (*On the Road: The Original Scroll* 226). The version published in 1957, however, has Sal stating, "And I agreed with him then" (124). As Hunt correctly comments, "The concluding phrase shows that Sal agreed with Dean at the time but leaves open the possibility that Sal is less sure about the matter retrospectively" (31). The Shrouded Stranger dream has no final meaning—it must be continually reinterpreted.

The Shrouded Stranger, and the enigma he represents, is thus at the heart of the novel. The reason Kerouac "shadows" Dean is the same reason he shadows all the others outside mainstream society who are "mad to live, mad to talk, mad to be saved" (*On the Road* 8). He is drawn toward their light, toward the promise of life. Yet as the Shrouded Stranger demonstrates, there is always an opposite pull toward the darkness. In the 1951 edition, after claiming that some "lost bliss" waits in death, Kerouac writes, "But more on this later" (225). He is most likely discussing a later scene in the novel, where Kerouac equates death with an ecstatic leap into the void:

> for just a moment I had reached the point of ecstasy that I always wanted to reach, and which was the complete step across chronological time into timeless shadows . . . and the sensation of death kicking at my heels to move on, with a phantom dogging its own heels, and myself hurrying to a plank where all the Angels dove off and flew into infinity. (274)

Though it occupies a mere page of description, the meaning behind this passage is the key to helping unravel all the unfinished searches the novel undertakes. The Shrouded Stranger becomes endlessly repeated as all the tropes that have come to be discussed in his work: Neal, the lost father, a more authentic America, and eventually death itself.

Understanding, for Kerouac, is always deferred. It has to be, in order for there to be more to write. There is an assumption running throughout Kerouac's writings that this negativity, while explainable, is always contingent. Employing the metaphor of light and dark in his journal, Kerouac queries,

> I know however that each of us is born in darkness, but dies in light. I have some doubts about an extension of this: is the darkness from whence we come, hell?—and is the earth in which we have our existence, heaven?—or purgatory? I believe it is heaven we live in, and that when we die we are buried here in heaven forever.—It is hell we come from. What is the Shrouded Dream? It is the vision of hell from which we come, and from which we tend, towards heaven, here, now. This needs further explanation, and is the most serious matter I can think of. (*Windblown*, April 1949, 322–23)

Shadows are the best metaphor for our world, a transitional space between the darkness of "hell" and the pure light of "heaven." Again, however, this is not the final answer but needs "further explanation." The

Shrouded Stranger is an important stimulus to thought, pushing Kerouac in new and invigorating directions. At one point, Dean himself takes on the persona, arriving in Denver unbeknownst to Kerouac in order to sweep him away into another adventure: "a burning shuddering frightful Angel, palpitating toward me across the road, approaching like a cloud, with enormous speed, pursuing me like the Shrouded Traveler on the plain" (*On the Road* 259). Shrouded Travelers are fearful but necessary. By never settling on one meaning, they reject the concept of closure and surety necessary to the maintenance of Cold War containment culture.

Kerouac's attempts to capture his Shrouded Stranger dream were important, if often overlooked, in both his thinking and his writing. Kerouac initially tried to make sense of the dream by capturing its "meaning" for the reader. As his subsequent writing developed, however, the interpretation of the Shrouded Stranger gave way to presentation, and by *On the Road*, Kerouac was more concerned with staging the dream and the "dark haunted thing" that it revealed. The goal was not to present a final version of this figure but to foist the act of interpretation onto the reader. Although Kerouac would abandon detailed discussion of the Shrouded Stranger as his career continued, the lessons he learned from his dream would reverberate throughout his writings. Kerouac's struggle to come to terms with this shadowy figure captured the zeitgeist of the American postwar period perfectly. There was still a desire for meaning in an anxious Cold War world, but at the same time there existed an uneasy sense that any such meaning was arbitrary and constructed—like an apparition, subject to disappear in a flash. Better, then, to perform this uncertainty than to contain it with a final resolution.

IN THE SHADOW OF FREUD

Any discussion of dreams, shadows, and shrouds must take into account the vast impact of a thinker whose presence cast its own shadow across the entire twentieth century: Sigmund Freud. Ginsberg's and Kerouac's attempts to write the Shrouded Stranger could not avoid Freudian theories since Freud's work was omnipresent. When not acting as an explicit influence, Freud's thought was there implicitly, creating the cultural background against which Ginsberg's and Kerouac's formulations took shape. Ginsberg and Kerouac did not dismiss Freud—they adapted him. The Shrouded Stranger was, in many ways, a coming to terms with the concept of the unconscious as Freud and his proselytizers conceived it. Writing and rewriting their dream of the Shrouded Stranger, Ginsberg and Kerouac attempted to reclaim the unconscious as a space for imagination and possibility.

Freud examined the role that ghosts, shadows, and other hauntings have to play in revealing unconscious processes in his highly influential study *The Uncanny* (1919). This piece, one of the few that Freud wrote on the subject of art, attempts to explain the uncanny effects that E. T. A. Hoffman employs so brilliantly in his short story "The Sandman" (1816). Dismissing Ernst Jentsch's contention that the uncanny is the result of a "lack of orientation" toward a "thing or incident" (8), Freud instead searches for meaning in the hidden depths of the unconscious.[7] One of the most useful artistic techniques for Freud is Hoffman's employment of the double. Drawing on the work of fellow psychoanalyst Otto Rank, who linked this motif with "mirror-images, shadows, guardian spirits, the doctrine of the soul and fear of death," Freud observes that originally such images were a "defense against annihilation" (*The Uncanny* 142). He invokes the Egyptians specifically as a people who wholeheartedly embraced this connection between the double and the soul as a means of protection. But such a state, Freud argues, can exist only in the "primordial narcissism that dominates the mental life of both the child and primitive man" (142). Now that modern man has surpassed this stage of development, the double takes on a new significance as "the uncanny harbinger of death" (142)—a theme that Kerouac and Ginsberg explore in their discussions of the Shrouded Stranger but ultimately reject.

Freud's argument hinges on the idea that there is a "*compulsion to repeat*" operating in the unconscious, and "anything that can remind us of this inner compulsion to repeat is perceived as uncanny" (145). Freud provides two possibilities. "Repressed childhood complexes" occasioned by earlier trauma might be unconsciously remembered with the introduction of certain objects or events, or "primitive beliefs that have been *surmounted*" (155) might appear to be confirmed when we witness an uncanny occurrence. It appears as though ghosts and shadows clearly fall into the second category, given their connection with ancient beliefs in the soul. But as Freud concludes, "It is sometimes impossible to distinguish between the two species of the uncanny" because "primitive convictions are closely linked with childhood complexes" (155). Shadows and shrouds are eerie doubles that return us to an earlier moment in a shared collective development, but they are also bound up in childhood fears of those darkened spaces we thought we outgrew but that sometimes return to inspire an uncanny feeling of dread. Such repetition is a reminder of the fears and desires operating in the unconscious.[8]

While Freud read the uncanny as the "return of the repressed," Ginsberg and Kerouac were more interested in what the Shrouded Stranger revealed about the current state of their mind and, by extension, the society that helped to inform and shape it. These Beats leveled the playing field—dreams were not a clue to something repressed that lay buried within the self. Rather, they were reality itself, already on the surface. This point was crucial for the subsequent development of their writing. Instead of trying to turn these images into abstractions, into allegories that only added another layer of signification, Ginsberg and Kerouac (after some initial struggles and false starts) used such revelations as starting points.

Kerouac and Ginsberg were initially very much interested in the work of Freud and practiced psychoanalytic theories both formally and informally. Kerouac, Ginsberg, and their friend and mentor William S. Burroughs were all analyzed. These three Beat writers would routinely practice psychoanalysis on each other, and their early correspondence from the 1940s and 1950s is littered with psychoanalytic terms and concepts.[9] Their degree of commitment to the process, and the reasons they went, varied. Ginsberg, who was trying to sort out family and sexual issues in his early years, seems the most engaged: "I went to a Reichian around that time myself [1944–45]. Burroughs was at that time being psychoanalyzed by a Doctor Federn, who had been analyzed by Freud, so he had in a sense a direct transmission to the source of psychoanalysis. And he psychoanalyzed us" (*Composed on the Tongue* 82). Many of Ginsberg's letters during the late 1940s and early 1950s advise analysis. In his letter explaining his thoughts on dreams to Holmes, Ginsberg writes, "This as you see is actually the same as the new psychological formulation, and I think that in proper hands (perhaps only Freud himself was deep enuf) it is a sufficient key; that is why I trust analysis for myself, whereas most do not, really. (Jack, Ansen, etc.)" (*Letters* 45). Kerouac, admittedly, was far more circumspect about the benefits of the analysis he underwent in a Bethesda, Maryland, naval hospital while under review for refusing to perform his military duties (Nicosia 105–6). Kerouac's mistrust of his superiors and of the medical experts assigned to his case would eventually lead to his rejection as unfit for military service. Nevertheless, Freud figured prominently in his thinking. According to biographer Gerald Nicosia, Kerouac had read Freud (134). While Freud's importance for the Beats waned as the Cold War continued, in the late 1940s and even into the 1950s Freud exerted a considerable influence on the lives and thoughts of Kerouac and Ginsberg.[10]

Despite this interest in Freud, Ginsberg and Kerouac were by no means Freudian. For Freud, the dream was normative, a scientifically understandable phenomenon that provided insight into the proper functioning of the human mind. By forcing his patients to confront the repressed thought, Freud hoped to mitigate their symptoms. Ultimately, Freud exchanged the dream for an understanding of the past. The dream was the key that opened the door to childhood, which laid bare the repressed desires at the center of the unconscious. In the concluding paragraph of his *Interpretation of Dreams*, Freud differentiates his work from the myriad of dream explicators that had come before him:

> And what of the value of dreams for our knowledge of the future? Of course that is out of the question. Instead, one should rather ask: for a knowledge of the past. For in every sense, dreams come from the past. It is true, the ancient belief that dreams show us the future is not entirely without some truth. For by representing a wish as fulfilled, a dream does indeed take us into the future; but this future, taken by the dreamer to be in the present, is shaped by the indestructible wish into the image of that past. (412)

The dream is the ticket back into the past, a means of recovering the "indestructible wish" that is the dream's origin and the source of the mystery to the waking mind. Thus the ancient belief in the prophetic power of the dream works only in reverse—its cataclysmic revelation is a glimpse into the self, not beyond it into the futurity of the world.

The core reason for Kerouac's and Ginsberg's rejection of Freud was the feeling that his work was too stifling—by rewriting the psyche along oedipal lines, Freud was felt to have closed off avenues of exploration that they were very much interested in examining. In their book *Anti-Oedipus*, Gilles Deleuze and Felix Guattari take Freud explicitly to task: "An unconscious that was capable of nothing but expressing itself—in myth, tragedy, dreams—was substituted for the productive unconscious" (24). For these two postmodern thinkers, the problem with Freud is that he renders the unconscious passive. Rather than "produce" something new, the Freudian unconscious can only repeat what has already formed it. As Fredric Jameson mentions apropos of Deleuze and Guattari's critique,

Freudianism is "characterized as a reduction and a rewriting of the whole rich and random multiple realities of concrete everyday experience into the contained, strategically prelimited terms of the family narrative" (6). Ginsberg and Kerouac, struggling not only to define themselves as writers but to find themselves in a conformist Cold War culture, came to view Freud as part of the same uptight, constrained, and limiting society they were struggling against.

Freud argued for an understanding of the dream based on a compromise—day thoughts negotiate with repressed desires to craft a dream that fulfills a sexual demand while leaving the sleeper physically undisturbed. Kerouac took direct issue with this belief. For Kerouac, "Mind Essence" was not reducible to such infantile sexual demands. The crux of Kerouac's denial of Freud resided in his disavowal that the unconscious operates on the basis of a limited set of desires. For Kerouac, the unconscious was the repository of all that was spontaneously free and thus authentic.[11] In a January 1951 letter to Cassady, Kerouac outlines his own theory of dreams, one that does away with any concern for a hierarchical structure for the unconscious:

> When a man dreams, he can't pluck his dream-image from the air that surrounds his bed; no, on the contrary, the image and the whole material in which it sits, is already in his mind . . . it comes from that part of his brain which has stored up a subconscious vision of an actual experience. Many's the time I've dreamed of ancient scenes in my babyhood distorted only by that forgotten vision that in babyhood I conjured up. . . . There is no distinction between memory and dream other than levels of consciousness. There is no such thing as a pipedream; all dreams come from visions of experience; they are released because they are already there in the mind. (*Selected Letters, 1940–1956* 268)

It should come as no surprise that Kerouac, known as "the Great Rememberer" to Ginsberg for his extensive memory, should equate dreams with memories. Kerouac leveled the playing field of the mind, making its entire range of phenomena—memories, experiences, visions, and dreams—of equal import. The only distinction Kerouac made was how and when that experience was accessed. He gave an example of a childhood bike ride that was exhilaratingly fast. Although he enjoyed it, "since then countless dreams of going too fast on a terrible bicycle have come to me, and no doubt this was on the other level I perceived the ride" (268). But there was no distinction between the conscious enjoyment of the ride as it occurred, the pleasant memory of the ride, and the unconscious perception of the ride as dangerous. All were co-present in the mind, and more important, none were taken as a sign for a "deeper" level of significance.

Both Freud and Kerouac agreed that something was being displaced—for Freud, it was the repressed dream thoughts finding vent through the dream work, while for Kerouac it was this reshuffling of associations between levels of consciousness. But whereas Freud nevertheless pushed for an ultimate truth lying at the center of the unconscious that was authoring the dream, Kerouac was less concerned with finding a final meaning than with using dreams as a chance to begin again.

Ginsberg was more willing to engage Freud and psychoanalysis than Kerouac. But in the end, Ginsberg came to much the same conclusion as his friend concerning its relevance. The dream provides a chance to challenge fixed notions of identity in order to reveal new possibilities to the dreamer. In a 1948 letter to Kerouac, Ginsberg explains that

> if I did not have faith in the mechanical procedure of psychoanalysis as a way of making me face myself I would no longer wait here in the City for a vision. . . . It may seem anachronistic for me to combine such ambitions spiritually with psychoanalysis but I believe that something will happen to me in psychoanalysis that will change everything—towards that goal. (*Jack Kerouac* 39)

Ginsberg used psychoanalysis not to uncover an original trauma that might point the way back to normality through a clearing of neuroses. Rather, the unconscious was being explored in order to produce "vision," to call into being a new state of mind that would lead the way to a "spiritual" shift in existence, and thus in his writing. For Ginsberg, Freud's conception of the unconscious as the clue to a more stable self ran counter to his project as a writer—analysis was a means to explore new conceptions of self and, with them, new ways to write. As writers constantly seeking new experience, Kerouac and Ginsberg viewed their dreams of the Shrouded Stranger as opportunities to reconfigure their sense of self.

While Freud saw the dream as a key to the past, Ginsberg read his dreams in terms of the possibilities they held for the future.[12] Discussing his celebrated September 1961 "Brain Damage" dream where he undergoes "a total loss of identity" (*Journals* 243), Ginsberg comments, "The dream is prophetic taste of true identity loss I will undergo later on . . . poetry be useful to maintain continuity and consult for memory . . . really necessary later, tho?" (244). The dream, rather than being the site where the truth of the unconscious is revealed, becomes the space for annihilation. The "message" of the dream is a tangible, "prophetic taste" of the future that awaits everyone. Ultimately, however, Ginsberg casts doubt on writing's efficacy for the dream. If the dream foreshadows death, what good can come of transcriptions of the near-death experience of dreaming? Just as his room dreams erase the past, the moment of death comes to erase the subject, and while he may try to "maintain some continuity or memory over to another state" (244), the lesson of the dream is to let go of fixed notions of self. For Kerouac and Ginsberg, the dream does not need to "say" anything. The language of the dream, when properly recorded, is simply a force that creates an *opening* for both writer and reader.[13]

In the early postwar years, Freud stood for everything the Beats were fighting against—scientific rationalism, the weight of the past, and the authority of the expert. Kerouac's and Ginsberg's "rewriting" of Freud's master narrative at midcentury can be seen as a reconceptualization of how this "culture of spontaneity," to use Daniel Belgrad's phrase, imagined history not as the mastery of experts but as the full expression of individual consciousness in each moment. Not only did the dream of the Shrouded Stranger allow Ginsberg and Kerouac to explore the depths of their own identities, but the difficulty in capturing this figure pushed them beyond a Freudian desire to interpret and into a new form of writing better able to stage this encounter with difference for the reader. Only by allowing the hidden fears and desires of the unconscious to be revealed in all their complexity could true communication, and thus great literature, be achieved.

SHADOWS MADE SOCIAL: JUNG

Part of what made the Shrouded Stranger so compelling was that both Ginsberg and Kerouac shared him, thus reinforcing each of their beliefs in his universal relevance. Both believed that the Shrouded Stranger represented a fundamental archetype that was at work in the minds of their fellow Americans. Ginsberg and Kerouac thought that if they could just portray the Shrouded Stranger in his immediate uncanniness, their work would become instantly accessible to readers who were likewise haunted by his presence. In an unpublished letter to Neal Cassady in 1950, Ginsberg discusses the ubiquity of the Shrouded Stranger, observing that "the important thing is that everyone has someone with deep socketed eyes and/or a green glassy visage, staring at him, in a crowd, in a dream, or following him unseen in a desert, or seeking though the windowpane" (Cassady, letter). Ginsberg's and Kerouac's repeated discussions concerning this shroud reinforced the desire of each to capture this enigmatic, yet universal, figure.

Kerouac and Ginsberg shared this dream to such an extent that they feared their consciousnesses were becoming inseparable. According to Schumacher, Ginsberg "had long been fascinated with the idea of a mysterious, inexplicable ghost presence, his interests dating back to the days of his youth, when he walked past the shadowy hedges along Graham Avenue in Paterson" (128). Ginsberg was surprised to discover that Kerouac, too, had similar fantasies. According to Schumacher, "Much of his 'Shroudy Stranger' poem, he pointed out, could be attributed to his and Jack's conversations" (141). The anxiety of influence these two writers felt toward Freud is repeated in their relationship to each other. In a March 1952 letter, Ginsberg writes to Kerouac, "My phantasies and phrases have gotten so lovingly mixed up in yours, Jack, I hardly know whose is which and who's used what" (Ginsberg, *Jack Kerouac* 145). Kerouac agreed. In a reply a week later, he says, "When you realize that the 'shrouded stranger' itself was my original phrase . . . there's nothing we can do about it—I think I could find some of my prose which uses some of your feelings" (147). Given that both Ginsberg and Kerouac discussed the character at length, ascribing ownership to a particular author was difficult. Later that month, Ginsberg responds, "You bastard I outright deny you made up phrase Shroudy Stranger, you'll hear from Brooks the lawyer tomorrow. I natcherly steal from you. But didn't you and I make it up together that day on York Avenue? Don't you go stealing my glory. Hole" (154). Ginsberg's tone is mocking and playful, but a hint of competition remains.[14] In a final rebuttal, Kerouac writes to Ginsberg later, "Yes, shrouded stranger you make up yourself talking to me that spring morn" (157–58). Such overlap may be expected from two writers who spent much time writing, sharing, and collaborating. Yet it is clear that they both considered the Shrouded Stranger as more than just a "Beat" phenomenon.

The idea that a Shrouded Stranger was haunting the collective unconscious of a culture would not have surprised Carl Gustav Jung. The Swiss psychiatrist was initially attracted to the work of Freud, as his findings seemed to validate and support Freud's theories. Freud, in his turn, viewed Jung as the heir apparent to his burgeoning psychoanalytic movement. But by 1913, Jung had broken with Freud, a devastating blow for both men. One of the major reasons for this split was their disagreement over the unconscious. As Jung himself explains, Freud made the unconscious "really nothing but the gathering place of forgotten and repressed contents" ("Archetypes" 3). For Jung, this "personal unconscious" is founded on an even "deeper layer, which does not derive from personal experience and is not a personal acquisition but is inborn" (3). Jung believed that the Freudian approach to the unconscious was too reductive. Not only was it entirely sexually motivated, but for Freud the unconscious was solely personal.

Jung's belief that the unconscious was actually the repository of an ancient history that exceeded the personal history of the subject put his ideas into direct conflict with those of his mentor. Jung posited his own notion of a "collective unconscious," which he described as "the ancestral heritage of possibilities of representation, . . . not individual but common to all men" (qtd. in Bilsker 32). According to Jung, this collective unconscious is filled with what he termed "archetypes," or "universal images that have existed since the remotest times" ("Archetypes" 9, 5). These archetypes are innate, universal psychic structures that send signals to the conscious mind in dreams, visions, and other moments when consciousness is receptive. Psychological symptoms develop not because of a prior history of trauma but as a means to regulate the function of the psyche.

For Jung, one of the most important archetypes was that of the shadow. A term Jung also used to refer to the unconscious as a whole, the shadow represents the obverse side of consciousness, a symbol of all the dark, malevolent, and evil feelings and emotions that the individual does not want to confront. The goal of Jung's psychotherapy was to get the patient to accept who he or she was in his or her totality, a process he called "individuation." A key component of that process was the analysand's encounter with the shadow. The shadow makes its appearance in Jung's work as early as 1928, when he was reformulating the aims of his analytic psychology. In "The Problems of Modern Psychotherapy," Jung queries, "How can I be substantial without casting a shadow? I must have a dark side too if I am to be whole" (59). The shadow represents all that is cast off, forgotten, or projected onto others in an attempt to deny the troubling characteristics in ourselves. The goal of this first stage of treatment is to become aware of the problem, to glimpse "those dim representations which detach themselves in the darkness from the invisible realm of the unconscious and move as shadows before the inturned gaze" (59). The unconscious is too dark to allow direct understanding, but shadows are those "dim reproductions" that allow the "internal gaze" to finally discern its own mental processes. Knowledge of the shadow is a necessary, if unpleasant, task.

Jung would repeatedly return to the theme of the shadow throughout his career. In "The Archetypes of the Collective Unconscious" (1934), Jung explains, "The shadow is a tight passage, a narrow door, whose painful constriction no one is spared who goes down to the deep well. . . . For what comes after the door is, surprisingly enough, a boundless expanse full of unprecedented uncertainty, with apparently no inside and no outside, no above and no below . . . no good and no bad" (21). The journey to discover the shadow is one of "unprecedented uncertainty," bereft of not only spatial orientation but also moral compass. The ambiguous shadow, by challenging borders and disrupting assumptions, provides an opportunity to reconceive the self. As Jung writes in a later piece, *Aion* (1951), becoming conscious of the shadow is "essential for any kind of self-knowledge" (*Portable* 145). Ironically, it is this attack on the normally fixed borders of the self that allows the individual to finally discover the reality lying within. The shadow is a portal through which the unconscious becomes conscious, allowing the individual to "become what he always was" ("Archetypes" 40).

The shadow is collective in more than one sense. Not only does it draw on a shared human inventory of myth, but the aggregation of individuals has the potential to produce a sort of collective shadow within society itself. In his 1946 British Broadcasting Corporation talk titled "The Fight with the Shadow," Jung takes on the "indescribable events of the last decade" ("Fight" 218)—the horrors of World War II. Drawing on his observation that the "psychopathology of the masses is rooted in the psychology of the individual" (218), Jung sees the mass appeal of Hitler's nationalism as the result of a collective attraction to the enticements of the shadow. Instead of integrating the negative attributes the shadow represents into their lives, the Germans chose to embrace it. As Jung explains, "Hitler's significance lay, that he symbolized something in every individual. He was the most prodigious personification of all human inferiorities. . . . He represented the shadow, the inferior part of everybody's personality, in an overwhelming degree, and this is another reason why they fell for him" (223). Jung's solution is simple. War could be averted if "everybody could see his own shadow and begin the only struggle that is really worthwhile: the fight against the overwhelming power-drive of the shadow" (224). But recognizing and dealing with the shadow is a difficult project that most humans have trouble achieving. Jung even takes Christianity to task for its failure to deal with its own shadow. As Ann Conrad Lammers argues in her work *In God's Shadow*, for Jung, "the consciousness of the traditional church has been psychologically split off from its collective shadow. Failing to take its own evil into account, the community of faith frequently projects its negative side onto scapegoats and exercises the prerogatives of moral perfection" (162). Even the concept of God possesses a shadow, and if humanity is to avoid error it needs to remain vigilant against the desire to view the world in terms of absolutes—ambiguity must be acknowledged and accepted.[15]

Jung's myth criticism should have struck a chord with the Beats, especially his work on the shadow. Jung's "shadow" looks very much like Ginsberg's initial portraits of himself as the Shrouded Stranger and is precisely what Kerouac calls "the dark haunted thing." Both writers knew of Jung's work. In a June 1959 column titled "The Last Word" written for *Escapade*, Kerouac starts off by complaining that he feels constrained by the "conventional English sentence," which to him seems "so ironbound in its rules, so inadmissible with reference to the actual format of my mind as I had learned to probe it in the modern spirit of Freud and Jung, that I couldn't express myself through that form any more" (*Good Blonde* 159). Kerouac is clearly aware of Jung and even cites him as an influence along with Freud, though both represent figures of authority that must be transcended in order to reach a more presentational style of writing. In the Beat film *Pull My Daisy* (1959), the voice-over narrator speaks the names "Jung. Freud, Jung, Reich" while the viewer glimpses a woman's hand holding a book. Jung is clearly part of the accepted pantheon of psychoanalytic thinkers whom those in Beat circles were reading. Ginsberg never explicitly mentions Jung, but in a May 1952 journal entry, he speaks of his desire to "include in Shrouded Stranger all archetype dreams as episodes" (*Martyrdom* 377). In fact, Ginsberg repeatedly uses the word "archetype" throughout these early entries, and while Jung was certainly not the inventor of the term, Ginsberg is clearly using it in a way Jung would approve. In the letters between Ginsberg and his father, Louis, collected in *Family Business*, Louis Ginsberg makes repeated mention of Jung and his concepts, so Ginsberg was clearly aware of Jung's existence (May 1959, 123; August 1960, 138). But despite Jung's presence, neither Kerouac nor Ginsberg ever engages his concepts. Why?[16]

One potential reason for this omission is the anxiety of influence Ginsberg and Kerouac might have felt toward Jung's work. The similarities that Jung held to Ginsberg's and Kerouac's own version of the Shrouded Stranger might have given them pause for thought. Yet the confessional Beats, who left us copious notes that were more than willing to reveal the most unflattering self-details, would have no reason to hide any connection to a writer whose work was so like their own. Perhaps the reason can be found in Norman Holland's work, which, according to Jameson, claims that myth criticism "works only if we have been told the work is mythic ahead of time, the unquestionable 'resonance' of the mythic rewriting presupposing not the operation of some mythic unconscious but rather our own preliminary conscious 'set' toward the reading in question" (52). In other words, myth criticism demands the same sort of acceptance of first principles that Freud asks of his readers, a demand that Kerouac and Ginsberg were not so willing to accommodate. Besides, Ginsberg and Kerouac needed their vision to be distinct in order to give their writing a mark of personality that would set them apart from their predecessors. Ultimately, these two writers wanted the freedom to define their own myth apart from the influence of both Jung and Freud and felt that the way in which these psychologists conveyed their conclusions lacked the immediacy, and thus the impact, they were seeking in their own work.

What makes this omission even more surprising is that Jung himself had a dream very much like Kerouac's and Ginsberg's Shrouded Stranger dreams. Traveling in Tunis in 1920, Jung described a dream that he had the night before he left for Marseilles: he finds himself in an "Arab city," and as he attempts to cross the bridge leading to the "citadel" he is accosted by a "handsome, dark Arab of aristocratic, almost royal bearing" (*Memories* 242–43). They proceed to wrestle, and during this struggle Jung pushes his head under water. The dream then changes scenes, and Jung finds himself "in a large vaulted octagonal room in the center of the citadel" (243). On the floor is a book, which Jung "forces" the young man whom he has just beaten to read (234). The similarities to Kerouac's dream are striking. The protected city, the Arab pursuer, and the danger are all present. The only difference is the outcome—where Kerouac remains afraid of this apparition, Jung is able to tame him.

Like both Kerouac and Ginsberg, Jung glamorizes nonwhites as somehow more authentic. The corollary to attacks on the European as "compensat[ing] for the loss of gravity and the corresponding *sentiment d'incompletitude* by the illusion of his triumphs" is an analogous belief that the non-European is closer to the earth (*Memories* 240). This leads Jung to compare the Arab to "game who do not see the hunter but, vaguely uneasy, scent him" (240). The Arab represents a second self that comes into conflict with the first. Jung explains, "My being European gave me a certain perspective on these people who were so differently constituted from myself. . . . But I was not prepared for the existence of unconscious forces within myself which would take the part of these strangers with such intensity" (245). The struggle between Jung and his Shrouded Stranger is the struggle between two selves—the European whom Jung feels himself to be consciously, and an Arab whom his unconscious identifies with. Critics from Edward Said onward have correctly read such binary divisions as a means to support European dominance, even when couched in such seemingly positive terms. Suffice it to say, the lauding of such "unreflective peoples" (242) as somehow more invigorated and alive, seen in both Jung and Kerouac (and to a lesser extent in Ginsberg), is an issue.

Given the rampant fear of wholesale nuclear destruction in the early Cold War years, an appeal to the "primitive" as a more useful alternative to an overly developed Western culture held much appeal. In his piece "Sharing a Shadow," James T. Jones argues that the Shrouded Stranger allowed Kerouac and Ginsberg to construct a notion of community that went beyond the binary of "us versus them." Drawing on Jung's political reading in his essay "The Fight with the Shadow," Jones declares,

> Kerouac and Ginsberg abstracted the image of the Shrouded Stranger in such a way that they extended its range, first to the basic community of each other and their friends (like Ed White and Neal Cassady), where it served as a means of bonding, and then to the community of their readers, where the image mirrored not only the personal psychic tensions that gave rise to it but also social anxiety about nuclear weapons and the Cold War. (239)

Jones's argument is compelling. The Shrouded Stranger, as a manifestation of the Jungian shadow cast onto the society as a whole, provides a critique of a technologically "superior" West that threatened the future of the planet with its nuclear devices. Cold War rhetoric was built on metaphors of exclusion, containment, and binaries. Jung's admonishment to acknowledge the shadow is an important step toward appreciating, and ultimately overcoming, such distinctions, even if the Jungian shadow sometimes relied on unquestioned assumptions about so-called primitive societies.

But the truth is that Ginsberg and Kerouac already had a myth that helped them negotiate fears of the apocalypse through an appeal to those outside Western cultures: Oswald Spengler's *Decline of the West*. As John Lardas aptly demonstrates in *The Bop Apocalypse*, Spengler's work found a much clearer resonance that made a more direct claim regarding the link between the West's increasing denial of its "fellaheen" Shadow. For Spengler, "all human communities follow the same organic pattern of birth, growth, decay, and death" (39). The West was headed toward its preordained end, a message that Burroughs, Ginsberg, and Kerouac picked up on in the early 1940s. According to Lardas, these Beats "replaced the material discourses of technological gadgetry, corporate liberalism, and nuclear proliferation with Spengler's emphases on the capacity of the human body, individual refinement, and the ways of the 'Cultural' soul" (41). The "Faustian" West was over; the "primitive" people of the earth were now ready to usher in a new world.

When it came to thinking the social, Ginsberg and Kerouac did not need Jung. As Ginsberg glosses Kerouac's enthusiasms over being in the Mexican jungle in his afterword to Kerouac's *Visions of Cody*, "At last the conception of 'Fellaheen Eternal Country Life'—Out of Burroughs' copy of Spengler" (Ginsberg, "Visions" 424). The fellaheen inhabitants of Mexico provided Kerouac with a real-life stand-in for dusky Arab travelers chasing him across the desert of the mind. The West's redemptive vision was, ironically, located just below the border. Ginsberg, as his celebration of American outsiders in poems such as *Howl* make clear, was equally in thrall. Overly rationalized and intellectualized America was over, and it was time for a new vision of the country gleaned from those who stood outside it. The Shrouded Stranger was a call for all to bring their own buried fears and desires to the surface in an attempt to create a more balanced and sane postwar world.

Ghostly apparitions such as the Shrouded Stranger are absences made present. They provide new perspectives by presenting a lack that demands explication. In his book *Specters of Marx*, Jacques Derrida argues that while the idea of haunting is conventionally bound up with notions of the past, in the work of Karl Marx, haunting suggests a future, a foreshadowing or adumbrating of events to come. Playing with the French translation of ghost or specter as "revenant" or "literally that which comes back" (224n1), Derrida sees a futurity in the specter that allows it to become a spur to thinking. Derrida's conception of the specter as that which "points toward a thinking of the event that necessarily exceeds binary or dialectical logic" (78) helps us to see the Shrouded Stranger as something more than simply a re-presentation. He is himself an image that speaks to the possibility for thinking otherwise, for imagining new futures where the image's use is unconstrained by a search for origins. It is this space between trace and origin where such images perform their unsettling work. Ghosts, shadows, and the realm of dream become spaces of possibility, becoming, and imagination—gaps that create the opening necessary for new thinking to emerge that exceeds the terms of its parameters.

The myth of the Shrouded Stranger that Ginsberg and Kerouac developed served multiple purposes. The importance of this figure lay in his ambiguous outline. While his misty shroudiness propelled Ginsberg and Kerouac to search for its meaning, the desire to limn the Shrouded Stranger's airy wanderings also pushed their writing into productive directions. The two grand dream interpreters of the twentieth century, Freud and Jung, were too constrictive. Meaning was always already there, waiting to be discovered. But for Ginsberg and Kerouac, the Shrouded Stranger was more important as a stimulus to constant exploration. In their attempts to understand and convey the impact of the Shrouded Stranger, these authors found a means to turn their personal experiences and anxieties into poetic forms accessible to their postwar readers. By invoking this shadowy reminder of the troubles lying just below consciousness, Ginsberg and Kerouac gave their postwar world a vision of their own minds that was nevertheless universally applicable. The Shrouded Stranger complicated the "us versus them" thinking of the Cold War by forcing readers to recognize an otherness already inside them. The shadowy presence of this figure thus posed a challenge to the idea that borders and meanings were so easily definable.

4. THE GHOST OF HUMANISM

The Disappearing Figure in Postwar Photography

The art of photography has always been inextricably linked to the idea of capturing reality. From its very inception, photography fascinated because it seemed to be able to take a part of the fleeting world and render it stable. Joseph Nicéphore Niépce's very first photograph, for example, introduced a new art form by depicting nothing more than a view from a window. Yet difficulties quickly arose once the camera sought to represent the human figure. Due to the necessity for long exposures, photography initially had a difficult time rendering people. But as the technology developed, photographic portraits became increasingly available to a public unable to afford traditional likenesses. Even today, the camera is predominantly used to capture images of friends and loved ones, and digital photography has only increased the desire to "capture the moment" instantaneously. But not everybody wants to appear before a camera. Stories of people afraid to have their photograph taken lest it "steal" their soul have become legendary, and accounts of photography's origins are filled with examples of spirit photographs and other hoaxes perpetrated on an unwitting public that believed that the new medium had the ability to peer into other planes of existence. Representing its subjects in a way that goes beyond painting or drawing, the photograph's effect can be uncanny—it almost seems that subjects become trapped in the medium. Even for the less superstitious, the camera often seems to miss the essence of humanity or to misrepresent it. Photographs both celebrate and challenge the sanctity of the human image.

The similitude involved in photography allows the medium to portray a person in detail, but if a photographer chooses to manipulate the portrait, it can often appear a threat to the subject's very being. The contrast between respectful images that sought to dignify the human figure and stylistic manipulation that challenged photography's inherited role as a recorder of humanity became especially pronounced in postwar American photography. With the threat of nuclear apocalypse looming, there was much concern over humanity's future. Postwar photography initially sought to contain this threat of annihilation by providing comforting images of humanity that reassured audiences. In Edward Steichen's celebrated exhibition *The Family of Man*, for instance, people from around the world were depicted in dignified scenes that sent a universal message of hope. But by the mid- to late 1950s, photographers began to explore the disintegration of the human figure in their work, challenging the sanctity of such images in the process. The so-called street photography of Robert Frank and William Klein, along with the more staged work of Ralph Eugene Meatyard, took a tack opposite Steichen's, recording postwar anxiety in images that challenged reassuring portrayals. By increasing reliance on shadow, blur, graininess, and reflection, these photographers demonstrated a corresponding loss in the redemptive power of the human figure during the early Cold War.

The result of such disquieting images was to force the viewer to confront the difficult questions of the period. While much has been made of the "subjective" turn in postwar photography (and indeed in the arts in general), the focus has remained on the subjectivity of the photographer rather than on the viewer. Photographers like Frank, Klein, and Meatyard are seen as championing expression over didactic message, in part to escape the ideological conflicts rife during the period. What this argument misses, however, is that these photographers strove to awaken the anxieties and difficulties of the age in their viewers as well. The distorted and disintegrating human images that Frank, Klein, and Meatyard offered forced audiences to reconsider their own existential conditions. Frank, Klein, and Meatyard drew on the shadow world in order to challenge viewer expectations. The use of shadow, blur, graininess, and reflection in their work raises issues that exceed the photograph's literal status as representation. In a postwar world of ambiguity, only such distortion could properly portray the complexity of a nuclear world. Because these techniques both excite imagination while frustrating its desire for completion, the viewer is forced into an uncomfortable relationship to the photographic image. The Cold War, and the disturbing anxieties and paradoxes it fostered, required such obfuscation—clarity of presentation was a lie.

The photograph's ability to "capture" reality helps us to understand the impact that Frank, Klein, and to a lesser extent Meatyard had in the postwar period. If photography is capturing reality, then representations that gave the viewer a bleak vision of the world or portrayed people as shadows were destined to have a difficult reception, which was precisely the case with Frank and especially Klein, who both saw their work attacked as pessimistic. Meatyard is a bit of an anomaly here—his work was mainly ignored during his lifetime (and beyond) for reasons that have more to do with his status as an outsider than with the quality of his work. Because photography has such a direct claim on the real, manipulating those who appear before its lens is almost tantamount to an attack on their very person. Dehumanizing the human figure was a political choice for these three photographers, and one that would create hostility to a body of work that many believed undercut what was best in all of us.

CAPTURING SHADOWS

The capturing of the human figure by the camera seems to be a passive process or a witnessing rather than a construction. Yet the photograph is clearly a mediated image subject to its own rules and conditions. The photographer makes choices, and those choices necessarily influence reception. As commentators such as Joel Eisinger have demonstrated, this dichotomy between capturing an image and constructing it runs throughout the history of photography. Is the photograph a trace, a neutral object that documents the existence of the real world, or is it itself a transformation of this "true" world, an artistic reproduction? Of course there is no answer to this question, or rather, the answer is "both." At various points in the history of photography, each side of the debate has been championed. When photographers want to gain for their work the title of art rather than craft, they appeal to the argument of transformation—they add something to the image that pushes it beyond a simple copying of nature. On the other hand, when photographers want to stress the social impact of their work, arguments for the photograph as a record of what is happening in front of the lens come to the fore.

The disintegration of the human figure in postwar photography was particularly shocking because it went against the major photographic trends that preceded it. While other photographers might have used blur and shadow, in the prewar years these were generally used to further the humanity of the subject. Pictorialism, the dominant aesthetic at the turn of the century, turned to painting as the model for photographic craftsmanship. With its use of soft focus and classical scenes, pictorialism attempted to re-create the painterly masterpiece with the photographic lens. Pictorialists would oftentimes rework the negative in order to suppress unwanted details and to achieve blurry, cloudy aesthetic effects. Edward Steichen, Gertrude Käsebier, and Alfred Stieglitz all worked in this mode, but perhaps the best-known practitioner was Julia Margaret Cameron. In her work *The Gardener's Daughter* (1867), Cameron is able to create an almost swirling sense with her use of blur, drawing the viewer's attention to her subject. The "gardener's daughter" is herself placed in soft focus, though not enough to take away her specific features. Nor do the slight shadows she is in conceal her entirely. These techniques only serve to highlight the figure, creating a sense of tranquility, as the girl plucks what appears to be a flower from a bush. While pictorialists like Cameron sought to soften the medium's oftentimes sharp detail with techniques that lent softness to the photograph, the use of such devices served to heighten the humanism of their subjects.

The history of modern photography, both in Europe and in the United States, is the history of the reaction to pictorialism. This reaction took two forms. Insisting on the novelty of the photographic apparatus, many artists began to experiment with form by examining the medium's ability to manipulate light. In what was dubbed the "New Vision" (or "abstraite photographie" in France), photographers like Man Ray and László Moholy-Nagy began experimenting with the potential of the camera. This new movement was "characterized by free-wheeling experimentation, with such techniques as photogram, photomontage, and manipulation of light upon a photosensitive surface" and other techniques that highlighted the nature of the photographic medium—"chiaroscuro in place of pigment," as Moholy-Nagy claimed (Barnett 15). Since the photograph's basic aim is to capture light onto a sensitive surface, these experimenters were quickly drawn to chiaroscuro effects that relied heavily on the interplay between light and dark. Despite differences in approach, Man Ray and Moholy-Nagy relied on shadow effects to highlight new ways of seeing, new "visions," that the camera made possible.

Although avant-garde artists like Man Ray and Moholy-Nagy believed their art engaged the social and was therefore "humanitarian" in a broad sense, its execution oftentimes denied the human element. But the other trend following in the wake of pictorialism emphasized the documenting of the quotidian, human world. In European photography at the time, the "Neue Sachlichkeit" or "New Objectivity" investigated the human as subject. Stressing detail and tactile surface, photographers of the "New Objectivity" oftentimes took to the streets, seeking compositions that were more than the sum of their parts. Armed with new, lightweight cameras like the Leica, early "street photographers" like Henri Cartier-Bresson, Robert Doisneau, George Brassaï, Ilse Bing, Robert Capa, and André Kertész stressed the opportune moment, the chance encounter that would lead to a great picture. As Cartier-Bresson describes it in his essay "The Decisive Moment," "I crazed to seize the whole essence, in the confines of one single photograph, of some situation that was in the process of unrolling itself before my eyes" (*Mind's Eye* 22). While aesthetics were certainly not ignored, the focus was on capturing life as it unfolded. The New Realists were just as interested as their more experimental counterparts in the ability of the camera to capture light and shadow. The difference was that instead of turning their attention to processes that foregrounded picture-taking itself, they instead chose to train their attention on their fellow humans.

Americans, too, moved away from the pictorialist tradition of photography in the 1920s and 1930s. What subsequently emerged, however, was far different from the work of their European counterparts. While the Europeans were more interested in either formalist experimentation or a humanistic photography of everyday life, in the United States there was more of an insistence placed on the clear, realistic image. The champion of this new aesthetic was Alfred Stieglitz. Originally a pictorialist photographer himself, Stieglitz abandoned the style and began to champion the work of Paul Strand, whose sharp images of everyday objects would adumbrate the modernist style in America. As the later practitioner Edward Weston would put it, the goal of such "straight" photography became "to see the *Thing Itself*... the quintessence revealed direct without the fog of impressionism" (qtd. in Salvesen 38). These figures are admittedly part of a more avant-garde tradition in American photography. Yet the desire for precise images would become a hallmark of American photography as a whole in the first half of the century. In both formalist and popular circles, a good picture was defined as clear one.

Although documentary photography was the dominant aesthetic in America during these years, there was a wide range of practices within this field. The work of the most noted photographer of Franklin Delano Roosevelt's Farm Security Administration (1935–44), Walker Evans, was difficult to classify. While many in the FSA and the socially engaged Photo League (1936–51) used their work for direct social aims, Evans considered himself not as a strict documentary photographer but as working in the "documentary style." As Gerry Badger explains, "Evans's voice was loudest in advocating the creative independence of the photographer and the medium and in calling for a liberation of the traditionally-held role of documentary" (12). Evans's work is subtle, and viewing it as mere social statement does a disservice to its complexity and richness. Nor is Evans alone—numerous photographers of the period saw little need to distinguish between artistic and social statements. There is indeed subtlety in Evans's work, but it comes from the critical distance he was able to create in his photographs, and not from any sort of distortion, which is almost impossible to find in his corpus. Evans is universally admired, but his clear, focused "documentary style" was for the most part left behind by postwar photographers.

The experimentation with light as medium did occur in American photography, though it was never as dramatic as with Man Ray or Moholy-Nagy. The work of photographers such as Harry Callahan, Clarence John Laughlin, Aaron Siskind, and Minor White all evidence an interest in formalist abstraction, to varying degrees. In his book *American Photography*, Jonathan Green claims that these photographers challenged the documentary aesthetic based on "readability, accessibility, or social utility" with work that "emphasized symbol, ambiguity, private experience, abstraction, and art" (53). Callahan's portrait of his wife, titled *Eleanor* (1948), is done as a silhouette reduced to abstraction. She appears as a shadow, a dark outline discernible only by slight markers such as the curve of her fingers or a wisp of hair. Laughlin, on the other hand, is far more straightforward about his use of shadows, going so far as to caption his photographs with explanations of their symbolic import. Describing his photograph *The Portent in the Shadow* (1954), Laughlin writes, "A traffic sign throws a shadow on an ancient Vieux Carré wall in New Orleans. . . . This image speaks to us, disquietingly, of our confusion, or our loss of direction" (124). A definition of the ambiguity of the shadow could not be made any clearer. But perhaps the most influential figure here is White, who in his role as editor of the journal *Aperture* (1952–present) championed the subjective. White rejected the documentarian ethos of presenting humanistic images meant to foster social critique or change. Instead, the photograph was seen as something to be read and, for the viewer, something designed to stimulate spiritual contemplation. White's change in aesthetic approach captured the zeitgeist of the 1950s perfectly, as American photographers moved away from the clear, sharp picture in the postwar period in order to present a more personal, and ambiguous, vision.

THE FAMILY OF MAN

The humanist tradition saw its final, and perhaps most glorious, realization in New York's Museum of Modern Art's 1955 exhibition *The Family of Man*. According to John Szarkowski, the museum's curator, "The three most important events in American photography during the 1950s were the founding of *Aperture* magazine (1952), the organization of *The Family of Man* exhibition (1955) and publication of Robert Frank's *The Americans* (1959)" (qtd. in Green 53). While White looked forward to a new subjective aesthetic, Edward Steichen, the curator of *The Family of Man*, looked back to the documentary impulse for the show's inspiration. Steichen saw the exhibit as a chance to celebrate the commonality of humankind in an effort to combat the divisiveness arising during the Cold War in the 1950s. As Steichen himself puts it in his catalog introduction, the photographs ran the "gamut of life from birth to death with emphasis on the daily relationships of man" (n.p.). While individual photographs could indeed present the viewer with the feeling of ambiguity, taken as a whole, the exhibition conveyed a sense of connectedness through shared universal feelings and situations. The photographs were divided into sections, with accompanying captions: "creation, birth, love, work, death, justice, the search for knowledge, relationships, democracy, peace, and opposition to brutality and slaughter" (Green 47). The show was also an attack on the American avant-garde as represented by people like White, a movement that many in the mainstream thought sent a disloyal message of angst and unhappiness. Overall, *The Family of Man* was an upbeat celebration of humanity that highlighted similarities while glossing over difference—to its critics, a "sentimental" amalgamation of photographs in the waning documentary style.

While some photographs in the exhibit raised issues of ambiguity that challenged the postwar status quo, the majority of images in *The Family of Man* served to reinforce middle-class consensus. The show itself included a range of photographers that was quite large, with figures like Cartier-Bresson, Doisneau, Frank, Callahan, Diane Arbus, and Garry Winogrand exhibiting alongside many now lesser-known artists. Most of the photographs, however, were brightly lit depictions of individual subjects that presented them in a sort of simple humanity. Shadows, shade, or darkness were rarely seen. This makes sense, given the note of human understanding that Steichen was attempting to strike—people are clear, they make sense, they are understandable, and communication with them is indeed possible. There are few shadows in the exhibit because there are no ambiguous or difficult spaces. As Green notes, *The Family of Man* was very much "in the tradition of the photo-essay" (40). Like its *Life* and *Look* counterparts, the show (which drew heavily on the work of photo-essay photographers) was more interested in providing an uplifting message than in truly examining social problems. As one critic puts it, "By the mid-1950s many issues of *Life* and *Look* were filled, cover to cover, with nothing but good news about the nation's economy and prosperity—all illustrated with pictures of the satisfied consumers, happy families, grinning young people, and smiling workers who inhabited what *Life*'s editors called, in 1947, 'This Pleasant Land'" (Guimond 207). Even the more controversial photographers in the show saw the sting of their work denuded when placed next to such an overwhelming collection of humanist photographs. Overall, the show sent a reassuring message of universal harmony—a message that comforted many while raising the ire of those both to the right and to the left of Steichen's middle-of-the-road position.

Steichen's *Family of Man* exhibit was, and to a certain extent remains, a controversial exhibit. Although liberal in content, the show left open the question of exactly how such a peaceful society as his images suggested could actually be achieved. For those engaged in leftist politics, *The Family of Man* lacked the critique necessary to effectively promote social change. As Lili Corbus Bezner relates in *Photography and Politics in America*, "Steichen diluted social documentary photography to the point of dissolving it into an all-encompassing metaphor for universal harmony. With specific partisan issues of class and race largely lost, even conservative forces could appropriate the show as their own." Yet Bezner is quick to note that the show was "a noble, though flawed, endeavor—with this project, Steichen tried to offset cold war fears of 'otherness,' Soviet aggression, and general cultural difference" (121–22). In a polarized world, the show sought common ground and even included many photographs taken in the Soviet Union. In fact, Bezner notes that viewed within the context of the anti-Communist fifties, *The Family of Man*'s attempt to bring together all the peoples of the world under a liberal humanist umbrella actually offended many on the right who wanted to exclude Communists from the show (139). *The Family of Man* was meant to be upbeat, to bring people across the world together, not to reveal the flaws and difficulties that keep them apart. Although the images in Steichen's show were intended to inspire confidence in the future of humankind, their uncritical nature made them appear sentimental, a hopelessly naive gesture in a world teetering on the brink of destruction.

The image that garnered the most controversy and posed a direct challenge to the complacency of the rest of the exhibit was a photograph of an atomic bomb blast. According to Bezner, toward the end of the show Steichen had placed a "dramatically lit color transparency of an H-bomb explosion" (154). This image was much discussed at the time, although it did not make it into the show's catalog. For Steichen, the message was clear—we must learn to live together or face the potential for mutual destruction.[1] Opinions were mixed. While some felt that the decision to include such a disturbing image was a bold one, others believed it was of the "too little, too late" variety. After an entire show devoted to uplifting images of humanity, the photograph of the atomic blast seemed a bit too easy. In any case, Steichen's decision to include the photograph and to place it at the end of the show in a room where everybody had to pass by it demonstrates the extent to which the bomb was an unavoidable reality by the mid-1950s. Despite complaints by both the Left and the Right, Steichen's show was a popular success, attracting "almost 3,000 [visitors] a day in New York and over nine million in the forty countries around the world" (Green 48). Steichen, always in tune with popular taste, was able to produce an exhibit that appealed to mainstream America and even induced those who normally stayed away from museums to attend.

Despite its commercial success, *The Family of Man* was the last gasp of the documentary impulse in postwar America. By the late 1950s, this humanistic belief that the photograph was a socially progressive tool began to look naive. The possibility of instantaneous destruction had rendered documentary photography, with its faith in the dignity and "wholeness" of humankind, hopelessly sentimental, a nostalgic desire for a prenuclear world where collectivism mattered. In an era of increasing political tension, *The Family of Man* touched a chord with a public who wanted to feel that a better world was indeed possible. Though reassuring, Steichen's vision for photography would be replaced by another far more cynical and far less sure about the possibilities for a united world. American photography now turned inward, replacing social vision with subjective statement. While photographers still roamed the streets in search of pictures, what they found there was not dignity and optimism but a people tainted by their acceptance of middle-class values in an attempt to forget the awful fate potentially looming overhead.

SUBJECTIVISM AND THE POSTWAR PERIOD

As the work of postwar photographers like Frank, Klein, and Meatyard become ever more personal, the subjects depicted in their work, including themselves, become ever more vague. We have to wonder why a photography so concerned with documenting the interior world chose to do so with photographs that utilized shadow, blur, grain, and reflection to destroy the presence of their subjects. Why is the shadow the apt metaphor for postwar photography? To answer this question, we must first discuss the importance of subjectivism as the dominant practice in the postwar arts. Szarkowski attributes the shift from "public to private concerns" to photographers' increasing distaste for magazine publication, where the photographer received financial support for his or her work but was forced to give up a good deal of control over the finished product (*Mirrors* 11). As compelling as such institutional explanations are, they fail to explain why artists in other mediums likewise turned to self-expression in the postwar period.

Daniel Belgrad notes in *The Culture of Spontaneity* that the postwar arts were galvanized by a return to the ever-changing moment. As his title implies, those living in this postwar culture relied on spontaneous decisions to guide their work. Given the atrocities of the previous wars and the possibility for nuclear destruction, art that relied on rigid systems or appeared to provide one final meaning became suspect. Personal expression was lauded as a necessary corrective to such overarching attempts to delimit and explain. Moreover, such personal statements were deemed authentic—anyone creating from the spontaneous moment was believed to be creating work untainted by ideology and politics. Capturing the essence of the moment was a method particularly suited to the medium of photography, where the instantaneousness of the shutter's snap called for quick and intuitive decisions that seemed to leave little room for overt calculation and manipulation.

This return to subjective, personal expression also has a darker interpretation. The giddy optimism of the immediate postwar years was replaced by conservatism characterized by a desire to preserve, rather than to challenge, the status quo. Events like the Korean War, the Suez Canal crisis, the Soviet Union's nuclear detonations, and McCarthyism produced a dampening of spirits immediately following the war. Thus many critics argue that the turn toward the subjective actually signaled a retreat. Rather than fight the dominant rhetoric that the Cold War produced, these artists chose to make personal statements that, while indeed an assault on such ideology, had little direct political impact. Discussing the work of Robert Frank, Bezner claims that "Frank might be called the perfect cold war photographer—his work walked the tightrope between social consciousness and political awareness while it remained invested with enough irony to obscure any didactic political clarity" (191). Although Bezner is correct in charging that intense focus on the personal oftentimes limits the political effectiveness of a photograph, ultimately it is a matter of perspective. Bezner is more interested in recuperating the more overtly political work of the Photo League, and so Frank's personal work must give way to a more didactic style. Frank is indeed a highly ambiguous photographer, but that ambiguity is itself a method of critique.

Style is in many ways itself the message. Postwar photography did not attempt to replace one flawed vision with another equally problematic. Rather, by focusing so intensely on personal subjectivity, it created a space that folded the desire for meaning back onto the viewer, forcing a productive relationship with the difficulty of the photograph. None of these photographers was particularly politically engaged, but their lack of didacticism is precisely the point. They engaged in a more subtle, and more pervasive, questioning through their style. The fiction of progress, civilization, and coherence was undermined in the Cold War by two world wars and a bomb. These photographers contributed to that critique, albeit obliquely. The disappearance of human figures in these photographs points to a larger social problem in postwar American cultural life: the anxiety caused by the Cold War and America's reactionary response to it denuded citizens of their humanity. As many artists and dissenters of the period found, the only recourse was to strive to get out of that cycle, to somehow disengage from America in order to not be tainted by its discourse of fear and paranoia. Photography had the power to shock the viewer out of complacency and into the realization of the ambiguities the Cold War fostered. Shadow, blur, grain, and reflection were techniques useful in allowing Frank, Klein, and Meatyard to leave their personal mark on the photograph. Frank possessed a more classically "artistic" style, Klein drew on the language of fashion and advertising to produce brash photographs, and Meatyard eschewed contemporary references to delve into "romances" more characteristic of literary antecedents. Yet despite their extreme differences in style, they all ended in the same place—with vague, ambiguous, shadowy images that challenge viewer expectations.

While many critics have noted the ambiguity inherent in these photographers, the ways in which Frank, Klein, and Meatyard produced their unsettling effects are far less discussed. In order to elucidate their practices, it is useful to invoke the work of critic Roland Barthes, and not just because his is a critical voice in photographic theory. Barthes is, in many ways, the ideal viewer. His understanding of the nature of photography is so compelling precisely because it encapsulates what many feel about the sanctity of the photographic image. As his discussion of the image of his mother in the celebrated "Winter Garden Photograph" in *Camera Lucida* illustrates, for Barthes the photographic image, with its ability to "ratify what it represents" through its apparent literalness, has the potential to "engulf" the viewer (85, 63). Barthes's praise for such photographs is hyperbolic. The Winter Garden Photograph captures his mother's essence: "It achieved for me, utopically, *the impossible science of the unique being*" (71). This viewpoint that the photograph's power stems from the fact that someone was actually there before the camera must necessarily find trouble accepting the blurred, the grainy, and the reflected, which is exactly what happens when Barthes discusses these techniques. Barthes unequivocally rejects such manipulations of reality as antithetical to the sort of feeling that great photographs elicit, stating, "The (rare) artifice [the photograph] permits are not probative; they are, on the contrary, trick pictures: the photograph is laborious only when it fakes" (87). Given this insistence on the clear and unmanipulated photograph, it comes as no surprise that the majority of the photographs in *Camera Lucida* could be considered sentimental portraits done without blur, grain, or reflection.

Barthes is correct to locate the meaning of photography in what it does to the viewer. His concept of the "punctum" or "that accident which pricks me" is extremely useful in explaining photography's (or at least some photographs') hold on the viewer (27). But the exact nature of this trauma deserves further examination. Barthes will go on to declare that "ultimately, Photography is subversive not when it frightens, repels, or even stigmatizes, but when it is *pensive*, when it thinks" (38). While this definition seems straightforward enough, Barthes makes it clear that he does not consider effects such as grain, blur, or reflection conducive to the pensive. Contrasting the punctum invidiously with the concept of "shock," Barthes declares,

> A fourth surprise is the one which the photographer looks for from the contortions of technique: superimpressions, anamorphoses, deliberate exploitation of certain defects (blurring, deceptive perspectives, trick framing); great photographers (Germaine Krull, Kertesz, William Klein) have played on these surprises, without convincing me, even if I understand their subversive bearing. (33)

Ultimately, it is the inadvertent that commands attention for Barthes, leaving photographers to receive the accolade of "great" only when they fail to recognize their own genius. Discussing another picture by Klein, Barthes illustrates that the punctum often goes beyond good taste: "William Klein has photographed children of Little Italy in New York (1954); all very touching, amusing, but what I stubbornly see are one child's bad teeth" (44–45). Leaving aside the fact that the "deliberate exploitation of certain defects" was often the result of precisely the sort of "accidents" Barthes prescribes in the work of these three photographers, I argue contra Barthes that techniques like blur, grain, and reflection can actually constitute a punctum for the viewer.

The use of blur, grain, and reflection does violence to the image by not allowing the sort of identification Barthes finds in the photograph of his mother. Thus "pensive" means something else here. It implies thinking, but through disruption; it inaugurates thought, but through a break rather than through an identification. Barthes calls his Winter Garden Photograph a "just image" (70). The images of Frank, Klein, and Meatyard are not "just" to their distorted subjects, but the world these photographers were living in was not just either. In an era when instantaneous annihilation was an ever-present possibility, Frank, Klein, and Meatyard captured their subjects in a manner appropriate for the times. When discussing the idea of the pose, Barthes explains that the viewer gets the idea that "someone has seen the referent (even if it is a matter of objects) *in flesh and blood*, or again *in person*" in the real moment when the photograph was taken (79). Barthes represents exactly the sort of thinking these artists were striving to disrupt. Frank, Klein, and Meatyard force the viewer to acknowledge the existence of the monstrous not through realistic pictures of the abject but through a form that renders their subjects abject. Barthes cannot accept this in these artists, since his idea of disruption, of the pensive, is based on a desire to reconnect with the image as conveyor of the "that-has-been" (77). These photographers chose to break such identification in order to draw attention to the disturbing nature of the present. Thus it makes sense that though Barthes considers Klein a major photographer and includes several of his photographs in *Camera Lucida*, most of his commentary on Klein is critique. The use of such "artifice" does not constitute either the "laborious" or the "fake," as Barthes claims, but rather seeks to better represent the unsettling and immediate truth of the postwar world in the work of these three photographers.

Ultimately, Frank, Klein, and Meatyard offer the viewer a novel position to occupy. For Barthes, the photograph gives viewers back to themselves, but for these photographers, the photograph gives viewers back a refraction of themselves, and in that distorted recognition the photograph has the power to evoke a questioning of the reason for that disjunction. These photographs create visual problems that lack tidy, or indeed any, solution. On the contrary, they rehearse the anxieties of a culture in ways that allow their viewers to reflect on their own circumstances and conditions. This explains Frank's, Klein's, and Meatyard's aversion to the sort of didactic photographs championed by Steichen, on the one hand, and the sort of objectivity professed by Henri Cartier-Bresson, on the other. By making their work highly subjective, these photographers offer their viewers not just a peek into their own view of the world but an opportunity to draw their own conclusions. Rather than comfort the viewer with images that disavow the problems of the Cold War, these photographers strove to provoke their audience into confronting the anxieties and difficulties that their photographs elicit. If such a strategy sometimes created anger and vitriol, it also produced an opening for viewers to rethink Cold War rhetorics.

ROBERT FRANK

Robert Frank stands at the center of this new postwar aesthetic. A German-speaking Swiss of Jewish ancestry, Frank was already an outsider to America upon his arrival in 1947. He quickly developed a subjective style that posed a challenge to standard photographic practice at the time. According to Sarah Greenough in the collection *Looking In: Robert Frank's*

"The Americans," "Frank is often praised for being the first to transform documentary photography into a mode of personal expression that prized the primacy of intuition over reason, experience over fact, and action over contemplation" ("Resisting" 9). While this outsider status propelled Frank into the spotlight as the dominant photographer of 1950s America, Greenough and Bezner both note that Frank was likewise well connected to the photographic world, with important friends like Steichen, Kertész, Louis Faurer, and especially Walker Evans (3). Despite commercial success in the photojournalistic world, by the mid-1950s Frank became more and more interested in the subjective photography that would become his signature style. He was not alone in this tendency—the same shift toward spontaneous, subjective expression could be seen in abstract expressionist painting, bebop jazz experimentation, and the writing of Beat writers like Jack Kerouac and Allen Ginsberg, both of whom Frank encountered in New York.

At the center of this shift in aesthetic was Frank's rejection of Steichen, who had been his mentor and one of his biggest supporters. Frank comments, "I just didn't agree with his sentimentality about photographs anymore. . . . I was aware that I was living in a different world—that the world wasn't as good as that—that it was a myth that the sky was blue and that all photographs were beautiful" (qtd. in Bezner 179).[2] Frank found his new aesthetic in the personal revelations that were the central concern for postwar American artists. Although deeply affected by the photo-essay format during his early years in Switzerland, Frank rejected the style, claiming, "I wanted to follow my own intuition and do it my way, and not make any concession—not make a *Life* story" (219). In fact, Frank rejected the work of Cartier-Bresson, whose ideas about the camera capturing the "decisive moment" came to define the street photography that was a direct precursor to Frank's work. For Frank, despite Cartier-Bresson's insistence on the spontaneous moment, his work was not subjective enough: "I've always thought it was terribly important to have a point of view, and I was also sort of disappointed in him [Cartier-Bresson] that that was never in his pictures" (qtd. in Guimond 242). Frank's work thus epitomizes what we come to think of as postwar American photography—subjective feeling rendered objectively onto the photograph.

Frank's work found its most cogent statement in *The Americans*, a book that came to define postwar photography. With the help of Walker Evans, Frank was able to procure a Guggenheim Fellowship that allowed him to make a photographic record of his travels throughout the

United States. Evans's work, along with other FSA photographers and Photo League professionals, is best seen within a context of exposing a "real" America that largely went ignored. Frank's (and Klein's) work, however, had as its backdrop the celebration of America in magazines like *Life* and *Look*, where America stood for progress and superiority among nations. Documentarians tended to dignify their subjects in an effort to reveal their hidden humanity, but the depiction of Americans who appeared in *The Americans* was far more ambiguous. Frank claimed that he did not want the "blaring confrontation of William Klein's *Life is Good & Good for You in New York*" nor "the emotional distance he saw in Henri Cartier-Bresson's *Les Européens*" (Greenough, "Disordering" 132). What he did capture is something more subtle and personal but also highly ambiguous.

As Greenough notes in *Looking In*, many of Frank's photographs were a homage to his mentor Evans, who shared Frank's aesthetic as well as his disgust of sentimentality, but the differences between their work are telling. *The Americans* includes a photograph that Frank took of a barbershop, a clear reference to Evans, but "unlike Evans, who had included a lucid and lovingly rendered image of the interior of a barbershop in his 1938 book *American Photographs*, Frank allows the viewer to see inside his barbershop only through his shadow" (Greenough, "Disordering" 123). While Evans's work evokes pathos for the simplicity and dignity of rural life, Frank's use of his own shadow adds a further layer to the photograph that leads it down the path of indecipherability. Is Frank eclipsing the work of his mentor, calling attention to the role of the photographer, or simply informing us that such homespun images are now relegated to nostalgia? Neil Campbell discusses the difference between Frank and his mentor in this photograph, observing that Frank is "offering a productive ambiguity of multiple frames and screens that serve to 'recode' the image" (149).[3] By offering multiple perspectives, Frank forces the viewer to interpret the many layers of meaning that this photograph evokes. As we will see, the use of such shadowy effects confounds final meaning in *The Americans.*

The ambiguity in Frank's work is no accident. He purposely courted a style open to interpretation. The main reason that his photography is so difficult to pin down, and why it has been the subject of so many reinterpretations over the years, is that *The Americans* lacks any sort of captioning. Roland Barthes discusses the role of the caption as a means to delimit the range of possible interpretations of a visual image. *The*

Americans, according to Frank's own wishes, does not include captions. Frank desired ambiguity, and captions would only serve to lead the viewer into certain interpretative directions. In *Black White and Things*, an earlier book Frank made in 1952, he allows the images to speak for themselves by providing only minimal captions. As Frank observes, "Something must be left for the onlooker. . . . He must have something to see" (Greenough, "Resisting" 31). Tired of the didacticism of magazines like *Life*, Frank instead produced a book in which meaning is made by the viewers as they scan the photographs.

Like Evans, Frank relies on the sequencing of photographs to provide some structure to his work. Frank, according to Greenough, learned sequencing through Evans's *American Photographs*—"He saw how Evans, eschewing texts and extensive captions, had constructed meaning in *American Photographs* through a rigorously organized sequence of photographs" ("Resisting" 36). When *The Americans* was first published in France in 1958, Frank's photographs were printed on right-hand pages that faced texts culled from writers such as Alexis de Tocqueville, Simone de Beauvoir, John Dos Passos, and Walt Whitman. Text and image fought for attention, leading to a confusing experience. Moreover, editor Robert Delpire organized the book into sections such as "space," "isolation," and "Blacks," for example, clearly at odds with Frank's organizational style (Greenough, "Disordering" 137–38). When later published in America, such devices were removed, leaving *The Americans* more open to interpretation.

The effects of such ambiguity can clearly be seen when Frank deals with the vexed issue of race in America. Frank wanted to capture America in all its complexity and did not shy away from recording its social problems during his travels. The mid-1950s were a watershed time for African American struggles for equality. Frank began his travels in 1955, the year that saw public school desegregation; bus boycotts start in Montgomery, Alabama; and Martin Luther King's rise to prominence as a civil rights leader. As the trip progressed, Frank became even more concerned with exposing social problems such as race, wealth, and the abuse of power in America. Unlike the standard *Life* and *Look* photo essay, *The Americans* is filled with difficult images that challenged America's perception of itself as a free and democratic nation. One such image even made it onto the cover of the American edition, released in January 1960. It depicts a New Orleans trolley car filled with passengers—the front three windows occupied by white passengers, the back two by African Americans. The implications are clear: African Americans are second-class citizens, forced to remain behind while white individuals occupy superior positions.

Ambiguity, however, denudes the photograph of its potential force. Frank claims he wanted to "not only comment on the perverse presence of racism but also . . . reveal the affinity he felt for African Americans and . . . celebrate their openness and lack of suspicion" ("Disordering" 122). And it is true that despite their position, the faces of the African American passengers do appear friendlier than those of the white figures, who seem filled with disdain. Bezner admits that many of Frank's images of African American men and women unsettle and disturb the status quo (206–10). Yet her main complaint is that these images, in the end, remain at least partly ambiguous. In an effort to avoid calling attention to himself in a paranoid decade that gave us the McCarthy witch hunts, Frank opts for a political vision far less radical than that of earlier documentarians such as those working in the Photo League. Frank is not a humanist, because according to one social documentary and Photo League critic, "he dwelled on *de*humanization in his deconstructive analysis of alienation and defeated souls" (qtd. in Bezner 212). The problem with Frank's work is that it cannot point the way to change. The African Americans on the trolley seem stuck in their seats. This is also the case with another celebrated image of a black nurse holding a white baby. The intense whiteness of the hospital hall in the print, set against the darkness of the nurse's face, seems to suggest that the entire institutional structure is against her. Again the social critique is clear—the woman is compelled, through economic forces, to care for the baby who is not her own. But there does not seem to be any hope in the photograph. Bezner argues that "cold war hypocrisy, fears of nuclear annihilation, and Frank's own existential angst, perhaps, make such idealism impossible" (213). Frank's images raise the specter of racism in America but leave the question open as to how to deal with it.

Despite this equivocal message, Frank's *The Americans* was a much-needed corrective to a postwar culture mired in racism, alienation, and skepticism over politics and consumer culture. His book was lionized by a 1960s counterculture that was fighting exactly these issues, but upon its publication, reviewers scorned the photobook as an aggressive attack on America, its people, and its way of life. Of course the timing of the release did not help matters. *The Americans* was delivered to a culture experiencing what was perhaps the height of the Cold War. Castro had just taken over power in Cuba, the controversy over the status of West

Berlin was pushing leaders to the brink of war, and weeks later the Soviet Union would shoot down an American U-2 spy plane and capture its pilot. It is small wonder that in such a climate Frank's book received such negative press. The editor of *Popular Photography*, Bruce Downes, published seven short reviews of it, and only one was moderately sympathetic (Szarkowski, *Mirrors* 19). These reviews give a general indication of the level of vitriol *The Americans* created (and are still the most often cited quotes in academic treatments of the book's reception). Descriptions of Frank's book include phrases like "a warped objectivity," "an attack on the United States," "marred by spite, bitterness, and narrow prejudice," and "a sad poem for sick people" (19). Clearly, Americans were offended by *The Americans*, seeing it as an unfair attack by a foreigner on his adopted country. Many were unhappy with the title, feeling that the America depicted by Frank was too marginal and did not include them. According to one reviewer, "Chicago has more valid facets to its personality than haranguing politicians, New York more than candy stores and homosexuals, Las Vegas more than gaming tables and quick weddings" (qtd. in Greenough, "Blowing" 315).

Frank also managed to offend his colleagues. As Szarkowski notes, "The angriest responses to *The Americans* came from photographers" (*Mirrors* 20). Frank's style was an affront to the accepted standards of photography—the clear and precise rendering of unambiguous subject matter. Frank's work, by contrast, seemed "tentative, ambivalent, relative, centrifugal; the photographer's viewpoint and the disposition of the frame seemed consistently precarious and careless—lacking in care" (20). What the photographic community failed to grasp was that the "problems" they saw with Frank's work—the "out-of-focus" shots, "unnecessary" grain, absence of "normal" composition—were in fact the essence of a new subjective aesthetic. Rather than defend his new style, Frank's rebuttal addressed the reviewers' attacks on the social meaning of his work in words as ambiguous as his photographs: "Life for a photographer cannot be a matter of indifference. Opinion often consists of a kind of criticism. But criticism can come out of love" (qtd. in Greenough, "Blowing" 315). Frank refused to be pinned down. In a manner characteristic of his photographs, Frank turned the burden of interpretation over to his critics.

Although Frank may not have been indifferent to the images he photographed, given the ambiguity inherent in his subjects it is easy to see how they could provoke a myriad of responses in their viewers. This is perfectly illustrated by a photograph Frank took of a deli window in New York sometime between 1947 and 1951. An early piece that did not make it into his book, *Wall Street* nevertheless sets up the sort of aesthetic that Frank would employ throughout *The Americans*.[4] At first glance, the image seems simple enough. The sign at the top of the window states "Welcome Home! General MacArthur," a reference to the famous general who helped lead America to victory in World War II and attained a series of critical successes in the Korean War before being removed by Harry S. Truman for his public disagreement with the president over war policy. The five stars on the sign refer to his rank, and the patriotic tenor of the placard is reinforced by the American flag hanging below it. However, even here ambiguity arises. Underneath the flag is written the word "MEATS," a reference, one assumes, to the store itself. Yet "MEATS" also offers a sardonic comment on the preceding images. General MacArthur will be "met" upon his arrival home by Americans, here represented by their flag. This wordplay was undoubtedly noticed by Frank and offers a humorous counterpart to the message of the sign. Yet "MEATS" is not "meet." Pushing further, the word "MEATS," signifying dead flesh, could also be read as an unintended reference to the occupation of the arriving general, whose work resulted in untold death. The juxtaposition of these visual cues creates instability in the message of the photograph. Is it patriotically supporting the American war effort, or inadvertently critiquing the cost in human lives it enacts? Frank's photograph, without caption or comment, leaves the viewer guessing.

The ambiguity of the photograph does not end here, however. Frank sets up a second scopic regime within the frame of the photograph that further complicates any attempt to establish a definitive understanding of it. The viewer is first struck by the prominence of the written signs and, above all, by the American flag. Upon closer inspection, a second world opens up—Frank's shadow world. We see the photographer's shadow caught in the window's reflection while in the act of snapping the shutter. We can see "Wall Street" behind him, including a parked car and the bust of a figure over a doorway. Just as the objects inside the window combined to produce a nexus of meanings, the images outside the window confront the viewer with a series of possibilities. Knowing what we do about Frank's travels, one wonders if it is his car behind him. If so, we get a glimpse into the process of the photograph normally denied us. A narrative forms in our minds—Frank was driving through New York, happened upon this window (and why this window?), and stopped and photographed it. We see Frank himself "meeting" a situation that would itself become the photograph. And why the lonely street? Is it a comment on loneliness and lack of companionship that occurs in America, an ironic comment on the "welcome" offered in the window, or simply a lazy downtown Sunday afternoon patrolled only by a Swiss photographer looking for an America of his own? Moreover, one wonders about the significance of the shadow. What does it mean to see Frank in the act of taking the picture? By bringing together two separate realms, Frank creates a gap that quickly becomes filled with conjecture.

Although critics may have wanted such questions answered, part of Frank's importance as a postwar photographer was in his knowing how not to answer them. The ambiguity of Frank's work is precisely the point here, not any particular meanings that the photographs may or may not generate. As Greenough observes, Frank "recognized that shadows or out-of-focus forms need not be legible—could even approach abstraction—and still be highly evocative. With this understanding, his photographs became not merely unclear in their subjects and casual in their style but also potent, deeply haunting, and deliberately ambiguous" ("Disordering" 123–24). There are two realities here—the one of the deli counter and the one the window reflects. Frank, epitomizing the situation of the postwar artist caught in an indecisive world, holds both possibilities open. Here is a picture trying to discover its own context; photography is becoming self-reflective. Frank is not given back whole but rather through the figure of the shadow. The moment is arrested at the point where a gap begins to yawn, where meaning begins to unravel as realities multiply. But at this point in the Cold War, it takes only one alternative reality to precipitate the collapse. Here is the beginning of an ambiguity that will have its conclusion in our own postmodern world of relativity and lack of origin. The meaning of the photograph is that its meanings are many, or at least two, which is enough to render it impossible to decide what the photograph is "saying." The Cold War was the beginning of a multiplicity that would increase in the postmodern, to the point where the search for origins and meanings, at least absolute ones, has been abandoned.

It is important to note, however, that Frank did not immediately use these techniques to introduce ambiguity into his photographs. On the contrary, many early pieces employ grain, haziness, and blur to bring the viewer closer to the subjects he depicts. Take, for example, a 1952 photograph of a female cigarette seller in Barcelona. The out-of-focus quality of the photograph, combined with the dark fabric of the woman's dress, serves to highlight her face and hands. An absence of detail around her likewise highlights the contrast between the only two really visible elements of the photograph—her face and her hands holding the cigarettes. While the woman does seem to be fading away in the same manner we witness in *The Americans*, the treatment given her by Frank is compassionate. Greenough notes that Frank began experimenting with the effects of blur, grain, and haziness even as an apprentice in Switzerland: "When attempting to impart a sense of immediacy and action, he utilized abruptly cropped, sometimes slightly out-of-focus forms at the edges of his pictures, suggesting that the viewer, like Frank himself, was a participant in the event" ("Resisting" 11). Frank's experimentation was also encouraged by his tenure under the Russian-born émigré Alexey Brodovitch, who hired him to work at *Harper's Bazaar*. Brodovitch, who had also done André Kertész's book *Days of Paris* (which influenced Frank), pushed those under his charge to experiment freely and encouraged them to use techniques such as blur and imprecise focus, to radically crop and distort their prints, and to use large foreground forms (Greenough, "Resisting" 18). Brodovitch's tutelage, as well as Frank's friendship with fellow struggling photographers like Louis Faurer, gave Frank the courage to experiment with his work and print negatives that might otherwise be considered failures.

Despite this earlier use of grain, in *The Americans* the technique is used to a different purpose: to distance and confound meaning. Frank abandons straight, clear, posed pictures that convey a sense of order and dignity to the subject in favor of blur and grain, which instead of imparting dignity to an individual "debases" their presence. Of course such techniques were not the only factor that made Frank's work an attack on America in the 1950s. Frank likewise selected certain scenes and characters that would not have made it into magazines like *Life* or *Look*. Consider his use of cars, for example. Rather than photograph the shiny new model that might be seen in a magazine advertisement, Frank focuses on older models, junked cars, or accidents on the side of the road. As James Guimond notes, "All the 1950s signs of American democracy, prosperity, popular culture, and success are in *The Americans*. . . . Seen in 'real life,' however, through the lens of Frank's Leica, without the flattering techniques and selectivity of the picture magazines, these icons of the American national identity all seem disappointing or debased" (234). But Frank's use of grain and blur contribute to such derogative representations. Not only does he forgo magazine techniques that would show subjects in their best light, but he goes a step further, deliberately obscuring his images to distance them even further from the viewer. Frank is not just showing the reality behind "American national identity"; he is intensifying it in order to reveal the instability in these seemingly American images.

Frank's ability to take mundane Americana and turn it into a highly controversial image can be seen in a double-page spread taken on Pennsylvania Avenue that depicts two displayed photographs of Dwight D. Eisenhower and Richard Nixon. *Pennsylvania Avenue, Washington D.C., 1957* was first collected in *The Lines of My Hand.* Composed between 1955 and 1956, the years of Frank's Guggenheim Fellowship, the photograph was not included in *The Americans* but pleased Frank enough that it was subsequently published again in both *Moving Out* and *Hold Still: Keep Going.* By themselves, these two images seem to connote postwar American authority and, given America's postwar dominance, economic and political prosperity.[5] However, behind the photograph of Eisenhower stands a young boy holding a camera. Like the shadow of Frank in the window, the boy becomes Frank's doppelgänger, a fellow photographer "caught in the act" of holding his camera. Moreover, his face bears an uncanny resemblance to Eisenhower's, though his appearance is not one of smiling familiarity but is rather a bit on the incredulous side as he looks directly back at the photographer with intensity. Behind the photograph of Nixon stands the figure of a young girl whose own face mimics Nixon's, though again she is even more withdrawn than the boy, with an air of scrutiny and suspicion. What are we to make of these intersections? Is Frank telling us that the young couple is the "real" America standing behind the supposed friendly, comforting smiles of its leaders? The truth about America would then be that despite the posed faces, deep down lies a world of suspicion and animosity. Or maybe the photographs are somehow projections of the hopes and fears of the couple. From here a myriad of readings could be produced, focusing on the America that the young couple represents, the political machine that the photographs call to mind, or the interstices between the two. Perhaps it is all just a joke—two young Americans happened to get caught behind two pictures that bear them slight resemblance.

Appeals to the photographer offer little aid in answering such questions. There is an American flag in the background, as well as what looks like a lunch counter menu, both images that run throughout *The*

Americans. There is also Frank's interest in photographs of photographs, as well as in photographs of subjects behind glass. But as all of these images are used ambiguously throughout his book, we are no closer to understanding the meaning of *Pennsylvania Avenue, Washington D.C., 1957,* if there is one. The same could be said about Frank's use of grain. In fact, graininess complicates things further, adding even more layers of ambiguity to the photograph. The "meaning" of the photograph is in the faces of the couple and in their relationship to those in the photographs of Ike and Nixon. But grain softens features, making it increasingly difficult to make sense of the look. Normally the use of such out-of-focus shots serves to humanize the subject, to remove sharp edges and clear detail that might render the subject brash or overly striking. But here grain does not make the subject more accessible. On the contrary, it starts to detract from the humanity of the couple. As the details of their faces fade, they seem less noticeably human, and our sympathies recede. Compared with the cigarette seller in Barcelona (or perhaps with Kertész's woman in a café), these two seem to be dissolving. All that is really left is suspicious eyes and disdainful mouths—other individualizing marks have melted away.[6]

The out-of-focus style, once it goes beyond a certain point, denudes subjects of their humanity. This is especially true when they are left alone, as they almost always are in Frank's book. In one of Frank's favorite images, the American diner, he portrays a lone waitress in what appears to be a nighttime shot with glowing fluorescent lights reflected off the shining metal. The diner is devoid of customers, and the waitress turns to confront the camera from behind the counter. But she is very far away, and again Frank uses grain to emphasize and expand this distance, both physical and emotional. What do we know about her? Almost nothing. Encased by the objects of the diner, its pies and sugar dispensers and straws, the woman appears as just another object for our vision. Her details escape us. We do not know if she is happy or sad, since we cannot see her face with any degree of clarity. Nor do we even know her race. Grain does not soften here; it distances for Frank. After a certain point, and when used in certain contexts, grain starts to detract from the humanity of the subject, leaving us with people who are more object than person. Describing the photographs of gang members by Bruce Davidson, Patricia Vettel-Becker comments that the grainy nature of the prints "conceals parts of their bodies" partly in an effort "to entice"—graininess distorts in order to draw the viewer closer (139). But this "enticement" is not a call for us to identify with the subjects in their humanity, as earlier documentarians attempted. Rather, we are invited to look upon them as objects, or at least as subjects who are interesting for reasons other than their humanity. Frank is not offering us a social statement with this photograph. Rather, we want to know about the waitress not in order to feel something for her but to solve the mystery that he has created in our minds—who is she?

In his introduction to Frank's book, Jack Kerouac registers exactly this curiosity in the details of the subjects that Frank manages to hide from the viewer.[7] Kerouac is fascinated with the America that Frank captures with his camera. For Kerouac, *The Americans* is poetry written with images instead of words. While it is true that Kerouac's praise is overflowing and refuses to acknowledge the sharp critique that Frank's pictures call to mind, nevertheless Kerouac is able to detect the mystery that lends *The Americans* its particular force. Describing Frank's technique, which he saw firsthand during his brief travels with the photographer, Kerouac writes, "And with the agility, mystery, genius, sadness, and strange secrecy of a shadow [Frank] photographed scenes that have never been seen before on film" (*Good Blonde* 20). Kerouac's recourse to the metaphor of shadow to describe Frank and his work is appropriate. Unseen and unbidden, the photographer slips beside the subjects to capture them almost unaware. But the metaphor of shadow also describes the type of photographs Frank produced—vague, undetermined, and "mysterious." As we have already seen, Kerouac also employs shadows in order to give imagination a wider reign. Frank's shadowy world draws viewers in, offering them a chance to produce meaning in the vague outlines of his subjects. For Kerouac this is the function of art, while for critics at the time it was an underhanded attack on the solidity of a supposedly transparent and bright America.

The ambiguity that the shadow creates is illustrated in the various readings generated by a famous photograph in *The Americans* of an elevator girl. She stands in focus in the center of the photograph while two other subjects, a man and a woman, frame her. Frank likewise employs his grainy aesthetic here, but even more to the point is his use of blur. While the elevator operator is basically in focus, her two patrons are captured in a blur that makes them appear almost like ghosts. The man is in profile, and we can make out what appears to be glasses and probably his suit, while the woman has her back to us. Describing this photograph in lines that were added just prior to publication in a sort of postscript that appears alone on the last page, Kerouac concludes: "AND I SAY: That little ole lonely elevator girl looking up sighing in an elevator full of blurred demons, what's her name & address?" (*Good Blonde* 23). Kerouac imagines her as "lonely," no doubt in order to maintain the fantasy of her availability. But surrounded as she is by "blurred demons," she does appear lonely. Kerouac's reading remains playful and upbeat—the conclusion of this narrative sees her finishing work and going out for dinner. Yet "blurred demons" is an unsettling description of the other two subjects. Why demons? Certainly not due to the faces or attitudes of the subjects, since they are too blurred to discern. Quite the contrary. It is because of our inability to make out their faces, to see the details of their being, that they become demonic. They are ghosts, apparitions trailing through life. The mass of America's citizens are like shadows, flitting through a world of doors and elevators where encounters are transitory and small talk is meaningless.[8] This is precisely why Frank's work is so "sad" for Kerouac—it records the loss of humanity, as people, the photographer included, fade from being.

WILLIAM KLEIN

The disappearance of figures into shadow becomes even more aggressive in the work of William Klein. Although they never met, Frank and Klein share a number of similarities. They both spent a good deal of time in Europe, became defining examples of the postwar "street photography" aesthetic, and, most important, published books in France in the late 1950s that produced shock and outrage over their presentations of Americans. However, Klein's *Life Is Good and Good for You in New York* pushes the shadowy aesthetic both photographers employed even further to the point where his subjects become inseparable from the light and darkness that surrounds them. Although some critiques of Frank and Klein focused on the supposedly "poor" quality of their prints, questionable content was usually the charge brought against them. For supporters of the United States, Klein's unhappy faces and dull and blurred looks and the preponderance of guns in the hands of children (he has a section titled "Gun" to bring the point home) undercut the myth of a successful America. Yet, as with Frank, the power of Klein's images rest in form as much as in content. Klein's use of grain, blur, and flash draw his images toward an abstraction that, once we are aware of the cultural context, become as potent a means for critique as the content of the images themselves.

Klein was no stranger to New York. Born to Jewish immigrant parents from Hungary, Klein grew up in a lower-middle-class family on the edge of Harlem (Heilpern 10–11). According to Klein, New York was a "city I thought had excluded me" (13). As a Jewish kid in an Irish neighborhood, Klein always had to fight his way to Hebrew school. Sandra S. Phillips relates in her introduction to the 1995 edition of *Life Is Good and Good for You in New York* that for Klein, "New York was both enormously exhilarating and essentially hostile" (3). Despite growing up poor, Klein was sent to the prestigious Townsend Harris High School, and he roamed the relatively new Museum of Modern Art, where he came into contact with Cartier-Bresson's work, FSA pictures, and modernist filmmakers (3). But perhaps the most important change for Klein came with his enlistment in the army. After a brief stint in Germany, Klein was then sent to France in 1946, a country where he chose to settle.

Klein's discovery of his unique brand of photography can be traced back to Europe. After being demobilized, Klein remained in Paris to study art with GI Bill funds. He chose as his teacher the cubist Fernand Léger, an iconoclastic painter who encouraged experimentation in his students (Heilpern 13). While he did not remain long with Léger, Klein took his lessons to heart. Arriving in Milan to work with a group of painters on a mural project, Klein accidentally discovered the aesthetic he would employ later in *Life Is Good*. Phillips relates that "Klein decided to rotate a panel during a long exposure, and discovered that the geometric forms were modified, producing an abstract blur . . . they published a portfolio of the revolving murals he made with Mangiarotti" (4). Klein would use this blurred aesthetic throughout *Life Is Good* to add another dimension to his work. At this point in his career, it was Klein's good fortune to accept a job offer from Alexander Liberman, the art director at *Vogue* magazine. Liberman encouraged Klein to return to New York to work as a graphic designer. Although *Vogue* never ran Klein's New York pictures, the magazine's financial support allowed him to complete *Life Is Good.* Klein returned to his native city in order to, as he himself put it, give New York "a kick in the balls" (qtd. in Phillips 4).

This aggressive stance can be seen even in the book's organization. Klein designed the book himself, modeling the layout on the *New York Daily News.* In a conscious reaction to Cartier-Bresson's notion that photography should be objective, Klein chose to make his photography a subjective record of his own thoughts and experiences. He explained that Cartier-Bresson was "making decisions and choices every second. I thought, if you're doing that, make it show" (qtd. in Heilpern 21). Klein's confrontational attitude toward the city he abandoned for Paris comes through in both content and form. Blur, grain, contrasts, strange framing—all of these techniques allow Klein to demonstrate his feeling for New York. As Klein states, "I saw the book I wanted to do as a tabloid gone berserk, gross, grainy, over-inked, with a brutal layout, bull-horn headlines" (qtd. in Phillips 4). In fact, the book reads as a sort of travel guide. The last page of the book begins with "Manhadoes" in boldface, then includes a mock description of the island, which, while accurate, is a send-up of the travel brochure: "Island of the Hills, is located on the SE corner of what is now the state of New York in what has long been the United States of America, further, as we used to say, the western hemisphere, center of the world, the Universe, etc." (n.p.). The text is interspersed with gaudy advertisements for things such as "Hypnotism" and "How to Get a Good Job." The layout of the photographs likewise mirrors the *Daily News*, with multiple images of various sizes on a single page, photographs blown up to cover a two-page spread, and the use of comic strip rows of photographs complete with text bubbles. *Life Is Good* is an ambiguous text, and one that provides a portrait of New York City that is always being undercut and challenged by its very format.

The subtitle of Klein's work, "Trance Witness Revels," helps explain his aesthetic. The term "witness" aligns Klein with earlier straight photography, where emphasis is placed on the clarity of the image as a direct record of experience. *Life Is Good* does indeed record a postwar New York. However, the other two terms mark a change. "Trance" and "revels" signal a moving away from the documentarian impulse and into the realm of the subjective. According to Colin Westerbeck and Joel Meyerowitz in *Bystander: A History of Street Photography*, the subtitle is also a reference to the often-used line "chance witness reveals," "a stock phrase commonly found in the subheads on the front page of papers like the *News*" (347). Even the table of contents is ambiguous, with one chapter simply labeled "?" For Klein, such ambiguity was precisely the point—if life is untidy, why should photographs be any different? As Klein himself explained, "I decided that anything would have to go. A technique of no taboos: blur, grain, contrast, cock-eyed framing, accidents, whatever happens" (*New York* 4). Klein's "anything goes" aesthetic fit perfectly into the spontaneous postwar zeitgeist.

While Klein's work is certainly more confrontational than Frank's, it is interesting how both of these postwar photographers became fascinated with similar subjects captured in a similar aesthetic. One commonality that becomes obvious throughout both works is the positive representation of African Americans. While Klein turns to depictions of African Americans less frequently, these depictions, like Frank's, are positive. In fact, *Life Is Good* begins with a section called "Album de famille" (Family album), where an African American woman, dressed in her Sunday best, poses for a photograph. The face of the woman appears happy and proud, while her companion, seated for a shoeshine, has his face half covered in shadow. The photograph does create uncertainties. The race of the seated man remains difficult to determine. The shoeshine man is himself fully in shadow and thus unknowable. The darkness the shadow creates does seem to lend a somber note to the otherwise happy-looking couple, a point emphasized by the somewhat dilapidated building the woman stands in front of. But the figures themselves appear proud and face the camera directly. In many other photographs, Klein's white subjects are either caught off guard or appear unflatteringly. In a photograph taken in a baseball stadium, for example, a man and his boy pose, but the creepy smile of the father, along with the suspicious and sinister looks of other fans behind them, belies the image of a wholesome father-son outing.[9] But in the shoeshine photograph, the humanity of the African American subjects is not in question. Shadows may represent the creeping darkness of American racism, but the couple seem to defy it triumphantly with their smart apparel and proud looks.

Klein also pays homage to his documentarian forebear Walker Evans. Klein references Evans's "subway photos" with a shot of a small man in a suit sitting in the subway. The figure, like many of Evans's, appears slightly comic. A small man with glasses, he nevertheless sports a large-lapelled, double-breasted suit. Hunched over, hands folded in lap, the man appears to be in somber thought sitting under a sign for Brooklyn (in *New York 1954.55*, Klein calls him "Woody Allen's sad uncle" [8]). For Evans, these subversive photographs (taken with a hidden camera) strove to capture the loneliness of people even in the midst of crowds and traffic. Unlike Evans, however, Klein employs grain to render his subject even more lost and remote. Klein's use of grain softens features, allowing the focus to be more on the mood of the subject than on the physical details of his circumstances, though they do obviously come through. Here we see Klein's belief in "witnessing," as his subtitle suggests. But this witnessing is more subjective, as the camera catches a mood that says just as much about the photographer as about the subject photographed. Like Frank's barbershop photograph, Klein's nod to Evans's subway photographs highlights the change in aesthetic as the documentarian impulse turned inward.

Other similarities between Frank and Klein abound in *Life Is Good.* Klein likewise has an eye for photographs involving glass and reflection. In one shot of an antique store, two women wear incredulous smiles behind a counter, while the reflection off the store's glass window front reveals a hazy man walking down the opposite side of the street. Klein seems fascinated by subjects behind glass, oftentimes capturing them unaware as window signs overwrite their faces.[10] Discussing a photograph of several somber men at a lunch counter shot from outside the glass window, Klein, forty years later in his reprint of *Life Is Good*, relates, "I motioned to the group within to pose. The ambiguity of a photograph: the men convinced they were all portrayed close-up and advantageously, not lost in a mess of signs, neons, and reflections" (*New York* 9). And he is also a connoisseur of crowds. In one photograph, a pretty woman's face is in grain while the rest of the crowd looks on at some unseen event. Of course these postwar photographers were not the first to capture such images. But the prevalence of reflection in their work does point to something important occurring in the postwar period. The contrasts that such images set up are telling, speaking to a lack of a fixed reality to guide the viewer in making meaning of the photograph. Again, ambiguity is precisely the point here. The multiplication and overlapping of images serve to highlight the loss of foundation in the Cold War era. As images proliferate, one wonders where to locate reality. This is demonstrated in Klein's photographs of advertisements, which do not serve an ironic purpose, as in the work of Evans, but simply present the overwhelming preponderance of images themselves. In such a world, how do we know that humans are not just another image, a fleeting reflection in a shop window?

What does distinguish Klein from Frank is the former's willingness to push photographic techniques that blur and distort to an even greater extreme. In a section titled "Parade," Klein captures a crowd of elderly onlookers standing in front of a large building. This photograph is reminiscent of Frank's opening photograph in *The Americans*, which is titled *Parade—Hoboken, New Jersey* and depicts bodies with concealed faces behind windows and an American flag. Klein pushes even further by employing grain. The images of these people seem to be caught in the act of disappearing, even though they stare directly back at the camera. When Klein combines this use of grain with blur, his subjects seem to transcend themselves, a point Klein brings home by labeling this section of his book "Extase." Here Klein specifically focuses on children, halting their movement and play with his camera in order to produce photographs that appear transcendent. The most famous of these is a picture taken on the street in front of a billboard for Ballantine's whiskey (fig. 4.1). Two children, a boy and a girl, appear to be dancing or playing; the girl has an arm raised in the air while her head moves to the side.[11] The boy's movement is rendered even more strangely by a blur emanating from his face, as if Klein caught his head in the act of moving. The graininess of the print renders many of their features indistinct, but this movement, especially of the boy, is what lends the photograph its particular force. Westerbeck and Meyerowitz claim that street photographers came to use blur to their advantage as a "way to express the energy of the street" (35). Here blur goes beyond capturing movement—it speaks to a strange transcendence. The ambiguity derives from the uncertainty as to the reason for their "ecstasy." While they appear to be dancing or playing, it is the distortion in the processing of the photograph that makes them appear otherworldly. The girl's eyes, for instance, seem to be rolling into

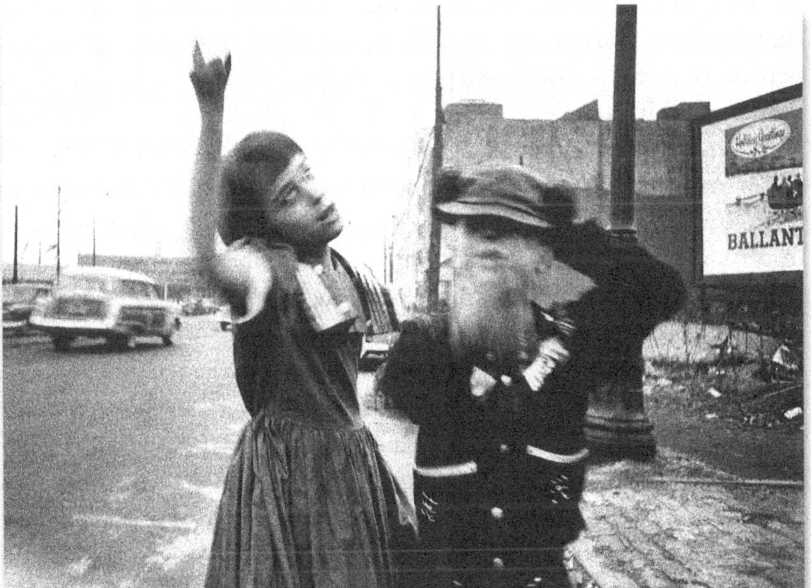

Fig. 4.1. With the photographer's extreme use of blur, it is difficult to tell whether William Klein's "revelers" are experiencing divine connection or satanic possession. Klein forces the viewer to decide. Klein, *Brooklyn, New York (Ballantine's Whisky)*, gelatin silver print, 1955. © William Klein.

her head, as if possession has taken hold of her. The boy's eyes are hidden in the shadow of a cap, but his blurred face trails downward almost as if he were wearing a beard. Is this Christian mystical redemption, idiocy, or a comment on the state of society that drove the children to act this way? Who is to blame, if blame even needs to be given? No other context in the photographs exists to provide a clue. Their faces struggle to represent—almost as if they are drowning in the medium itself.

The "Extase" section of *Life Is Good* is filled with such pictures. In another, a boy seems to be in the act of hailing a man across the street. But because of the blur Klein uses, defining features become lost. The photograph achieves the status of a dream. We know we are witnessing a street, a boy, and a man, but the precise connection between them remains vague and uncertain. Klein's use of overexposure creates a contrast between the black of the boy's legs and head and an overly white torso whose arms seem to blend into the sidewalk above them. Is he hailing the man or waving in danger? In another contrast, the man's torso is in a dark shadow rendered even darker by blur and overexposure, while the upper part of his body remains in light. Thus we have no hand gestures to guide us, and though his parted hair and eyes remain discernible, they lack any readable characteristics. The same aesthetic is at work in perhaps the most transcendent picture of the collection. A girl appears to be dancing with arms over her head. However, Klein's use of grain, blur, and overexposure lends a transcendent feel to the photograph. The tops of her arms, overexposed to the point of whiteness, blend into the pure white background of the photograph. More important, while her facial features are indeed specific, grain and blur render her eyes almost as black holes. She takes on the appearance of a dancing ghost, an apparition appearing from nowhere and destined to fade back into that nothingness from which she came in the blink of an eye. Klein's use of overexposure bleeds his subjects into their backgrounds, making it feel like they are about to disappear into the blacks and whites of the photograph itself.

The use of children in this section is important. Although the ecstasy they present to the viewer is highly ambiguous, coming as it does from children it seems to be innocent of any didacticism on the part of the subjects themselves. Of course the idea of the child as a marker of untainted innocence is itself a myth. Yet these "trances" that the children perform might be read differently if undertaken by an adult. Coming from a child, they seem unallied to any overt comment or purpose and simply the manifestation of a phenomenon whose cause the viewer must provide. In a book highly critical of American society, these revelers could be pointing the way out of the impasse. Amid the crass materialism and self-involvement of Klein's other subjects, these young revelers seem to offer an escape, a focus on the otherworldly rather than on the materiality of American society. Their revelries exist on the thin line between this world and utopia.

Just as easily, however, we could read these revelries as symptom. Children are the barometer of the culture, more sensitive registers of the anxieties and fears permeating society than the adults who know how to bury this unease with social convention and denial. In *Shooting from the Hip*, Vettel-Becker claims that there are parallels between Klein's aesthetic and existentialist motifs that are "symptomatic of widespread masculine anxiety. The alienation and loneliness of modern man, the chaos and absurdity of modern life, and the sense of paranoia and dread that permeated modern existence were widespread preoccupations on both sides of the Atlantic" (82). Following this logic, it is easy to see Klein's ecstatic photographs as evidence of anxiety. The children's bizarre postures and their disappearance into the photograph call a society to account for the levels of stress and fear that push children down the path of neurosis. Ecstasy can also be read as neurotic, a symptom of the pressure occasioned living under the shadow of the Cold War.[12]

Klein becomes far less ambiguous when dealing with the rich. *Life Is Good* contains several photographs of high society collected under the title "Dream." Here Klein pushes his use of grain, overexposure, and flash to the extreme in order to create photographs that turn his subjects into grotesques. In one photograph, two women sit at a table while a man in a tuxedo stands behind them. As with previous photographs, the use of grain transforms these people into mere shadows. Klein heightens this effect by overexposing the photographs during printing. The contrast between black and white becomes intensified, sometimes to the point of eroding a face altogether. Even when discernible, Klein's faces take on a faded appearance, reinforcing the effect of the graininess and rendering his subjects as pale ghosts.

In another photograph, a single woman sits at a table with a cigarette holder in hand (fig. 4.2). Her bracelet, earrings, and dress mark her as wealthy, and although she is recognizable as a woman by her profile, Klein turns her into a ghost. Her features denuded by grain and the side of her face eroded by overexposure, the woman becomes a caricature of feminine wealth. Shot on assignment for *Vogue* at Elsa Maxwell's charity Toy Ball, these are not kind photographs, and they anticipate much of Klein's later fashion photography and filmmaking that take a satiric stance toward the industry (*New York* 11).[13] Yet nothing rivals the disdain Klein shows in his first book. Of course it is easier to feel this way toward rich adults at a dinner party than toward poor African Americans or children dancing in the street. The socialites are, in some sense, the cause of the problem, or at least the beneficiaries of the powerful. Labeling the section "Dream" is ironic—"nightmare" is more apt. While the socialites seem to have achieved the American dream, the

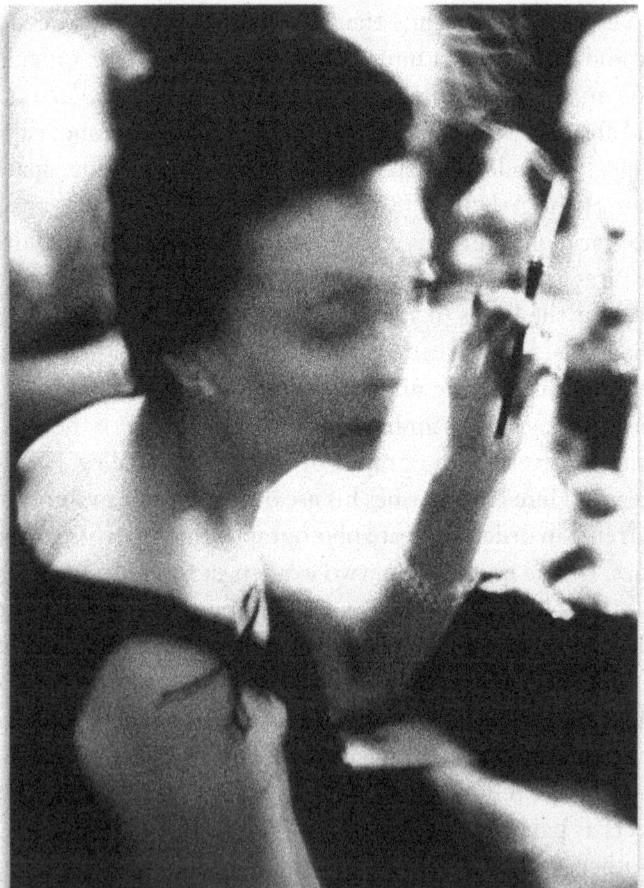

Fig. 4.2. Klein's excessive use of blur turns this portrait into a grotesque, burdening the viewer with the task of attempting to decipher the photograph. Klein, *Woman with Cigarette*, gelatin silver print, 1955. © William Klein.

way Klein renders them appears more like a nightmare. They are faces fascinating in their repulsiveness, subjects with whom it makes more sense to observe than to empathize.

Ultimately, what is most unsettling about Klein's images is their indeterminacy and the uneasiness they create in their viewers. In one photograph, Klein catches a man in the act of standing on top of a fire hydrant in what appears to be an attempt to catch the fading rays of the sun. His lower body is in shadow—only his face, straining upward, remains in light. The shadow seems to represent engulfment, an ever-increasing tide of darkness that must always be struggled against. Thus the man's reaching toward the sun can be read as a valiant attempt to transcend, to lift oneself out of doubt and fear. Yet the shadow seems to wrap the man like a blanket. His face wears a smile of contentment, as if shadow and sun were merely two opposing possibilities, one not necessarily worse than the other. Klein's book champions such indeterminacy. As Klein himself states, he wanted to "make photographs as incomprehensible as life itself" (qtd. in Guimond 244). *Life Is Good* achieves that goal. Klein's subjects become fascinating because we are not sure how to read them. Such ambiguity drives our interest, propelling us toward novel interpretations of faces and bodies that are in varying degrees of disintegration. Because viewers must read themselves into the photograph, Klein's work always keeps the question of existence and its meaning open. We see ourselves in the metaphor of disintegration. Like Klein's subjects, we too are not given whole and must fill in the outline of our image. In the postwar years, this personal message had political undertones because it subtly raised the questions as to how Americans had gotten to such a state and what could be done about it.

Klein is reticent about the impact of the 1950s on his work. He lists a series of things "going on" at the time such as "McCarthy's Soviet style witch hunts, CIA putsches in Iran and Guatemala, Levittowns, and H-bombs" but ultimately concludes that "my priority was coming to terms with myself" (*New York* 5). Given Klein's own ambiguous relationship with his childhood city, such ambiguity is understandable. Yet such uncertainty is likewise bound up in the Cold War world. Forty years after the publication of *Life Is Good*, Klein seems to have changed his mind about the book's formatting. A newer version of *Life Is Good*, retitled to a more classic-sounding *New York 1954.55*, drops these stylistic innovations in favor of a more straightforward format. Section titles like "?" now become numbers, and much of the sardonic commentary and loud formatting is omitted. Klein's decision is curious, since he himself sees the original book positively, as "pseudo-ethnography, parody, and Dada" (4). An older, more established Klein relates, "I was surprised to find that New York didn't look as bad as all that" (5). But this change in format can likewise be explained in terms of changed cultural contexts. The ambiguity that informed the first book seems unnecessary to the second—the book moves from an attack on the Cold War to a classic.

RALPH EUGENE MEATYARD

At first glance, Ralph Eugene Meatyard seems a poor choice of photographer to accompany the likes of Robert Frank and William Klein. Between them, Frank's and Klein's work defines postwar photography, and their "street" style has become the hallmark of 1950s photography in America. In contrast, Meatyard—a photographer who stayed home, never really venturing outside the Lexington, Kentucky, area—certainly was not working in the mode of street photography. While he did turn to a spontaneous, Zen style, Meatyard was more concerned with creating visual narratives of his friends and family and delving into metaphoric and experimental abstractions. Meatyard was more of a "photographer's photographer," an outsider who ceaselessly experimented with new forms and techniques. Despite these differences, all three of these photographers share a similar aesthetic. Meatyard also played with the line between light and dark in order to challenge viewer expectations, and many of his photographs employ blur and double exposure to question the place of the human in the photograph. Despite his outwardly stable and by all accounts happy family life, Meatyard's images betray something darker beneath the surface. If the shadow is representative of the uncanny, of the disclosure of something vaguely known that nevertheless remains hidden, then Meatyard's work presents us with the notion that the seemingly complacent, normal middle-class existence that many share is a lie. This is what makes Meatyard's work so unnerving at times. Seemingly innocent, it hints at problems welling up to the surface.

In contrast to Frank's and Klein's European backgrounds, Meatyard's life is classically American. Born in Normal, Illinois, in 1925, Meatyard entered the navy in 1944 and two years later became an optician's apprentice, a field that was to become his livelihood for the remainder of his life. After the navy, Meatyard settled in Lexington to raise a family, and it was in this city where he would take the bulk of his photographs. Meatyard began his photography career as many others did in the postwar years—by photographing his wife and kids. But he quickly became intellectually curious and joined the Lexington Camera Club under the tutelage of its leader, Van Deren Coke (Young, introduction 9). With the support of Coke, Meatyard began experimenting with his camera. Not only did Meatyard manipulate the apparatus itself to achieve blurred images and out-of-focus effects, but he began posing his friends and family in ruined mansions found outside of Lexington. The poet and scholar Guy Davenport recalled one such trip: "He used us as models and he moved us about, and was clearly interested in light. Several of those photographs were in motion, so that we are erased, except for a hand or a foot, as if we are ghosts" (Young, "Interview" 21–22).[14] Though outwardly Meatyard's life as an optician with a wife and children might have seemed conventional, it is clear from Davenport's interview, as well as from Meatyard's work itself, that it was anything but. In fact, it was Meatyard's ability to interject uncertainty and doubt into the seemingly ordinary that accounts for the disturbing and unsettling nature of his work. According to Davenport, Meatyard was "a photographer who got many of his best effects by introducing exactly the right touch of the unusual into an authentically banal American usualness" (16).

Meatyard's work, though still in print, has received scant attention, even in recent years. In 1989 photography celebrated its 150th anniversary, but among the many publications and exhibits, Meatyard is noticeably absent. As David L. Jacobs claims, "No Meatyard photographs appear in *Photography until Now*, in *On the Art of Fixing the Shadow*, or in *Decade by Decade*, and only in the last book is Meatyard even mentioned. Among the major sesquicentennial publications, only Adam Weinberg's *Vanishing Presence* features the work of Ralph Eugene Meatyard in a significant way" (63). Such lack of attention clearly affected Meatyard. Feeling slighted that Beaumont Newhall had excluded him from the 1964 edition of the *History of Photography*, Meatyard dry-mounted one of his own prints onto a blank page in the front of his own copy. The reasons for this dismissal are varied. Certainly Meatyard's regionalism plays a part. Although Meatyard did exhibit in larger cities like New York, he remained outside the influential art circles that helped to propel figures like Robert Frank or Diane Arbus to national prominence. For Jacobs, however, Meatyard's lack of notoriety can also be explained by the content of his work. Meatyard's work is difficult, "challenging both aesthetically and psychologically," and while there are more upbeat photographs, "the pictures that stay most vividly in mind are those that reach down into dangerous psychological territory" (63). What can disturb the viewer most about Meatyard's work is that it calls subjectivity into question. For the majority of viewers, photography is supposed to present the subject to us in an understandable manner. Meatyard challenges this idea, providing instead images of people that unsettle and disturb.

In a 1959 lecture at the Louisville Photographic Society, Meatyard claimed that he had "twelve methods, series, subjects" that he was working on ("My Aims" 34). Two of these types he termed "uncanny photographs" and "emotionalist photographs." The former he defined as "not surreal, but which give the feeling of being not quite of this world," while the latter was characterized by "three or more objects that have definite emotions attached to them," arranged such that "an entirely different emotion is attached to the entire group" (34). Meatyard's self-portrait, taken sometime between 1955 and 1956, fits both definitions perfectly. Titled *Self Portrait—Citizen—Night Deposit*, this photograph records the photographer but does so through reflection. Meatyard, like his fellow postwar photographers Frank and Klein, prefers to capture himself as a reflected image. In another 1955 self-portrait, the shadow of Meatyard's head appears as a reflection on a guitar standing behind a pane of glass. But *Self Portrait—Citizen—Night Deposit* takes the use of reflection even further to open up a series of ambiguities that the viewer is left to decipher.

The title itself is a hint at such uncertainty. There are indeed three figures in the photograph, and while the figure of Meatyard hunched over his apparatus is undoubtedly the "self portrait" being referred to, the image of a child sitting next to a tricycle and a blurred man seen from behind loading an object into a night deposit box are more difficult to attribute. One assumes that the "night deposit" refers to the man, though that term could describe the object itself. Thus the viewer is left with the question of who represents "citizen." Such a title is odd when applied to a child but certainly possible. "Citizen" seems to connote a sense of the adult, which the older man involved in some sort of business transaction better fulfills. Meanings become even more difficult to ascribe once the photograph begins to be read. The difficulty arises because we are able to see both the back of the man making the deposit as well as the front of the photographer taking the picture. How is this possible? The use of reflection seems to be an obvious answer. But when looking at the image of the photographer, it becomes unclear where exactly he is standing. Meatyard is behind a pane of glass, but it is impossible to tell where that pane is located. Moreover, there is another pane of glass in front of

Meatyard's camera, on which registers part of a car that does not appear in the rest of the shot. It is possible that Meatyard manipulated the negative to create an optical illusion, though according to Davenport, Meatyard was more interested in camera manipulation than outright deception (Young, "Interview" 27). But the point here is not to simply determine if this photograph was the result of darkroom experimentation or an interesting use of reflection. What this photograph reveals through its use of refraction and shifting of perspectives is the ambiguity inherent in the period. Meatyard labels this photograph a "self portrait" and then goes on to present himself in such a manner that he is difficult to locate within the photograph.

The confusion the photograph creates comments not just on Meatyard but also on the shifting audience expectations in the postwar period. If pictorialism presented idealized subjects and documentarians authentically real ones, then postwar photographers demonstrated what occurs when subjectivity comes under pressure—a sense of wholeness is lost. While the photographic subject is always by definition a trace, since the image on paper is not a real person, postwar photography takes this a step further by offering reflection in the place of verisimilitude. Meatyard's image certainly exists within the frame of the photograph, but upon closer inspection he is not so easy to locate as the picture seems to suggest. He is really a trace of a trace—a stand-in for the "real" Meatyard who is not even stabilized within the frame of the photograph but floats as a vague reflection between panes of glass. Photography began with an appeal to the use of actual molecules hitting a sensitized piece of paper as a means to literally "capture" something of the essence of humanity. However, the light emitted from the real Meatyard reaches the negative through a series of refractions, an apt metaphor for a period struggling to secure a personal (and national) identity in a reconfigured world. The viewing subject is even less sure. The fiction of coherence and wholeness that photography oftentimes offered was replaced in the postwar period by an insistence on the indeterminability of meaning. Subjectivism meant greater freedom not only for the photographer but for the viewer as well. No longer a passive enjoyer of the beautiful object, the postwar art patron was invited to participate in the act of making art. But along with such freedom comes its concomitant anxiety—what if there is no order or meaning at all?

The role of the viewer as participant in meaning-making rather than as passive consumer of the artist's vision becomes even more pronounced in Meatyard's "No-Focus" series. In response to criticism of artistic photography as a weak medium, in 1958 Meatyard began his no-focus work in order to "seek out new characteristics of vision that were unique to the camera's lens," or, in his own words, to explore "new aspects of art belonging only to photography" (Tannenbaum 30). His no-focus work went beyond his previous out-of-focus pictures that nevertheless retained recognizable outlines. Instead, Meatyard opted for images that did away with lines entirely, allowing masses to blend and mix together. As Barbara Tannenbaum notes, this effect was not easy to achieve. Meatyard "spent three months walking around looking through an unfocused camera before he felt ready to capture an image on film" (31). Although his choice of subjects was left more or less to chance, the processing of the print was carefully controlled in order to produce a clear and sharp image. Waiting two or three months before developing his negatives, the photographer was "no longer able to identify the scenes or objects by looking at the works" (31). The subjects of these no-focus pictures deteriorate into shadow, leaving nothing but vague outlines that became indeterminable even to the photographer himself.

An untitled photograph from 1959 presents a typical example (fig. 4.3). Three figures inhabit a white background, with a dark silhouette on the right edge of the frame. Although they are amorphous, one could read the figures as human silhouettes. They appear to have the general shape of a blurred human, and something like legs and perhaps even heads can be discerned. Young describes these projects as hinting "at the balance of the barest amount of information needed to ascertain something recognizable—when soft black shapes become a human form" (introduction 10). Of course this formula is reversible; Meatyard's photograph can also be read as revealing the moment when human shapes dissolve into amorphous forms of darkness. In either case, it becomes the viewer's job to make sense of these shapes that do appear to gesture toward the human but that, in the end, cannot be read with any degree of certainty.

Meatyard is not the first photographer to produce such images. As Tannenbaum notes, these figures recall Harry Callahan's 1953 exploration into focus. But while Callahan's figures are "readily identifiable," Meatyard's work is "far more abstracted and distorted" (31). Meatyard pushes the disintegration of the figure to new lengths. This deliberate courting of the ambiguous defines Meatyard's aesthetic. According to Davenport, Meatyard was reticent about providing explanations of his work, preferring instead to stand back and gauge audience response: "For

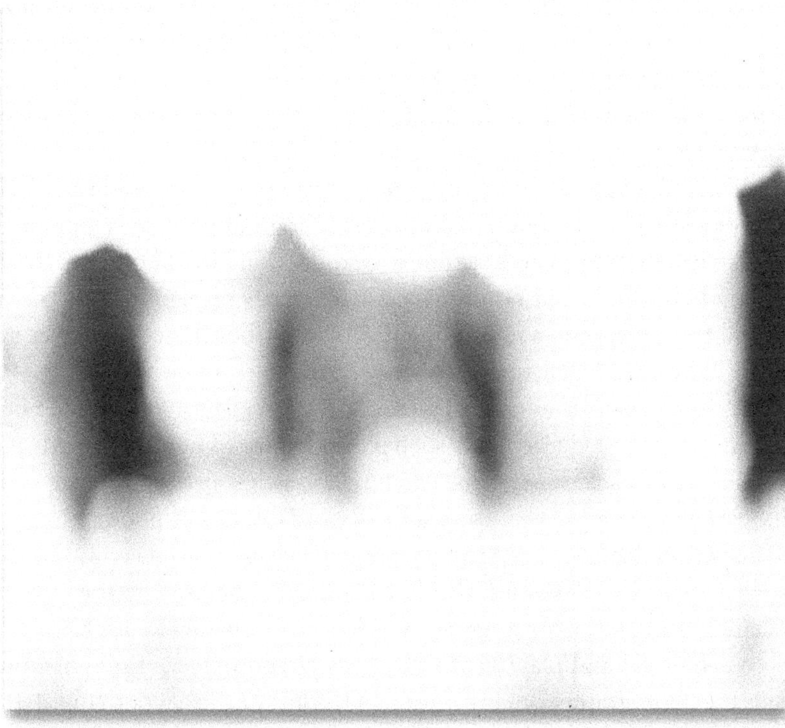

Fig. 4.3. Ralph Eugene Meatyard's "No-Focus" series reduces human figures to the point of abstraction, challenging the viewer to determine just where the "human" begins. Meatyard, *Untitled (no-focus: three figures with dark band on right edge)*, gelatin silver print, 1959. © The Estate of Ralph Eugene Meatyard, courtesy Fraenkel Gallery, San Francisco.

nine years I would see the new pictures as they were printed and mounted, always in complete silence from Gene" (15). Meatyard's enigmatic stance is partly a result of his interest in Zen. At the same time he was making his "No-Focus" photographs, he was also experimenting with what his son Christopher describes as "Zen Twigs": "studies that capture nature's movement and energy in simple, linear, gestural strokes" (Tannenbaum 32). There is an ambiguity in these photographs that forces the viewer to become an active maker of meaning in order to decipher them. While there is no final "meaning" to these photographs, they invite viewers to actively engage them, to attempt to separate light from dark in order to draw their own figures and readings from the intersection of masses. In fact, Meatyard did return to caption these photographs in 1969, but these captions are themselves elliptical and illusory, more like Zen koans than descriptions (Tannenbaum 32). Meatyard's abstractions are meant not only to challenge his own abilities as a photographer but to challenge the viewer as well. Eschewing photography that provides a quickly discernible meaning, Meatyard instead offers his postwar audience difficult work that is meant to be actively engaged.

Meatyard retains difficulty and ambiguity in his more representational work as well. Throughout his career, he photographed what critics have come to call his "Romances" (Young, introduction 11), photographs that employ his friends and family in created scenes set against locations around the Lexington area. Tannenbaum describes these Romances as "koanlike scenes that are a cross between parables and paradoxes" (40). Tannenbaum traces these staged scenes to the turbulent 1960s, the period when Meatyard produced many such photographs: "The struggles Meatyard shows were made at a time when relationships between young and old, parent and child, were especially discordant. Other photographers of the period, from Diane Arbus to Larry Clark to Bruce Davidson, addressed this same alienation through different styles and themes" (40). Discussing a print of a young boy, hidden in the shadows with his head slightly blurred and playing with a shiny round object, Tannenbaum reads the photograph as an invocation of the lost magic of youth (fig. 4.4). She focuses on the expectations the photograph creates for the future: "The viewer is left wondering about the next moment, once the circle has worked its magic. Will a genie arise? Will the object take off and swoop up into the stratosphere? Will the child change in size, like Alice in Wonderland when she bites off different sides of the magic mushroom?" (40–42). These are all plausible readings. But as with all of Meatyard's images, their ambiguity quickly leads to divergent possibilities.

This shadowy child can also be read as a disappearance, his blurred arm as evidence of a fit. Perhaps the object's "magic" is sinister—after all, Alice's adventures were often as disturbing as they were pleasurable. Meatyard was fond of found objects, and this orb was actually a hubcap, scratched on the outside. This magical object, this "mushroom," can also be read as a dangerous object to be avoided. Following this line of thought, the viewer watches as the child is exposed to its effects, the shadowed face the negative results of its influence. This is not the chance photography of Frank and Klein. Meatyard staged his photographs and carried in his car objects that struck him forcibly, ready to be deployed in his photographs. Although Meatyard relied on momentary inspiration, he nevertheless directed his subjects where to stand and how to pose. As

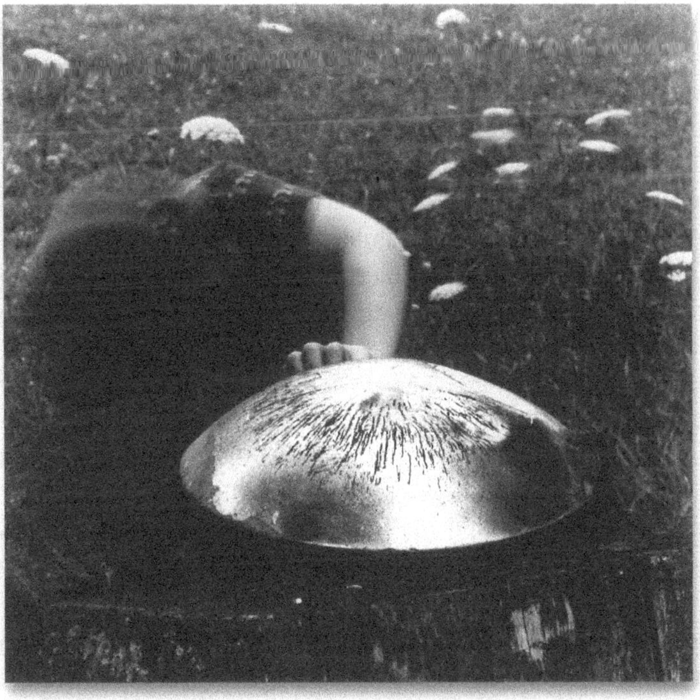

Fig. 4.4. Meatyard was fond of staging photographs, using found objects and interesting locales to place his subjects in scenes that maximized possible readings of his work. Here, the use of shadow begs the viewer to make sense of the shiny object and the boy's relationship to it. Meatyard, *Untitled (child with hubcap)*, gelatin silver print, circa 1959. © The Estate of Ralph Eugene Meatyard, courtesy Fraenkel Gallery, San Francisco.

Tannenbaum relates, "When it came time to print . . . he would 'read' the negatives to choose the best shots" (42). Nevertheless, Meatyard was not looking for one formal meaning behind these photographs. Clearly, what struck him most was the possibility for divergent readings to be created from the images. The child with the magical hubcap creates a set of readings, none capable of commanding advantage over the others.

Meatyard's desire for ambiguity makes the use of shadow and blur especially important to his work. Shadow and blur hint at transformation, but whether this transformation is figured as a movement toward death or as the reemergence after it remains unclear in Meatyard's photography. Meatyard was fond of employing blur to "mask" the faces of his subjects.[15] In a 1964 photograph, an older boy stands against a wall, his face captured as if in the act of quickly turning his head. Otherwise, the photograph is clear and distinct. Meatyard's mentor Van Deren Coke described such shadowy images as the "'reveries of a wandering soul'" (qtd. in Tannenbaum 46). Meatyard, however, saw in them "merely acceptance," declaring in his notes simply, "'It is'" (qtd. in Tannenbaum 46). A man who suffered a serious heart attack at age thirty-six and was diagnosed with cancer in 1970, Meatyard lived with the fact of death on a daily basis (48). His use of children as subjects further complicates matters, as the viewer is left wondering whether to read them as symbols of a redemptive future or as tragic innocents unaware of the fate that lies before them, or both.

Meatyard can be approached as the farthest orbit of the sort of work Frank and Klein were engaged in—subjectivity that still holds humanistic interest. In another self-portrait, taken in 1970, we see an image of Meatyard coming out of newspaper-covered stairs, half his body in shadow and his face in a slight blur (fig. 4.5).[16] The image of the photographer becomes the symbol of the unconscious, the repressed arriving from the cellar amid the detritus of yesterday's banal headlines pasted to the walls. Meatyard as image straddles the gap between a recognizable subject, the self-portrait of the artist, and a ghostlike figure onto which viewers can project their own emotions and concerns. The photograph thus serves a schizophrenic function—it oscillates between the subjectivism of the photographer that the viewer struggles to interpret and at the same time calls on the viewer to read himself or herself into the photograph. This is the power of Meatyard's images—his ability to draw the viewer into a relationship with the photograph that, in the end, reveals as much about the viewer as it does about the photographer. Shadows are instrumental in that process. Their vague outlines beckon viewers into the image by enticing them with the half-formed. The mind struggles to finish the shape, to lighten the dark and darken the light, and the result is that the very process of filling in gaps becomes the "meaning" of the photograph.

What Frank, Klein, and Meatyard saw in the human figure was not its inherent universality but a chance to question the boundaries of subjectivity in order to highlight the anxieties of their Cold War age. These three photographers replaced a static, universalist viewpoint with an active gaze that brought the photographers' subjectivity to the fore. In the process, these photographers turned their viewers' gaze away from what they were supposed to look at and drew attention instead to the inadvertent, clandestine, and supposedly irrelevant. The result was an

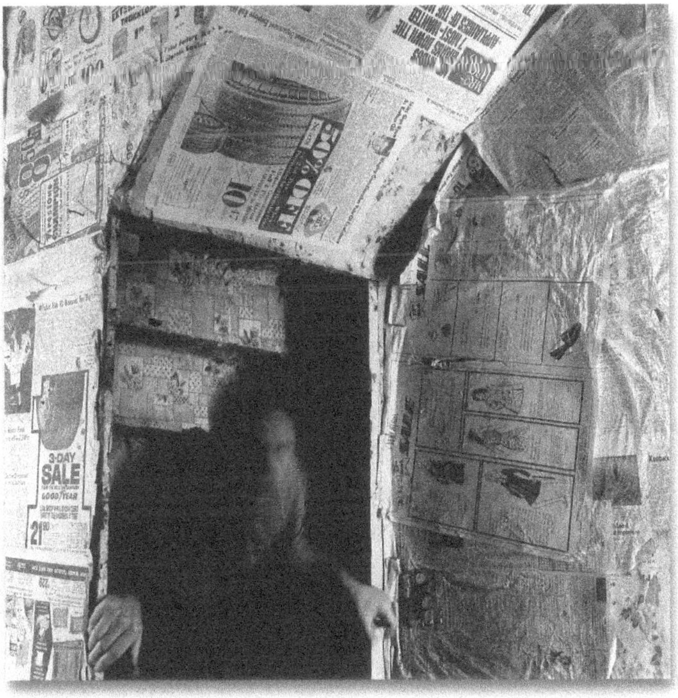

Fig. 4.5. The image of the photographer emerging as a ghostly figure from the cellar offers the viewer multiple vantage points from which to view this self-portrait. Meatyard, *Self-Portrait with News*, gelatin silver print, 1970. © The Estate of Ralph Eugene Meatyard, courtesy Fraenkel Gallery, San Francisco.

engaged look; the viewer could no longer consume the photograph passively as beautiful object or clearly as social statement but was forced to take sides and make decisions. Viewers were invited to love or to hate these images, but complacency was out of the question.

Yet despite Frank's, Klein's, and Meatyard's concern with experimentation and abstraction, they were nevertheless unwilling to completely jettison the human. While their figures disintegrate and blend with their surroundings, they still remain human figures. Their individuality, while perhaps muted, is never fully erased. What makes their work so compelling is that we stare at these figures, trying to make sense of their outline in a vain attempt to connect with another human being. It is this failed attempt that grabs our attention and makes us realize the very real desire we have for photographs that present our fellow humans clearly. That disruption is precisely the space that these photographers needed to highlight the anxieties of their postwar milieu. Authentic connections and the narratives that supported them were fading—a point that these photographers emphasized with their ghostly images of disappearing figures. For these photographers, that loss is figured as a shocking call to engage postwar anxiety rather than as nostalgia for a supposed prewar collectivity.

Looking back from the twenty-first century, Frank's, Klein's, and Meatyard's works can now be seen as classics of postwar photography. But given the level of attack Frank and Klein originally received, it is clear that for the mid-1950s viewer, their work was indeed an affront to accepted notions of America. Viewers wanted to identify with the subjects depicted in their work but were unable or unwilling to find themselves in a world of grain, blur, shadow, and reflection. With the advent of postmodernism, the desire for such identification receded. Andy Warhol's repeating Elvises, Cindy Sherman's performative reappropriations, and Garry Winogrand's enigmatically banal portraits demonstrate the erasure of the individual subject's humanistic importance. We realize we do not have to "identify" anymore at all—we can watch, safe in an irony that has transported us to a "meta" level of thought that opens questions of image, commodity, and spectatorship but evades personal questions of identity and subjectivity. Registering the uneasy anxieties of a nuclear age, the disintegration of the human figure in the work of Frank, Klein, and Meatyard was part of a larger zeitgeist that expressed anxiety over the place of the human in a world where immediate annihilation was a daily possibility.

5. THE BATTLE OF LIGHT AND DARK

Chiaroscuro in Late Film Noir

Consider a classic film noir image: a shadow on the wall slowly creeping up the stairs, its silhouette distinguished by a fedora hat and the outline of a gun. We know from these signature flourishes that it must be the killer whom we met earlier in the picture, arriving late at night to commit a crime. What makes such images so engaging is that they represent both presence and absence simultaneously—the figure is both there and not there, a mere trace on the wall that nevertheless heightens viewer suspense. Film noir presents a world of hidden motives and dark purposes, and shadowy imagery is essential to capturing this mood of intrigue. Shadows might gesture toward their origins, but they also open up a space for the imagination to consider other possibilities. Film noir revels in this gap, using it to create an unease and uncertainty that work in tandem with the dark purposes of its plots and the twisted intentions of its characters. Film noir uses shadows to both hide and reveal, forcing the viewer to continually revise assumptions and expectations.

Alternating between illumination and darkness, cinema is able to control this uncanny world of shadows in order to explore not just the visible but the invisible as well. In his article "Invisible Cities, Visible Cinema: Illuminating Shadows in Late Film Noir," Tom Gunning explains that while the film theory that came out of the 1970s focused on "visual mastery" of the gaze, "cinema also offers an exploration of the vulnerability and limitation of vision. As an art of the visible, film must necessarily become an art of the invisible" (319). Although the visual is often associated positively with revelation, Gunning draws attention to the ways in which the medium of film is able to hide as well as to disclose. Nowhere is this truer than in film noir, where shadows and darkness are made to speak where light must often remain mute. This chapter explores the challenge that shadows pose not only to the medium of film but also to the Cold War world as a whole.

Shadows are integral to the film noir aesthetic. While the production of film noirs was on the decline by the early 1950s and the rich chiaroscuro that characterizes the genre was on the wane, the mid- to late 1950s nevertheless gave us some of the most-discussed film noirs ever: *The Night of the Hunter* (1955), *Kiss Me Deadly* (1955), and *Touch of Evil* (1958). What unites all three of these films is their return to the heavy shadow imagery characteristic of film noir's beginnings. In earlier film noirs, shadows were often employed for more subtle effects—to create a mood of despair, to highlight the moral degeneracy of a character, or to evoke a sense of uneasiness. In later film noirs, however, we see a much more deliberate use of light and darkness. By this late date, noir filmmakers were becoming aware of the characteristics of the genre. The success of these three films lies in their ability to harness the stylistic use of shadows of early film noir in order to address contemporary social problems. Self-consciously aware of the film noir tradition, these films adapt the uses of the shadow bequeathed to them in order to make more subtle comments on their Cold War cultural milieu.

Echoing a Cold War world divided along strict binary lines, these three films create a world of light and dark, a world where the fight becomes who can master illumination and control darkness. In *The Night of the Hunter* this takes its most simplistic, Manichaean form—the battle between the innocent children and the dark force of the preacher. As the opposing tattoos on the preacher's own hands testify, it is a world divided between "love" and "hate," a world in constant struggle. In *Kiss Me Deadly*, the plot centers on the "great whatsit," a nuclear device capable of unleashing a potent force. But while we normally consider darkness as a force of evil, here the opening of Pandora's box releases a destructive light, calling into question the very binaries that we have come to consider essential and unchallenged. *Touch of Evil* becomes an exercise in the control of such light, of knowledge and power that go astray when used for malicious purposes. This is clearly seen in the figure of the corrupt detective Quinlan, who justifies his dark means through their result, in the process finding all that he has built destroyed by the shadows in his life that return to haunt him. In all of these works, chiaroscuro lighting effects work in tandem with plot to create a critique of Cold War binaries.

COLD WAR NOIR

Cold War film noirs look very different from their earlier counterparts. Film noir can be divided up into roughly three periods: an early expressionist stage occurring mainly during and right after World War II, a social-realist period directly following the war, and a later phase in the early to mid-fifties that signaled film noir's final flowering before its demise with *Touch of Evil* at the end of the decade.[1] Commenting on this final phase of film noir's development, Sheri Chinen Biesen argues in *Blackout: World War II and the Origins of Film Noir* that "Cold war noir is distinctive from wartime 1940s film noir, reflecting different cultural anxieties (xenophobia, organized crime, communism, the atomic bomb). Postwar noir took on a new tone—and ultimately a different, grayer film gris aesthetic, no longer the deep, shadowy blacks and flickers of light from the war years" (210). Social themes had more of an impact on late-1950s noir than did the expressionist style of the genre's earlier counterparts, resulting in films that raise social issues rather than evoke atmosphere. Shadows are considered too subtle, and the viewer is given more direct (and better-lit) scenes that reinforce dominant messages rather than a chiaroscuro that would cloak them in ambiguity. Yet shadows nevertheless make their appearance in later film noirs, and when they do their impact is pronounced. As Brian McDonnell notes, "There were . . . a handful of exceptional films from that period [mid-1950s] that looked back to the experimentation seen earlier in the cycle" (79). He then lists the three film noirs under discussion here: *The Night of the Hunter*, *Kiss Me Deadly*, and *Touch of Evil*. These films harken back to the lighting effects of earlier noir style that, by the 1950s, were beginning to wane. What accounts for this change in film noir style, and why would these films consciously imitate an expressionist aesthetic that film noir had virtually abandoned years before?

The answer, in its most basic form, is that America was undergoing a change in its national myth. Early film noir captured a more downbeat mood. The Depression was still a conscious memory, the war that fueled the economy was also exacting its toll in loss of life, and the returning veteran, traumatized by the war and unable to reclaim his place in society, became one of the standard characters in 1940s film noir. Production of film noirs reached its peak in 1950, when they accounted for 8 to nearly 15 percent of Hollywood production (Spicer 28). By the 1950s, however, America had a new myth, a utopian vision of a better life through technological advancement and suburban relocation. As Biesen declares, internal confidential film industry memos containing audience survey information suggested to producers that American audiences were tired of brutal, "downbeat" pictures filled with unsympathetic and psychotic characters (211–12). Filmgoers had grown weary of the standard film noir depiction of a chaotic world populated by deviants and misfits and instead wanted something more upbeat, more in keeping with the mood of the times. Film noir's dark shadows had no place in a brighter America.

Hollywood responded with more lighthearted fare, much of it in color. James Naremore, in his seminal study *More Than Night: Film Noir in Its Contexts*, observes that in 1947, when the noir chiaroscuro style was at its peak, only 12 percent of US films were in color. With the development of color film by Eastman Kodak in the early 1950s, more films began to be photographed in color—"by 1954, at least half of the films produced in Hollywood were shot with Eastman color" (186). According to Naremore, due to the "relative brightness of the Eastman color photography, the transitional years between 1955 and 1970 were ill suited to atmospheric color movies about murder and psychological violence" (186). Part of the reason for Hollywood's focus on color, CinemaScope, biblical epics, and other superproductions was the increasing dominance of television. This new medium, whose low-contrast form was at variance with film noir's rich chiaroscuro, chipped away at Hollywood's market share. Moreover, an increasingly teenage market flocked to science fiction and horror films rather than to the more adult film noir offerings. Biesen correctly remarks that wartime noirs were intellectually provocative:

> They demanded thinking from filmgoers just to figure them out. Their elaborate, even convoluted plots, foggy mysteries with open questions, oblique dialogue, murky shadows, and adult themes for viewers to actively piece together, like psychologically flawed criminals and detectives investigating a problem, would change in the face of the postwar years. (215)

Viewers demanded an escape from the anxieties of Cold War life, and thus film noir was replaced with entertainment that was far less disturbing.

Political realities were not conducive to the production of film noirs either. The effects of Senator Joseph McCarthy's anti-Communist campaigns on Hollywood filmmaking are well documented. McCarthy's attack on suspected Communists kept many émigré filmmakers, the majority of whom were deeply indebted to the expressionist effects that characterized early film noir, from making films in America. Not only did this limit the talent pool for classically expressionist noir films, but it sent a message to the industry as a whole that film noirs (both expressionist and social-realist) were too dangerous to make and thus should be avoided. Biesen notes that "as Washington's House Un-American Activities Committee [HUAC] investigations fueled the Red Scare and industry blacklisting of creative talent from late 1947 into the 1950s, cultural xenophobia and cold war paranoia encouraged major studios to be more conservative, pro-American, or upbeat—in their films and in their labor force" (210). Foreign-born directors working in a disturbing film noir mode were out.

Ironically, such censorship had initially contributed to the film noir aesthetic. The Hollywood "Production Code," instituted in the 1930s and not abandoned until 1968, governed what could and could not be shown on the silver screen. Critics like Raymond Borde and Etienne Chaumeton argued in their influential *A Panorama of American Film Noir* (1955) that "censorship actually heightened the effectiveness of certain films by forcing directors to rely on the power of suggestion; sexuality was displaced onto a shadowy and seductive mise-en-scène" (xvi). The HUAC hearings, however, had a different effect, blunting radical experimentation and making for films that shied away from social messages. As Michael Walker notes, by 1950–51, with a second round of HUAC hearings, "one can discern a clear shift away from the radicalism of the late 'forties.' The social problem film virtually disappeared, and the crime film in general became much more conservative: the forces of law and order were now more likely to be shown as worthy of esteem than criticized" (37).[2] Containment culture made sure that Hollywood depicted America in a positive light.

Film noir, however, was not entirely silenced. It continued to critique and question, although the issues that film noir addressed in the 1950s looked substantially different from its 1940s concerns. Americans' move to the suburbs in search of a more wholesome and stable life, the "paranoia" surrounding McCarthyism in the 1950s, and the anxiety caused by the ever-present threat of a nuclear attack were leitmotifs of the period. Film noir quickly picked up on these trends. *Desperate Hours* (1955), starring Humphrey Bogart as an escaped criminal who takes a family hostage in their suburban home, demonstrates film noir's new concerns perfectly. As the tension rises and an emasculated father must prove his worth to his family, the use of shadows increases as the film draws to its ultimate showdown between the criminal and the suburban male. *Pickup on South Street* (1953) and *Sweet Smell of Success* (1957) both tackle the specter of McCarthyism, albeit in different ways. *Pickup on South Street*, a more right-wing film, seems to condone fears of Communism as well founded, while *Sweet Smell of Success*, a strange picture that is perhaps only marginally noir, presents McCarthyism as simply opportunistic and calculatingly ruthless. And the threat of nuclear annihilation haunts many film noirs from this late period, including those discussed in detail below. Even when the bomb is not directly mentioned, it is hinted at in numerous catastrophes that seem to be beyond the control of the protagonists. Films like *Odds against Tomorrow* (1959) even begin to take up the issue of race. In the film, a black jazz musician and a white racist both have their shadows etched against walls after a bungled robbery, and in the end both are burned beyond recognition to the point where the police cannot identify who is who. Such cultural concerns pushed late film noir into very different directions from its predecessors, leading to films at the end of the cycle that come across as very strange, oftentimes only discernible as film noirs at all by their chiaroscuro lighting features or pessimistic plots.

Nowhere is this strangeness more apparent than in late film noir's use of shadowy mise-en-scène. In early film noir, shadows were most often used to set a tone or a mood. They connoted a sense of uncertainty or foreboding, either in the events of the plot or in the portrayal of the characters. But by the 1950s, audiences had grown aware of film noir lighting, and its use in this period became almost nostalgic, meant to signal that the film resided within an earlier artistic tradition. However, in some of the more interesting film noirs of the 1950s, such as the films we will shortly examine in more detail, shadows created a new effect: they became symbols. Rather than create an atmosphere as in 1940s film noir, films like *The Night of the Hunter*, *Kiss Me Deadly*, and *Touch of Evil* use shadows more purposefully. Shadows become a distinct image, one that is harnessed by the film to contribute to its overall meaning. This was possible in part because film noir had become more self-conscious. Shadows were not cast because of production exigencies nor because that was how film noirs were "made." They were cast with specific purposes in mind, as images that helped to subtly guide viewer reaction and response. This is not to say that late film noir is any better than early film noir. It simply represents the culmination of an understanding of how shadows might be used most forcibly in the film's development.

Although there is still much debate about what exactly defines film noir, one element that consistently appears in discussions is film noir's use of chiaroscuro lighting effects.[3] The use of high contrast lighting is by no means the exclusive test of "noirness," but no other feature so connotes film noir to us than darkened faces, strangely lit scenes, and highly defined shadows. Not all of these choices were conscious decisions by directors or producers. Film noirs seldom enjoyed large budgets. In the terminology of earlier Hollywood cinema, film noir usually fell somewhere between the "A" films, which were the studios' major draws, and the "B" films made on tight budgets and short production schedules. Some of film noir's lighting effects can thus be traced to production values. As Paul Kerr has noted, economic exigencies spurred the creation of "B" noirs, which used low-level lighting and unusual angles to mask minimal or borrowed sets and employed night-for-night shooting to bring films in on time and to economize on fixed assets and rentals (228). But the main reason that low-key lighting continued was that it expressed a mood that later film noirs were trying to capture. Naremore demonstrates that the use of black and white was a conscious choice rather than a materialist necessity for artists and filmmakers of the period. Although color film was available and technologically advanced by the early 1940s, black and white still retained legitimacy for two reasons: "It suggested both gritty realism and the highest aesthetic refinement" (*More Than Night* 172). As Naremore rhapsodizes, film noir photography reminds us that "the medium itself originated in shadow play, or in the primitive fascination of hot fire gleaming in cold blackness" (175).[4]

Noir lighting continued to be used even into the late 1950s because this "shadow play" of black and white, despite its seeming simplicity, was capable of conveying subtle moods and emotions that film noir was striving to capture. Janey Place and Lowell Peterson, in their influential article "Some Visual Motifs of Film Noir," discuss the uses to which film noirs put their distinct cinematic features. Examining the rejection of high-key lighting characteristic of the 1930s that was meant to glamorize studio stars, Place and Peterson explain that "the low-key noir style opposes light and dark, hiding faces, rooms, urban landscapes—and, by extension, motivations and true character—in shadow and darkness which carry connotations of the mysterious and unknown" (66). Film noir plots typically revolve around suspense. We either do not know the identity of the villain or are unsure of his or her motives or whether he or she will succeed in the end. Lighting works with such plots, heightening uncertainty and drawing the viewer into this "mysteriousness." The same is true for camera angles. Traditionally, the key light is positioned high and at about a forty-five-degree angle to the actor. However, "because the attractive, balanced, harmonious face thus produced would have been antithetical to the depiction of the typical noir moods of paranoia, delirium, and menace, the noir cinematographers placed their key, fill and back light in every conceivable variation to produce the most striking and offbeat schemes of light and dark" (66). Film noir lighting is clearly a conscious choice. Chiaroscuro effects intertwine with noir plots to heighten the sense of the uncanny and disturbing, which is their hallmark. Not every film noir uses such cinematography to its advantage, and sometimes the use of such effects is gratuitous to the plot, but the best film noirs are those that are able to support their plots with a lighting style geared to unsettle and provoke their viewers.

The conscious manipulation of light and dark is most evident when film noir creates shadows that cut the frame into a series of distorting planes. While classical cinema strives for a harmonious balance within the frame, film noir oftentimes creates strange and menacing compositions that disrupt viewer expectations. This odd mise-en-scène disturbs the viewing experience, helping to impart the uneasiness and imbalance that is a hallmark of film noir and its characters. As Place and Peterson comment,

> The "dark mirror" of film noir creates a visually unstable environment in which no character has a firm moral base from which he can confidently operate. . . . Right and wrong become relative, subject to the same distortions and disruptions created in the lighting and camera work. Moral values, like identities that pass in and out of shadow, are constantly shifting and must be redefined at every turn. (69)

Shadows literally conceal characters and, by extension, their thoughts and emotions. When not obscured completely, characters are oftentimes "pierced" by diagonal shadows in a manner that seems almost aggressive. Shafts of light interlaced with dark shadows make it difficult to develop a straightforward understanding of the relationship between characters. Carried to an extreme, shadows suggest entrapment, as in the use of "bar" motifs in the final scene of *The Maltese Falcon* (1941), where the elevator door casts shadows over the femme fatale in the form of bars before she is led to prison.

This use of shadows to unsettle and disturb viewer expectations culminates in the stand-alone shadow doubles that seem to haunt a great number of film noirs. These shadows tend to function as alter egos for characters, uncanny second selves that cohabit the space of the frame to challenge any unity of meaning. In *Die lange Nacht der Schatten: Film noir und Filmexil*, Barbara Steinbauer-Grötsch traces the shadows of film noir back to their German expressionist origins. She argues that such shadows are linked closely to death, both in German silent cinema and in their subsequent use in film noir. Steinbauer-Grötsch claims that "the death-symbolism of the shadow in the Classical and Christian world became adapted in the literature of the 'dark' Romantic period and found, from this connection, an entrance into the German silent film. Shadows, as harbingers of death or as a symbol of a deathly threat, spread from there even wider" (141).[5] As we have seen in the introduction, the shadow has a long history as a representation of a second self without which a human cannot function. To see this visibly expressed on the screen, whether sharing the frame with its owner or standing alone as his or her representative, calls to mind this link with the other world. To raise this specter is to raise all the concomitant associations it entails—fear, a sense of unease, and even the notion of fate—which the shadow seems to trail in its wake.

Naremore, in his excellent treatment of film noir and its history in *More Than Night*, argues that in the end there is no satisfactory means of defining film noir: "Nobody is sure whether the films in question constitute a period, a genre, a cycle, a style, or simply a 'phenomenon'" (9). Naremore instead follows the work of Michel Foucault and sees film noir as a discourse, a set of competing strategies for making sense of a body of films that share traits and characteristics. Thus Naremore questions the "genre function" that has come to drive much film noir criticism and, instead of asking which films are noir, attempts to explain a paradox: "Film noir is both an important cinematic legacy and an idea we have projected onto the past" (11). Late-1950s film noir represents the beginning of that nostalgic process. This is precisely why *The Night of the Hunter*, *Kiss Me Deadly*, and *Touch of Evil* appear as such noir classics—coming at the end of the cycle, they are able to reflect back on their predecessors while simultaneously responding to the new demands of the Cold War. In the process, they reveal what film noir might "mean" along with the uses to which it can be put.

THE NIGHT OF THE HUNTER

The Night of the Hunter is a strange film. The author of the source novel, Davis Grubb, described the story as "a Christian mural," while director Charles Laughton has called it a "fairy-story, really a nightmarish sort of Mother Goose tale" (qtd. in Callow 9, 26). And like most fairy tales and folktales, it deals in stark contrasts. Set in the Depression, it tells the story of the trials and tribulations of a brother, John (Billy Chapin), and sister, Pearl (Sally Jane Bruce), set upon by an evil preacher (Robert Mitchum) who is after their dead father's (Peter Graves) stolen money. With their mother, Willa (Shelley Winters), murdered by the preacher, the children are hounded from their home, are forced to travel by river to escape the preacher's machinations, and ultimately find refuge in the home of an older widow, Rachel (Lillian Gish). While the plight of innocent children driven nearly to starvation and ruin is ostensibly the film's main theme, the realities of Cold War concerns can be read in almost every frame. *The Night of the Hunter* provides a nostalgic retreat away from the harsh realities of the Cold War by displacing contemporary concerns onto an imagined past. The plight of these two innocents becomes the plight of all those living under the threat of nuclear ruin—"saving the children" has as much to do with the atomic bomb and the fears of the Cold War 1950s as it does with the starvation theme of the Depression 1930s. The film invokes the figures of shadows, silhouettes, and darkness as markers of the fears that it will then go on to exorcise. But the invocation of the shadow world cannot be so easily dismissed—by calling up fears to vanquish them, a residue always remains. *The Night of the Hunter*, in true Gothic fashion, seeks to foist such fears onto the past, but reading these shadows into their Cold War present reveals just how much the film is commenting on the cultural conditions of its making.

But the return to a rural, depressed America as subject matter for a film historically situated in the flush postwar years is not the reason for *The Night of the Hunter*'s odd feel. The idiosyncrasy of the film is mainly the result of its unique style. The film is a hybrid, drawing on a range of cinematic techniques to create a look that is unclassifiable. The cinematographer, Stanley Cortez, proposed shooting in color, but Laughton opted for stark contrasts: "Working with very few lights of great intensity, throwing startling shadows across faces and surfaces, [Cortez] entered with great relish into the German expressionist style with which the American pastoral manner alternates in the film" (Callow 46). Cortez and Laughton draw on the film noir tradition but take it a step further by creating scenes not only filled with shadow but harkening back to the highly stylized German expressionist tradition. Jeffrey Couchman's *"The Night of the Hunter": A Biography of a Film* likewise notes the stylistic debt to the German expressionist tradition, including the Universal horror films of the 1930s and D. W. Griffith's interest in landscape as further influences (despite the fact that Cortez discounted Griffith's influence) (118–26). *The Night of the Hunter* also recalls *Gone with the Wind* (1939), another film that projects itself onto an imagined agrarian past to perform a social critique of contemporary society. Like director Victor Fleming's masterpiece, *The Night of the Hunter* is fond of nature imagery and especially of silhouettes set against a pastoral backdrop. Even stranger, *The Night of the Hunter* contrasts these scenes with a pastoral tradition that emphasizes outdoor shots and close-ups of animals. The film continues in this vein throughout, employing voice-overs, underwater photography, and sets rather than locations for many shots.

All these choices led to a look that is obviously artificial. As Callow observes, the film received mixed and complex reviews, since "nobody seemed to know what kind of picture it was" (53). The film, like many others during the Eisenhower years, was caught between the arty and the commercial, with some praising (or deriding) it as a thriller while others, prompted by its unconventional style, argued for its status as a great "art" film (52–53). Its ability to employ several styles simultaneously allows *The Night of the Hunter* to make social comments that might appear hackneyed in a "straighter" film.

The film begins almost melodramatically, with an image of an older woman superimposed on the starry night sky. She is explaining Bible stories to a group of children, whose own faces then appear as hers recedes. Ending with her admonition to "beware of false prophets," the film then moves into an aerial tracking shot across a farm. We see more children playing in what looks to be a bucolic summer, the sun throwing long shadows alongside trees and bodies. The camera zooms in closer to the farmhouse, and we see one child pointing into the cellar. As the camera approaches, we see the legs of a woman, in heels and pantyhose, lying on the cellar stairs. The camera then pans out and back to a long aerial shot of a man in a car driving along a tree-lined country road. It is the preacher, who we soon discover is the killer of the widow in the cellar.

This opening scene sets up the basic dichotomies that will fuel the rest of the film. Although we will later discover that we are in the throes of the Depression, for the most part the film presents the rural American countryside in nostalgic terms. The children are playing hide-and-seek under the summer sun in what appears to be a scene filled with innocence in an idealized country setting. Yet very quickly the presence of evil is felt, as the dark secret emerges from the cellar. Despite this wistful opening, all is not right here. The cellar certainly carries Gothic connotations of a hidden secret coming to light, "unhoming" the seemingly perfect American farmhouse. But for a 1950s audience, the half-hidden body on the cellar stairs also calls to mind the fallout shelter, even more so because we do not know initially her cause of death. *The Night of the Hunter* deals in contrasts, but its unique power lies in its ability to keep such contrasts from slipping into easy binaries by working on multiple levels simultaneously. The rural setting is both safe and unsettling, summer picnic and dark cellar alike. Thus the film is able to keep us in two simultaneous presents—the Depression of the film's setting and the Cold War of its production and reception.

The preacher himself represents the idea of evil lurking within the good. A duplicitous character, the preacher is not really a preacher at all but, in the words of one character, a "wolf in sheep's clothing." Espousing a special brand of religion that "the Almighty worked out betwixt us," the preacher is a killer of widows who twists the Lord's words to fit his own diabolical purposes. As such, all of his actions cloak a doubled meaning. The Cold War is literally inscribed onto the preacher's very hands—a Manichaean world of "love" tattooed onto his right hand and "hate" depicted on his left, though he has distorted their meanings to the point where the one has become the other. The film divides characters along these lines, with the preacher representing darkness and John, Pearl, and the widow who receives them standing for goodness. The majority of the townspeople are then caught somewhere in the middle, from the Spoons' (Don Beddoe and Evelyn Varden) gullible support of the preacher (and their subsequent leading of the lynch mob once his purposes are revealed) to Uncle Birdy's (James Gleason) kind but ineffectual attempts to help John escape.

Though it is difficult not to read these binaries into Cold War terms, assigning characters ideological values becomes somewhat complicated. It would be tempting to read the preacher as an outside influence come to the heart of America to wreak havoc. He thus could stand for an undefined enemy, someone even more to be feared as his persuasive powers are so tremendous and take in so many of the townspeople, at least initially. As such, he could be read as a stand-in for Joseph Stalin, hiding behind a mask of seeming benevolence a true pursuit of power that will stop at nothing to attain its goals (and for an untrustable Russia in general). But the hypocrisy of the preacher hits even closer to home. As Callow notes, "When thinking of the film in its historical context it is hard to banish thoughts of another hunter, equally complex and oddly persuasive, who stalked the land of America, causing fear and anxiety in, amongst others, Charles Laughton and Robert Mitchum" (66). Callow is referring to that other Joseph, Senator Joseph McCarthy. By the film's premiere, his anti-Communist activities were coming to a close, but as Callow rightly comments, his "legacy was everywhere" (66). Callow exonerates the director, cowriter James Agee, and the novel's author, Davis Grubb, claiming, "It is not suggested that Laughton and Agee—nor indeed Grubb—were making a conscious parallel," but goes on to conclude that there is nevertheless a "striking resonance" (66). Like McCarthy, the preacher might sound forthright and upstanding, but behind his message we discover evil lurking.

The preacher's words hide another secret—he is not after salvation but money, pure and simple. Within the logic of the film, the secret of the father's stolen money could be read as the secret "names" of Communists that McCarthy wanted revealed. But the stolen money can also be interpreted as a comment on postwar materialism, a tainted gain that drives the evil of the preacher, captures the attention of the jaded townspeople, and creates havoc in the lives of innocent children like John, who does not want the money anyway. Grubb, whose 1953 novel formed the basis for the screenplay, comments that "Willa's obsession with the money once he's [her husband] in jail is another manifestation of the 'economic neurosis of those times'" (Callow 29). John's father professes to stealing the money so that his children will never have to know hunger and want. While this admission somewhat softens his act and creates pity for his subsequent execution, the preacher's greed could easily be read as a comment on the materialism of the 1950s, one not even born out of necessity but from a simple desire for acquisition and accumulation. His desire for money seems to have no endpoint. In fact, he remains a figure of impotency throughout, both in his inability to consummate his marriage with Willa and in his lack of any larger meaning for his actions. He becomes simply a juggernaut bent on the destruction of the children and the acquisition of the loot.

This fact is rendered literal in a scene where Pearl is caught by John making silhouettes out of the stolen money that their father had stashed in her doll. As the children cautiously attempt to stuff the money back into the doll, we see the preacher speaking to them from the porch. The tension builds, and as the scene comes to a close we see the silhouettes of the money drift across the feet of the preacher. In the logic of the film, the preacher must remain oblivious to such an innocent and childish use of money—he can conceive of it only in the abstract. In a later scene the irony is brought to a close. The preacher is arrested, and John takes the doll and beats him with it until the money spills out, urging him to take the ill-gotten gain and the burden it placed on him. John never wanted the money; he wanted the love provided by a happy home that his father squandered and that Rachel the widow ultimately provided. Salvation lies in human-to-human contact, not in secreted wealth.

The first battle between John and the preacher takes place in the world of shadows. In response to Pearl's request for a bedtime story, John looks to the flickering shadows on the wall cast by tree branches through the window. He begins a tale about a rich king in Africa who tells his son to kill anyone who tries to steal his gold, a thinly disguised veiling of his and Pearl's own predicament. The space of the shadow on the wall seems to literally and figuratively draw John into his tale. As he walks toward the wall, he is provided a space for imagination to play. As we have seen, shadows offer an opening into another world where the rules of realism are loosened. John stares at his own shadow as he unfolds his tale, but as he turns to face Pearl a larger, more sinister shadow eclipses his—the preacher's (fig. 5.1). Pearl points to this disturbing shade, the music highlights its sinisterness, and all John can do is go to the window to stare at a stranger leaning on a lamppost. While John tries to dismiss the event, he is clearly unsettled, and the preacher's shadow announces his forthcoming role as nemesis. Shadows are the spaces where light fights with dark for supremacy, where good battles evil for control. John meditates on his own shadow as a site for thinking through his newfound role as protector and literal man of the house, but the preacher's dark shadow engulfed this narrative, leaving only a space of darkness. John's knowledge of how to harness the darkness is only beginning, while the preacher displays a more robust understanding.

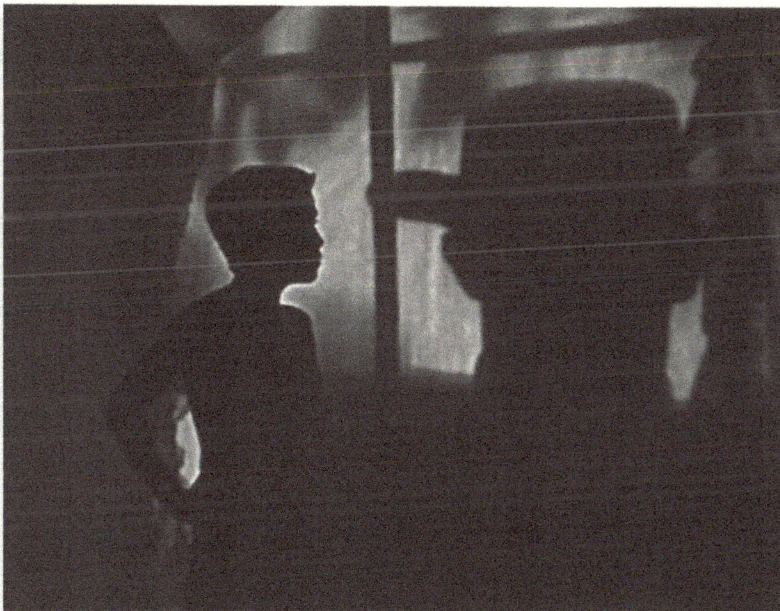

Fig. 5.1. John stands in silhouette as the large shadow of the preacher's head announces the beginning of their struggle. Frame enlargement from Charles Laughton's *The Night of the Hunter.*

This scene is important not just for what it tells us about shadows but because Grubb ends his novel with a return to it. Director Charles Laughton borrows liberally from the novel, but what he changes is telling. In the book, John's first encounter with the preacher leaves him far more disturbed than the film seems to warrant: "Using his hands to create a shadow play, John summons up a horse prancing, a soldier, a clown. His own shadow looms up menacingly, which he quells with his toy pistol, running back to bed. But when he looks up, the shadow man is still there 'Go away, man!' whispered John, his flesh gathering for a paroxysm of trembling" (Callow 13). Here we see the slippage between the child's shadow world and that of the adult realities that will come to supersede it. John is literally "afraid of his own shadow," but with his toy pistol he has a means to combat it. He rules his own world. But the preacher's arrival sends him into a "paroxysm of trembling" because it represents the moment when shadows take on a life of their own, when we no longer are masters of our imaginations. In the film, Laughton chooses to downplay this encounter, saving suspense for the battles ahead. But Grubb is interested in such shadow play, and the novel ends with a return to the scene of the initial trauma. As Callow writes, the film ends "with the Christmas card image of Rachel's snow-covered house, which is a poor substitute for the novel's return of John to his shadow-filled bedroom and his understanding that the nightmare has finally ended" (77). Laughton vanquishes the preacher in the light of day, while in the novel John is left to contemplate the shadows.

The Night of the Hunter brings the expressionist theme to its apex in the murder scene. Set in a claustrophobic attic bedroom, Laughton literally paints the scene with light. Callow admits that "the team's desire for visual distinction sometimes operates independently of meaning" (67), and in scenes like this the bizarre nature of the film is given full vent. Nevertheless, the use of light works within a certain economy here. Willa lies in bed, knowledgeable about the preacher's true state but blissfully secure in her newfound faith in the Lord. Her innocence is highlighted, literally drawn, by a shaft of light that illuminates her face as she stares heavenward. The preacher, by contrast, stands half in shadow and half out, stretching out his hand of "hate" in what looks like an effort to block the light. He temporarily succeeds—in a highly stylized gesture, he moves to the bed and covers his wife, dealing her the deathblow with the knife firmly clutched in his "hate" hand that only a moment ago strove toward the light streaming through the window. Both characters appeal to a light that seems to connote divine approval. But whereas Willa enjoys the light passively, almost as a divine gift, the preacher strives to reach it, absorb it, and then re-harness it for his diabolical purpose, a move that is consonant with his double-sidedness, his two-faced appropriation of God's word to work his evil deeds. Thus this murder scene encapsulates the economy of light that the film deploys as a whole—in keeping with biblical themes, light stands for God's divine grace and a moral regime that the preacher tries to manipulate to his own ends.

The murder of Willa sets in motion another strange series of scenes where the children are forced to flee their home in search of shelter. The film consciously recalls Mark Twain's *Huckleberry Finn*, with two innocents set adrift on the river, forced to rely on their wits and the kindnesses of others. The threat the preacher poses to domestic security is everywhere. After the murder, we see him in daylight, standing against a tree facing the house. In a diminishing keyhole shot, darkness engulfs him as he approaches the home in search of John and Pearl. The entire town, including close friends the Spoons, has left him in control of the household after Willa's death, and the inevitable results—he threatens

John, makes Pearl cry, and is kept from harming them in a scene characteristically occurring in the cellar only by the inadvertent arrival of Icey Spoon carrying dinner. This "darkening" of what should be a safe refuge sends the children running, and the "night of the hunter" begins as the preacher follows the children so relentlessly that at one point John quips almost jocularly, "Don't he ever sleep?" Given that the preacher represents pure evil, he probably does not need to, and certainly not at night.

Throughout the search the preacher appears as a dark silhouette against the night sky, a shot that effaces any semblance of humanity and makes him an archetype, the seminal "bogeyman" come to haunt children's dreams in the form of darkness and shadow. The figure of the silhouette appears repeatedly in these scenes. As John and Pearl arrive at one farm, they observe the silhouette of a bird in a cage hanging in a farmhouse window. This scene is highly stylized, in keeping with the rest of the film, but it seems unclear how the image is to be taken. Pearl wants to sleep there, but John feels it would be better to bivouac in the barn. The bird in the cage stands for security, and the house is rendered as peaceful and secure, and indeed the children are safe there for the night. But the silhouette is also a symbol of their plight—poor and innocent, they are at the mercy of their masters.

The film employs binaries squarely in the Gothic mode. The home is both a place of security but also a potential trap, as the threat of the preacher makes abundantly clear. John tricks the preacher into thinking the stolen money that his father gave him is hidden in the cellar of their home and then locks the preacher into the cellar to facilitate his and Pearl's escape. In fact, the filming of the house that the preacher comes to usurp makes the entire residence claustrophobic, from the cellar to the attic, where the murder is committed. It is not until John and Pearl make it to the widow Rachel's home that the figure of the house becomes welcoming. This reliance on the Gothic trope of houses as secret repositories for terror is in keeping with the overall theme of the film. In a fashion reminiscent of Edgar Allan Poe, cellars are where secrets are repressed, be they murders, money, or the threat of survivors huddled in the wake of nuclear destruction. The relevance of this trope for the Cold War is not hard to detect. The home, especially the suburban home, came to stand for a sense of security and prosperity during the period, but one that was always subject to attack, either in the form of economic loss or through outside aggression. The preacher represents both. Emptying homes of their mothers, the preacher comes to stand for an attack waged both from without and from within. A "wolf in sheep's clothing," he is the stranger who nevertheless insinuates himself into the household to destroy it from the inside. In a Cold War world that felt it had to fight Communism both at home and abroad, the preacher could be seen as that double threat made single—an evil shadow come to darken the security of the home by corrupting its very members.

It comes as no surprise that the preacher's final showdown occurs at night. The children have sought refuge with a widow who has taken in a number of children as part of her "brood." But unlike the widows whom the preacher normally murders, this one is willing to fight fire with fire. The preacher arrives initially during the day and tries to take the children through cunning. A pious woman herself, Rachel easily sees through the preacher's demonstrative tale of "love" and "hate" that so captured the hearts of the Spoons. Humiliated and irritated, the preacher then threatens, "I'll be back, when it's dark!" This makes sense within the logic of the film, since it is in the darkness where his evil is most effective. But unlike his other widows, this one arms herself in defense of her newly found children.

The final altercation is another lesson in the fight between light and darkness. In the next scene, in front of the house, we see a shot of the preacher's silhouette from behind, and then the shot jumps to the silhouette of Rachel in a rocking chair. The light in her lap illuminates a shotgun. The preacher begins to sing "Leaning on the Everlasting Arms" and the widow joins in, but her verses all mention Jesus, whom the preacher fails to acknowledge. Following quick facial shots of Rachel and the preacher comes a medium shot with both in the frame, the preacher half in darkness and the widow in darkness again, except for the shotgun, which is illuminated. Ruby, one of the widow's charges, has fallen in love with the preacher and arrives with a candle that ironically allows him to escape under the cover of light. We then see a shot of Rachel walking in and out of the shadows holding a shotgun, the children against the wall in the light. The preacher arrives as a shadow and a voice; when his head quickly appears, Rachel shoots, and he runs out into the barn in agony. The widow guards him with a shotgun, and the police appear in the morning light to take him to jail.

The use of chiaroscuro in the film is calculated. While Rachel is clearly associated with the good that light entails, she herself manipulates the darkness to ultimately capture the preacher, tricking him at his own game. Yet it is important to emphasize that she remains compassionate and understanding throughout, never fully succumbing to the darkness that the preacher so clearly represents. Although it is Ruby who allows the preacher to guess the whereabouts of John and Pearl and also Ruby who brings the light that allows the preacher to escape back into the night, the widow understands that she is doing so out of a desire for love and in the end rewards her at Christmas with the trinkets she is so desperate to have from men. On the most literal level, Rachel represents a call for a different sort of mother, one who loves deeply but is willing to battle for her children. The problem with the preacher's other widows, one supposes, is that they were too easily taken in by desire and thus were unable to adequately care for their families. The townspeople fare no better. In the end, it is the Spoons themselves who yell loudest for the preacher's death, demonstrating not only their fickleness and poor judgment of character but also their lack of compassion.

The battle between light and dark has geopolitical consequences as well. In a world where darkness threatens to engulf, it is ludicrous to trust too fully, especially strangers who are untested. Sometimes militancy is the best policy; sometimes the enemy can be defeated only by turning his own tactics against him. In the mid-1950s of this film's production, such a message would not have been lost on viewers—the only way to ensure the safety of the American homeland from an encroaching Soviet threat was to fight fire with fire, a policy of mutual deterrence that worked by letting others know that, when it came to ensuring the survival of one's children, compassion and understanding would only go so far.

KISS ME DEADLY

Robert Aldrich's *Kiss Me Deadly* begins as oddly as *The Night of the Hunter*. On a highway at night, a woman (Cloris Leachman) wearing only an overcoat tries to flag down a ride. Car headlights illuminate her as they approach and then leave her in darkness as they recede. Desperate, she finally resorts to standing in front of the next oncoming car. The car's headlights become brighter and brighter; at the last minute, the vehicle swerves to miss her and stops. After she gets in the car we get a shot from the backseat looking forward through the windshield. Nat King Cole comes on the radio singing the lines "I'd rather have the blues than what I've got" as we listen to the woman's exasperated breathing and muffled cries. In true noir fashion, the scene is meant to raise more questions than it answers, placing us into confusion about where we are and what is happening, questions that the film will go on to solve. But then the opening credits appear. Not only is it odd to watch the credits unroll amid the sounds of a woman's troubled voice backgrounded by a blues tune, but the credits themselves scroll down the screen "backwards," so that the title reads "Kiss Me" and is followed by "Deadly," the words coming from a somewhat tilted angle from the top of the screen and slowly disappearing at the bottom. Coupled with the use of sound and the disorienting mise-en-scène, the inverted titles lend the opening scene a disturbing, uncanny feel that signals the viewer to expect the unexpected.

The inverted titles of *Kiss Me Deadly*'s opening scene epitomize the sort of inversions that the film as a whole will go on to make to the film noir genre. The film revolves around the search for the "great whatsit," a box of nuclear material that places *Kiss Me Deadly* squarely in a Cold War setting. But in the process of critiquing its postwar milieu, the film likewise interrogates the means by which film noir operates. Challenging some of its most celebrated tropes, *Kiss Me Deadly* performs a deconstruction of film noir that calls into question our assumptions about the role of the detective, his search for meaning, and the supposed stability of the Cold War world. Detective Mike Hammer's (Ralph Meeker) search for the "great whatsit" does not validate the existential quest that is so prevalent in film noir. Rather, it reveals the faults of such "go it alone" thinking and the ramifications it has for those around him. Light and dark become the sites for this critique, the spaces where commonplace beliefs become interrogated. The bright headlights of the film's opening are only the start of a sundering of the bond between light and its connotations of truth, goodness, and security. In *Kiss Me Deadly*, light can also bring annihilation. The dark spaces of shadow, far from simply representing evil, can call forth revelation and understanding, if only characters learn how to properly read them. Confusing light with dark and dark with light, *Kiss Me Deadly* presents an ambiguous world with an ambiguous ending. In the process of this unraveling, the ironies and inconsistencies of film noir and the real world it reflects and refracts are laid bare.[6]

This strategy of inversion can be seen in the film's treatment of its source, Mickey Spillane's 1952 best seller, *Kiss Me, Deadly*. This novel features one of Spillane's best-loved characters, the hard-boiled detective Mike Hammer. As Naremore comments in *More Than Night*, it is important to realize the immense commercial success of Mickey Spillane, a novelist who "wrote seven of the ten best-selling books" published between 1948 and 1955 (151). But Spillane's Hammer was also a controversial figure. A war veteran who fights corruption threatening American democracy in governmental circles, he reflected the paranoia and fears of the Cold War era. Meant to be a patriotic figure, Hammer was nevertheless associated with the sort of ideology practiced by McCarthy. In addition, Spillane's novels were extremely violent and pornographic. Despite his commercial success, Spillane's work was considered vulgar and without any redeeming cultural critique.

Kiss Me Deadly revises Spillane's novel. As Naremore comments, Aldrich, a liberal, created a film ambivalent about Spillane's reactionary protagonist: "Most writings on noir describe it as a critique of Spillane. No doubt it *had* to be critical or revisionist to a degree if it wanted to achieve acceptance among reviewers and mainstream exhibitors; but within the limits of movie censorship in 1955, it also tried to give Mike Hammer's fans a good deal of what they expected" (152). Censorship problems turned Hammer's search for hidden narcotics into the "great whatsit" of atomic material in the film. Hammer himself underwent a change as well. While Spillane tries to make Hammer an admirable protagonist in his works despite his violence and sadism, according to Naremore, the film makes Hammer seem "vaguely repellent" (153). Working with his partner Velda (Maxine Cooper), Hammer is transformed from a tough, hard-boiled detective into a slick operator working divorce cases, a "bedroom dick," as one FBI man sneeringly jokes, a man who is not above using entrapment to gain incriminating photos. This updated Hammer is not out to make things right or to save America but cynically asks, "What's in it for me?" As Edward Gallafent argues, "What [Aldrich and writer A. I. Bezzerides] have done is to create a different model of the hero and then offer a critique of that figure, rather than treating Spillane's hero from an oppositional point of view" (241). *Kiss Me Deadly* could have offered a patriotic Hammer devoid of the violent sadism of Spillane's character and in the process given us a vision of a noble American who is a model to emulate. Instead, the writer and director kept Hammer's misogyny and added a dash of self-interest to it, in the process creating a figure who better encapsulates the tensions and dilemmas of the 1950s Cold War world.

Mike Hammer is not the typical film noir detective. Combining a deep mistrust of women with an even deeper desire for material gain, he exemplifies a type that would find its best expression in the covers of Hugh Hefner's widely circulated magazine—the playboy. First published in 1953, *Playboy* magazine catered to the adult male who felt that marriage was too confining and that a single lifestyle was more fun. As Elizabeth Fraterrigo explains in *"Playboy" and the Making of the Good Life in Modern America*, "*Playboy* promoted an image of the young, affluent, urban bachelor—a man in pursuit of temporary female companionship and a good time, without the customary obligations of marriage or fatherhood" (1). The magazine helped fuel a lifestyle revolving around the acquisition of material objects, a sense of cultured sophistication, and the enjoyment of sexuality unencumbered by marriage vows—"a little diversion from the anxieties of the Atomic Age" (1), as Hefner himself explained. The magazine was a huge success commercially but also triggered a backlash from those who felt that it undercut American values associated with the home and family. Hammer fits squarely into the image that the magazine sought to cultivate. In the opening scene, his response to the desperate woman Christina's predicament is simply, "You almost wrecked my car." Christina understands immediately whom she is dealing with, claiming, "You're the kind of a person who never gives in a relationship, who only takes." The earlier hard-boiled detective could be equally callous, but usually only to the femme fatale, and then only at the end of the film, as the depth of her trickery is revealed. Later 1950s noirs tended to downplay this independent streak, opting for images of the detective that supported the role of the family in the Cold War. In *Kiss Me Deadly*, however, Hammer views women as just another commodity available for purchase. In a later scene, upon leaving the hospital after being beaten and left for dead by the thugs who murdered Christina, Hammer sees two beautiful younger women walking down the street, and though he is escorting Velda to a taxi, he has no problem remarking, "Look at all the goodies."

Aldrich "modernizes" his detective, bringing him into line with mid-1950s trends. This is even clearer when one considers Hammer's penchant for technology in the film. His smart apartment is equipped with all the latest devices needed for his work, including a series of cameras and a state-of-the-art audio tape recorder for his telephone. His car, which gets a lot of attention in the film, is a foreign convertible that is the envy of his mechanic, Nick (Nick Dennis). As Gallafent remarks, unlike earlier detectives, Hammer has little competency with regard to the past—he does not know the poem that is the clue to the mystery, the music of Tchaikovsky, or opera.[7] In fact he even breaks an album. But cars he understands, and technology (243). Previous noir detectives were not necessarily cultural sophisticates, but they did not seem as aggressively hostile to the past as Hammer, either. *Kiss Me Deadly* thus presents a detective who comes to represent the problems plaguing America as a whole—a selfish desire for accumulation; lack of respect for home, family, and tradition; and the desire for ostentatious display.

Despite Hammer's playboy lifestyle, he appears strangely impotent throughout the film. While he and Velda have the power to disrupt marriages, they are unable to generate one. Hammer personifies the joke of the man always talking about sex but never able to actually have it. After picking up Christina, the couple is stopped by unknown assailants, and the next scene finds Christina, her feet dangling, screaming as the men torture her. Hammer lies on the bed until kicked onto the floor, where he revives but is unable to move. What would normally have been the carnal fulfillment of their meeting has instead turned into a sadomasochistic display of torture, Hammer ineffectual, forced to watch shoes make shadows across the floor.

Such impotency repeats itself later at the beach house, where Hammer lies tied face-down to the bed, in shadow. The same man as in the beginning enters, but again all Hammer sees is his shoes and the shadows they cast across the floor while he injects Hammer with sodium pentothal. This time he manages to escape, but the homosexual implications of the scene are clear. Even with Velda, Hammer is more interested in getting her to seduce other men in order to gain evidence for his cases. Velda clearly is in love with him, but though they are often alone together, nothing seems to happen. Only at the end of the film does he display his love (or at least concern) by rescuing her. But even here the point remains ambiguous—they escape into the sea as the bomb detonates, but can they really escape the mental trauma of their adventure or the nuclear fallout that the bomb unleashes? Will Hammer amend his ways and start contributing to American society? Can he physically? We are left wondering.

The ambiguity inherent in *Kiss Me Deadly* is highlighted by its use of chiaroscuro lighting effects. As Naremore notes, visually the film looks backward to earlier noir: "At a time when low-budget movies were increasingly turning to color and wide screens, Aldrich and cinematographer Ernest Laszlo . . . used a grainy, black-and-white film stock that deglamorizes Hammer's world, and they photographed most of the action on location, mapping the shadowy decadence of Los Angeles" (*More Than Night* 154). The use of light here is important. More than simply producing atmosphere, the manipulation of light and dark serves as a metaphor for the internal struggle that the discovery of Christina alone on the highway creates for Hammer. Gallafent makes the point that "Aldrich presents the landscape of the street as a series of screens and frames—opaque windows, a mirror, the bars of a news-stand outlining a figure—walking these streets is a matter of seeing, of knowing how light falls and how it is reflected" (242). In the bedroom scenes, for example, Hammer struggles to read the shadows cast on the floor but can get no higher than legs and voices.

This inability to decipher the meaning of shadows has led many critics to view Hammer as a man unable to come to terms with his own sexual repression. In another scene, Hammer catches a man "shadowing" him down a street. As soon as Hammer exits his automobile, shadows of him and an automobile appear along the wall. He continues to a newsstand, where in a medium shot a lone lightbulb appears over Hammer's head while in the background we see Hammer "doubled" by a man in a suit approaching him from behind. Hammer then turns the corner, and we cut to a shot of the man striking a match as he casts a perfect shadow against the wall. A series of alternating shots follows: jump cuts between both men's feet and shadows as well as shots of Hammer's "tail" both become visible, and then the man tailing Hammer is merely a silhouette as he moves in and out of the shadows. Hammer catches a glimpse of the man in a mirror (this time the lightbulb is above the man) as he stops to buy something from a vending machine, and we realize that Hammer is aware of his presence. The man flicks open a switchblade knife, and a fight ensues in the shadows. This time Hammer comes out victorious. The man drops the knife he is holding at waist-height upon Hammer's command, Hammer takes it and closes it, and as the man tries to make a final assault, Hammer sends him (and his shadow along the wall) tumbling down a long flight of stairs.

Although the image of two men fighting is a fairly common film noir trope, by emphasizing the figure of the double this scene suggests that Hammer is not simply fighting an opponent but that that opponent is himself. The scene achieves this by drawing out the encounter so that we begin to focus not just on the fact that Hammer is being followed but on the myriad ways in which the film signals this to us. The lightbulb above Hammer's head, an almost comic sign for illumination and understanding, becomes inverted when Hammer observes his opponent in the mirror, as if he is seeing his own image doubled. The excessive use of shadows likewise hints at this instability between selves. Shadows are the spaces where distinct parameters dissipate, where figures blend into one another. Of course we know who is who based on who wears which shoes, but the jump cuts that show Hammer's assailant as alternating between having a distinct face and look and being simply a silhouette or outline leave room for the imagination to wander.

The battle over the knife in the fight sequence can be read as a battle for sexual control. Robert Lang, in his contribution to *Perspectives on Film Noir*, "Looking for the 'Great Whatzit,'" views the scene as evidence of Hammer's homophobia (172). Hammer's shadow becomes Jungian, the repressed side of his personality that he is unable or unwilling to acknowledge. Thus Lang comments, "Mike Hammer's fear, then, is not just a fear of women, but of the woman (the feminine) in himself, and of the feminine position that (he perceives) homosexual desire puts him in" (174). Hammer might wear a smug smile as he closes the knife and sends his opponent's shadow sprawling down the stairs, but the joke is ultimately on him—it is this repression that makes him unable to connect with anyone outside himself, especially the myriad of women in the film that he treats so despicably.

Hammer's solipsism is the inevitable result of his inability to communicate with himself. In an image that is repeated throughout the film, Hammer casts a distinct shadow on the wall as he listens to his recording machine. Alain Silver, in his article "*Kiss Me Deadly*: Evidence of a Style," notes that "he and the machine are on the right and left of a medium shot with his shadow between them. The machine becomes a second shadow, another self, an embodiment of the mechanistic, emotionless aspect of Hammer's psyche" (221). To the viewer, it appears almost as if he is listening to his own conscience. The machine looks like a human face, so when it speaks it is as if three people are present: the machine, the shadow, and Hammer. Despite his ability to use technology to screen his calls, Hammer nevertheless remains passive. Hammer is unable to listen to himself, and it is only at the end, when Velda is in trouble, that he realizes his mistake.

Although critics have pointed to the repressed nature of Hammer's character in *Kiss Me Deadly*, they rarely equate this discussion of sexuality with the larger postwar world. Carol Flinn, in her article "Sound, Woman and the Bomb: Dismembering the 'Great Whatsit' in *Kiss Me Deadly*," argues for the importance of reading the double-sided nature of Hammer's character: "To analyze a film like *Kiss Me Deadly* as a product of only cold war politics deflects and ultimately obscures the fear of feminine sexuality which displays itself so lavishly across this and other examples of film noir" (qtd. in Lang 173). Yet what critics like Flinn miss is that in the 1950s, such sexual concerns were intimately connected with discussions of the nation as a whole. *Kiss Me Deadly* is very much an entry into the debate about what makes an appropriate family, and thus a strong nation. The independent bachelor detective of the past needs updating. While *Kiss Me Deadly* deconstructs the film noir detective in order to show that the model of self-sufficient male trails behind it a Jungian shadow of misogyny and perhaps homosexuality, Hammer is also a comment on the fears and insecurities of the postwar years, where distrust of femininity, either in oneself or in women as a whole, ironically led to a less stable America as the family structure was thereby eroded. The use of shadows raises the issue of Hammer's repression not only to perform a subtle critique on the violence and misogyny of Spillane's novels but also to point out the flaws of such thinking in America as a whole.

By lightening the dark spaces and darkening the light ones, shadows act as a sort of mediator in *Kiss Me Deadly*, allowing characters to glimpse the reality that is occluded by stark contrasts. The climactic scene of the film, where the "great whatsit" is finally opened and its power unleashed, demonstrates what occurs when such arbitration ceases. At the beach house, Gabriel (Gaby Rodgers) is warned by Dr. Soberin (Albert Dekker) not to open the box by a series of metaphoric examples—Lot's wife, Pandora's box, and the Medusa's head—that point to curiosity (particularly female curiosity) as the cause of one's downfall. Gabriel disregards this advice and, after killing Dr. Soberin and wounding Hammer, opens the box. The viewer witnesses a bright light, but in keeping with the conceit that such light is destructive, we then move via a jump cut to a low-angle medium shot of Gabriel behind the box, its light quickly throwing a shadow on the wall and illuminating her face as she screams. Shortly thereafter, she bursts into flames. As Lang correctly comments, "The only way to see it (and this is precisely the point, if we remember what it is that is ultimately desired) is in a reflection, a shadow, or through a filter" (182). Truth resides in the shadows. Hammer finds Velda, who is locked in a room, and runs with her outside to the beach. The ending, however, is highly ambiguous (fig. 5.2). Like Lot's wife, both Velda and Hammer repeatedly look back to the house, but the bright light that is emitted forces them to avert their gazes. This intense light alternates with darkness as the material in the box seems to flash on and off. Shadows do occasionally exist, but the emphasis is on the alternation of light and darkness, one eclipsing the other, Velda and Hammer becoming engulfed in both. Deadly light and its dark absence signal a closing off of possibilities for the characters, and though they make it to the baptismal waters of the Pacific Ocean, they seem far from safe. In the final scene, the pair stand shivering in the water as the words "The End" appear on top of them, unable to go farther and afraid to reapproach the home, now destroyed by the final blast. Although they seem to have escaped, given postwar fears of nuclear fallout, the viewer is left with the suspicion that both Velda and Hammer are doomed to a slow death by radiation.

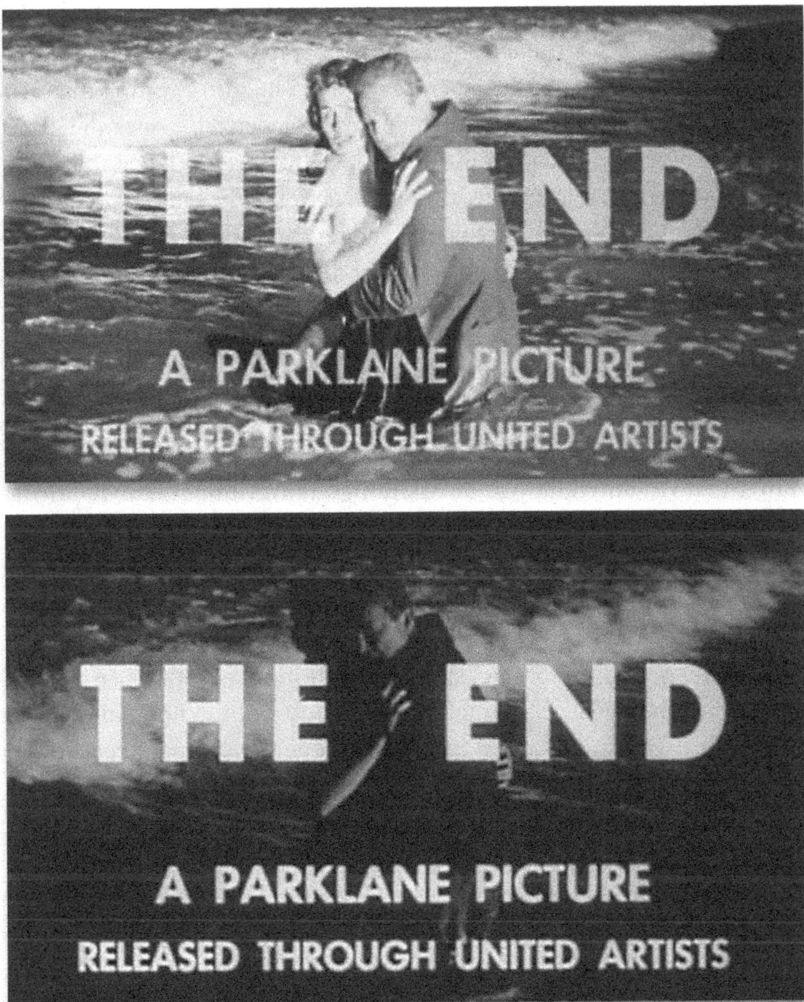

Fig. 5.2. Intense light alternates with engulfing darkness as Hammer and Velda face a world without the mitigating shadow in the final scene of *Kiss Me Deadly*. Frame enlargement from Robert Aldrich's *Kiss Me Deadly*.

Kiss Me Deadly's ending points to a political reading, not only because of its invocation of the nuclear but because of the way it sets up the binary between light and dark. The problem, for all the characters except Velda, is their excessive, monomaniacal behavior. Even Nick, Hammer's auto mechanic, is not immune. His love of speed, of the comical "Va-va-voom!" that he repeats throughout the film like a mantra, deftly characterizes all the characters' obsessive search for the "great whatsit." But as Nick's own brother warns him, going too fast results in death, as he ultimately discovers for himself as he is killed under the very symbol of his desire—a car. In fact, all of these characters are ironically killed by the very things they so desperately seek. The film's ending maps the possible cataclysmic result of such compulsive behavior onto the global political stage, as two opposing powers vie for a supremacy that could easily devolve into mutually assured destruction. The truth of Hammer's love of gadgetry is that there is one gadget standing behind them all—American technology is founded on not just a will to mastery but a will to war. His comfortable lifestyle, flashy clothes, and nice cars do not save Hammer (or America) from himself, from his curiosity and inability to trust others, or from his vanity in discovering the secret alone. Though Hammer seems to have learned his lesson and amended his actions by the end of the film, the final move away from the destroyed house and into a vast ocean could just as easily signal annihilation as baptismal rejuvenation. The hope that shadows in the film have signified comes to an end, as Hammer and Velda stand shivering and trembling, watching the house, a space of their symbolic union, being blown apart.

Thus the film leaves us with an ambiguous politics. If the box represents the possibility of nuclear Armageddon that Hammer is helpless to contain, the message is simply that it is best not to know. In the logic of the film, Hammer should have helped the government recover the "great whatsit," even if it hurt his ego and deflated his sense of superiority. The message implicitly becomes "trust the government," since it really knows what is happening and one might become an innocent (or not-so-innocent) bystander, the way Hammer does. Yet this reading is fundamentally disturbing, since the film implies that the government itself had lost control of the device in the first place and was unable, even up to the end, to recover it or render it harmless. Hammer himself repeatedly mocks Pat (Wesley Addy) and his colleagues' attempts throughout the film—they are not to be trusted because they are unable to get the job done. The existentialist theme of independent action, which is so prevalent in film noir, leads to an uncharacteristically bleak end. Early in the film, Hammer lies for Christina in order to get past a roadblock that has been set for her. But Hammer does not know what or whom exactly she is running from, and Christina is reluctant to tell him. "You know the old saying," she says, and Hammer answers correctly, "What I don't know can't hurt me." Of course the irony is that remaining "in the dark" is not an option for Hammer, as he is captured and almost killed despite his lack of knowledge. If the darkness is not safe, even less so is the light.

The ending of the film calls the idea of light as a metaphor into question: understanding does not equal goodness, kindness, or security; it equals annihilation. The "great whatsit" is the ultimate secret that represents all the desires that the characters ascribe to it. Quentin Tarantino, in his appropriation of this image in *Pulp Fiction* (1994), reduces it to this basis—desire. Pushing the "great whatsit" to its postmodern limit, we do not even need to know what is inside the briefcase; it is enough to know that all the characters want it. The ultimate source of light, like the reasons for the characters' desires, is unknowable. Even worse, there is nowhere else to turn, since the government, so often a force for good in 1950s noir, is equally ineffectual. The world spins out of control, subject to the whims and desires of those searching for the "great whatsit," the placeholder for all petty desires that can quickly lead to wholesale destruction. *Kiss Me Deadly* mirrors the ambiguity and uncertainty of the Cold War that inspired it. Viewers were left with the same anxieties over the nuclear that they brought with them into the theater—only now those fears were rendered conscious.

TOUCH OF EVIL

Touch of Evil is a film about borders—borders between countries, between races, and between right and wrong. Shadows, in *Touch of Evil* as well as in the other films discussed, represent these borders. They are transitional spaces made manifest, fluid spaces that allow movement from one side to another. Symbolic of the ambiguities that exist at such border crossings, shadows make visible another liminal space that is repeatedly crossed in the film—the border between light and dark. Like *The Night of the Hunter* and *Kiss Me Deadly*, *Touch of Evil* also presents the viewer with a Manichaean world where light struggles with dark to form gray spaces that are somehow both definable and vague. But director Orson Welles's unique genius resided in his ability to film scenes in such a way that the struggle between light and dark itself comes into clear focus. Consciously manipulating film noir's rich tradition of chiaroscuro, Welles created a film that critiques the binary thinking of the postwar America that he found upon returning from ten years abroad in Europe. *Touch of Evil* is often seen as the last and perhaps greatest film noir ever made, mainly because it pushes the use of light (and its occlusion) to its limits. Folding the film back upon its own generic precedents allowed Welles to use the established tropes of film noir to comment on the postwar conditions of the film's making and, in the process, to create shadows that provided the space for rethinking not just the history of film noir stylistics but also the role that that history had to play in revealing the social anxieties of the time.

Welles was no stranger to shadows. He was, after all, one of the first voices of "the Shadow" on radio, and shadow imagery appears throughout Welles's corpus, from his earliest boyhood plays, to his time directing and acting on the stage in his Mercury Theater productions, to what Naremore calls the "grotesque visuals" (*Magic World* 88) of *The Magnificent Ambersons* (1942) and of the dream sequences of *The Stranger* (1946). Naremore reads Welles's penchant for shadows as an insight into his difficult political views. Although conceding that Welles is clearly liberal in his viewpoint, Naremore finds it difficult to ultimately classify Welles politically.

> His preference for the Gothic or "expressionist" mode is a further sign of an emotional dualism: Gothic writers have typically been political rebels of a sort, trying to depict the corruption and degeneracy of an entrenched order; even so, . . . the tyrants at the center of Welles's films are usually more fascinating and sympathetic than the naïve, commonplace figures around them—this in spite of the fact that Welles puts many of his own political sentiments into the mouths of "starry-eyed idealists" like Jed Leland, Michael O'Hara, and Mike Vargas. (49)

Welles's Gothicism resides in his desire to give evil full vent, all the while knowing that, ultimately, good will triumph in the end. The ambiguous space of the shadow allows Welles to have it both ways, indulging his fascination with the power of darkness while ultimately siding with a flawed but morally correct liberal position. It is thus no accident that Welles chooses the expressionist mode—as we have seen, shadows can easily contain such contradictions.

The irony of Welles's classic is that it was poorly received upon its 1958 release. Critics gave it mixed reviews, often complaining of the difficult and convoluted plotline. Audiences were not much kinder to what amounted to a "B" film, and box office receipts were minimal. Over the years, the reason for its lackluster performance has been ascribed to the fact that the original release was not entirely Welles's film. While Universal executives originally responded positively to the picture, problems began to emerge during editing, where Welles was notoriously slow. The studio took control of the process, making Welles's unconventional narrative style more linear and even calling for extra footage to be shot (Armstrong 135). This led Welles to respond with his now-famous fifty-eight-page memo in which he detailed the corrections necessary to restore the film to coherency, most of which were ignored (136). Thus the film languished, Welles's vision being lost in the editing. It was not until 1998 that the film was reedited using Welles's memo and most of his original footage.[8] Since then, *Touch of Evil* has taken its rightful place as a film noir classic, and one that arguably closes the original cycle of film noir until neo-noirs such as director Roman Polanski's *Chinatown* (1974) began to emerge in the 1970s.

As persuasive as this appeal to the auteur status of Welles may be in explaining *Touch of Evil*'s initial reception, the fact remains that film noir as a genre was on its way out by the time *Touch of Evil* made it to theaters. As Stephen Armstrong puts it, "By 1958, . . . film noir had become box office poison" (133). Welles, returning from a ten-year hiatus in Europe, may have been unaware of this shift in popular taste. According to Armstrong a change had occurred, "fomented, perhaps, by advances in technology, the spread of television and the ending of the Korean War. This change—a collective, national turn toward confidence about the present and optimism for the future—seems to have crystallized shortly after the U.S. Senate's 1954 censure of Joseph McCarthy" (139–40). As America entered the late 1950s, it did not want films that reminded them of the corruption and twisting of justice that McCarthy represented. Hollywood instead turned to escapist entertainment, and as Welles himself observed, studio executives believed *Touch of Evil* to be "too dark and black and strange" (Armstrong 137). But the film noir style, with its emphasis on the darkness of American life, also gave Welles a vehicle that questioned the uses and abuses of power.

In his discussion of *Touch of Evil* in interviews, Welles never explicitly equated the film with the rise and fall of McCarthy. Yet it is difficult not to read a film that deals with a corrupt detective (Welles) who plants evidence to convict those who his "game leg" tells him are guilty against this very public figure. The film was adapted from Whit Masterson's (a pseudonym for Robert A. Wade and H. Billy Miller) hard-boiled novel *Badge of Evil*, a story in which a district attorney investigates the planting of evidence by a corrupt police officer. While the title *Badge of Evil* was changed to *Touch of Evil* to tone down the antiestablishment message, Welles also made numerous changes that added depth to the script. In the film, the detective Hank Quinlan frames the suspect, but he turns out to be correct—the suspect is indeed guilty. To further complicate matters, we find out that Quinlan has been framing suspects all along, as a sort of payback for his inability to capture his wife's murderer. In addition to deepening the character of Quinlan, Welles has Mike Vargas (Charlton Heston), the Mexican district attorney who becomes involved in Quinlan's case, question his own love of the law when his wife becomes framed by Quinlan for a crime involving drug use and murder. Welles moves the novel's location of San Diego even closer to the Mexican border, in the process evoking complicated discussions about race. In short, Welles increases the level of ambiguity in the screenplay, making every character susceptible to corruption in the fluid space of a border town.

Touch of Evil is ultimately a film about ethics, as Welles has made clear in numerous interviews. Although he complicates Quinlan, Welles is quick to disclaim the sort of redemptive possibility that the death of his wife or the guilt of his victim might entail, explaining, "It's a mistake to think that Quinlan finds any favor in my eyes. To me, he's hateful. There's no ambiguity in his character. . . . But because he's a man of a certain breadth, a man of courage, you can't prevent yourself from feeling sympathy for him" (Comito 204). Vargas, on the other hand, is described by Welles as his "mouthpiece": "Personally, I believe in everything that's said by the character played by Heston" (qtd. in Comito 205). The film begs to be read not only against the memory of McCarthy but also against the ends-justify-the-means thinking fostered by the continuing rise of Communism (both as a literal threat and as a psychological fear) that would reach its apex with the Cuban missile crisis in 1962. But this contextualized reading still does not explain why Welles picked the film noir genre to convey such a message about morality.

Welles does not just make another film noir; he makes a film noir that is highly conscious of its status as a film noir, perhaps even the last film noir. Welles's heavy reliance on the use of film noir lighting effects not simply is a visual nod to his earlier work but calls attention to the reasons that these techniques were effective in the first place. Light, dark, and the shadows between them are not used simply as markers of "noirness." True, they help define film noir and can be seen in numerous productions. But such lighting effects worked in earlier films because they produced a mood that supported the malaise and uncertainty of the pictures in which they occurred. Welles distills chiaroscuro into its very archetype, and this distillation process has the further uncanny effect of not only disturbing us but also showing us why and how we are disturbed. This deconstruction mirrors the deconstruction of power that the film undertakes. As the film reveals film noir to us, it reveals the corruption of power that Quinlan represents. We see how Quinlan works his effects, how evidence is planted, how confessions and convictions are constructed.

The doubling that the film enacts on the level of cinematic technique runs parallel to the uncovering of corruption in its thematic content. The deconstruction of light that *Touch of Evil* performs technically is part and parcel, then, of the deconstruction of the evil that figures like Quinlan and McCarthy represent. The folding back of filmic technique that allows us to see just how persuasive chiaroscuro is in film noir also allows us to see how figures like Quinlan (and, by extension, McCarthy or Stalin) are able to manipulate appearances to serve their own ends. Welles, just as in *Citizen Kane* (1941), was ahead of his time. The fact that it is Welles himself playing Quinlan reinforces the connection—framing subjects in the picture while putting film noir into a "frame" outside of it. There is now little doubt that Welles's changes make for a better picture, but it is also our present distance from both the final days of the film noir cycle and the Cold War that informed its production that allows us to see *Touch of Evil* in ways a 1958 audience could not fully appreciate. *Touch of Evil* is a reworking of the classic tropes of film noir that performs a meta-critique on abuses of power that occurred in a postwar era that was ready to accept certain ethical losses if they would ensure survival in a nuclear world.

Touch of Evil's self-reflectedness can be seen when it deals with the issue of race. The film continually calls attention to its own politics and in the process signals the viewer to watch the film both as an entry into the vexed question of race that dominated domestic discussions in the 1950s and as a meta-commentary on that discussion. This sort of Bakhtinian, double-voiced discourse serves to raise racial stereotypes in order to critique their artificiality. According to Stubbs, in the novel the hero is not a Mexican at all but a white Anglo-Saxon assistant district attorney. His wife, however, is Mexican. The young shoe clerk who plants the bomb, Sanchez (Victor Millan), is not Mexican, either, in the book. Although there is some treatment of the theme of race in the novel, it is Welles who incorporates the theme of American racism into the film. Thus we have a Mexican character (Sanchez) who lives in the United States planting a bomb made of dynamite stolen in the United States in an American's car while he is with his mistress in Mexico. The car then explodes in the United States, which sends Quinlan into occasional forays into Mexico and brings the Mexican investigator Vargas into America to look into the case, spoiling his honeymoon with his American wife, Susan (Janet Leigh), in Mexico. Welles heightens this sense of fluidity by continually crossing the border with his camera so that we get jump cuts back and forth between Quinlan's investigations, Vargas's investigations of Quinlan, and Susan's tribulations from one side of the border to the other.

Such border crossing would be a model of the sort of openness, diplomacy, and cosmopolitanism that Welles as a historical person stood for, if all of the characters were not so anxious about these crossings. Quinlan is forced to confront his dark past in Mexico in the figure of Tanya (Marlene Dietrich), an old friend from his drinking days who is part madam, part fortune-teller. Vargas is worried about the political fallout of the case and registers this fear almost unconsciously, claiming after the car bombing that "this could be very bad for us." His new wife, Susan, responds, "For us?" and a distracted Vargas replies, "For Mexico I mean." Susan, during her difficulties with Uncle Joe Grandi (Akim Tamiroff) and his relatives on both sides of the border, slips into bigotry, calling one of Grandi's boys "Pancho" and forcing her husband to move her to the (supposed) safety of an American hotel (actually owned by Grandi). The border might be an open space, but its meaning remains ambiguous, at least at the narrative level.

Touch of Evil needs to be seen against the fear of infiltration that characterized the discourses surrounding 1950s containment culture. The anxiety of the Soviet threat was omnipresent, manifested in a world of spies and double agents, covert operations in the Third World, missile gaps, and the space race. Permeable borders were something to be distrusted. Internally, American borders between black and white were likewise being challenged through integration. *Touch of Evil*'s depiction of a border filled with ambiguities also mirrored the racial situation America found itself in during the late 1950s. Although most agreed that something must be done about intolerance in a supposedly free America, how deep that shift would be and whether it should occur gradually or drastically (or for some, not at all) was fiercely debated. By locating itself at a border crossing, *Touch of Evil* plays on those fears, making the anxiety associated with the threat of otherness and difference manifest. The bombing itself is the most obvious example of this fear, a piece of home-grown terror that, despite its being planted "over there" in Mexico, nevertheless comes back home to roost. The plot also has obvious political ramifications when one considers the numerous covert operations the United States was engaged in across the globe in its fight against the evils of Communism. The question of borders was thus a question about how open America should be in the highly volatile postwar period. Welles seems to come down on the side of openness, but the ambiguity of *Touch of Evil* leaves the viewer ample space to question this conclusion.

It is on the meta-level that *Touch of Evil* performs its most effective critique of such isolationism. The film's artificiality openly mocks the idea of closed borders, easy binaries, and obvious conclusions. Welles's character, for example, sarcastically sneers to his colleagues that Vargas "don't look Mexican." The joke, of course, is that he is right—it is the actor Charlton Heston playing a Mexican, a well-known star who would have been immediately identifiable to the audience. Later, Welles again quips with regard to Vargas's wife that "she don't look Mexican either," and he is again correct—she is white. Jill Leeper notes in her article "Crossing Musical Borders: The Soundtrack for *Touch of Evil*" that the film is one in which "the WASPish Charlton Heston and a very well-known German actress, Marlene Dietrich, both play Mexicans, and a Russian, Akim Tamiroff, plays an Italian Mexican American" (233). Of course Welles's own rotund persona would have been equally identifiable to moviegoing audiences from his command performance in *Citizen Kane* (among others), despite his absence from Hollywood. This sort of meta-commentary on the film extracts the audience from the narrative, calling attention to the film qua film and ultimately undercutting any notion of a stable border between on-screen and offscreen. Terry Comito notes that the film slips into comedy, melodrama, and farce and that this instability mirrors the larger visual instability of *Touch of Evil* (31). The film becomes almost camp, as well-known actors take on roles that their stardom does not allow them to play with any degree of reality.

Touch of Evil is not realistic but rather creates a fantasy zone around the Mexican border that breaks the cinematic illusion of verisimilitude. Leeper thus concludes, "When characters are overdetermined by discrepancies between their real-life personas, their filmic identities, their appearances, their voices and accents, and their associated musical motifs, spectators cannot form a simple, sutured emotional identification with those characters" (240). In other words, Welles keeps the border open. Just as the characters jump between Mexico and America, viewers move from Heston the Mexican to Heston the Hollywood star. By calling attention to itself, the film rejects the idea of closed, final meanings. In the process, it subtly argues for a more nuanced view of America, one that questions the sort of "us versus them" binaries that characterized both race relations and foreign policy in the 1950s. Offering ambiguity in the place of certainty, *Touch of Evil* is an attack on binaries in general, binaries that people like McCarthy fostered. The fact that Quinlan is right is not a vindication of McCarthy's methods, only a reminder that nothing, even evil, is so simple.

Welles sets a tone of uncertainty in the opening scene. Much has been made of the famous aerial tracking shot that he employs, but equally important is his use of chiaroscuro lighting effects. We begin with a close-up of the bomb itself, as the killer sets the timer on the device. Welles creates a superb tension in the scene, following the path of the car with the bomb in its trunk as it weaves in and out of traffic and among the frolicking crowds. As Comito correctly observes, "We are not confused, as we are by the opening of *Kiss Me Deadly*. We are disoriented, dizzy. . . . With everything apparently in motion, there is no fixed point of reference by which to chart or rationalize any single trajectory" (9–10). We know there is a bomb about to explode, but Welles's shot gives us too much information, too much to look at and decipher.

This emphasis on motion begins even before the tracking shot as we follow the large shadow that the killer casts against the brick wall when he runs to place the bomb in the trunk. This will be the first of many shadows that occur throughout the film, but its presence in the opening seconds is pivotal. Not only does it invoke the motif of the shadow world of illusion and hidden motive juxtaposed with daytime reality, but its quick movement along the wall sets up the "dizzying" pace that makes Welles's opening shot so effective. The shadow seems to take on a life of its own as its pace outstrips that of its maker. It is also an indication of the haste of the killer set against the mood of a relaxed Friday night. Thus when the aerial shot begins to track the car, its slow pace in relationship to the shadow of the bomber helps create the tension that drives the scene forward. As John Stubbs notes, "Welles changes the dancer's shadow of the screenplay into a gigantic, expressionistic shadow of the dynamiter. Linnekar's convertible moves out of sight momentarily behind a building and then moves in and out of pockets of shadows during its progress to the check point" (34). According to Stubbs, these shadows "unsettle us and play nicely against Welles's refusal to speed up time" (34). The movement of the car as it weaves through the darkness and the light is an apt image for the path that Welles will take us in the course of the film. Oftentimes critics relegate this use of shadows to mere background, such as in Gilles Jacobs's assertion that "what does it matter if the shadow is arbitrary, if the lighting is arbitrary; all that counts is the dramatic illusion thus attained" (qtd. in Beja 169). But critics such as Jacobs who want to view such a use of chiaroscuro as simply a background effect miss the point. Welles is not just creating mood; he is consciously using shadows to create an ancillary world within the frame that he then can use to play against the primary one. These shadows create the gaps and occlusions necessary to demonstrate the ambiguities inherent in the plot.

This use of shadows as markers of ambiguity only heightens when the bomb actually explodes and Quinlan arrives to investigate. As in *Kiss Me Deadly*, the release of light functions in several registers simultaneously. The car's burning hulk illuminates, but not with the light of understanding. On the contrary, it inaugurates the secret that will drive the plot forward. Flashlights and headlights play across the crash scene, trying to shine a ray of light in a random attempt to establish meaning, to define causality in the otherwise incomprehensible moments following the bombing. In the process of the film's unraveling, we will become privy not just to the identity of the killer but also to the "evils" of the various characters. *Touch of Evil*, like the previous films discussed, is ultimately a battle for the control of light. Characters continually move in and out of shadows, or cast shadows on top of someone else, sometimes even forming a clear pattern on another's chest. As Quinlan and his followers gather around the crime scene, their verbal confrontations are doubled by their shadows as the smoke of the fire sporadically darkens their conversation through further shading. This constant doubling and indeed proliferation of shadows not only heightens the confusion of the scene but prepares the viewer for the struggle that will ensue between Quinlan and Mike Vargas, the Mexican district attorney who involves himself in the case.

The use of shadows to mirror ambiguity repeats itself in the scene where Quinlan interrogates his suspect, the hapless Sanchez, the Mexican boyfriend of the murdered man's daughter. The scene is a cacophonous battle for control as a jumble of voices jockey for position, with shadows subtly mirroring this confusion. As Stubbs remarks, "Lighting comes from below eye-level and throws shadows on the far wall, in effect, doubling the number of figures in the room" (34). Thus the uncertainty and disorder of the plot is constantly highlighted visually by a calculated use of chiaroscuro. Welles's camerawork reinforces this unsettling by avoiding the eye-level medium shot that Hollywood uses to generate a "realistic" feel to its films. As Comito remarks, "Quinlan looms up in extreme low angle or is dwarfed in empty space or in networks of light, shadow, and architectural detritus" (13). Later in the film, Vargas convinces Quinlan's followers to question him regarding the dynamite used on his ranch, and again the scenes are claustrophobic and shadow-filled. As they leave Vargas's hotel room and cross a large common area, Quinlan's shadow elongates and then becomes highly defined, standing behind him like a double. The same happens to Pete Menzies (Joseph Calleia), Quinlan's sergeant, who literally stands by him, body and shadow. Finally, Vargas comes out, his shadow less defined but looming over the other two, as he argues with Quinlan. Welles consciously places us in a world off-kilter, forcing his viewers to search for meaning without guideposts. We know from his meeting with Grandi that Quinlan is trying to frame Vargas's wife, just like he framed Sanchez, but we are not sure about his guilt with regard to his other cases, or whether or not he really believes Sanchez is guilty. This ancillary world of distorted shadows is the visual complement to such uncertainty.

In *Touch of Evil*, whoever controls light controls the other characters. This struggle is played out most dramatically in the scenes involving Susan, Vargas's new bride. Welles turns Susan's struggles to free herself from the influence of Uncle Grandi, the brother of the man Vargas is attempting to prosecute in Mexico, as a conscious attempt to control light and its sources. Summoned by one of Grandi's nephews, Susan has her picture taken on the street. As the flashbulb erupts in her face, her "escort" stands next to her in a shot that will later be used for blackmail purposes. Entering Grandi's shop, Susan engages in a heated argument filled with innuendo and threats. Throughout the scene the lights dim and brighten, an indication that we are in an in-between space where the outcome of the encounter is uncertain. Although she escapes, she is clearly unsettled by the meeting. Later, as she settles into her Mexican hotel, Susan attempts to turn the tables on her tormentors in a scene that encapsulates the film's use of light. In the room across from hers, one of Vargas's relatives shines a flashlight in her face, throwing a clear shadow on the wall behind her while he remains hidden in the dark. Susan then turns her own light on, yelling, "See any better this way?" The man continues to illuminate her face with the flashlight, at which point Susan unscrews the bulb and throws it at him. Although she attempts to assert control, Susan is clearly the victim and is saved only when her husband arrives and agrees to take her to an American hotel.

Susan's predicament is presented through an economy of light. She is the passive recipient of illumination, but an illumination so bright that rather than render things understandable they are instead hidden. She is unaware initially that the photo will be used against her, and the feeble attempt to "fight fire with fire" by throwing the lightbulb at her assailant is, within the logic of the film, the wrong way to retaliate. Susan's ineffectuality as a character is demonstrated by her inability to control sources of illumination. Turning her own light on is an attempt to play the game, but it is a losing move—it does not illuminate her antagonist and still leaves her susceptible to his probing flashlight. By throwing the bulb Susan is either making light a literal weapon or attempting to take a higher moral ground, but either strategy is doomed to failure. Without its power to illuminate, the bulb is an ineffectual weapon, and conceding defenselessness is equally useless since no quarter can be expected from Grandi and his relatives. The power of light is that it makes its object clearly visible while rendering its user invisible at the same time, a lesson Susan will repeatedly fail to learn throughout the film.

Susan's inability to control light means that she will have to suffer in darkness. This experience begins in earnest when her husband deposits her in the American hotel. Unbeknownst to both, the motel is actually controlled by Grandi, and it is here that Susan will begin her harrowing descent into "evil." In a scene reminiscent of both *The Night of the Hunter* and *Kiss Me Deadly*, Susan hears a female voice coming from the other room. It beckons her closer, and as she moves to the wall it appears as though she is discoursing with her own shadow (fig. 5.3). The voice asks, "You know what the boys are trying to do, don't you?" In a voice less fearful than inquisitive, Susan responds and discovers that the revelers next door are using drugs. Comito notes that "Susan's whispered dialogue with her own shadow ('What's that got to do with me?') suggests that the most fearful antagonist stirring within the depths of Los Robles is the alien or uncontrollable side of her own sexuality" (23). Like the orphan John and the detective Hammer, Susan's discussion with her shadow can be seen as a peek into the unconscious. This is her honeymoon, and while she certainly does not want the sort of party the Grandi boys are planning for her, nevertheless the mood here is charged with sexuality. She is, after all, a newly married bride awaiting her husband in her motel room. But the sort of consummation she can expect with Vargas is overshadowed by her tormentors, both literally and figuratively. As the rock-and-roll music increases in volume, the Grandi boys enter, casting dark shadows across Susan's face.[9] She struggles to leave the darkening room for the light of the outside, but both the window and the door are blocked by Grandi's nephews. Access to light is denied her. Vargas is equally ineffective. Arriving late to the motel after the party is over and Susan has been abducted, he finds the night watchman sitting in the dark and asks, "What seems to be the trouble? . . . The lights seem to be out in all the cabins." The night watchman responds that "somebody's been monkeying in with the fuses." Of course, the viewer knows it must have been the Grandi boys cutting the lights in order to drug and abduct Susan. Vargas attempts to assert control with his (phallic) flashlight, but it is too late—Susan is already gone.

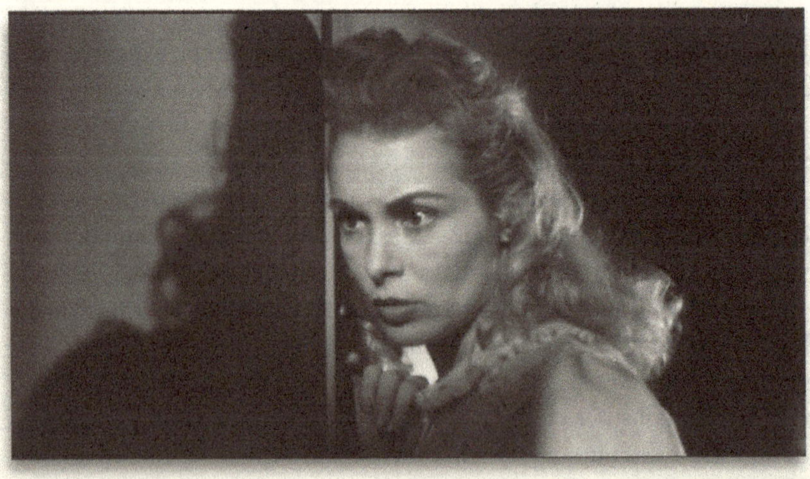

Fig. 5.3. What appears to be Susan's discussion with her own shadow reveals that her curiosity might have less to do with what is going on in the next room and more to do with her own repressed feelings and desires. Frame enlargement from Orson Welles's *Touch of Evil*.

In contrast to Susan, Quinlan displays a more robust understanding of the uses of light and dark. Quinlan plans to frame Susan in order to discredit Vargas, and to cover his tracks he will leave the body of Grandi behind as well. In the final showdown between the two master manipulators of light, we see a drugged Susan lying on the bed of a cheap hotel while Grandi motions in Quinlan from the shadows of the hall. Quinlan's first statement is telling: "Turn out the light," he says. Such nefarious business needs to be transacted in the dark, where only Quinlan and Grandi can see what is occurring. Grandi, his partner, understands this all too well, immediately answering, "Nobody can see up here." As in the scene at Grandi's office, an outside light pulsates on and off, one minute throwing shadows of the two against walls and the next leaving them in total darkness, a visual metaphor of their dark purposes and Quinlan's duplicitousness, even to his partner Grandi. Quinlan commits the murder, and Susan wakes to an image of Grandi's face above her, his eyes bulging as the light alternately reveals and hides his hideous visage. Once again, Susan remains the passive recipient of a constructed scene. William Johnson is only half right when he asserts in "Orson Welles: Of Time and Loss" that it is in a "mechanical pulsing rather than in the light and darkness themselves that the underlying symbolism is to be found" (23). Both work in tandem. This pulsation of light, coming from a source outside the room, becomes the perfect metaphor for the helplessness of Susan. But Welles's use of chiaroscuro is at its most calculated in the final scene of the film. Menzies, finally realizing that his longtime friend and partner Quinlan is guilty of murdering Grandi, decides to help vindicate Vargas and his wife by attempting to get Quinlan to admit to the murder and various framings on tape. This climactic scene is thus one of betrayal. Though an honest cop at heart, Menzies admires and, according to Tanya, even loves Quinlan. He is filled with doubt and remorse at the prospect of tricking Quinlan, claiming, "Hank is the best friend I've ever had." As Welles himself observes in an interview, "The possible ambiguity is not in the character of Quinlan, it's in the betrayal of Quinlan by Menzies" (Comito 206)—an odd statement, given the fact that Quinlan needs to be brought to justice and Menzies is an honest cop and the only one capable of rectifying the situation. But in a film in which every character is tainted, it only makes sense that Menzies, too, must be implicated.

Vargas, on the other hand, betrays not a friend but his own principles. In his attempt to bring Quinlan and his crimes "into the light," Vargas thus far has relied on fair police procedures such as straightforward questioning of suspects and appeals to records and evidence. The idea of sneaking behind someone's back to record him without his knowledge is beneath him. As he tells Menzies, "I hate this machine, spying, creeping . . ." But in *Touch of Evil*, everything happens at night, in the dark spaces where shadows dwell. Daytime is simply a reprieve, a time to solve the problems the film poses in a more rational manner that does not produce results. Menzies and Vargas have to cross the border into the murky world of Quinlan's "game leg" and hunches in order to capture their killer.

Shadows are the visual sign that the principles guiding Menzies and Vargas are collapsing. When we first encounter Tanya earlier in the film, it is by way of Quinlan entering her house through its darkened porch. As Comito observes, Tanya's is a "shadowy portal marking the boundary between two worlds: Quinlan is framed by it as he hesitates, turned to silhouette" (24). In the final scene, Vargas approaches the same door, but this time Quinlan sits inside, bathed in light, while Vargas slinks around in the shadows. Menzies, too, stands in these shades in order to lure Quinlan out. This step into the darkness is important, for it connotes that both characters have moved into the dark world that Quinlan represents. This scene is filled with doublings that undermine the stability of all three characters. Menzies, wearing a wire, follows Quinlan through a maze of shadows that Comito rightly terms a "labyrinth." Vargas, carrying the recording device, then "shadows" Menzies and Quinlan as Menzies attempts to extract the confession. Throughout the scene the characters weave in and out of shadows as they themselves cast another set of shadows across walls and the ground. As Stubbs comments, the scene "has the potential to be visually rich, whereas in the novel, the episode was physically static and almost completely given over to the dialogue" (32). Sound as well as shadow gets doubled—Vargas's recording device produces an echo of Quinlan that causes his "game leg" to surmise that he is being recorded. Shadows function not just as a means to add "richness" to the mise-en-scène; they also provide another layer of commentary on the action of the film. Although Menzies and Vargas are bringing a killer to justice, they are forced to use the same sort of deceit that Quinlan employed to frame his suspects. Thus, like Quinlan, they get their man but at the cost of losing part of themselves in the process. Shadows represent that other world where compromises are made between truth and expediency—a world of hunch, deceit, and a bending of the rules.

This ambiguous result is captured in the title of the film. What exactly does "touch" signify? At the end of the film, Menzies "touches" Quinlan with his bloodstained hand, an act that eventually brings a solitary tear to Quinlan's eye. After Quinlan is shot by Menzies, he looks up at the bridge to see his partner's finger pointing down at him, complete with a shadow doubling the accusation. Quinlan's deceptions have "touched" the lives of many and in the end come back to haunt him. But the title also carries a more subtle message: "touch" refers to the way in which evil insinuates itself subtly into every character, from Vargas's need to sneak around and record Quinlan, to Menzies's betrayal of a dear friend and mentor, to the effects of the story on the honeymoon of Susan. "Touch" also carries with it the sense of adulteration. Everyone has a little evil in them. The bombing, and its subsequent events, unleashes this taint. Susan's slight racism, Vargas's loss of control, and Menzies's betrayal all hint at the fact that, deep down, everyone has a darkness waiting for the right conditions to call itself up. The finale's shadows become the symbol of this "touch" in both of its senses, the place where darkness encroaches on light, clouding and obstructing it. In shadows, the evil lying dormant in the various characters is revealed, even to the last ambiguous words of Tanya, the old fortune-teller friend of Quinlan's who abandons him to his fate and whose epitaph fails to provide the moral closure that would render the film a comment on something—"he was some kind of a man."

It is precisely this sense of uncertainty that shadows represent in all three of these films. Shadow imagery becomes a placeholder for the inconsistencies and paradoxes that defined the postwar world. Shadows' opaqueness reminds the viewer that the simple dichotomies between good and bad, light and dark, that Cold War rhetoric attempted to police was a myth. The darkness that the preacher represents in *The Night of the Hunter* can be exorcised only through even more darkness as the widow must combat the preacher throughout the night before the children can see the light of day. The blinding light of *Kiss Me Deadly* is destructive rather than redemptive. The film's invocation of the nuclear did not calm Cold War anxieties but rather left viewers even more disturbed as to the fate of their atomic world. The shadows of *Touch of Evil* remind the viewer that in the Cold War world, there were no unadulterated absolutes or clear borders. All truth is, at least in part, built on lie and deceit. In all these films, the reality of the world is best represented not by an illuminating brightness but through a shadowy darkness that troubles rather than reassures the viewer. Highly conscious of their expressionist predecessors, these last three great film noirs self-consciously use the chiaroscuro that defines the genre to comment on their Cold War milieu, in the process demonstrating the adaptability of the film noir aesthetic to postwar concerns.

6. A JOURNEY INTO THE SHADOWS

The Twilight Zone's Visual Critique of the Cold War

The use of light and dark as a means to critique the binaries of the Cold War reached its crescendo in what is perhaps the most celebrated television series of all time—Rod Serling's *The Twilight Zone* (1959–64).[1] Aired during the height of the Cold War, *The Twilight Zone* challenged viewer assumptions by forcing its audience to consider the existential, social, and political problems of the day. In order to discuss such delicate matters as nuclear anxiety, racial tension, and suburban conformity, Serling had to refract his messages through a fascinating combination of the film noir and science fiction genres. Imagination became the tool to pry open public opinion. Serling asked viewers to journey into what he termed a "twilight zone" where normal rules and expectations broke down, a "land of shadows" where ideas and concepts were liable to bend and invert. *The Twilight Zone* drew on the shadow imagery running throughout American culture at midcentury to create a subtle, aesthetic critique of Cold War binaries.

The Twilight Zone was a provocative series where thematic content and innovative visual style were mutually reinforcing. Most treatments of *The Twilight Zone* focus on Serling and the thematic content of the episodes. The show was Serling's brainchild, and it was due only to his tireless efforts at both promoting and writing that *The Twilight Zone* achieved its impact and success. Despite Serling's importance, however, *The Twilight Zone* was very much a joint effort, requiring not only the writing skills of Serling and his fellow contributors but also the arresting visual effects developed by the various directors and his director of photography, George T. Clemens. Focusing so exclusively on Serling has shifted criticism toward the thematic content of the scripts. This has lent monotony to academic treatments of the subject. Critics tend to begin with a short biographical sketch of Serling and then move into a set of themes running throughout the episodes, culling examples from the various seasons. This allows discussion to turn toward Serling's intellectual preoccupations and oftentimes draws on his earlier teleplays and his later, mainly problematic, attempts to reassert creative control over his other television and film projects. Such approaches are compelling, but they nevertheless elide one crucial consideration that, given the show's title, ironically goes unnoticed in the scholarship—the look of the show itself.[2]

What makes *The Twilight Zone* unique is that camera and plot work together to create something more than the sum of their respective parts. As J. P. Telotte argues, the series is able to weld the aesthetics of film to the subversive power of its scripts: "It repeatedly demonstrates how those cinematic possibilities might be used in concert with language, how words and images might function together to move audiences in a way that for various reasons most broadcast television in the US had up until that time little explored" (15). In order to achieve this success, Serling had to rely heavily on the expertise of his crew. According to his biographer Gordon Sander, Serling was a very flexible producer. As Sander concludes, "Serling also had total confidence in George Clemens, who, as director of photography, was probably more responsible than anyone else for the distinctive 'metaphysical' look of the show" (163). Contractually obligated to produce 90 percent of the weekly scripts, Serling focused on the writing, and as the show progressed he became even less concerned with his role as producer until the fourth season, when he was actually removed as coproducer. According to Douglas Heyes, who directed nine episodes, including "The Eye of the Beholder," Serling "encouraged you to give your best. Many of the things I tried would not have been possible in any other atmosphere. . . . They worked right with you on the cutting, and it came out the way you wanted it" (qtd. in Sander 153). Serling was certainly involved, but his genius resided in knowing when to let others do their own jobs. Of course as a writer for television, Serling was also acutely aware of the camera when crafting his scripts. Discussing the practice of excessive cutting on the part of some directors in a 1975 lecture at Sherwood Oaks, Serling cited John Frankenheimer as a counterexample, providing an insightful analysis of his shots. Serling was clearly fluent in the vocabulary of cinematography, and his remarks demonstrate that he had an eye for how scenes were put together. Ultimately, however, the uncanny visual feel of the episodes was not solely the result of Serling.

Although shadow imagery can be seen in almost every episode of *The Twilight Zone*, this chapter examines three representative episodes where the use of shadow effects is most pronounced. The pilot, "Where Is Everybody?" (October 2, 1959), employs an extensive use of shadows that sets the tone for the rest of the series. This episode, which has not received the attention it deserves, uses shadows to mirror the psychological breakdown of its protagonist and, in the process, subtly questions many cultural assumptions of the time. "The Eye of the Beholder" (November 11, 1960) has been much more thoroughly discussed, but little attention has been paid to the ways both shadows and chiaroscuro effects create an indeterminate space that prepares the viewer for the episode's celebrated "twist" ending. "The Shelter" (September 29, 1961), though perhaps a lesser-known episode, uses shadow imagery to heighten viewer suspense as a neighborhood is plunged into nuclear Armageddon and to provoke viewers to question their beliefs and assumptions. In all three of these representative episodes, shadow imagery works with plot to challenge the convictions of the Cold War age. The success of *The Twilight Zone* rested on its ability to challenge viewers to reconsider their beliefs and assumptions in a seemingly depoliticized "zone" lying outside the stark realities of the Cold War.

A STRUGGLE FOR THE AIRWAVES

The Twilight Zone's critique of the Cold War was made all the more subversive by the fact that the nascent medium of television had the unique power to reach directly into the homes of millions by the late 1950s and early 1960s. Television was a highly contested domain in the 1950s, and Americans were fascinated by it. Discussing the "scale of the invasion" of television into America's homes, Thomas Doherty, in *Cold War, Cool Medium*, relates that "in 1949 television was a luxurious indulgence in one out of ten American homes; in 1959, television was essential furniture in nine out of ten" (4). With such direct access to the American home and its families, television was poised as a key battleground in the Cold War ideological fight against Communism. Doherty details a series of atomic bomb explosions caught on the small screen to fascinate and terrify an ever-larger number of viewers. Two Los Angeles stations "transmitted the first live images of an atomic blast" in 1951, and more such images were to follow throughout the first half of the 1950s (8–13). Increased viewership also brought on increased fears of Communist infiltration. In 1950, the right-wing journal *Counterattack* issued *Red Channels: The Report of Communist Influence on Radio and Television*, providing a long list of suspected Communist Party members in the industry (or those associated with them) and suggesting that the Soviet Union was plotting to utilize the new media to foment dissent and indoctrinate American citizens (7–8). The era of television had arrived, trailing with it all the hopes, fears, and anxieties of the nuclear age.[3]

Serling was at the right place at the right time. While many established Hollywood actors, directors, and writers shunned what they saw as an inferior medium, television was in its infancy and desperately seeking talent. Serling, with his proven success in the medium during its "golden age," was in an excellent position to dictate terms in this fledgling industry. He began writing early, contributing scripts for the Armed Services Radio while in the military (he saw combat in the Philippines as a paratrooper) and managing the radio program at Antioch College while an undergraduate (Zicree 5). After a stint in Cincinnati doing more radio work, Serling started selling scripts to television programs to earn a living (7). He made his name and career with *Patterns*, a television play that explored the corrupt values of American business and the ethical dilemmas it creates for those who want to succeed. It was produced on *Kraft Television Theatre* in 1955 and made Serling a much sought-after commodity. Serling, though producing a multitude of poor scripts written quickly for money, topped *Patterns* with another hit, *Requiem for a Heavyweight* (aired October 11, 1956). Despite this success, censorship of his work, along with a changing program format, forced Serling to begin looking for an alternative. Although *The Twilight Zone* was never a "ratings bonanza," it nevertheless received immense critical acclaim and garnered a number of industry awards while producing one of the most lasting critiques of the Cold War era (Presnell and McGee 16–17). *The Twilight Zone* would become Serling's masterpiece, making him both famous and rich by the end of the show's run in 1964.

Serling turned to the realm of shadow and imagination in order to avoid the censorship that plagued his earlier work as a writer of television screenplays. Always provocative and challenging, Serling quickly ran into trouble with both network executives and corporate sponsors. In *Noon on Doomsday*, produced on the *United States Steel Hour* in 1956, Serling explored racial prejudice in small-town America with the story of an elderly immigrant grocer's murder by a white townsman. Lawrence Venuti explains that Serling drew inspiration for the story from the case of Emmett Till, "a Negro boy from Chicago who was apparently kidnapped and murdered by two white men after he whistled at a white woman during a visit to relatives in Sumner, Mississippi" (358). As in Serling's story, the murderers were acquitted despite clear evidence of their guilt. Although Serling had changed the details in order to avoid censure, when news of the connection became known, public outcry led to the show's sponsors requiring changes, even though most of the complaints came from "White Citizens Councils" (359). According to Erik Barnouw, such "race-relations stories" were "regarded—by many, including the FBI—as a likely symptom of communist leanings. This explains the extraordinary brouhaha over *Noon on Doomsday*" (50). Discussing the practice of precensorship, Serling declared in his 1959 interview with Mike Wallace that "we just do not write those themes which we know are going to get into trouble" (season 2, disc 5). Television writers of the 1950s like Serling had to be extremely aware of the issues that their scripts raised or else deal with the censorship that went along with the medium. This would not be the last of Serling's teleplays to receive such treatment, but it certainly appeared to be the most egregious.

While Serling's constant battles over censorship and his championing of divergent views would seem to mark him as politically leftist, his politics were by no means exclusively liberal. Serling clearly indicted corporate America and the business culture that forced its employees to either embrace unethical and cutthroat practices or be crushed underneath the juggernaut. He was also a sincere advocate for civil rights. David Cochran observes that Serling, of Jewish descent himself, "occasionally fell victim to anti-Semitism" (199). In addition to his opposition to racial intolerance, Serling also "publically opposed the nuclear arms race" (206). Yet Serling believed in America and its democracy, flawed though it was, as the better alternative to a collectivist Soviet Union. While Serling was "outspokenly critical of right-wing Cold Warriors" and went as far as writing a letter to the pro-McCarthy *Cincinnati Enquirer* in 1954 that stated "not all of us who flinch at McCarthy's methods are Communists, or even Communist excusers," many of Serling's scripts are strongly anti-Communist (201). Cochran uses the apt term "consensus liberal" to describe Serling, though one could argue Serling was simply a maverick who was determined to make his own decisions regardless of what others felt. Cochran relates the interesting anecdote that Serling was "both banned from a non-Jewish fraternity and expelled from the Jewish fraternity for dating Gentile girls" (199). Such Cold War ironies were not lost on Serling and would continue to reverberate throughout his *Twilight Zone* scripts.

In addition to overt censorship brought on by Cold War ideology, Serling faced another problem. By the late 1950s, the nature of television was changing. In the early part of the decade, television was based on the anthology model, with writers contributing scripts that would change from broadcast to broadcast. As Jon Kraszewski notes in his well-researched article "Do Not Go Gentle into That Twilight: Rod Serling's Challenge to 1960s' Television Production," with the postwar American theater struggling, television filled the gap and generated much-needed income and work (345). This "golden age," however, gave way to "series drama" that favored "narrative formula and repeatable characters" (347). *The Twilight Zone* clearly followed the anthology model. Each episode was self-contained and did not build viewership through an interest in characters or situations that repeated themselves across episodes. Rather, what drove interest was the show's format, style, and, ultimately, the appeal of Serling as writer, producer, and recognizable host. When *The Twilight Zone* aired in 1959, only four anthology shows remained on the air, and by the time *The Twilight Zone* finished its run in 1964, none was left (347). Television had a new production model, which favored efficiency and profits rather than quality of output.[4]

While overt political pressure was an issue for Serling, even more insidious was the influence of sponsors on the new medium. Barnouw explains that writers like Serling, Paddy Chayefsky, Reginald Rose, and Gore Vidal produced work that was complex and lacked tidy solutions, whereas "the commercials featured products that solved problems of business and pleasure in a minute or less" (106). Quality shows made the commercials appear fraudulent. The networks instead turned to lighter fare, with recognizable characters and plots meant to build a repeat audience from week to week. Producers, not writers, were now in charge. Discussing this shift from anthology to episodic series, Barnouw explains that despite their critical success, the former "made sponsors restive . . . the dilemmas sometimes had wide social implications, which might make them meaningful, and win critical enthusiasm, but also produced angry letters. With the rise of McCarthyism, organized letter-writing became the order of the day" (106). Serling, in his interview with Mike Wallace, blamed not only the networks, agencies, and sponsors but also the audience, a "wild lunatic fringe of letter writers" who could have a disproportionate impact on shows.[5] Wallace pushed Serling on the issue, asking whether *The Twilight Zone*, too, had come under either precensorship or network censorship, but Serling was clearly hesitant, stating that "because they deal in the areas of fantasy, and imagination, and science fiction . . . there is no opportunity to cop a plea, or chop an ax, or anything." Wallace pushed further, asking Serling if he was not going to delve into social issues, to which Serling confirmed that he was not, though he still considered the show "important" (season 2, disc 5). Serling, exhausted from fighting the network and sponsors, attempted to steer clear of branding himself an iconoclast in the hopes of avoiding difficulties in getting his show on the air.

Creating a "zone of imagination" populated by shadows, *The Twilight Zone* was able to obliquely raise social questions that were not permissible in more straightforward treatments. As Venuti concludes, "Instead of relying on realism to convey his message, Serling embodied it in fantasy and managed not only to avoid the censorship which had plagued his earlier writing, but also to maintain his integrity as a socially concerned writer" (355). Serling opted for an oblique criticism. Describing Serling as one of the "underground" writers and filmmakers of his study, Cochran observes that "the binary oppositions marking the official Cold War paradigm—between, for instance, communism and democracy, good and evil, totalitarianism and freedom—drove out of public discourse darker and more morally ambiguous visions, such as film noir" (217). Serling reintroduced ambiguity by creating a realm that was neither the brightly lit epitome of American optimism nor the darker pessimism of an earlier film noir. *The Twilight Zone* was instead a space where light and dark struggled for dominance, with some episodes ending in an upbeat way and others somberly. Serling made shadows the site of critique, a liminal space of ambiguity where other possibilities could be thought.

SHADOWS IN *THE TWILIGHT ZONE*

Thomas Wartenberg, in his contribution to *Philosophy in "The Twilight Zone,"* discusses the impact that entering this indeterminate realm had on him as a child. Wartenberg explains that after watching "The Odyssey of Flight 33," an episode where a plane gets lost in time, whenever he heard the sound of a plane he could not see he had the disturbing thought that perhaps the plane was Flight 33 from the show. Wartenberg argues that *The Twilight Zone* "destabilizes the distinction between fiction and reality" (125). The use of shadow imagery is essential to creating this destabilizing effect. Wartenberg discusses Serling's opening narration on-screen, commenting, "Although Serling and the stewardess do not both appear in one frame, when Serling appears on the screen we see him partially covered in the stewardess' shadow. The shadow that covers the lower portion of his body and that also appears on the wall is not his, but that of the stewardess who has just walked out of the frame" (132). Here, the shadow itself becomes a "twilight zone" of indecidability. It signals the "real" presence of a fiction character (the stewardess) while simultaneously covering Serling, a "real" person standing on the set of a fiction. In this zone of indecipherability the show does its work, unsettling binaries between the real and the imaginative so that the viewer must reexamine his or her assumptions.

The uncertainty Wartenberg describes is integral to the show's success and is captured both visually in its various openings and aurally by Serling's voice-over introductions.[6] The show utilized several permutations of both, but the consistent thread that binds them all is the conceit that the viewer is traveling to another "dimension." In the first season, Serling locates this "dimension of imagination" in "the middle ground between light and shadow, between science and superstition, and it lies between the pit of man's fears and the summit ["sunlight" in Serling's alternative opening narration for the pilot] of his knowledge." Serling would alter this introduction repeatedly, but the insistence on the journey to a "wondrous land whose boundaries are that of the imagination," as he claims in season 2, would remain consistent. Serling invokes shadows when describing this domain. In an unused voice-over, Serling puts the viewer on a "highway leading to the shadowy tip of reality," while in seasons 4 and 5 Serling explains that "you're moving into a land of both shadow and substance of things and ideas. You've just crossed over into the Twilight Zone." Intangible yet visible, unnerving but alluring, shadows provide Serling with both the dislocating feel he wishes to impart to the viewer and the indeterminate and unstable frame of reference he needs to prepare the viewer to have an open mindset when watching the episode. *The Twilight Zone* is a liminal space where imagination trumps reason, and shadows are instrumental in allowing possibility full rein.

Although critics have discussed Serling's on-camera introductions, little attention has been paid to *The Twilight Zone*'s opening graphics. Here, too, shadows are important for setting the mysterious and uncanny tone that characterizes the episodes. The first season opening begins with what looks like circles of fog, slowly clearing to reveal a set of clouds in a dark sky. As the foggy lines disperse, a flat horizon appears across the middle of the screen, as do rock formations (as in a Salvador Dali landscape) that throw long shadows across a flat ground. As Serling's narration gets to the phrase "pit of man's fears," there is a quick jump cut to a cave that is slowly zoomed in on and then an abrupt shift upward toward the sky as Serling hits "imagination." The viewer then sees a series of twinkling stars while the show's title gradually appears, piece by piece, as Serling concludes with "an area which we call the Twilight Zone" (fig. 6.1). The opening graphics serve to reinforce the show's title by invoking the indeterminate. Shadows, caves, and a twilight sky signal to the viewer that he or she is entering a space both alluring and unsettling.

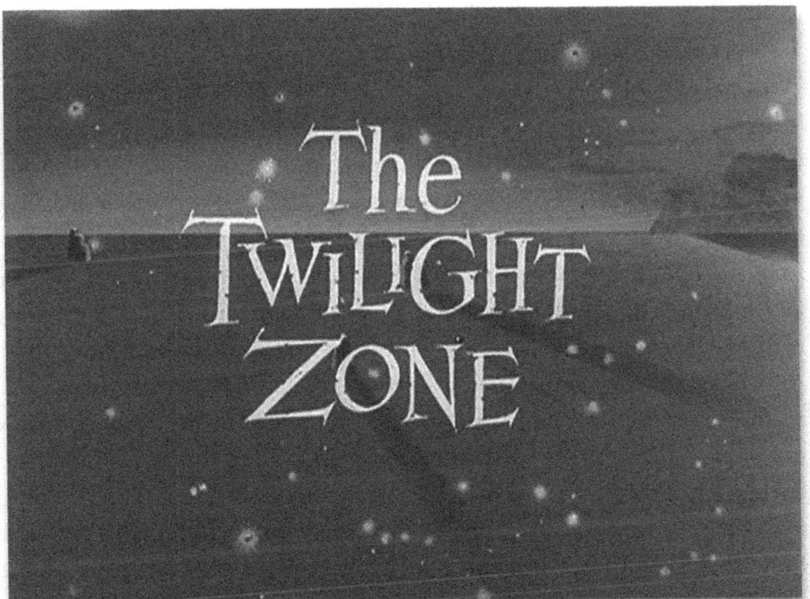

Fig. 6.1. The shadowy graphics of *The Twilight Zone*'s first season set a mood of uncertainty for the episode that would follow and were redeployed as intertitles throughout the show's run. Frame enlargement from Rod Serling's *The Twilight Zone.*

This opening also captures the motif of transition that is crucial in breaking down binaries and preparing the viewer for the sudden switches and juxtapositions that the show uses to make its points. In the second season, the foggy mist separates, but instead of revealing a flat plane with shadow-casting rocks, we instead see a black line slowly traverse the bottom of the screen as an image of the sun appears. As the voice-over progresses, the sun sinks below the black line, the sky darkens, and stars emerge, and when Serling speaks the words "that's the signpost up ahead," the show's title appears, rushes toward the viewer, and splinters. Season 3 employs essentially the same voice-over narration as in season 2, but this time a black-and-white cone spirals away from the viewer as Serling's voice introduces the show. All of these openings, however, bring the viewer into the episode by panning down from the starry sky of the opening into the "reality" of the episode, as if the viewer is being physically transported from the unreal world of the opening artwork into the very real world of the episode's setting. The effect is uncanny, blurring the line between fiction and reality by carrying the viewer on a journey from the darkness of space to the progressively lighter reality of the show's opening scene.[7]

"WHERE IS EVERYBODY?"

The idea of traveling to a disorienting land of shadows as a means of unsettling viewer expectations is inaugurated in the pilot episode.[8] The viewer arrives at the episode in medias res, the camera slowly panning down from the opening credits into the reality of an earthly sky that grows brighter until it reveals treetops and then, finally, a man walking along a road. Serling's trademark voice-over then remarks, "The place is here, the time is now, and the journey into the shadows we are about to watch could be our journey." Serling's characteristic introduction to the episode creates a no-man's-land that draws the viewer into the character's predicament and sets the tone for the anxiety he must face. "Where Is Everybody?" is the story of a man (Earl Holliman) who finds himself alone in an empty town, struggling to remember who he is and how he arrived there. Though written by Serling, the episode is a bit of an anomaly, as it was produced by CBS executive William Self and photographed by Joseph La Shelle (Presnell and McGee 21). Director Robert Stevens, a veteran of *Alfred Hitchcock Presents* (1955–62), had already directed the film noirs *The Big Caper* (1957) and *Never Love a Stranger* (1958) and was thus aware of how lighting effects could influence mood and tone. Though none of these people would continue with the show, *The Twilight Zone*'s classic feel is present at the outset.[9]

The viewer follows the man into a café as he struggles to understand his situation. After realizing that he must be an American since he has American money, the man explains, "There's some question about my identity. Let me put it to you this way, I am not sure who I am." The character addresses the empty café in his longing for self-understanding, a comment not only on the human condition in general but on the specifically postwar anxiety over the isolation fostered by the move to the suburbs and the relentless striving of the executive in his "gray flannel suit." The man finds his way to a town that, as the title suggests, is devoid of people. Heightening this uncanny effect is the fact that the man feels that he is being watched. By setting the episode in a picturesque version of small-town America, "Where Is Everybody?" comments on a vanishing communality. From today's perspective, it is easy to see why nobody is downtown—they are all ensconced in their own isolated postwar suburban homes. While it would be inappropriate to attribute such authorial intention to Serling, who admitted that the idea came to him while touring a vacant studio back lot that he found strangely unsettling, those viewers who had recently experienced this shift in postwar demographics might very well have seen a vacant downtown in just such terms.

In a series of brilliantly filmed scenes, the protagonist confronts endless traces of people but no real "souls": he mistakes a mannequin sitting in a car as a person, receives a telephone call from an unknown figure, and even sees a burning cigar. These absent presences haunt the episode, creating both the mystery that drives the plot as well as an uncanny feeling that invites the viewer into the protagonist's disquieting quest for understanding. He is both desperately trying to find someone to talk to and dreading such an encounter. Staring into the mirror of a soda fountain, the man, in a moment of levity, addresses himself: "Sorry, old buddy, I don't recollect the name. The face is vaguely familiar, but the name escapes me." The mirror image or double is repeated throughout the episode, heightening the uncanny effect of a second self who, in this case, is the protagonist's only friend and confidante. His is an existential struggle to understand this second, shadow self as the only clue to his "true" identity.

The sense of anxiety is heightened by the recurring motif of time passing, exemplified by the man's accidental breaking of a clock in the café and given impetus by the continual chiming of the town clock.

Time progresses, bringing at first shadows and then complete darkness, which serves to highlight his growing fears and precipitates his mental collapse. Images of spatial entrapment reinforce this temporal anxiety. As the camera pans across the town, mimicking the protagonist's point of view, his vision comes to rest behind a chain-link fence, and he steps back, concerned. He almost gets trapped in a phone booth, is unable to find the keys to a parked car, and eventually runs around the town disoriented and stumbling. The irony here is that while the town is entirely his, the character simply wants out, but he cannot find a means of escape.

Shadow motifs are less prominent at the outset of the episode, mainly due to the fact that the show begins in the daytime. But as time progresses and tension builds, they multiply, mirroring the internal turmoil of the protagonist. Entering the local police station, the man goes to investigate the jail, where a single light illuminates the cells and the bars throw shadows across him and the walls. In typical film noir fashion, the image of shadow and darkness reinforces this sense of claustrophobia and entrapment. As he steps into a cell to investigate the running water and freshly applied lather on a shaving brush, the protagonist casts a full shadow on the wall. Muttering to himself, "Time to wake up now, time to wake up now," he glances at his own shadow to see shadows of the cell bars slowly creeping across it and rushes out just before he is trapped in the cell (fig. 6.2). Running out into the light, he comes up to the camera for a close-up and screams, "Where is everybody?" as the show cuts to the intertitle image of the aforementioned illustration of a cave with the show's title lettered across it. Serling equates shadows with the space of imagination, but here they also function as the site of dread.

The original pilot reveals even more shadow play than the subsequently televised version (Bonus Features, "The Original Pilot," season 1, disc 6). After the break, in a shot that did not make it into the final televised episode, the viewer first sees the shadow of the protagonist slowly appear on the sidewalk, turn, and bring his hand to his face for a smoke before a pan-out reveals the man himself quickly looking around in the hopes of catching somebody following him. The protagonist's shadowed double appears repeatedly, but as it is cast against a wall it is difficult to tell if such presences are intentional. But focusing on this cast shadow on the sidewalk as the opening image of the second half of the episode is clearly an attempt to harness the motif in the service of a growing anxiety over the protagonist's predicament. In another scene excised from the televised version, we see the protagonist in a long shot

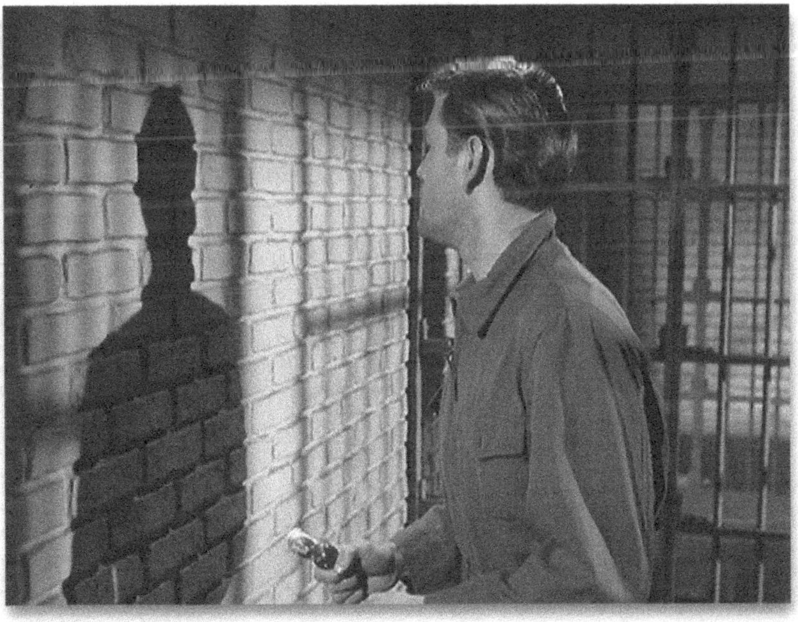

Fig. 6.2. The shadows of cell bars on the walls visually encapsulate the predicament of the protagonist. Frame enlargement from Rod Serling's *The Twilight Zone.*

as he comes out of a deep shadow cast by a building. Watching through the glass of a store, we—the viewers—appear to be the antagonistic other he so clearly imagines exists just outside his vision's periphery (fig. 6.3).

As night falls and the town's lights appear, the protagonist's anxiety increases and the episode races toward its denouement. Entering a movie theater, the protagonist notices a movie poster with a man directing a plane and realizes that he too is in the air force. This joy at self-discovery is short lived, since he immediately begins to contemplate the ramifications of this new fact. As his face becomes shadowed, he muses that there must have been a bomb attack but then corrects himself, since if there had been a bomb "everything would be destroyed and nothing is destroyed." As the film in the theater begins, he rushes to the projection room to see who is running the picture but finds nobody. Hurrying out of the theater, he immediately runs into a full-length mirror in the lobby, effectively colliding with himself.[10] With canted angle shots reminiscent of film noir chases, the viewer follows the protagonist as he stumbles down the now-darkened streets, racing around in a useless attempt to escape his existential predicament.

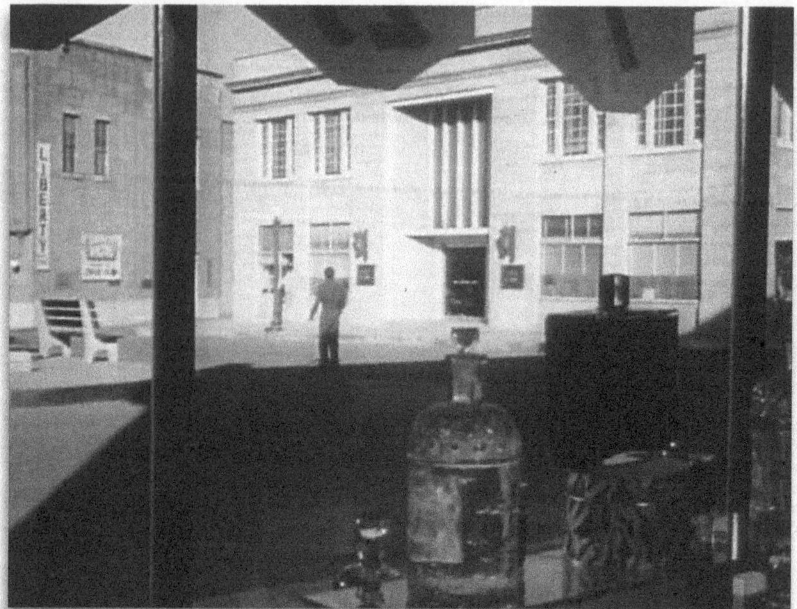

Fig. 6.3. A deep shadow separates the viewer from the viewed as we are invited to occupy the space of an unknown tormentor. Frame enlargement from Rod Serling's *The Twilight Zone*.

The protagonist begins pushing a crosswalk button frantically, exclaiming, "Somebody please help me, somebody is looking at me somebody is watching me please help me." In characteristic *Twilight Zone* fashion, the episode ends with a twist as a jump cut reveals a room filled with men in uniforms watching the protagonist on a large screen. Their faces are in shadow, and in an eerie moment that doubles our own viewing experience, we realize that the protagonist is indeed being watched. The ending then explains all. The protagonist is in the air force, a test subject put in a metal container for "484 hours" in order to simulate the isolation of space flight that he will soon endure. The broken clock in the café is mirrored by the smashed clock within the container, which the protagonist endlessly pounds despite the fact that it is already broken. The crosswalk button is the button he is supposed to push when he cannot stand the isolation any longer. While the military audience within the episode has witnessed only his breakdown, the viewers have seen the hallucination brought on by such isolation. Ultimately, this suffering is redeemed. The general (James Gregory) considers the experiment a success, since it simulates the time it takes to reach the moon, orbit it several times, and return, as he explains to the press. Despite the fact that his "imagination ran away with him," as the general remarks, Mike (as we now know him) looks to the moon as they carry him out and says, "Next time it won't be a dream or a nightmare; next time it'll be for real," ending the episode on a note of hope, optimism, and good old American pluck.

Serling's recuperation of the troubling anxiety the episode produces by placing it within a patriotic theme of American space exploration is characteristic of the sort of displaced social commentary that many of the episodes conduct. *The Twilight Zone* operates in precisely such dichotomous spaces. The uncanny effect of the majority of the episode is not exactly erased by the ending, since despite Mike's optimistic claims, he has suffered a horrendous ordeal and the viewer comes to understand that space travel, while glamorously patriotic, would indeed be lonely and probably unnerving in its isolation and danger. The episode is also strangely complicit in nuclear anxiety. Although it attempts to reassure the viewer that American authorities are capable of rendering such threats minimal, it invokes a postapocalyptic world devoid of people that is the nightmarish outcome of nuclear war. The metal container, for example, has connotations of the bomb shelter, calling up the question of whether survival is even desirable in a deserted, postnuclear world. The episode's own politics is thus as schizophrenic as its protagonist: it simultaneously calls up fears of nuclear destruction while seeming to claim that such fears are necessary for American technological superiority. As with many late film noirs of the period that felt obliged to provide an explicit public warning at the beginning and the end of such unsettling films, the episode's conclusion attempts to smooth over the anxieties created in the episode, but viewers are nevertheless left with an unsettlingly apocalyptic vision of America.[11] Although the first human space flight would not occur until two years after the episode, when the Soviet cosmonaut Yuri Gagarin orbited the earth in 1961, the topic was on Americans' minds due to the Soviet Union's successful launch of the first satellite on October 4, 1957. By yoking the existential theme of loneliness and the Cold War arms race together, the episode makes a salient comment on the anxieties of the age.

"THE EYE OF THE BEHOLDER"

Shadows function through concealment, creating an indeterminate zone that allows many of the episodes' endings to unsettle and disturb the viewer. In perhaps the best-known *Twilight Zone* episode ever, "The Eye of the Beholder," Serling takes on the Cold War issue of conformity. Collaborating with his mainstays Buck Houghton and George T. Clemens as producer and director of photography, Serling enlisted Douglas Heyes, whose credits include the film noir–inspired television series *Naked City* (1958–63), to direct. Serling's team created an episode that examines both the pressure to adhere to social norms and the mechanisms that allow such conformity to be perpetuated. With its use of shadows, "The Eye of the Beholder" forces its viewers to address these issues.

As in "Where Is Everybody?," the camera slowly pans down from the sky to bring the viewer into the world of the show, in this case, a hospital bed with a patient (Maxine Stuart) whose face is wrapped in gauze. An overhead bulb and a desk lamp cast stark shadows as a nurse enters and quickly moves behind a screen, her actions visible by the shadow she casts along the fabric. The introduction here sets up the motif that will govern the entire episode—the viewer never gets to see anyone's face until the end. The patient remains wrapped in a bandage while the doctor and nurses strategically move through shadows and screens, providing only bodies and outlines, with shadow oftentimes addressing shadow. According to Marc Scott Zicree, "To accomplish this, Heyes and George Clemens worked together to block every movement of camera and actor perfectly" (148). Serling himself maintains this conceit when delivering his opening narration in front of the camera. He arrives from behind a screen, an elongating shadow that terminates as he steps out to inform viewers that they have entered "the Twilight Zone" (fig. 6.4). In an emotional interchange with the nurse, the woman, we discover, has undergone an operation to fix a problem with her face. She not only seems troubled by her temporary inability to see but also frets about the outcome of the procedure, explaining, "I never really wanted to be beautiful . . . I just wanted people not to scream when they looked at me." By the end of the episode her face is unveiled—she is beautiful by the viewer's standards but appears grotesquely deformed to the now-revealed monstrous doctor and nurses.

The episode gives us more than simply a comment on social norms. The pressure that the "disfigured" character faces is intensified by a totalitarian regime that reinforces such cultural expectations with political propaganda. Not only does the woman look different, but that difference is proscribed by the government. The viewer gets the idea that more is at stake here than simply fitting in when the doctor complains that "eleven is the mandatory number of experiments; we are not permitted to do

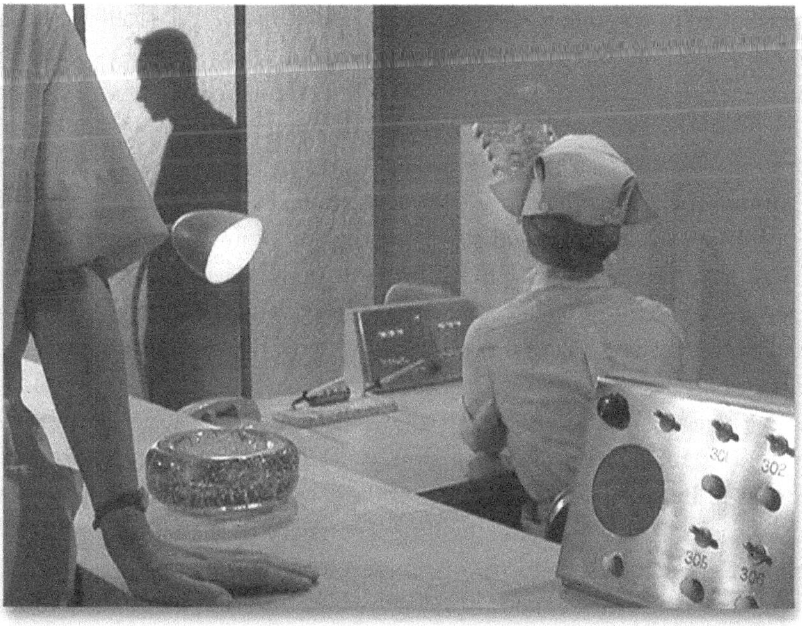

Fig. 6.4. Serling arrives via shadow to deliver his opening monologue to the camera while the nurses look away. The viewer sees their faces only at the end of the episode. Frame enlargement from Rod Serling's *The Twilight Zone.*

any more after eleven." The alternative, as the doctor explains, is for her to live with "people of her own kind" in a special area. She rightly sees this as a form of "segregation," though the doctor claims that there is nothing else to do, and besides, the state has been kind enough to help her try to become "normal" through multiple operations. The doctor, while frustrated and willing to question the rule that everyone must be the same, ultimately accepts this mandate to fit in, as does the patient, who cries on his shoulder, "I want to be like everybody." Later in the program, the doctor and nurse watch their "leader" give a talk about "glorious conformity" on their television screen, and as the patient attempts to escape down the hall, we see the leader, his hideous face now revealed, preach "a single norm, a single approach, a single morality . . ." Social programming has done its job; this is a show not about rebellion but about a character trying desperately to fit in and failing in her attempt.

Serling originally titled his script "A Private World of Darkness," a phrase he redeploys in his opening monologue to the episode. The "darkness" of the alternative title thus comes to represent a mental darkness, a conceptual prison that forces the woman to live in a world of self-loathing and self-hatred. The metaphoric unwrapping of the bandages, though it brings an ever-increasing amount of light, ends in disappoint rather than illumination as she discovers, in the shocked responses of those present, that her face has remained as "hideous" as before. If there is any illumination here, it is for the viewer, who finally gets to see the face of conformity in the deformed visages of the doctor and nurses as the doctor orders, "Turn on the light." The irony here is that, according to the viewer's standard of beauty, the patient is actually stunningly beautiful and the nurses and doctor correspondingly ugly. But the episode is subtle. Though the viewer reacts with a sort of reflexive horror to the repugnant faces (heightening by the jarring tone of the music that accompanies the unveiling), to view the ending as simply an ironic twist where a normally beautiful human has to live in a world of freaks is to miss the point of the episode. Mary Sirridge, in "The Treachery of the Commonplace," observes that "the dramatic revelation scene and Serling's epilogue suffice to undercut the viewer's unthinking assumption that judgments about personal beauty and ugliness are no less objective than other complex perceptual judgments" (69). The viewer realizes that from the nurses' and doctor's perspective, the protagonist really is unattractive, despite the fact that she conforms to the viewer's own standards of beauty. But the ultimate point is a political one, an attack on the idea of conformity to a single standard, law, or ruler. The real problem is that the hospital staff have fallen victim to the totalitarianism of their leader, either due to fear or indoctrination. Even the doctor, who realizes that he is complicit in the functioning of the state and questions its methods, chooses not to rectify the situation.

While Sirridge traces Serling's use of the authoritarian leader preaching a doctrine of purity to the Nazi regime, this figure could just as easily be read into a Cold War context. The episode manages to be a comment both on the anti-Communist hysteria of McCarthyism and on the racism prevalent in a segregated postwar society. Viewers are subtly asked to reevaluate their attitude toward the supposed enemies of America and, closer to home, to rethink their conception of minority groups that may look different but hold the same sort of common beliefs as any other Americans. The use of shadows, then, creates a sort of indeterminate zone that the viewer occupies, breaking down assumptions so that the final revelation can work its effects unburdened by prejudices. Had Serling established any one group as dominant by making its members visually identifiable at the outset, viewers would immediately have ascribed some sort of attitude toward them and thus rendered the ending less effective. But shadows are vague enough to serve as abstract placeholders for a general notion of a "human" devoid of specific characteristics. Thus shadows not only conceal here but create a clearing that opens the way for an unbiased encounter with the episode's denouement.

In tandem with a judicious use of camera angles, shadows allow the suspense necessary for the episode's unveiling to be maintained. Sirridge goes on to ask why the viewer is able to fall for the surprise ending. In order to do so, the viewer must ignore the strange mise-en-scène that makes a point of hiding the faces of the doctors and staff.[12] Sirridge argues that part of this can be attributed to our commonplace assumptions about perception; in the real world, we are often denied such points of view but casually fill in the blanks. The other reason the viewer remains credulous, according to Sirridge, "has to do with the director's fairly heavy use of the visual techniques and familiar narrative types of film noir" (73). The film noir style provides a rationale for viewers, and they are willing to play along. Serling and his crew were certainly aware of the conventions of the film noir genre. For instance, in the sales pitch to prospective sponsors, Serling explained the story "Escape Clause" (November 6, 1959), a tale centered on one character's pact with the devil. Serling is filmed with a low-angle shot and typical noir lighting that casts deep shadows behind him and partially obscures his face in darkness. Pulling a "charred" contract from the file cabinet, Serling's face erupts in bright light as the diabolical nature of the story is reinforced with chiaroscuro in keeping with the narratorial conceit. The whole thing is slightly campy, but the lighting achieves the desired effect, highlighting the sinister nature of the tale. The film noir technique encourages us to accept the diegetic reality.

Yet the shadowy mise-en-scène of "The Eye of the Beholder" does more than just maintain illusion. It visually reinforces the episode's questioning of what constitutes beauty, or any value judgment, by disrupting viewer expectation and positing an ambiguous zone that allows conventional thinking to be challenged. Lewis R. Gordon, in "Through the Twilight Zone of Nonbeing: Two Exemplars of Race in Serling's Classic Series," concludes his discussion of *The Twilight Zone*'s exploration of racial issues with the figure of the shadow. As he rightly observes, "The themes considered in *The Twilight Zone*, including the metaphor of the title, are ultimately penumbral. They are both there and here, but they are also not fully here and there. This is because they are at the edge or liminal points of what we are willing to face. Shadows, after all, can occur where there is also light" (120). Gordon sees *The Twilight Zone* as a useful call to reexamine racial anxiety, a means of thinking about social amelioration through a return to those "penumbral" places that subvert binaries. While Gordon is analyzing the episodes "The Big Tall Wish" (April 8, 1960) and "To Serve Man" (March 2, 1962), his remarks are just as pertinent to that other *Twilight Zone* marathon mainstay, "The Eye of the Beholder." By establishing a "twilight zone" of indeterminacy that is neither light nor dark, shadows prepare the viewer for the shift in thinking that the ending attempts to achieve.

"THE SHELTER"

The use of shadows to signal the dark, occluded side of 1950s optimism occurs in several episodes. "The Shelter" employs shadow imagery to explore the ramifications of a breakdown of the social order. The episode presents the unthinkable—nuclear attack. Serling again partnered with producer Buck Houghton and director of photography George T. Clemens and brought in Lamont Johnson to direct an episode that many critics feel is a bit didactic but that nevertheless employs a forceful use of chiaroscuro to make its point. Johnson, a veteran of *Naked City* and the noir-ish television series *Peter Gunn* (1958–61), complained that the episode's "devices and its general style of writing were a little too pompous" (qtd. in Zicree 227). Sander relates that this episode "was inspired by the then topical atom bomb shelter craze, and one cleric's comment that Americans would be justified in keeping their neighbors out of their shelter during an actual atomic attack" (181). Serling had explored this territory before in the classic episode "The Monsters Are Due on Maple Street" (March 4, 1960), where a peaceful suburban block is thrust into both literal and metaphoric darkness when space aliens tamper with citizens' technological devices. "The Shelter" also pits neighbor against neighbor but uses the trope of the shadow more poignantly to highlight the disintegration.

After the opening title explodes into fragments, the camera again pans down from the starry sky into the "reality" of the episode, in this case a peaceful suburban street. A birthday party is in progress for a doctor named Bill, attended by several couples who are his friends, neighbors, and patients. The happy proceeding is interrupted, however, by a public service announcement that warns of the approach of unidentified flying objects and the civil defense authorities' request that everybody go directly to their shelter or basement. The party disbands amid fearful cries and worried glances, each couple to their own home, and Serling comes on-screen to state, "What you are about to watch is a nightmare. It is not meant to be prophetic, it need not happen, it's the fervent and urgent prayer of all men of goodwill that it never shall happen, but in this place, in this moment, it does happen. This is the Twilight Zone." Aired between the Bay of Pigs fiasco in August and the Cuban missile crisis in October, postwar viewers witnessed a trial run of nuclear holocaust in a neighborhood that was probably very much like their own.

Shadows darken along with motives as the neighborhood becomes prey to nuclear fear, and the American tradition of individualism becomes an all-out rush for self-preservation at all costs. Shadows begin appearing on the walls, the lights flicker, and as Bill and his family enter their shelter, their faces slowly become correspondingly darker. Commenting on such use of chiaroscuro in the show, M. Keith Booker remarks that "numerous episodes had a distinctive film noir look . . . no doubt largely because the hundreds of film noirs made during the 1940s and 1950s had already demonstrated that dim lighting and exaggerated shadow effects could produce precisely the air of mystery and foreboding that *The Twilight Zone* was striving for" (55). The shadows in "The Shelter" produce just such an effect. At this early stage of the episode, the doctor's wife begins to voice some of the concerns of the nuclear age, such as, "Might it not be better to be killed outright than to survive into a world of rubble and death?" The increase in shadows mirror this increase in doubt, and even though the good doctor assuages his wife by arguing for survival's necessity because of their young son, this is clearly the beginning of the "nightmare" that Serling announced in his introduction. Shadows become those spaces where the hidden fears and prejudices of the neighbors emerge, as well as the blank screen where viewers can project doubts about how they would react in such a situation.

Things begin to really unravel when Bill's neighbors arrive seeking refuge in his shelter. Each has his or her own reasons and justifications for inclusion. Jerry, Bill's closest friend and the sanest of what will eventually become the mob, has the newest house on the block. Unfortunately, such modernity does not include a basement. In a heated exchange, the doctor casts his shadow across a pleading Jerry in a dimly lit basement entrance to the shelter. He yells, "I built that for my family," to which Jerry shouts, "What about mine?" Marty arrives with his wife and children as the lights flicker and dim. As he pleads, Marty casts his own shadow against the shelter's door, his shadow self a representation of the "real" personality that is now emerging as social decorum collapses. Marty pleads, cajoles, and then angrily admonishes Bill for failing to let him in. Marty pounds on the door, screaming, "You're a doctor, you're supposed to help people!" Bill, his eyes wide and his face strangely lit against the darkness surrounding them, whispers, "That was a million years ago." Suburban America has retreated, literally as well as figuratively, into a new Dark Ages. Forced to go underground for protection, the social structure collapses as allegiance shifts to oneself and immediate family.

The neighbors assemble, the debris of the night's dinner party providing an ironic contrast to their deliberations as they try to determine their course of action. What little light is provided by candles and flashlights throws stark shadows against the walls. As in the previous scenes, these uncanny doubles mirror the increasing terror of their owners, providing an eerie comment on the hidden sides of their personalities as neighbor turns on neighbor in a final bid for survival. The discussion turns ugly as each family makes a plea for their inclusion in the shelter, Marty claiming that his three-month-old baby needs saving, while Frank, another neighbor, castigates Marty as a foreigner, claiming, "That's the way it is when the foreigners come over here, pushy, grabby, semi-Americans." Shadows crowd on top of each other as the men almost come to blows over the exchange. A strange tribalism prevails. They eventually decide to batter down the door, which ironically would render the shelter useless for everyone. During their discussions, the neighbors are reluctant to seek help from their friend Phil Kline from Bennet Avenue for fear of involving him in the spoils, concluding, "That would get him in the act too, and who cares about saving him?" Marty's wife concurs: "What right do they got to come over here? This isn't their street; this isn't their shelter." This encounter exposes the lie of a "United" States, proving that, in the end, conceptions of community are often a self-serving means of excluding others.

Shadow imagery builds as the hysteria mounts. We see the mob armed with a long length of pipe, shadows following the men and women down the street and into the house as they upset the dinner table and rush into the basement. Just as they break through the shelter door, the lights come back on. The door of the shelter frames their faces as the radio announces that it was all a false alarm. Although the return of light has seemingly eclipsed the literal and symbolic darkness, the damage has been done. The neighbors attempt to return to normal. Families unite, apologies are made, and pleasantries exchanged, but as Bill summarizes, "We were spared a bomb tonight, but I wonder if we weren't destroyed even without it." Even Bill's actions are open to critique. While he is clearly the victim, he must still live with the fact that he would have allowed his neighbors to die in order to save himself and his family. The fact that he is a doctor who took an oath to save lives makes this lapse even more disturbing.

The transition in "The Shelter" from light to dark and back again provides viewers with a chance to experience the potential horrors of nuclear war in the comfort of their living rooms. The episode, however, offers more than a glimpse into the possible outcomes of a nuclear attack. The "fallout" of the nuclear arms race can be seen not only in radiation but in the threat of a dehumanizing fear that unjustly places certain people above others. Though the episode takes place in "the twilight zone" of imagination, it speaks directly to Cold War concerns about the Other. The need to remain "civilized," as Serling comments in his final voice-over, also extends beyond the suburban American neighborhood, since the threat of nuclear destruction links this block with the Soviet Union through the threat of mutually assured destruction. "Neighborliness is international" is one of the implied, if unstated, lessons of the episode. Shadows serve to reinforce this message of tolerance by providing a glimpse into a darkness lying just underneath the surface of a supposedly superior American society. At any moment, that evil can, with the slightest provocation, escape into the light of day.

The Twilight Zone has repeatedly been hailed as one of the greatest television series ever produced. The fact that the show works within the often-maligned genre of science fiction makes these accolades even more impressive. While Rod Serling's writing and tireless promotion of the series is unquestionably a large part of its success, the appeal of *The Twilight Zone* is as much visual as thematic. Strange openings, interesting graphics, and a deft interplay of light and dark are integral to the uncanny feel of the majority of episodes. While shows like *Alfred Hitchcock Presents* and *The Outer Limits* (1963–65) strove to unsettle the viewer in similar ways, *The Twilight Zone*'s ability to weld the shadowy aesthetic of film noir to the science fiction genre created an even more successful version of the uncanny. *The Twilight Zone* demonstrated that big-screen visual effects, when used judiciously, had a place in the small-screen world of television.

The concept of a "twilight zone" of undecidability has entered the American consciousness as a phrase describing an indeterminate, ambiguous space where the normal does not apply and the uncanny reigns. The show launched the term into the popular lexicon with no less a figure than Secretary of Defense Robert McNamara stating in 1962 that "the force of world Communism operates in a twilight zone between political subversion and quasi-military action" (qtd. in Field 1). The success of the term can be traced to Serling's and his cowriters' scripts, which offer strange, twisting tales intended to catch viewers off guard. The visual feel of the majority of the episodes, populated by shadow and chiaroscuro, work in tandem with the show's content to create a world where common assumption is interrogated and oftentimes overturned. The show's use of such imagery creates a clearing for viewers, allowing them the critical space necessary to rethink their beliefs. Shadows, as vague markers of the liminal, are instrumental in this aesthetic strategy, allowing *The Twilight Zone* to deliver a critique of Cold War ideology that resonates straight into the American home.

CONCLUSION

Adumbration, Penumbra, Foreshadowing

Cold War artists were not the first to use shadows, nor will they be the last. The shadow is much too common and ubiquitous to be relegated to a single moment in history. Shadows are a never-ending source of fascination and, as such, will continue to catch the attention of generations to come. But what the artists of the Cold War did bequeath is a particular way of using shadows. Earlier uses typically sought to recontain the unsettling import of a shadow through assigning it a negative value as an absence or by giving it a specific meaning such as a "spirit" or a "soul." The artists of the postwar period, however, used shadows as a productively ambiguous space that questioned rather than answered. Shadows were everywhere in the Cold War, and by folding the anxiety they produced back onto their viewers, these Cold War artists used shadows as a liminal space where thinking could continually be rethought. Shadows became a gap that demanded to be filled, and as each reader or viewer arrived with a new set of assumptions, this gap was in constant flux and renewal. What made shadows so volatile was that the space of imagination they opened up could plummet readers or viewers into an abyss of fear or catapult them into an entirely new mode of thought. With shadows, one never knows which direction the penumbra might take him or her.

The early Cold War use of shadows as placeholders for the indeterminate had a direct effect on how subsequent shadow imagery would be deployed. Individuals in the 1960s tended to reject the black and white of their parents' generation, opting instead for Day-Glo colors and tie-dyed patterns that mirrored the exuberance and playfulness of the era. Despite this brief sojourn, the sobering facts of Vietnam and the real possibility of nuclear destruction meant that shadows quickly returned to public consciousness. Andy Warhol, for example, made his name in the 1960s with a "pop" style that stressed irony, color, and the celebration of quotidian Americana. But Warhol also produced numerous shadow paintings and photographs in the 1970s, including a series of representations called *Hammer and Sickle* (1976–77) that relied heavily on the use of shadows. Warhol placed these two tools in various positions against a white background and then with a strong light photographed the shadows they cast (fig. 7.1). Warhol's use of the symbol is playful and in keeping with his overall pop art mentality that conflates the high

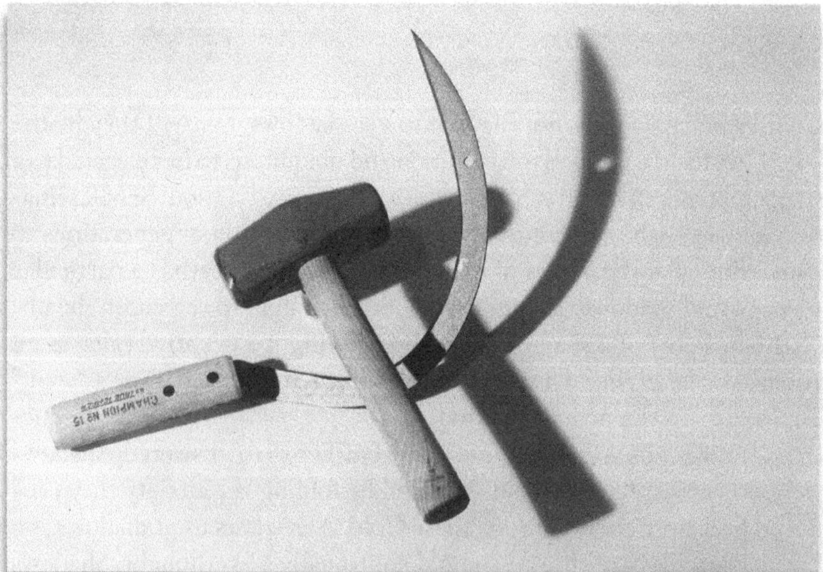

Fig. 7.1. Andy Warhol's *Hammer and Sickle* series utilizes shadow imagery to add a depth that is missing from many of his other works. The shadow stages a number of gaps here that leave the piece an ambiguous comment on the Cold War. Warhol, *Hammer and Sickle*, circa 1977, black-and-white print, 4 × 8 inches. © The Andy Warhol Foundation for the Visual Arts, Inc. / Artists Rights Society (ARS), New York.

and the low. The hammer and sickle, unmistakably laden with Cold War connotations, nevertheless appear next to a pizza, a McDonald's Big Mac container, and even a dildo. The Soviet image, reproduced around the Communist world as a symbol of collective production that adorned flags, monuments, and statues, became just another image to be manipulated.

But shadows, by their very nature, add both literal and figurative depth to the work of an artist generally considered to deal in blank or flat representational models. By doubling the hammer and sickle, the ambiguous shadows invoke the specter of the Cold War in ways that question the seemingly obvious use of this Soviet icon. In a series of notes collected in *Shadows and Other Signs of Life*, Benjamin Buchloh has little to say about these shades, reducing them to elements in Warhol's overall presentation. While Buchloh is correct in reading them as another image that Warhol can manipulate visually, at the same time these shadows speak to the "reality" of the hammer and sickle as objects and to the role of shadows as cultural markers in the Cold War. While Warhol's work usually deflates such gaps by equating every image as consumable product, shadows function as both image and metaphor simultaneously. Overburdened as signifiers, the shadow of a hammer and sickle does more than just comment on the interchangeability of signifiers in a postmodern consumer society; Warhol's shadows serve as a direct reference to Cold War anxieties always lurking just beyond the periphery. While the 1970s was an era characterized by the uneasy rhetoric of "détente" and Strategic Arms Limitation Treaty accords, the possibility for nuclear apocalypse always remained present. Like the examples discussed throughout this book, the shadow of Warhol's hammer and sickle testify to the unease lying just below the surface of American society.

The shadow's ability to question dichotomies made it an important figure for artists of the early Cold War who wanted to call attention to the binaries ruling the atomic age and to the paradoxes they fostered. This use continued in Alan Moore and Dave Gibbons's graphic novel *Watchmen*. The election of Ronald Reagan in 1980 signaled a return to hard-line Cold War policies occasioned in large part by the Soviet invasion of Afghanistan in the same year. *Watchmen* is a direct intervention into the Manichaean public rhetoric of the 1980s. Borrowing what by the mid-1980s had become a well-recognized motif of the haunting shadows left on the remnants of Hiroshima and Nagasaki, *Watchmen* invokes the image of nuclear destruction created in the early postwar period in order to adumbrate the apocalyptic end of the novel's conclusion, where an attempt to forestall an atomic war between the United States and the Soviet Union through a fake alien invasion results in massive destruction to New York City. For some, the silhouettes of the two lovers spray-painted on city walls represent love triumphing over destruction, for others, the futility of human embrace in the face of massive destruction. Reagan posited a return to the "us versus them" world of the early Cold War, claiming in his 1983 "Evil Empire" speech that the struggle against Communism was a moral one "between right and wrong and good and evil." Shadows, however, fold such easy binaries back onto viewers, forcing them to make sense of an image that raises more questions than it answers. *Watchmen* enjoyed a huge popularity and critical success and prompted the wide dissemination of the novel's classic tagline, "Who watches the watchmen?," a statement meant to question the trust placed in leaders like Reagan and Margaret Thatcher who were tasked with maintaining world peace and security. Such a reception demonstrates that Moore and Gibbons's examination of the return to Cold War binary rhetoric struck a sensitive chord.

With the collapse of the Berlin Wall in 1989 and the end of the Soviet Union in 1991, it would appear that the legacy of Cold War shadow imagery had reached its conclusion. Yet shadows linger. With the fears of "rogue" Soviet warheads being sold to the highest bidder and the threat of the terrorist replacing the menace of the Communist, shadow imagery has proven highly amenable to the post–Cold War world. George W. Bush, for instance, repeatedly drew on the image of the shadow when referencing the threat posed by terrorism in the post-9/11 world. In a 2001 speech to cadets at the Citadel in South Carolina, Bush remarked that "when the Cold War ended, some predicted that the era of direct threats to our nation was over. . . . They were wrong. . . . We are fighting shadowy, entrenched enemies" (qtd. in Field 1). Bush would return to this theme in 2003, declaring in another speech about Saddam Hussein that "shadowy terrorist networks are not easily contained" (qtd. in Field 11n7). It is no surprise that Bush, very much an inheritor of Cold War logic, would have recourse to the trope of the shadow. Such appeals demonstrate the unconscious legacy of early Cold War thinking and its mutability to changing contexts and situations. Such use of light and dark ultimately reinstates the binary oppositions that were so prevalent in the early years of the Cold War and that form an irresistible stock of metaphors for post–Cold War rhetoricians.

Shadows, as markers of the occluded and marginal, also continue to reverberate with the racial overtones that characterized their use in the early postwar period. The African American artist Kara Walker has updated the silhouette tradition by creating highly charged racial images from life-sized black paper cutouts traced from shadows. Beginning in the 1990s, Walker produced images designed to evoke "stereotypical images from historical novels, folklore, minstrel shows, cartoons, movies, and even modern-day Harlequin romances" (Williams-Forson 204). These silhouettes rely on racially charged features that allow viewers to quickly locate each figure in its stereotyped context. Such imagery is discomforting in the extreme and made additionally so by Walker's placing them in situations involving "fornication, cunnilingus, defecation, murder, and suicide" (201). The result is a comment on race that is even more troubling for its ambiguity. Given the silhouette's ability to hide extensive information, viewers of Walker's art often have a difficult time assigning a coherent meaning to the stereotypes her figures portray. Such liminality forms the perfect vehicle for raising difficult-to-discuss topics like race. Walker's use of shadow imagery points to a third way—by visually illustrating the paradoxes and difficulties of race in America, her figures allow these topics, in all their disturbing specificity, to again be discussed. I am not arguing that Walker's work is a direct result of Cold War shadow imagery. She draws extensively on a wide range of source material that often predates the sort of concerns we have seen in the Cold War. But Walker's use of shadows to create an indeterminate, liminal space that allows her to generate an anxiety that raises undisclosed issues that would otherwise remain hidden places her use of shadow imagery squarely in the mode we have been examining.

The power of Walker's work is that, like many of the artists under discussion in this volume, it forces the difficult process of understanding racial representation back onto the viewer. Shadows call forth the culturally repressed, forcing the viewer to deal with race and its troubled relation to sex, identity, and nation. We do not see the reality of the "pickaninnies, sambos, mammies, mandingos and mulatto slave mistresses" (280) that inhabit her walls and canvases. Rather, we see our reaction to them. The silhouette's lack of depth and contextual vagueness allow Walker to create the ambiguity necessary to force the burden of interpretation onto her viewers. Such ambiguity ensures that Walker's art will never be simply didactic or give in to easy commonplaces around the topic of race. As Hamza Walker sums up Walker's method, "The work's refusal to acknowledge shame when dealing with issues of race and desire[,] set within the context of slavery, allows Walker to challenge, indeed taunt, our individual and collective historical imaginations" (280). The silhouette form casts its shadow onto the viewer, implicating him or her in the disturbing racial formulations that Walker's work manipulates.

Perhaps the most striking use of early Cold War shadow imagery occurs in David Foster Wallace's novel *Infinite Jest*. Wallace draws directly on earlier shadow imagery to update the paradoxes of the Cold War. One of the plot lines of this purposely ambiguous novel consists of a political discussion between Rémy Marathe, an agent for a Quebecois separatist cell whose superiors believe he is posing as a double agent but is actually betraying them, and Hugh Steeply, an operative for the U.S. Department of Unspecified Services, who disguises himself in horribly unflattering women's attire. Their all-night discussion centers around a film titled *Infinite Jest*, which is supposedly so entertaining that the viewer becomes instantly addicted and will forgo basic human necessities in order to watch it repeatedly. For Marathe, the film encapsulates American desires to be entertained at all costs; he believes that personal sacrifice to something larger than individual desire is essential for a functioning society. Steeply disagrees, arguing that what Marathe calls selflessness is really just the trained response to totalitarianism, and while American self-interest may contain problems, nevertheless the freedom it represents is ultimately more important than the conformity expected from collectivist regimes. The debate, while taking place on an outcropping high above the city of Tucson in the near-distant future, is an updated version of the ideological arguments of the Cold War.

Wallace, however, goes on to explicitly link the scene to the fears of Cold War nuclear apocalypse by invoking the figure of the shadow. The debate begins as the sun sets, focalized through Marathe as "an explosion . . . swollen and perfectly round, and large, radiating knives of light when he squinted" (88). Wallace describes the sunset in apocalyptic terms that call to mind descriptions of the nuclear that we have seen earlier. This brilliant light forms the literal backdrop to their discussions, sending their elongated shadows forward to meet the encroaching darkness of night. Marathe in particular becomes enamored with the inordinately large shadow he casts across Tucson, thinking of it in terms of Goethe's Brockengespenst that the author describes in a footnote as "ghostly light- and monster-shadow phenomenon particular to certain mountains" (994n38). To further highlight the role of such eerie shadows, Steeply arrives as another large shadow eclipsing Tucson that slowly merges with Marathe's own. Set in the American desert, this narrative thread thus recalls both the piercing light of aboveground nuclear testing and the shadows (both literal and figurative) that the nuclear produced, locating this political discussion squarely in a Cold War framework.

Wallace uses this postwar shadow imagery to provide a sort of metacommentary on the novel as a whole. *Infinite Jest*, as its title suggests, is a work that endlessly circles around themes and issues while never fully providing a final meaning or offering the reader closure. In typical postmodern fashion, the novel forces the reader to attempt to assemble the parts into a coherent whole, though such completeness is impossible. Cold War shadows symbolize these aporias. One of the central questions Wallace raises is to what extent citizens should be given freedom in society, especially when they have demonstrated that such freedom leads only to addiction. The shadows that Marathe and Steeply cast over the populace symbolize the power wielded by those covert forces set on determining the outcome of people's lives. The average citizen did not opt for the nuclear bomb; its construction was decided for them. But the vague space of the shadow allows more than one reading. The shadows of these two post–Cold War secret agents likewise open up a space for questioning their motives, allegiances, and actions. Which is right, Marathe's collectivism or Steeply's individual freedom? The novel refuses to answer the question resolutely. Like the ambiguous shadows of the Cold War it invokes, *Infinite Jest* is meant to stimulate thought and open debate, not close it with a solution.

The nuclear detonation that sent bright piercing light racing across the New Mexico desert in 1945 cast a long shadow into the ensuing decades, a shadow that nobody at the time could possibly have foreseen. The late 1950s became fascinated with this light, using it in ways that would be revisited whenever fears and anxieties of the Cold War resurfaced. The power of shadows to disturb our expectations and to provoke our imaginations was not discovered in the early Cold War era; it has been there since humans pondered the enigmatic figures cast by sun and fire. But many of the artists of the 1950s and early 1960s drew on a history of shadow imagery to question a world that both frightened and captivated them. Realizing that the shadow could mean more than simply a false sign or a precarious soul, these artists crafted shadows into images that drew on all these associations simultaneously. They made shadows into a space where fear mingled with fascination, where the banal slid into the uncanny, where assumption bled into awakening. Shadows thus became an opening for the imagination to think beyond the actual. While this meant a letting go of the desire to control meaning, it also meant that readers or viewers could now share the responsibility for coming to terms with their textual experiences. In the process, the world as they knew it and the world they could envision had the possibility to change places.

NOTES

BIBLIOGRAPHY

INDEX

NOTES

INTRODUCTION

Shadows and Their Place in Postwar America

1. Masco, in *The Nuclear Borderlands*, provides a string of such quotes. I. I. Rabi claimed that "it blasted; it pounced; it bored its way right through you. It was a vision which was seen with more than the eye" (57). Emilio Segre thought "the explosion might set fire to the atmosphere and thus finish the earth" (57), while Philip Morrison likened the blast to "opening a hot oven with the sun coming out like a sunrise" (58). Clearly, the atomic test was a watershed moment in history, reducing even the most articulate to cliché.
2. The US military was more pragmatic—archival footage taken by Japanese filmmakers shows physicists recording these shadows and using them to help locate the epicenter of the blast.
3. For an extensive study of shadows and their relationship to the perception of shape, see Baxandall's *Shadows and Enlightenment.* Baxandall offers a discussion both of eighteenth-century theories of visual perception and of modern notions of shadows derived from cognitive science. Sorensen's *Seeing Dark Things* provides a similar account of shadows and the questions of perception that they raise. What is missing in these and other works that address the topic of the shadow is their metaphoric use and its relation to the social. One notable exception is Avery F. Gordon's *Ghostly Matters*, which examines

the concept of haunting as a means to theorize both social life and its study.

4. Given the importance of the shadow in this founding myth of artistic representation, it is perhaps odd that painters have not always been quick to embrace its use. Pliny's tale has found its way into numerous painterly renditions over the centuries, from Giorgio Vasari's *The Origin of Painting* (1573), where a man is tracing his own image, to Vasily Komar and Alexander Melamid's work *The Origin of Socialist Realism* (1982–83), which depicts the drawing of Stalin's shadow on the wall. But as Gombrich notes, many painters "had studiously avoided inserting such shadows, as if they regarded them as a disturbing and distracting element" (19). While techniques of shading lent reality to depicted images and offered painters the opportunity to set moods and tones, cast shadows were often seen as disruptive. For more detailed accounts of shadows in the arts, see Stoichita; Gombrich; and the catalog for the exhibition "La Sombra (Shadows)" held at the Museo Thyssen-Bornemisza in Madrid, Spain, written by Stoichita and several others.
5. In 1757, Etienne de Silhouette was named finance minister of France, but his unpopular programs, modeled on those of England, made him hated throughout the country. A lover of profile cutting, his name became a derogatory term for this cheap form of portraiture (Laliberté and Mogelon 16). Appearing as they did in the Enlightenment period, with its logics of scientific and moral perfectibility, silhouettes also became something to be deciphered. For the Swiss Johann Caspar Lavater, silhouettes became instrumental in his discussions of physiognomy, the science of judging personal characteristics and mental attitudes through the analysis of facial features. The shadow became a condensation of inner nature that led to a more "precise" view of the soul than mere outward appearance could provide. While Lavater's method was presumptuous as well as lacking in rigor, it nevertheless enjoyed a huge popularity.
6. Von Chamisso is not the only one to explore this theme. In his fairy tale "The Shadow" (1847), Hans Christian Andersen describes a man who loses his shadow one evening. Years later, the shadow returns, now wealthy and respectable. As time passes, the shadow becomes healthier while the man slowly withers, until finally a proposal is made—the man can accompany the shadow on holiday, provided he acts as a shadow himself! Nor is this simply a nineteenth-century phenomenon. The motif of selling one's shadow occurs in Lord Dunsany's fantasy novel *The Charwoman's Shadow* (1926), where a young man barters his to a magician during Spain's golden age. In Carl Dreyer's silent film classic

Vampyr (1932), an uncanny moment occurs when a sleeping soldier has his shadow run away from him. Without a shadow, one loses the essential feature of humanity—the soul.

7. According to Martin Jay in his magisterial study *Downcast Eyes: The Denigration of Vision in Twentieth-Century French Thought*, the metaphor of the sun as the "giver of natural light" has "ruled metaphysics from Plato to Descartes and beyond" (509). Jay successfully demonstrates the resistance to such ocular centrism throughout the past century. While Derrida does not provide a wholesale rejection of the primacy of vision, as Jay notes he is certainly skeptical of the privileging of specularity, and thus his investigations into the spaces of light's occlusion makes perfect sense here.
8. Tanizaki's observations, however, do raise concerns. Discussing skin color, Tanizaki comments that "from ancient times we have considered white skin more elegant, more beautiful than dark skin, and yet somehow this whiteness of ours differs from that of the white races" (48). This launches him on a discussion of a particular "cloudiness" of skin in the "yellow races" where "dark, almost dirty, shadows gathered" (49). According to Tanizaki, such people came to prefer the darkness of shadows as a means of hiding this darkness in their very bodies. As we shall see throughout this study, the ambiguity of shadows makes them the perfect place to hide prejudice as well as to inspire its reconsideration. For a discussion of the trope of shadows as they pertain to Japanese cinema, see *The Aesthetics of Shadow: Lighting and Japanese Cinema* by Daisuke Miyao.

1. A FASCINATING ANXIETY
The Paradoxes of Life in the Shadow of the Bomb

1. For writers who did discuss the bomb directly, humor often provided the necessary distance to critique it. Beat poet Gregory Corso uses humor to defuse it in his poem "Bomb," celebrating the bomb's destructive power in a tone that playfully mocks America's fascination and fear. The same strategy informs Stanly Kubrick's 1964 film classic *Dr. Strangelove*, where the powers behind America's defense are treated as ridiculously patriotic, to the point where Slim Pickens actually rides a nuclear bomb to its target, whooping all the way. The famous paradoxes of Joseph Heller's *Catch-22*, such as anyone who realizes they are insane must really be sane, are actually products of the Cold War (see Stephen J. Whitfield's "Still the Best Catch There Is: Joseph Heller's *Catch-22*").

2. While the term "nuclear sublime" appears repeatedly in the literature, discussions of it are scant. See Masco, Hales, and Ferguson for more detailed discussions of the term and its implications.
3. Masco makes the interesting point that with the 1963 Atmospheric Limited Test Ban Treaty, the world lost direct access to the nuclear sublime. According to Masco, "Underground testing replaced a full sensory experience of the exploding bomb (producing fear and awe in the mode of the dynamic sublime) with a more limited form" (71). The underground tests in Nevada limited the sort of physical interaction that was necessary to produce feelings of the nuclear sublime but rather invoked what Immanuel Kant termed the "mathematical sublime," or "a flooding of the senses with overwhelming scale and complexity, rather than physical fear" (71). What they did provide, according to Masco, were huge, perfectly symmetrical craters.
4. Tom Gunning, whose work repeatedly returns to the question of the visible and invisible in media, discusses the fascination such images have for us:

   > The ghostly fascinates us as a complex of two fundamental fantasies. First, it envisions a phantasmatic body, fundamentally different from ordinary bodily experience, whose appearance seems to make us doubt or rethink the nature of our senses. . . . Second, the ghostly represents a fundamental untimeliness, a return to the past not in the form of memory or history but in a contradictory experience of presence. ("To Scan" 117)

   Gunning's observations hold true for these shadow imprints. They offer the viewer an uncanny perception of a vacated body that is both there and not there simultaneously.
5. *Return to Hiroshima* by Betty Jean Lifton and *Rain of Ruin* by Donald M. Goldstein, Katherine V. Dillon, and J. Michael Wenger both include such ghastly photographs. For a sampling of poetry inspired by the bombs, see *Atomic Ghost: Poets Respond to the Nuclear Age*, edited by John Bradley. This work contains several poems dealing specifically with the shadows of humans left in Hiroshima and Nagasaki. Fascination with nuclear apocalypse continues unabashed into the present day—witness the rekindling of interest in the nuclear sublime in the Reagan 1980s as the Cold War was again invoked politically through the "Star Wars" defense system and culturally through movies like *Red Dawn* (1984) or even the tongue-in-cheek *War Games* (1983). This trend continues into the present century; Cormac McCarthy's postapocalyptic novel of nuclear holocaust, *The Road* (2009), became a major Hollywood film.

6. Further complicating matters, as Pavitt explains, this phrase is actually a misquote from Hindu scripture. Oppenheimer himself recalled that these words "occurred to him in a documentary for US television made in 1965" (277n3). Thus there is no proof that he uttered them at the time of the blast.
7. Discussing the Dutch painter (and student of Rembrandt) Samuel van Hoogstraten, Stoichita demonstrates how the use of cast shadows became "demonized" through distortion and magnification. This is an important innovation, since shadows came to be used extensively in caricature to portray the hidden motivations and evil intentions of their caricatured subjects. The menacing shadow standing behind the seemingly benign public figure is a stock visual trope whose origins can be seen as early as the beginning of the 1600s. For an extensive collection of visual images dealing with political propaganda and violence, see Keen's *Faces of the Enemy.*
8. Palpable, yet not monolithic. As Cyndy Hendershot points out in *Anti-Communism and Popular Culture in Mid-century America*, although anti-Communist rhetoric was pervasive in American culture at midcentury, neither was it the sole topic of discussion nor were treatments of the theme univocal. J. Edgar Hoover and Senator Joseph McCarthy might have given voice to its most authoritarian dimension, but such rhetoric was also used as counter-subversive propaganda and parodic plot device (2). Science fiction films, for instance, that deal with the Communist threat create an ambivalent image of Cold War concerns. According to Hendershot, internal domestic issues were also represented, "complicating a simple view of the Soviets as evil enemy" (56).
9. For a fascinating account of how McCarthy's own rhetoric was shaped by postwar ambiguity, see Darsey's *Prophetic Tradition and Radical Rhetoric in America.*
10. Men, too, suffered from the stultifying effects of postwar conformity. The plight of the middle-class suburban male spawned a cottage industry of books that sought to analyze and redress these problems. David Riesman, Nathan Glazer, and Reuel Denney's *The Lonely Crowd* (1950) discussed the shift in the decade to "other-directedness," a term they used to describe people who defined themselves in relation to the group rather than through personal autonomy. Sociologist C. Wright Mills's *White Collar* (1951) explored social alienation in bureaucratic organizations, while the best-selling *The Organizational Man* (1956) by William H. Whyte Jr. examined the shift from rugged individualism to the collectivist ethic in American corporations that led to an empty, conformist life. In addition, Sloan Wilson's popular novel *The Man in*

the Gray Flannel Suit (1955) depicted the difficulties of an ex-serviceman trying to find contentment in a materialist and conformist postwar culture. All these examinations of the problems and plight of America's white-collar workforce were focused on the problem of conformity and the fear of becoming just a faceless shadow, a mere ghost of one's former or potential self.

11. Recent scholarship nuances May's findings while leaving her ultimate conclusions basically intact. De Hart views women and homosexuals in the postwar period not simply as products of Cold War logic but of a "larger, ongoing process of defining America," though she admits that "the Cold War may have given this particular construction of national identity its distinctive coloration" (128) and that "domestic containment is an appropriate metaphor" (130). Meyerowitz's collection, *Not June Cleaver*, takes issue with May's "conservatism-and-constraints approach," claiming that it "tends to downplay women's agency and to portray women primarily as victims," as well as "obscures the complexity of postwar culture" and "sometimes renders . . . other women invisible" (4). Nevertheless, Meyerowitz is forced to admit that "no serious historian can deny the conservatism of the postwar era or the myriad constraints that women encountered" (4). May and critics like her are describing a larger trend that had a vast influence on a huge percentage of white middle-class Americans and also formed an ideological backdrop that those lying without its perimeters likewise had to confront as a pervasive message in the culture.
12. In fact, the difficulties of American race relations were fodder for a Soviet propaganda machine that loved to call attention to the hypocrisies of "freedom." Edwin Marcus draws attention to such efforts in a cartoon titled *Playing It Up*, which depicts Khrushchev projecting a slide called "Segregation Issues" onto a screen. Such paradoxes as inequality in the supposed land of the free were used by the Soviet Union in attempts to discredit US influence abroad and to drive a wedge between various factions domestically.
13. Abel, in her wonderful essay "Shadows," explores the connection between shadow, blackface, and race in the films *The Jazz Singer* (1927) and *Swing Time* (1936). She argues that "'shadow' euphemistically replaces 'nigger' in the shooting script for the film" (166). Increased camera mobility in the 1930s created an abundance of shadows that became a mark of cinematicity itself. Films, cartoons, and musicals began playing with the body as a shadow, yet such figures also had the power to unsettle. Shadows demonstrated perspectival freedom but also "figured the decade-specific fears of deracination, dispossession, and material forfeiture" (169).

14. The literature on the Gothic is vast, but for a more extensive discussion of race and how it pertains to the genre Fiedler calls "a literature of darkness and the grotesque in a land of light and affirmation" (29), see Edwards's *Gothic Passages* along with Goddu's *Gothic America*. Current scholarship tends to take Fiedler as a starting point but oftentimes critiques his work for its emphasis on the psychological nature of the Gothic. These two studies opt instead for historical-cultural approaches to the important role race plays in the Gothic.

2. WHAT THE SHADOWS KNOW

The Return of the Crime-Fighting Hero the Shadow in Late-1950s Literature

1. The exact audience for the magazine is difficult to discern. The Shadow Club, with its decoded messages, was certainly targeted at young audiences, admonishing them to fight crime and obey the law—but advertisements for Gillette razors and shaving cream, tobacco products, Goodyear tires, and Ex-Lax, the "chocolated laxative," obviously addressed an older audience.
2. The Shadow is a prototype of later superheroes, most notably Batman. But he is also a precursor to master spies of the Cold War like James Bond. In one novel, he employs suction cups on his feet and hands to scale a building undetected. The suave crime fighter is likewise fond of gadgetry, like a pen that writes in disappearing blue ink.
3. Subsequent references to specific episodes are from this CD collection.
4. Part of the Shadow's ruthlessness might be seen as a sign of the times. In The Shadow Club, a reporter asks "Lieutenant L——, head of the detective bureau in a large Eastern city," about the profession of criminals. Discussing the use of the "third degree" to get them to talk, the reporter wonders about a rumor that it "isn't dead." The detective grins, "Not by a darn sight" (*Shadow Magazine* 126). The audience is invited to relish the justice that is meted out. Yet the magazine also appeals to the interest in the workings of the criminal underworld, describing, for instance, the "mock courts" held by the inmates themselves to reprimand and discipline each other (124–25). Contempt is mingled with fascination.
5. "The Shadow" was written for submission to literary periodicals from December 31, 1958, until January 7, 1959, while Plath was back in Boston (Ferretter 8, 112). According to Ferretter, despite Plath's dissatisfaction with her work, later stories like "The Shadow" represent "most of her best fiction" (7). Stevenson disagrees. In her biography *Bitter Fame: A Life of Sylvia Plath*, Stevenson believes that "Superman,"

written while at her final year at Smith College, is the better story: "Complaining of lack of ideas, lack of know-how, she wrote a story, 'The Shadow,' a less impressive evocation of her Winthrop childhood than her earlier 'Superman and Paula Brown's New Snowsuit'" (149). Plath herself seemed satisfied with "The Shadow." In her journals, she comments that she had "written six stories this year, and the three best of them in the last two weeks!" (*Journals* 307). Plath then proceeds to list them, and while "The Shadow" does not appear to be one of those "three best," she nevertheless appears upbeat and considers the story a product of her "magnificent sense of space, creative power, and virtue" (307). Plath was clearly interested in the trope. Ferretter notes that Plath also wrote a short story titled "Shadow Girl" in September 1961 about a woman who lives under the shadow of her father and is led out of that shadow by her lover (10, 162). The story was rejected by the women's magazine *My Weekly* in the following year, however (158).

6. Gothic and camp are not the only generic categories applicable to Kerouac's novel. As the subtitle makes clear, Kerouac considered his work to be "Faust Part Three." This classic German legend tells of a scholar who sells his soul to the devil in exchange for knowledge. But Kerouac supplements this Faustian tale with still other myths. The Snake can be read through the dominant influence of his early years, French-Canadian Catholicism. Within a Catholic schema, the Snake is clearly satanic, a fact that the text itself repeatedly claims. But *Dr. Sax* is also infused with Aztecan mythology. The novel ends with

   > Written in Mexico City,
   > Tenochtitlan, 1952
   > Ancient Capital
   > of Azteca (245)

   Discussing the figure of the snake in Aztec mythology, Nicosia remarks that "the serpent Quetzalcoatl is regarded as both the destroyer of earth and the messiah of enlightenment. In a similar way, instead of struggling with dualisms, Kerouac unites them in the play of images" (404–5). Whereas Catholicism pits good against evil, light against dark, here these binaries are united in a single figure. According to James T. Jones, such imagery is also indebted to a Hindu myth of a serpent residing under Mt. Meru (*Jack Kerouac's Duluoz Legend* 51). Such myths helped to resolve the dualities in his Catholicism without challenging the basic tenet of a supreme force benignly watching over the world.

7. Reviews were dismal. David Dempsey, writing in the *New York Times*, claimed the novel "runs the gamut from the incoherent to the incredible,

a mishmash of avant-gardism (unreadable), autobiographical (seemingly Kerouac's) and fantasy (largely psychopathic)" (qtd. in Maher 392). The review is overly harsh, but there is a kernel of truth. Meandering through different styles with difficult authorial perspectives, *Dr. Sax* is not the most accessible read. Barnaby Conrad of the *Saturday Review* concurred, calling it "stupefying in its unreadability" (qtd. in Maher 392). According to Charters, Kerouac's editor Malcolm Cowley described *Dr. Sax* as "an exercise in self-abuse" (Kerouac, *Selected Letters, 1957–1969* 68) in a Viking Press memorandum. Kerouac's own position is clear. In a letter to Lucien Carr a few years after *Dr. Sax* came out, he called it the "greatest book I ever wrote, or that I will write" (Nicosia 410).

8. While care must be taken not to push the connection between text and life too strongly, the disappointment the novel registers about the adult world echoes Kerouac's personal state at the time of writing. The text reverberates with biographical detail. The campy discussions of "blood" can easily be read in terms of Kerouac's own rising addiction to alcohol, as well as his stated use of marijuana throughout the writing process. Carrying several "unpublishable" masterpieces around in his suitcase, it is not too far a stretch to read the older narrator's disillusion with the world and his weariness as Kerouac's own. Jackie's entry into sexuality had, for the 1952 Kerouac, become somewhat jaded. Writing to Neal and Carolyn Cassady in May 1952, Kerouac discusses his meanderings around the city while writing *Dr. Sax*, including visits to "Organo the new whore street" where, he explains "to my sorrow in having to confess, there was a 17 year old girl name Luz who induced me to go upstairs with her" (*Selected Letters, 1940–1956* 359). If Mexico was a Cockaigne offering cheap liquor, drugs, food, and women, it also demonstrated the exhaustion of debauchery and just how far Kerouac had traveled from his innocent boyhood beginnings.
9. For a more detailed discussion of Kerouac's writing of memory into the present, see my book *Capturing the Beat Moment: Cultural Politics and the Poetics of Presence*. In chapter 4, I detail how Kerouac's spontaneous prose method seeks to reactivate the past in the present in an intermediary zone of "becoming." *Dr. Sax* is particularly effective in this regard, but some of Kerouac's later chronicles tend to stabilize narrative in an act of wistful remembrance.
10. William J. Harris, in his important work *The Poetry and Poetics of Amiri Baraka: The Jazz Aesthetic*, draws a sharp divide between Baraka's first collection and his subsequent work, stating, "Although the title *Hard Facts* only applies to one of Baraka's books, it suggests the direction of all his poetry after *Preface*. He wanted an art of hard facts that would

expose the evils of money, power, and luxury and would drive the black sane, that is, into political action" (94). In contrast to these "hard facts," Harris sees poems like "In Memory of Radio" as flights into "imagination" (50) rather than into reality. Jerry Gafio Watts, in *Amiri Baraka: The Politics and Art of a Black Intellectual*, discusses Baraka's lack of political commitment, bypassing "In Memory of Radio" altogether and concluding that "a bohemian, Jones was much more interested in the deviance of personal identity and the psychic costs" (51). Werner Sollors, in *Amiri Baraka / LeRoi Jones: The Quest for a "Populist Modernism,"* suggests that despite claims that Baraka abandons the earlier style of *Preface*, such "interpretations do not go far enough in explaining Baraka's pervasive use of popular mythology, both in his early poetry and in his literature of Black nationalism and Maoism" (53).

11. While "The Death of Nick Charles" and "Duke Mantee" include shadow imagery, the poems "The Bridge," "The Clearing," and "Symphony Sid" use such imagery to particular advantage.
12. Although care should always be taken to avoid equating the speaker of the poem with the biographical author, this distinction was challenged by the autobiographical nature of postwar writing. As Harris notes in reference to Baraka, "'I' in his poems is a fairly close approximation for himself. Rejecting the persona, he substitutes an autobiographical speaker" (40). Following Harris, this study identifies the speaker of Baraka's poems with the author himself.
13. Yet there are other possibilities. Lacey, in his work *To Raise, Destroy, and Create: The Poetry, Drama, and Fiction of Imamu Amiri Baraka*, reads this first line as evidence of camp. Baraka was indeed influenced by the New York School, and the use of such an exalted word like "divinity" to describe a radio character is reminiscent of Frank O'Hara's overenthusiastic tribute to movie stars like Lana Turner. But to read this line as camp is to denude the poem of its power, to strip away the realization that the final lines work so hard to create. Turning "Love" into "evol" is indeed a bit tongue in cheek, but this campy process does produce the revolutionary discovery that lends the poem its force. That evil hides within love is certainly not a mundane revelation.

3. TAKING BACK THE SHADOWS

Allen Ginsberg's and Jack Kerouac's Struggles to Reclaim the American Unconcious

1. These two authors also employed the term "Shroudy Stranger" as well as "Shrouded" or "Shroudy Traveler." For convenience, I will mainly use the Shrouded Stranger when referring to this figure.

2. Again problems in publication history arise. While the *Empty Mirror* version is undated and the *Gates of Wrath* poems are dated 1949, in *Collected Poems: 1947–1980* (as well as in the later *Collected Poems: 1947–1997*) Ginsberg provides more specific dates (and places) for both. These two early volumes now form a single section, collating Ginsberg's early work from 1947 to 1952. "Please Open the Window and Let Me In" has been updated from "1949" to "Paterson, May 1949." The *Gates of Wrath* version of "The Shrouded Stranger" is now "New York; 1949–1951," while the *Empty Mirror* version is dated "Paterson—New York 1949—September 1950." The *Empty Mirror* version comes later in *Collected Poems*, but its new date makes it clear that Ginsberg was still working on the *Gates of Wrath* version *after* he had given up on "The Vision of the Shrouded Stranger of the Night." While the *Empty Mirror* version seems to signal the final word on the Stranger, based on the dates included in both volumes of *Collected Poems*, it appears that Ginsberg was still working on a version of "The Shrouded Stranger" into 1951. To complicate matters further, in a February 25, 1951, entry, Ginsberg includes an earlier version of the first stanza from the *Empty Mirror* version, and in a May 3, 1952, entry he is still admonishing himself concerning the Shrouded Stranger despite the fact that he will no longer go on to write any more versions of the poem (*Martyrdom* 377). Despite this confusion, what remains clear is that the Shrouded Stranger was the central poetic concern for Ginsberg during the late 1940s and early 1950s, and he would continue to reference the figure throughout his life, such as in his sound recording of *The Gates of Wrath*'s "The Shrouded Stranger" on *The Lion for Real* (1989) and in his inscriptions to his works made for his fans. In a final twist, we know from the last page of the *Gates of Wrath* manuscript that its later publication was a matter of luck and circumstance—the manuscript "disappeared" in the early fifties and was miraculously returned by Bob Dylan in 1968, seven years after *Empty Mirror* appeared (56).
3. Ginsberg repeatedly refers to the line "shadow changes into bone" to discuss the role of concrete language in conveying meaning to a reader. In his letter to John Clellon Holmes, for example, Ginsberg states, "The phrase 'Shadow changes into bone' sums up the whole business" (*Letters* 50). In an October 1950 letter to Neal Cassady, Ginsberg discusses the death of his friend Bill Cannastra, who was killed while trying to climb out of a moving subway car, using the same lines, claiming, "Those who invite a shadow bone are those who possibly do not realize the seriousness of life and death, the depth of bone . . . the fact that you can't play around with nonexistence and ambiguity" (*As Ever* 71).

4. Although Kerouac does not mention it, another possible source is William Rimmer's painting *Flight and Pursuit* (1872). The painting depicts two figures running parallel to each other through an Orientalist building rich in detail. The figure in the foreground appears human, while the one in the background appears more ghostly, shrouded in white with an arm concealing his face. Both figures cast shadows in front of them, but off to the painting's right there are two more shadows that seem to suggest other figures hidden beyond the frame. Rimmer's title is ambiguous—it is unclear which figure is in "flight" and which is in "pursuit." It is impossible to know for certain whether Kerouac saw the painting or not before his Shrouded Stranger dreams (the painting was part of a Whitney Museum of American Art exhibit in New York, November 5–27, 1946, as well as part of an exhibition at Boston's Museum of Fine Arts from January 7 to February 2, 1947 [www.mfa.org]), but the similarities are striking.
5. Bloom's own Modern Critical Interpretation series includes an edition of *On the Road*, but against the critic's wishes, as the introduction to the work makes brutally clear.
6. Hunt ultimately stresses the oral nature of Kerouac's innovative style, and while he does not deal with the figure in *The Textuality of Soulwork*, the many discussions of the Shrouded Stranger that Kerouac maintained with Ginsberg may have played a role in Kerouac's desire to capture his performance on the page as well.
7. Jentsch reads shadows as uncanny precisely because of the slippage between the literal and imaginative that they call to mind.

   > The effect of the uncanny can easily be achieved when one undertakes to reinterpret some kind of lifeless thing as a part of an organic creature, especially in anthropomorphic terms, in a poetic or fantastic way. In the dark, a rafter covered with nails thus becomes the jaw of a fabulous animal, a lonely lake becomes the gigantic eye of a monster, and the outline of a cloud or shadow becomes a threatening Satanic face. (13)

   The uncanny is produced when boundaries break down, when a shadow becomes a satanic face or a shroud veils a figure in secrecy. Freud dismisses such an explanation, opting instead to read the uncanny "back" into the reminder of a repressed fear or desire. Where Freud sees ancient reminders, Jentsch sees an uncertainty of outline.
8. Critical response to *The Uncanny* has tended to focus on the rhetorical and narrative elements of Freud's paper. According to Hélène Cixous, Freud is haunted by the difficulty artistic works pose for his theories

and by his desire to be an artist himself. In her "Fiction and Its Phantoms: A Reading of Freud's *Das Unheimliche* (The 'uncanny')," Cixous reads Freud's text as a "strange theoretical novel" (526). Neil Hertz, in the chapter "Freud and the Sandman" in his book *The End of the Line*, problematizes Freud's use of figurative language. Samuel Weber's "The Sideshow, or: Remarks on a Canny Moment," which defines the uncanny as a "certain indecidability which affects and infects representations, motifs, themes, and situations" (1132), likewise has problems with the Freudian account's desire to ascribe a final meaning to Hoffman's polyvalent text. Further critics could be mentioned (see especially Bresnick's "Prosopoetic Compulsion: Reading the Uncanny in Freud and Hoffman" and Royle's *The Uncanny*), but the main point is that all read the uncanny as ultimately irreducible to a single narrative. As Martin Jay claims in "The Uncanny Nineties," the concept "has become a master trope available for appropriation in a wide variety of contexts" precisely because of its adaptability (20).

9. Ginsberg and Kerouac were not alone. The figure of Freud loomed large over the 1950s. The Second World War had sent a larger number of European analysts to America in order to escape the Nazis, and by the 1950s psychoanalysis was well established. But America was also receptive to this new trend—the American military, for example, used psychiatrists to "weed the psychologically unfit from the armed forces and to treat returning veterans from war neurosis" (Beaty 24). Such successes led to an overall trust in psychoanalysis, and by the late 1950s the discourse of psychoanalysis could be heard in influential magazines like *Life* and *Time*, on the movie screen, and even in everyday life in the street. For American intellectuals, Freud quickly replaced Karl Marx as the leading theorist at midcentury (Hale 291). Stalinist purges and the attack on Communists led by Joseph McCarthy (among other reasons) led to the discrediting of Marx in the 1950s, and Freud, an Austrian Jew who had fled the Nazi regime, lacked such negative associations. Thus no less a figure of the liberal intellectual establishment than Lionel Trilling pronounced Freud "the prime mover of modernism" in his 1955 book *Freud and the Crisis of Our Culture* (Robinson 2).

10. Although the name of Sigmund Freud can be found in many critical studies of Ginsberg, Kerouac, and the Beats in general, for the most part Freud and his work are given cursory treatment. Freud is brought in either to demonstrate larger cultural trends current at the time or simply as a foil against which Beat spontaneity can demonstrate its rebelliousness. A notable exception to this rule is James T. Jones's *Jack Kerouac's Duluoz Legend*, which reads Kerouac's corpus into the oedipal

myth that Freud likewise employs. While Jones is concerned with examining how Kerouac turned the oedipal elements of his life into prose, here I am more interested in Freud as collaborator, as Ginsberg and Kerouac react to his ideas in order to work through their poetic strategies at this nascent stage in their careers.

11. Kerouac and Freud also differ in their location of censorship. In Freudian terms, repression occurs in the space between the unconscious and the conscious, as the censor has to shield the latter from the disruptive tendencies of the former. Kerouac, however, sees repression occurring at the level of consciousness—we willingly inhibit our impulses in order to conform to preestablished social modes of thinking. Direct access to the unconscious, for Kerouac, is both possible and desirable.
12. Tony Trigilio, in *Allen Ginsberg's Buddhist Poetics*, offers an excellent discussion of the connection between Ginsberg's dreams and his Buddhist practice. Trigilio examines how later dreams of his mother, Naomi (along with the Snowmass Incident), became the basis for the poems "White Shroud" and "Black Shroud." At this stage of his career, Ginsberg had yet to discover Buddhism, and his struggles to make sense of the Shrouded Stranger took place in more of a psychological framework.
13. Kerouac's and Ginsberg's insistence on leveling distinctions can be seen in their discussions of their own writing processes. Trading Freud for his pupil Wilhelm Reich, these writers use the embodied concept of orgasm to help explain the effects their writing is trying to achieve. For Freud, libido is what spurs the artist to create. Rather than find an outlet in sexual activity, desire becomes sublimated into artistic creation. Ginsberg and Kerouac make that connection literal—writing is ejaculatory utterance. Reich took issue with Freud's idea that the curing of neuroses in patients required them to accept their hidden desires, no matter how troubling they may have been. On the contrary, Reich focused on the body, arguing that the orgasmic moment itself had the power to heal, to burst through repression and create a healthy, functioning individual. Ginsberg and Kerouac are squarely in the Reichian mode. Writing is not obliquely disclosing the deeper causes of neuroses—it is instantaneously expelling them in a moment of catharsis. For a more detailed discussion of the metaphor of orgasm in Beat works, see the third chapter of my book *Capturing the Beat Moment: Cultural Politics and the Poetics of Presence*.
14. Schadenfreude enters into the exchange as well. In "The Visions of the Great Rememberer," Ginsberg provides a series of lengthy notes on his rereading of Kerouac's *Visions of Cody*. As the narrator and Cody (Neal Cassady, aka Dean Moriarty of *On the Road*) enter Mexico City,

he relates the dream of the Shrouded Stranger, only this time "there is a dream of a little golden road, a house, a treeshade, the which Shroudy inhabits in the disguise of my mother and then projects himself over to a shade across the shimmering heat coming after me. . . . This is the city the Shrouded Stranger denied me, he smothered me to death in his dress" (Kerouac, *Visions of Cody* 384). Ginsberg's comment contains a hint of glee as he remarks, "But the shrouded stranger's his Mother, he's smothered by the shroudy stranger's 'dress'!" ("Visions" 426). It is almost as if Ginsberg, with a more masculine stranger, wins the battle of the shroud he fights with Kerouac. In the novel, Cody provides yet another gloss, claiming it could be "the eternal husband coming back to peek at the tortured lover who stole his wife away" (*Visions of Cody* 312), an allusion to Fyodor Dostoyevsky's 1870 novella *The Eternal Husband* as well as to a 1946 film based on Dostoyevsky's work.

15. The failure of Jung's followers (and perhaps of Jung himself) to address his own shadow—his alleged anti-Semitism and the difficulties of his dealings with the Nazi Party—is the subject of much debate. In *The Jung Cult*, Richard Noll goes so far as to argue that Jung "set out to design a cult of redemption or renewal in the period beginning as early as 1912. This was a mystery cult that promised the initiate revitalization through contact with the pagan, pre-Christian layer of the unconscious mind" (141). As his title suggests, Noll is critical of this project and castigates previous researchers for ignoring the historical conditions of Jung's work.
16. Jung appears in several essay collections devoted to the Beats. Bartlett's *The Beats: Essays in Criticism* contains several references to Jung. This Jungian viewpoint allows Bartlett himself to see Kerouac's work not as evidence of neurosis but as a marker of the numinous. Albert Gelpi's contribution, "Everson/Antonius: Contending with the Shadow," discusses the Jungian shadow in the work of Christian poet William Everson. Freud likewise makes brief appearances in several articles in the collection. In his book *The Daybreak Boys: Essays on the Literature of the Beat Generation*, Stephenson discusses the Jungian shadow in the context of Lawrence Ferlinghetti's book *Her*, as well as in Kerouac's *On the Road*. Stephenson sees Dean as "Sal's shadow, and in a larger context, the Cassady figure may be seen to represent the shadow of postwar American society" (158). In her article "ruth weiss's Desert Journal: A Modern-Beat-Pomo Performance," collected in *Reconstructing the Beats*, Nancy M. Grace does note the importance of both Freud and Jung to weiss's poetics. And in the same collection, Belgrad notes in "The Transnational Counterculture: Beat-Mexican Intersections" that

the work of Jung "had significant impact both on the Magic Realists of Latin America and on the avant-garde in the United States" (34).

4. THE GHOST OF HUMANISM
The Disappearing Figure in Postwar Photography

1. There is some evidence that Steichen wanted to push social issues a bit further. For example, he had also wanted to include a photograph of a lynching titled *Death Slump at Mississippi Lynching* (1937) by an unknown photographer. It was included in the opening but was removed due to an overwhelmingly negative response (Bezner 162).
2. For a comparison of Frank's work to Steichen's *Family of Man* exhibit, see Eric Sandeen's *Picturing an Exhibition: "The Family of Man."*
3. Ken Takata disagrees. In "Towards an Elegance of Movement—Walker Evans and Robert Frank Revisited," Takata draws on Todd Papageorge's 1981 book *Walker Evans and Robert Frank: An Essay on Influence* to argue that these two photographers are actually more similar than most critics believe. Takata takes issue with critics who generally contend that "the grain and blur of Frank's photographs, the deep and concealing shadows that dominate his photographs, have identified the presence of secrecy and illegibility that run through his work" (55). Takata instead maintains that "what connected Evans and Frank . . . was not just an embrace but a way of documenting the connections between people and their most common possessions that revealed how deep those connections were. And common to both also was that element of incongruity, idiosyncrasy, shock, obscenity, and surprise" (63). Evans can be shocking and surprising, while Frank is capable of quiet dignity. But Takata gets too involved in such equivalencies, failing to acknowledge the validity of the larger picture he criticizes. There is something very different about these two. Moreover, Frank often directly references his mentor, photographing in ways that are clearly a rejection of Evans's aesthetic, as in the barbershop photograph.
4. The photograph was eventually published in his autobiographical book *The Lines of My Hand*, which first appeared in Japan in 1972. *Wall Street* predates his Guggenheim Fellowship period and does not appear in later editions of Frank's work. Critical thinking on *The Lines of My Hand* sees the book as a personal, rather than social, work. Greenough claims that the photographs in *The Lines of My Hand* were selected "not so much for their historical or aesthetic value as for their personal importance" ("Blowing" 320). Brookman concurs, stating that "the fundamental power of Frank's art came primarily from his personal

response to his own experiences" (325). *Wall Street*, while perhaps personal, clearly invokes the Cold War conditions of its production with its reference to the American flag and General MacArthur. Regrettably, permission to reproduce the Robert Frank photographs discussed here was denied by the copyright holder.

5. Frank is fascinated with images of American political figures. In a photograph that made it into *The Americans*, a picture of Ike is posted next to a tuxedo in a shop window. The contact sheets also include photographs of Eisenhower's and Nixon's framed portraits hanging in front of what appears to be another window display of mannequins. *The Americans* even includes a pair of portraits of Washington and Lincoln hanging in a Detroit bar.
6. The ability that graininess has to detract from the presentation of the human is powerfully conveyed in another photograph from *The Americans*. A film actress is in a crowd of onlookers. We see the crowd of mostly feminine faces in clear focus. Their faces display a range of emotions—happiness, wonder, pride, and awe. They are the faces of the "average" person on the street, not unsympathetic, but not outstanding either. In the foreground we have the blonde actress in a dress wearing what looks like a beautiful necklace. But Frank has left her in grain, and while the larger details of her face are indeed visible, we are denied the nuances that make a face an individual. She ironically becomes a type, an "actress," while the lesser-knowns in the crowd behind her have their particularities and expressions registered and recorded.
7. Both this introduction and Evans's was rejected by the French publisher, but Kerouac's piece made it into the American edition, albeit not in the original form he had intended. The first, spontaneous introduction was dropped in favor of a longer, revised one (Greenough, "Disordering" 137–39).
8. Selection, of course, is everything in photography. The contact sheets included in *Looking In* indicate that the photograph Frank selected was only one of a series of fifteen shots he took of the elevator. In the others, passengers appear unblurred and, in many, the elevator girl is smiling and even posing for the camera. Given that Frank had a wide range of possible options, his choice to include blurred and grainy photographs speaks to a decision on his part to produce a more somber book.
9. Klein ultimately chooses to remain ambivalent about photography's role in capturing the world. Klein explains that a camera "can do lots of things, but it can do no more than it can do. It can show what things look like, not necessarily what they are. . . . It can be anything" (qtd. in Heilpern 18). Is there something sinister in the man's smile, or is

he truly a great father taking his son out for a game? The photograph can hint at possibilities but never will be able to answer such questions, according to Klein.

10. In the case of people behind glass, the photographer interposes a distance that calls us to observe and be fascinated but not to feel. The photography of Louis Faurer also employs this grainy effect, and as early as the late 1940s Faurer was taking shots of partial reflections in windows. But Faurer never entirely loses the documentarian impulse. The same can be said of Roy DeCarava. In *The Sound I Saw: The Jazz Photographs of Roy DeCarava*, we have figures put in shadow, out of focus, in an attempt to "see" the "sound" of the musicians. Rejecting more social or documentarian styles, DeCarava employs abstraction to convey the African American experience in a compelling and sympathetic manner. But DeCarava's use of such techniques never reaches the level of Klein, and his work overall sympathizes with his subjects. For both Faurer and DeCarava, the use of grain, blur, and shadow is seen as having more of a social purpose, one meant to celebrate the subject rather than to attack it.
11. Many of these photographs are undoubtedly "mistakes." But while blur, grain, and overexposure might not have been the focus of the picture, the choice to retain a mistake tells us that the image generated does indeed say something important. In his later edition, Klein claims that the shot of the girl and boy remains "one of my favorites" (*New York* 11). Klein explains that they were dancing as the sun was going down and he captured them with a "slow shutter speed" (4), crediting this picture with helping introduce him to chance and accident. Klein shot in near darkness or with flash using a long exposure, sometimes not even aiming in order to see what chance collected (Heilpern 16). In the end, however, he had the final decision about what to print and what to discard. The desire to use "flawed" photographs demonstrates that the aesthetic under discussion spoke to the cultural condition of the postwar years. Klein may have been simply looking for a new style, but this style was a necessary corrective to the idea of the "straight" photograph that preceded it.
12 Vettel-Becker's critique is more concerned with the particularly male viewpoint of Klein rather than with the larger social critique he might be making. She links his use of blur not to Cold War anxiety but to an attack on the feminine that must be overcome in the name of masculine order. Such pictures we have been examining thus come to signify an "alienating sea of matter" that, coded as feminine, the male photographer must negate (83). She writes, "Klein's body is absent, yet it is

everywhere, for it is signified by the photographs, which serve as physical evidence of his movement through space. The blurred shot is the most profound trace of this movement" (84–85). Vettel-Becker sees Klein as objectifying New Yorkers in a bid for control—though the gaze of the camera always creates an anxiety that the photographer, too, might likewise become objectified, and thus feminized. Thus Vettel-Becker links the moment of the shutter to ejaculation, as the photograph attempts to "impose order on chaos, to fix matter without representing its own matter" (85). Both readings work, though here I am more interested in the metaphors his pictures create rather than in what they might tell us about postwar masculinity.

13. *Life Is Good and Good for You in New York* was followed by *Rome* (1958), *Moscow* (1961), and *Tokyo* (1962). Though all of these books strove to capture the faces and images of a city, none of these later works was as abrasive or as stylistically challenging as *Life Is Good*. In addition to his fashion photography, Klein would go on to make several satirical avant-garde films, including *Who Are You, Polly Maggoo?* (1966), *Mr. Freedom* (1969), and *The Model Couple* (1977).
14. Meatyard was also an avid reader of such postwar avant-garde luminaries as Jack Kerouac, Henry Miller, Allen Ginsberg, Gary Snyder, Charles Olson, and Louis Zukofsky (Tannenbaum 35). He also counted among his friends Christian theologian and poet Thomas Merton, environmentalist Wendell Berry, and poet Denise Levertov. Meatyard was especially interested in William Carlos Williams's book *Paterson*, which, according to Davenport, he read while driving.
15. Meatyard makes this masking of the human face literal in his last series of photographs. As early as 1953, Meatyard began work on photographs that portrayed his family and friends, dressed in masks and props, amid the ruined antebellum mansions of the Lexington area, which led to one of his more famous series titled *The Family Album of Lucybelle Crater*. Although Young reads these scenes as an emphasis of "the similarity of people when their differences are gently erased" (introduction 12), one could argue that the masks' erasure of personality is not "gentle" at all. In fact, the *Lucybelle Crater* series produces a highly uncanny effect, as the faces of the posed subjects are all made both interchangeable and horrible.
16. Between 1967 and his untimely death from cancer in 1972, Meatyard also worked on an environmental project that recorded the effects of development on the Red River Gorge. At the same time, he was also experimenting with a new form that he called "Motion-Sound," photographs made "by moving the camera slightly to engage a sense of

movement" (Young, introduction 12). When the process is applied to human subjects, the result is disturbing. Describing a Motion-Sound picture Meatyard took of Wendell Berry, Tannenbaum relates that "Berry's body seems to be disintegrating; his head has already disappeared into the inhospitable rocks that cover the ground. Berry was actually laughing when the photograph was taken, but instead he appears as a dead man caught in the process of abandoning the materiality of the body" (37). In yet another self-portrait, Meatyard appears to be moving into the frame from the left, but the use of the Motion-Sound technique doubles him so that a faint image of his face appears to be leaving his body. In capturing motion, Meatyard produces photographs that depict subjects as a series of ghosts.

5. THE BATTLE OF LIGHT AND DARK
Chiaroscuro in Late Film Noir

1. Film noir, as a highly contested term, is itself no stranger to ambiguity and uncertainty. As the name implies, "film noir" was originally a French conception. According to Porfirio, the term was coined by Nino Frank in 1946 and comes from the "Série noire," a series of crime novels started in 1945 by the French publisher Gallimard and edited by Marcel Duhamel (119). The French saw the "noir" in film noir, the cynical darkness that has come to be one of its defining elements, but attempts to define the exact characteristics of film noir would prove futile. There are certainly classic film noir elements, such as fixed character types like the detective or the femme fatale, narrative patterns such as murder mysteries or unhappy endings, and stylistic features like chiaroscuro, but these elements can be combined in such a dizzying array that the term loses any value as a defining concept.
2. Naremore disagrees. For him, this change had more to do with the political situation of individual, leftist filmmakers than with a larger mood of repression. According to Naremore, the Left, "demoralized by Truman, the atomic bomb, and the HUAC investigations," responded with fatalistic films, and thus "the atmosphere of death and disillusionment in *The Asphalt Jungle* and most other crime pictures of its day has relatively little to do with the nation as a whole, and a great deal to do with a specific community that could no longer maintain its Depression-era faith that America would someday evolve into a socialist democracy" (130). Nevertheless, it is difficult to imagine that the impact of the trials would not have been internalized by those in the industry, leading to less risk-taking as an inevitable result of precensorship by producers and directors.

3. The origins of this style, like the origins of the term "film noir" itself, are vexed. The vast majority of critics point to the expressionist cinema of the 1920s, which flourished in Germany's Weimar Republic. There are, however, some problems with this claim. One antecedent that is largely ignored is the Weimar *Strassenfilm*, or street film, examples of which include *The Blue Angel* (1930), *M* (1931), and *The Street* (1923). These films were part of a movement termed the "Neue Sachlichkeit" or "New Objectivity" and focused on social reality rather than on Gothic expressionism of mood. According to Mark Bould, the sense of determinism inherent in Weimar culture continued in the American film noir context and is as much of a legacy for film noir as expressionist cinematic effects (32). Another argument against expressionism as the sole or even main origin of film noir's effects was that Hollywood already had a history of using expressionist techniques. Marc Vernet has maintained that such lighting techniques existed well before the arrival of European émigrés in early American cinema, most notably in the Gothic film. A final influence worth considering is French poetic realism as it occurred in the 1930s, whose lighting prefigures film noir but without the harsh chiaroscuro that came to embody the film noir style in America.
4. John Alton, a cinematographer who began work as a lab technician in the 1920s but went on to shoot many of the most memorable film noirs ever made, does Naremore one better in his classic study *Painting with Light*. Alton asks his audience to visualize the following scene: "The room is dark. A strong streak of light sneaks in from the hall under the door. The sound of steps is heard. The shadows of two feet divide the light streak. A brief silence follows. There is suspense in the air. Who is it? What is going to happen? Is he going to ring the bell? Or just insert a key and try to come in?" (56). Alton, a master at crafting with light, demonstrates that a small bit of illumination and shadow can speak volumes.
5. The German reads, "Die Todessymbolik des Schattens in der Antike und dem Christentum wurde von der Literatur der 'schwarzen' Romantik adaptiert und fand über diese Verbindung Eingang in den deutschen Stummfilm. Schatten als Vorboten des Todes oder als Symbol einer tödlichen Bedrohung erscheinen dort immer wieder."
6. As Spicer claims, "Robert Aldrich had a copy of Borde and Chaumeton's *Panorama* on the set of *Kiss Me Deadly* with him" (43). Clearly aware of film noir history, *Kiss Me Deadly* goes on to exploit that knowledge in order to craft one of the more self-conscious noirs produced in the period.
7. Thus the irony of the poem that Christina references and that ultimately leads Hammer to the key buried inside her body that opens the

locker containing the "great whatsit"—Christina Rossetti's "Remember." In a condensed and slightly amended version, Hammer repeats the penultimate couplet in order to discover the clue: "But if the darkness and corruption leave / A vestige of the thoughts that once we had." The "darkness and corruption" indeed leave a "vestige": her own body, which houses the key to the locker. But the film performs an inversion of the poem's meaning. Although it is titled "Remember," the poem advises forgetting the beloved. But it is hard to believe Hammer will ever forget, after what he endures at the end of the film. The "darkness and corruption" will remain, even as the light threatens to engulf them. Hammer confuses the physical, literal meaning of the message (the actual key inside her body) with the poem's more obviously metaphysical import (remembering her "soul").

8. The analysis presented here is based on sound engineer Walter Murch and producer Rick Schmidlin's 1998 restoration.
9. Leeper also demonstrates how the soundtrack for *Touch of Evil* reinforces the themes of the film. She claims that Henry Mancini's decision to use "race music" (i.e., rock and roll and jazz recordings) in the film was very new for the period and that the hybridity embodied in these recordings mirrored the sort of transgressions that were occurring in the film in general. According to Leeper, the soundtrack "reveals contradictions, increases the spectator's sense of discontinuity, exposes the construction of identity and ethnicity (both at the filmic level and in a broader social sense), and, in general, increases the awareness of the apparatus of filmmaking" (227). In other words, the soundtrack works to support the themes of the film, disrupting our assumptions regarding borders, in all of their senses.

6. A JOURNEY INTO THE SHADOWS

The Twilight Zone's Visual Critique of the Cold War

1. All episodes, interviews, and commentaries by Serling referenced here, unless specifically attributed to another source, can be found in the DVD box set titled *The Twilight Zone: The Complete Definitive Collection* (Image Entertainment, DVD, 2006). As the box set is divided into seasons that are themselves divided into a series of disks, I will reference both in the citations.
2. Emblematic of such treatments is Worland, who argues that "many *Twilight Zone* and *Outer Limits* episodes exude the dominant political ideals and broad social anxieties of their time, reverberating Cold War America in the Kennedy era" (104). While this is accurate, he confines

his analysis to cursory treatments of the plots of several episodes he connects to Cold War problematics. This lack of rigorous, in-depth analysis and disregard of visual stylistics is unfortunately endemic in the criticism. Hill goes a bit further, examining the ways the show's "reflexive turn" is able to "examine the potential of genre TV as an agent of contemporary myth" (111). Still, Hill's analysis, though more subtle, remains uninformed by extensive visual considerations. A notable exception to this trend is Telotte, who examines filmic aspects of the show. He argues that unlike most dialogue-driven television, *The Twilight Zone* is acutely aware of the cinematic gaze and employs it in ways that reinforce theme.

3. Television, however, was a volatile new medium. It opened the door to a broad array of opinions and talent, as Doherty's book makes abundantly clear. But it could also turn on its users, as Senator McCarthy himself discovered when the medium that helped propel him into the limelight televised his downfall: "The arc of McCarthy's political influence begins with a speech in Wheeling, West Virginia, in February 1950 and concludes definitively with his televised immolation at the Army-McCarthy hearings in June 1954" (Doherty 13). Everyone from President Eisenhower to Bishop Fulton J. Sheen saw the opportunity in a medium that could reach directly into people's homes, but not everyone was able to master this powerful new mode of communication.
4. Kraszewski argues that by making himself both producer and writer, Serling attempted to keep alive the old model of production and to protect himself from the incursions of the show's executives. Serling was able to take on this feat because of the money he made adapting his anthology work to the big screen and Broadway productions (349). Unfortunately, Serling had a difficult time holding down both writer and producer positions. In order to meet his schedule, the Ashley-Steiner Famous Artist talent agency brought in Buck Houghton to coproduce, allowing Serling to do his writing but also to remain coproducer and thus retain control over his revision of his own scripts (358). Serling also hired more writing help. After an open call for scripts produced an unworkable volume of material, Serling hired Richard Matheson and Charles Beaumont. With a later addition of George Clayton Johnson and Earl Hammer Jr., this team of four would script the majority of the *Twilight Zone* episodes. Ultimately, Serling could not keep up with either his production or his writing duties, and when unsettling charges of plagiarism had to be settled, "CBS executive Boris Kaplan cut Rod Serling's role as script supervisor for the series so that he could dedicate more time to writing" (361).

5. Fearing such product boycotts, sponsors and ad agencies moved quickly to ensure that nobody was offended, particularly those in the South. Serling himself sardonically relates that the script for *Noon on Doomsday* "was gone over with a fine-tooth comb to delete any possible reference to the South or southern thinking. . . . The extent of the fears was such that . . . the director was pointedly told to keep Coca Cola off the set" (Venuti 359). It was precisely such excessive scrutiny that led Serling to produce *The Twilight Zone.*
6. Serling's famous presence as on-screen narrator begins in the second season. During the first season, only his voice is heard. Interestingly, Serling was not the first choice for the position. As Presnell and McGee relate, "In early screenings of the series pilot, the narrator's rumbling voice belonged to Westbrook Van Voorhis of the *March of Time* newsreel fame, but his elocution just wasn't right. Interestingly, Orson Welles was then considered as narrator," but Welles and the producers could not reach an agreement with regard to salary (19). These on-screen appearances by Serling have now become iconic and even in his day made him instantly recognizable.
7. Seasons 4 and 5 forgo the pan down from this galaxy into the episode's beginning scene. They also employ yet another opening. This more familiar introduction begins with the background of a starry sky as a door, a window, an eye, the equation "$E = mc^2$," a painter's mannequin, and then a clock become superimposed upon it. Although these seasons do contain some interesting episodes, they are generally considered weaker than the first three of the show's run. The show experimented with a longer, one-hour format in the fourth season that proved disastrous to Serling's writing style. Moreover, for reasons of economy, the show switched temporarily to filming on tape, which destroyed *The Twilight Zone*'s interesting use of chiaroscuro effects. By the fourth season, Serling was distancing himself from the show. Though he continued to write, he involved himself even less in the show's production, preferring instead to lecture at Antioch College. Thus I have chosen to focus on episodes from each of the first three seasons, when the show was at its height and under the same producer, Buck Houghton.
8. "Where Is Everybody?" is actually the fourth pilot Serling wrote for the show. According to Don Presnell and Marty McGee in their history, Serling first submitted "The Time Element" in 1957, a story about a time-traveler who tries to warn authorities about the Japanese attack on Pearl Harbor (12–13). Although CBS purchased the script, it was not aired until a year later because executives were wary of the science

fiction format. Much to their surprise, the audience loved it, and the *Westinghouse Desilu Playhouse* "received more phone calls, telegrams, and letters for 'The Time Element' than for any other drama CBS ever aired" (13). Serling had planned on using the story as his pilot, but after it ran, he wrote "The Happy Place," which was rejected by CBS as too depressing. Serling pitched another story, "I Shot an Arrow into the Air" about "a young boy, a social outcast, who forms a bond with another outcast, a visitor from outer space," but executives considered the episode too weak to serve as a pilot. Serling, after a "summer vacation spent brainstorming," offered them "Where Is Everybody?" (13).

9. According to producer William Self in an audio commentary to the episode, Serling asked Self to continue as producer, but due to other commitments he declined, recommending Buck Houghton instead. Self said he believed the pair would work well together: "Rod would create the episodes, and Buck would know how to put them on film."
10. Mirrors and shadows as markers of anxiety over identity are also used to superb effect in the classic episode "The Dummy" (May 4, 1962), where a ventriloquist struggles to free himself from his dummy and alter ego, Willy. This fight for control of identity between the two takes place in the in-between world of reflection and shadow, where Willy eventually triumphs in an uncanny reversal of man and puppet.
11. Serling's written story, which he claimed he liked better in a Sherwood Oaks College lecture, retains the confusion of identity. While in the pilot we realize beyond a doubt that the protagonist was suffering from a delusion, in the story Serling has the character take a ticket stub from the theater, only to find the exact stub in his pocket after he leaves the isolation booth. In his typical self-deprecating manner, Serling was unfairly critical of the episode, claiming it could have been a knockout given two weeks to shoot but that the production had only six and a half days (season 1, disc 5). According to Zicree, by television standards, *The Twilight Zone* was given an "extremely generous schedule: one full day of rehearsal plus three shooting days" (35). Yet Serling repeatedly complained about temporal constraints. Speaking of the television writer's craft in another of his Sherwood Oaks lectures in 1975, Serling explained that "you don't have time to perfect," grumbling that, apropos of the episode "The Mighty Casey," with *The Twilight Zone* there was little time in which to revise his scripts. According to Serling, the network "doesn't want it good, they want it Thursday," implying that they cared more about the money than about the quality (season 1, disc 4).
12. The show's use of chiaroscuro is malleable. In another episode that explores conformity and state power, "The Obsolete Man" (June 2,

1961), the librarian Wordsworth is called to defend his existence before a menacing state magistrate. In a scene whose lighting is reminiscent of German expressionism, Wordsworth steps back into the shadows to hide but is called forth into the light to receive his fate. Sentenced to die, the viewer discovers that Wordsworth has set a trap for the magistrate by forcing the official to accompany him in his study as he waits for his televised execution—by bomb. A meta-commentary on television itself, Wordsworth bellows, "Let the whole country see how a member of the state dies—step into the light!" Here shadows signal concealment while illumination becomes the metaphoric space of disclosure.

BIBLIOGRAPHY

Abel, Elizabeth. "Shadows." *Representations* 84 (Autumn 2003): 166–99.

Abrams, Nathan, and Julie Hughes, eds. *Containing America: Cultural Production and Consumption in Fifties America.* Birmingham, UK: Birmingham UP, 2000.

Alton, John. *Painting with Light.* 1949. Berkeley: U of California P, 1995.

Annas, Pamela J. *A Disturbance in Mirrors: The Poetry of Sylvia Plath.* New York: Greenwood, 1988.

Armstrong, Stephen B. "*Touch of Evil* (1958) and the End of the Noir Cycle." *Film Noir Reader 4.* Ed. Alain Silver and James Ursini. Pompton Plains, N.J.: Limelight, 2004. 133–44.

Axelrod, Steven Gould. *Sylvia Plath: The Wound and the Cure of Words.* Baltimore: Johns Hopkins UP, 1990.

Badger, Gerry. "From Humanism to Formalism: Thoughts on Post-War American Photography." *American Images: 1945–80.* Ed. Peter Turner. New York: Viking and the Barbican Art Gallery, 1985. 11–22.

Baraka, Amiri. *Conversations with Amiri Baraka.* Ed. Charlie Reilly. Jackson: UP of Mississippi, 1994.

———. *The LeRoi Jones / Amiri Baraka Reader.* Ed. William J. Harris. New York: Thunder's Mouth Press, 1991.

———. *Preface to a Twenty Volume Suicide Note.* New York: Totem Press and Corinth Books, 1961.

———. *Transbluesency: The Selected Poems of Amiri Baraka / LeRoi Jones (1961–1995).* Ed. Paul Vangelisti. New York: Marsilio, 1995.

Barnett, Nancy C. *Ilse Bing: Three Decades of Photography.* Meriden, CT: Meriden-Stinehour, 1985.

Barnouw, Erik. *The Sponsor: Notes on a Modern Potentate.* New York: Oxford UP, 1978.

Barthes, Roland. *Camera Lucida: Reflections on Photography.* Trans. Richard Howard. New York: Hill and Wang, 1982.

Bartlett, Lee, ed. *The Beats: Essays in Criticism.* Jefferson, NC: McFarland, 1981.

Baxandall, Michael. *Shadows and Enlightenment.* New Haven: Yale UP, 1995.

Beaty, Bart. *Fredric Wertham and the Critique of Mass Culture.* Jackson: UP of Mississippi, 2005.

Beja, Morris. *Perspectives on Orson Welles.* New York: G. K. Hall, 1995.

Belgrad, Daniel. *The Culture of Spontaneity: Improvisation and the Arts in Postwar America.* Chicago: U of Chicago P, 1998.

———. "The Transnational Counterculture: Beat-Mexican Intersections." *Reconstructing the Beats.* Ed. Jennie Skerl. New York: Palgrave Macmillan, 2004. 27–40.

Bell, Daniel. *The End of Ideology: On the Exhaustion of Political Ideas in the Fifties.* Cambridge, MA: Harvard UP, 2000.

Bezner, Lili Corbus. *Photography and Politics in America: From the New Deal into the Cold War.* Baltimore: Johns Hopkins UP, 1999.

Biesen, Sheri Chinen. *Blackout: World War II and the Origins of Film Noir.* Baltimore: Johns Hopkins UP, 2005.

Bilsker, Richard. *On Jung.* Belmont, CA: Wadsworth/Thomson Learning, 2002.

Bloom, Harold. *The Anxiety of Influence: A Theory of Poetry.* Oxford: Oxford UP, 1997.

Booker, M. Keith. *Strange TV: Innovative Television Series from "The Twilight Zone" to "The X-Files."* Westport, CT: Greenwood, 2002.

Borde, Raymond, and Etienne Chaumeton. *A Panorama of American Film Noir, 1941–1953.* 1955. Trans. Paul Hammond. San Francisco: City Lights, 2002.

Borhan, Pierre. "The Double of a Life." Introduction. *André Kertész: His Life and Work.* Ed. Borhan. Boston: Little, Brown, 1994. 8–45.

Bould, Mark. *Film Noir: From Berlin to Sin City.* London: Wallflower, 2005.

Boyer, Paul. *By the Bomb's Early Light: American Thought and Culture at the Dawn of the Atomic Age.* Chapel Hill: U of North Carolina P, 1994.

Bradley, John, ed. *Atomic Ghost: Poets Respond to the Nuclear Age.* Minneapolis: Coffee House, 1995.

Bresnick, Adam. "Prosopoetic Compulsion: Reading the Uncanny in Freud and Hoffman." *Germanic Review: Literature, Culture, Theory* 71.2 (1996): 114–32.

Brians, Paul. *Nuclear Holocausts: Atomic War in Fiction (1895–1984)*. Kent: Kent State UP, 1987.

Brinkley, Alan. "The Illusion of Unity in Cold War Culture." *Rethinking Cold War Culture*. Ed. Peter J. Kuznick and James Gilbert. Washington: Smithsonian Institution, 2001. 61–73.

Britzolakis, Christina. "Conversation amongst the Ruins: Plath and Chirico." *Eye Rhymes: Sylvia Plath's Art of the Visual*. Ed. Kathleen Connors and Sally Bayley. Oxford: Oxford UP, 2007. 167–82.

Brookman, Philip. "The Silence of Recognition: Exhibiting Robert Frank's Americans." *Looking In: Robert Frank's "The Americans."* Ed. Sarah Greenough. Washington: National Gallery of Art, 2009. 324–32.

Brown, Lloyd W. *Amiri Baraka*. Boston: Twayne, 1980.

Buchloh, Benjamin H. D. Notes. *Shadows and Other Signs of Life*. By Andy Warhol. Cologne: Walther König and La Galerie Chantal Crousel, 2007.

Callow, Simon. *The Night of the Hunter*. London: British Film Institute, 2000.

Campbell, Neil. "Cold War 'Containment Culture' and Photography: Robert Frank's *The Americans* and the 1950s." *American Visual Cultures*. Ed. David Holloway and John Beck. London: Continuum, 2005. 142–49.

Cartier-Bresson, Henri. *The Mind's Eye: Writings on Photography and Photographers*. New York: Aperture, 1999.

Cassady, Neal. Letter to Neal Cassady [from Allen Ginsberg]. Box 2, file 1. 1950. Harry Ransom Center. Austin, TX.

———. Prose piece. Box 1, file 1. 1950. Harry Ransom Center. Austin, TX.

Charters, Ann. *Kerouac: A Biography*. New York: St. Martin's, 1987.

———. "The Past Is the Root of the Future." *Un Homme Grand: Jack Kerouac at the Crossroads of Many Cultures*. Ed. Pierre Anctil, Louis Dupont, Rémi Ferland, and Eric Waddell. Ottawa: Carleton UP, 1990. 181–94.

———. "'True-Story' Novels as Autobiography: The Influence of *The Shadow* on Jack Kerouac's *Doctor Sax*." *Writing Lives: American Biography and Autobiography*. Ed. Hans Bak and Hans Krabbendam. Amsterdam: VU UP, 1998. 97–105.

Cixous, Hélène. "Fiction and Its Phantoms: A Reading of Freud's *Das Unheimliche* (The 'uncanny')." *New Literary History* 7.3 (Spring 1976): 525–48.

Clark, Clifford E., Jr. "Ranch-House Suburbia: Ideals and Realities." *Recasting America: Culture and Politics in the Age of Cold War*. Ed. Lary May. Chicago: U of Chicago P, 1989. 171–91.

Clarke, Graham. "'Lost Connections': Post-war American Photography and the Imagery of Strangeness." *A Permanent Etcetera: Cross-Cultural Perspectives on Post-war America*. Ed. A. Robert Lee. London: Pluto, 1993. 70–85.

Cochran, David. *American Noir: Underground Writers and Filmmakers of the Postwar Era*. Washington: Smithsonian Institution, 2000.

Comito, Terry. *"Touch of Evil": Orson Welles, Director*. New Brunswick, NJ: Rutgers UP, 1985.

Communist Blueprint for Conquest. US Department of the Army. 1956. 16-millimeter black-and-white print. Fort Devens Collection, Harvard Film Archive, Harvard Library.

Communist Target Youth. US Department of Defense, Armed Forces Information and Education. 1961/1962. 16-millimeter black-and-white print. Fort Devens Collection, Harvard Film Archive, Harvard Library.

The Communist Weapon of Allure. US Department of Defense, Armed Forces Information and Education. 1956. 16-millimeter black-and-white print. Fort Devens Collection, Harvard Film Archive, Harvard University Library.

Coontz, Stephanie. *The Way We Never Were: American Families and the Nostalgia Trap*. New York: Basic, 1992.

Couchman, Jeffrey. *"The Night of the Hunter": A Biography of a Film*. Evanston, IL: Northwestern UP, 2009.

Cox, Jim. *Radio Crime Fighters: Over 300 Programs from the Golden Age*. Jefferson, NC: McFarland, 2002.

Creeley, Robert. Introduction. *Book of Dreams*. By Jack Kerouac. San Francisco: City Lights, 2001. v–xii.

Damon, Maria. *The Dark End of the Street: Margins in American Vanguard Poetry*. Minneapolis: U of Minnesota P, 1993.

Darsey, James. *The Prophetic Tradition and Radical Rhetoric in America*. New York: New York UP, 1997.

Davenport, Guy. "Ralph Eugene Meatyard." *Ralph Eugene Meatyard*. By Davenport. New York: International Center for Photography, Steidl, 2004. 15–19.

Davidson, Michael. *Guys Like Us: Citing Masculinity in Cold War Poetics*. Chicago: U of Chicago P, 2004.

DeCarava, Roy. *The Sound I Saw: The Jazz Photographs of Roy DeCarava: January 20 to March 20, 1983*. New York: Studio Museum in Harlem, 1983.

De Hart, Jane Sherron. "Containment at Home: Gender, Sexuality, and National Identity in Cold War America." *Rethinking Cold War Culture*. Ed. Peter J. Kuznick and James Gilbert. Washington: Smithsonian Institution, 2001. 124–55.

Deleuze, Gilles. *Negotiations*. Trans. Martin Joughin. New York: Columbia UP, 1995.

Deleuze, Gilles, and Felix Guattari. *Anti-Oedipus: Capitalism and Schizophrenia.* Trans. Robert Hurley, Mark Seem, and Helen R. Lane. Minneapolis: U of Minnesota P, 1983.

D'Emilio, John. *Sexual Politics, Sexual Communities: The Making of a Homosexual Minority in the United States, 1940–1970.* Chicago: U of Chicago P, 1983.

Derrida, Jacques. *Specters of Marx: The State of Debt, the Work of Mourning and the New International.* Trans. Peggy Kamuf. New York: Routledge, 1994.

Descartes, Renè. *Meditations on First Philosophy in Which the Existence of God and the Distinction of the Soul from the Body Are Demonstrated.* Trans. Donald A. Cress. Indianapolis: Hackett, 1993.

Diggory, Terence. "What Abstract Art Means in *Pull My Daisy.*" *Reconstructing the Beats.* Ed. Jennie Skerl. New York: Palgrave Macmillan, 2004. 135–49.

Doherty, Thomas. *Cold War, Cool Medium: Television, McCarthyism, and American Culture.* New York: Columbia UP, 2003.

Edwards, Justin D. *Gothic Passages: Racial Ambiguity and the American Gothic.* Iowa City: U of Iowa P, 2003.

Eisinger, Joel. *Trace and Transformation: American Criticism of Photography in the Modernist Period.* Albuquerque: U of New Mexico P, 1995.

Evans, Joyce A. *Celluloid Mushroom Clouds: Hollywood and the Atomic Bomb.* Boulder: Westview, 1998.

Fariña, Richard. *Been Down So Long It Looks Like Up to Me.* 1966. New York: Penguin, 1996.

Ferguson, Frances. "The Nuclear Sublime." *Diacritics* 20 (Summer 1984): 4–9.

Ferretter, Luke. *Sylvia Plath's Fiction: A Critical Study.* Edinburgh: Edinburgh UP, 2010.

Fiedler, Leslie. *Love and Death in the American Novel.* New York: Anchor, 1992.

Field, Douglas. Introduction. *American Cold War Culture.* Ed. Field. Edinburgh: Edinburgh UP, 2005. 1–13.

Filene, Peter. "'Cold War Culture' Doesn't Say It All." *Rethinking Cold War Culture.* Ed. Peter J. Kuznick and James Gilbert. Washington: Smithsonian Institution, 2001. 156–74.

Flinn, Carol. "Sound, Woman and the Bomb: Dismembering the 'Great Whatsit' in *Kiss Me Deadly.*" *Wide Angle* 8.3–4 (1986): 115–27.

Foucault, Michel. *Aesthetics, Method, and Epistemology.* Trans. Robert Hurley et al. New York: Penguin, 2000.

Frank, Robert. *The Americans.* Introduction by Jack Kerouac. 1958. Millerton, NY: Aperture, 1978.

———. *Hold Still: Keep Going.* Essen, Ger.: Museum Folkwang, 2001.

———. *The Lines of My Hand.* 1972. New York: Pantheon, 1989.

———. *Moving Out.* Ed. Sarah Greenough and Philip Brookman. Washington: National Gallery of Art, c. 1994.

Fraterrigo, Elizabeth. *"Playboy" and the Making of the Good Life in Modern America.* Oxford: Oxford UP, 2009.

French, Warren. *Jack Kerouac.* Boston: Twayne, 1986.

Freud, Sigmund. *The Interpretation of Dreams.* Trans. Joyce Crick. Oxford: Oxford UP, 1999.

———. *The Uncanny.* Trans. David McClintock. New York: Penguin, 2003.

Frizot, Michel. *A New History of Photography.* Cologne: Könemann, 1998.

Gallafent, Edward. "Kiss Me, Deadly." *The Movie Book of Film Noir.* Ed. Ian Cameron. London: Studio Vista, 1992. 240–46.

Gallant, Christine. *Tabooed Jung: Marginality as Power.* New York: New York UP, 1996.

Gay, Peter. *Freud: A Life for Our Time.* New York: Norton, 2006.

Gewirtz, Isaac. *Beatific Soul: Jack Kerouac on the Road.* London and New York: Scala and the New York Public Library, 2007.

Giamo, Ben. *Kerouac, the Word and the Way: Prose Artist as Spiritual Quester.* Carbondale: Southern Illinois UP, 2000.

Gibson, Walter B. "The Chinese Disks." *Two Classic Adventures of "The Shadow."* Encinitas, CA: Nostalgia Ventures, 2006.

———. "The Red Blot." *Two Classic Adventures of "The Shadow."* Encinitas, CA: Nostalgia Ventures, 2006.

———. "The Voodoo Master." *Two Classic Adventures of "The Shadow."* Encinitas, CA: Nostalgia Ventures, 2006.

Ginsberg, Allen. *As Ever: The Collected Correspondence of Allen Ginsberg and Neal Cassady.* Ed. Barry Gifford. Berkeley: Creative Arts, 1978.

———. *The Book of Martyrdom and Artifice: First Journals and Poems.* Ed. Juanita Lieberman-Plimpton and Bill Morgan. Cambridge, MA: Da Capo, 2006.

———. *Collected Poems: 1947–1980.* New York: Harper, 1984.

———. *Composed on the Tongue.* Ed. Donald Allen. Bolinas, CA: Grey Fox, 1980.

———. *Empty Mirror.* New York: Totem and Corinth, 1961.

———. *The Gates of Wrath: Rhymed Poems, 1948–1952.* Bolinas, CA: Grey Fox, 1972.

———. *Jack Kerouac and Allen Ginsberg: The Letters.* Ed. Bill Morgan and David Stanford. New York: Viking, 2010.

———. *Journals: Early Fifties Early Sixties.* Ed. Gordon Ball. New York: Grove, 1977.

———. *The Letters of Allen Ginsberg*. Ed. Bill Morgan. Cambridge, MA: Da Capo, 2006.

———. Letter to Neal Cassady. Box 2, file 1. 1950. Harry Ransom Center. Austin, TX.

———. Letter to Neal Cassady. Box 2, file 1. 1953. Harry Ransom Center. Austin, TX.

———. Letter to Jack Kerouac. Box 1, file 4. 1948. Harry Ransom Center. Austin, TX.

———. Letter to Jack Kerouac. Box 1, file 4. 1950. Harry Ransom Center. Austin, TX.

———. *Spontaneous Mind: Selected Interviews, 1958–1996*. New York: Harper, 2001.

———. Typescript. Box 1, file 2. No date. Harry Ransom Center. Austin, TX.

———. "The Visions of the Great Rememberer." Afterword. *Visions of Cody*. By Jack Kerouac. New York: Penguin, 1993. 399-430.

Ginsberg, Allen, and Louis Ginsberg. *Family Business: Selected Letters between a Father and Son*. Ed. Michael Schumacher. New York: Bloomsbury, 2001.

Goddu, Teresa A. *Gothic America: Narrative, History, and Nation*. New York: Columbia UP, 1997.

Goldstein, Donald M., Katherine V. Dillon, and J. Michael Wenger. *Rain of Ruin: A Photographic History of Hiroshima and Nagasaki*. Washington: Brassey's, 1995.

Gombrich, E. H. *Shadows: The Depiction of Cast Shadows in Western Art*. London: National Gallery, 1995.

———. *The Story of Art*. London: Phaidon, 2006.

Gordon, Avery F. *Ghostly Matters: Haunting and the Sociological Imagination*. Minneapolis: U of Minnesota P, 1997.

Gordon, Lewis R. "Through the Twilight Zone of Nonbeing: Two Exemplars of Race in Serling's Classic Series." *Philosophy in "The Twilight Zone."* Ed. Noel Carroll and Lester H. Hunt. Chichester, UK: Blackwell, 2009. 111–22.

Grace, Nancy M. *Jack Kerouac and the Literary Imagination*. New York: Palgrave Macmillan, 2007.

———. "ruth weiss's DESERT JOURNAL: A Modern-Beat-Pomo Performance." *Reconstructing the Beats*. Ed. Jennie Skerl. New York: Palgrave Macmillan, 2004. 57–72.

Green, Jonathan. *American Photography: A Critical History, 1945 to the Present*. New York: Abrams, 1984.

Greenough, Sarah. "Blowing Down Bleecker Street: Destroying *The Americans*." *Looking In: Robert Frank's "The Americans."* Ed. Greenough. Washington: National Gallery of Art, 2009. 314–23.

———. "Disordering the Senses: Guggenheim Fellowship." *Looking In: Robert Frank's "The Americans."* Ed. Greenough. Washington: National Gallery of Art, 2009. 120–39.

———. "Resisting Intelligence: Zurich to New York." *Looking In: Robert Frank's "The Americans."* Ed. Greenough. Washington: National Gallery of Art, 2009. 2–37.

Guimond, James. *American Photography and the American Dream*. Chapel Hill: U of North Carolina P, 1991.

Gunning, Tom. "Invisible Cities, Visible Cinema: Illuminating Shadows in Late Film Noir." *Comparative Critical Studies* 6.3 (October 2009): 319–32.

———. "To Scan a Ghost: The Ontology of Mediated Vision." *Grey Room* 26 (Winter 2007): 94–127.

Hachiya, Michihiko. *Hiroshima Diary*. Trans. Warner Wells. New York: Avon, 1955.

Hale, Nathan G., Jr. *The Rise and Crisis of Psychoanalysis in the United States: Freud and the Americans, 1917–1985*. Oxford: Oxford UP, 1995.

Hales, Peter B. "The Atomic Sublime." *American Studies* 32 (Spring 1991): 5–31.

Harris, William J. *The Poetry and Poetics of Amiri Baraka: The Jazz Aesthetic*. Columbia: U of Missouri P, 1985.

Heilpern, John. Profile. *William Klein: Photographs*. New York: Aperture, 1981. 7–22.

Hendershot, Cyndy. *Anti-Communism and Popular Culture in Mid-century America*. Jefferson, NC: McFarland, 2003.

Henriksen, Margot A. *Dr. Strangelove's America: Society and Culture in the Atomic Age*. Berkeley: U of California P, 1997.

Hersey, John. *Hiroshima*. New York: Bantam, 1986.

Hertz, Neil. *The End of the Line: Essays on Psychoanalysis and the Sublime*. New York: Columbia UP, 1985.

Hill, Rodney. "Mapping *The Twilight Zone*'s Cultural and Mythological Terrain." *The Essential Science Fiction Reader*. Ed. J. P. Telotte. Lexington: UP of Kentucky, 2008. 111–26

Hirsch, Robert. *Seizing the Light: A History of Photography*. Boston: McGraw-Hill, 2000.

Holdstock, Douglas, and Frank Barnaby, eds. *Hiroshima and Nagasaki: Retrospect and Prospect*. London: Frank Cass, 1995.

Holmes, John Clellon. Introduction. *Neurotica: 1948–1951*. Ed. Jay Landesman. London: Jay Landesman, 1981. 7–13.

Hrebeniak, Michael. *Action Writing: Jack Kerouac's Wild Form*. Carbondale: Southern Illinois UP, 2006.

Hunt, Tim. *Kerouac's Crooked Road: Development of a Fiction*. Hamden, CT: Archon, 1981.

———. *The Textuality of Soulwork: Jack Kerouac's Quest for Spontaneous Prose.* Ann Arbor: U of Michigan P, 2014.

Jacobs, David L. "Seeing the Unseen, Saying the Unsayable." *Ralph Eugene Meatyard: An American Visionary.* Ed. Barbara Tannenbaum. Ohio: Akron Art Museum, 1991. 53–78.

Jameson, Fredric. *The Political Unconscious: Narrative as a Socially Symbolic Act.* London: Routledge Classics, 2002.

Jay, Martin. *Downcast Eyes: The Denigration of Vision in Twentieth-Century French Thought.* Berkeley: U of California P, 1994.

———. "The Uncanny Nineties." *Salmagundi* 108 (Fall 1995): 20–29.

Jentsch, Ernst. "On the Psychology of the Uncanny (1906)." *Angelaki: A New Journal in Philosophy, Literature, and the Social Sciences* 1.2 (1996): 7–21.

Johnson, David K. *The Lavender Scare: The Cold War Persecution of Gays and Lesbians in the Federal Government.* Chicago: U of Chicago P, 2004.

Johnson, William. "Orson Welles: Of Time and Loss." *Film Quarterly* 21.1 (Autumn 1967): 13–24.

Jones, Janna. "Living with the Bomb: The Retreat to the Suburban Bomb Shelter." *The Impact of the Cold War on American Popular Culture.* Ed. Elaine McClarnand and Steve Goodson. Carrolton: State U of West Georgia P, 1999. 1–13.

Jones, James T. *Jack Kerouac's Duluoz Legend: The Mythic Form of an Autobiographical Fiction.* Carbondale: Southern Illinois UP, 1999.

———. "Sharing a Shadow: The Image of the Shrouded Stranger in the Works of Jack Kerouac and Allen Ginsberg." *Post-Jungian Criticism: Theory and Practice.* Ed. James S. Baumlin, Tita French Baumlin, and George H. Jensen. Albany: State U of New York P, 2004. 223–41.

Jung, C. G. "The Archetypes of the Collective Unconscious." *The Collected Works of C. G. Jung: The Archetypes and the Collective Unconscious.* Trans. R. F. C. Hull. Vol. 9. Princeton: Princeton UP, 1977. 3–41.

———. "The Fight with the Shadow." *The Collected Works of C. G. Jung: Civilization in Transition.* Trans. R. F. C. Hull. Vol. 10. Princeton: Princeton UP, 1964. 218–26.

———. *Memories, Dreams, Reflections.* Ed. Aniela Jaffé. Trans. Richard Winston and Clara Winston. New York: Pantheon, 1973.

———. *The Portable Jung.* Ed. Joseph Campbell. Trans. R. F. C. Hull. New York: Penguin, 1976.

———. "The Problems of Modern Psychotherapy." *The Collected Works of C. G. Jung: The Practice of Psychotherapy.* Ed. Sir Herbert Read, Michael Fordham, and Gerhard Adler. Trans. R. F. C. Hull. Vol. 16. London: Routledge and Kegan Paul, 1954. 53–75.

Kackman, Michael. *Citizen Spy: Television, Espionage, and Cold War Culture.* Minneapolis: U of Minnesota P, 2005.

Kavka, Misha. "The Gothic on Screen." *The Cambridge Companion to Gothic Fiction.* Ed. Jerrold E. Hogle. Cambridge: Cambridge UP, 2010. 209–28.

Keen, Sam. *Faces of the Enemy: Reflections of the Hostile Imagination.* San Francisco: Harper and Row, 1986.

Kerouac, Jack. *Book of Dreams.* 1960. San Francisco: City Lights, 2001.

———. *Dr. Sax: Faust Part Three.* 1959. New York: Grove Weidenfeld, 1987.

———. *Good Blonde and Others.* Ed. Donald Allen. San Francisco: Grey Fox, 1993.

———. "Letters from Jack Kerouac to Ed White, 1947–68." *Missouri Review* 17.3 (1994): 107–60.

———. Letter to Neal Cassady. Box 2, file 2. 1955. Harry Ransom Center. Austin, TX.

———. *Mexico City Blues (242 Choruses).* New York: Grove Press, 1959.

———. *On the Road.* 1957. New York: Penguin, 1976.

———. *On the Road: The Original Scroll.* New York: Penguin, 2008.

———. *Selected Letters, 1940–1956.* Ed. Ann Charters. New York: Penguin, 1995.

———. *Selected Letters, 1957–1969.* Ed. Ann Charters. New York: Viking, 1999.

———. *Visions of Cody.* 1972. New York: Penguin Books, 1993.

———. *Windblown World: The Journals of Jack Kerouac, 1947–1954.* Ed. Douglas Brinkley. New York: Penguin, 2006.

Kerr, Paul. "Out of What Past? Notes on the B *Film Noir.*" *The Contemporary Hollywood Reader.* Ed. Toby Miller. London: Routledge, 2009. 223–39.

Kirstein, Lincoln. *William Rimmer.* Catalog. New York and Boston: Whitney Museum of American Art and Museum of Fine Arts, 1946–47.

Kiss Me Deadly. Dir. Robert Aldrich. 1955. MGM Home Entertainment, 2001. DVD.

Klein, William. *Life Is Good and Good for You in New York.* 1956. San Francisco: San Francisco Museum of Art, 1995.

———. *New York 1954.55.* Manchester, UK: Dewi Lewis, 1995.

Kraszewski, Jon. "Do Not Go Gentle into That Twilight: Rod Serling's Challenge to 1960s' Television Production." *New Review of Film and Television Studies* 6 (December 2008): 343–64.

Kristeva, Julia. *Powers of Horror: An Essay on Abjection.* Trans. Leon S. Roudiez. New York: Columbia UP, 1982.

Kuznick, Peter J., and James Gilbert. Introduction. *Rethinking Cold War Culture.* Ed. Kuznick and Gilbert. Washington: Smithsonian Institution, 2001. 1–13.

Lacey, Henry C. *To Raise, Destroy, and Create: The Poetry, Drama, and Fiction of Imamu Amiri Baraka (Le Roi Jones)*. Troy, NY: Whitston, 1981.

Laliberté, Norman, and Alex Mogelon. *Silhouettes, Shadows, and Cutouts: History and Modern Use*. New York: Reinhold, 1968.

Lammers, Ann Conrad. *In God's Shadow: The Collaboration of Victor White and C. G. Jung*. New York: Paulist, 1994.

Landesman, Jay. *Neurotica: 1948–1951*. Introd. by John Clellon Holmes. London: Jay Landesman, 1981.

Lang, Robert. "Looking for the 'Great Whatzit': *Kiss Me Deadly* and Film Noir." *Perspectives on Film Noir*. Ed. R. Barton Palmer. New York: G. K. Hall, 1996. 171–84.

Lardas, John. *The Bop Apocalypse: The Religious Visions of Kerouac, Ginsberg, and Burroughs*. Urbana: U of Illinois P, 2001.

Laughlin, Clarence John. *The Personal Eye*. Philadelphia: Philadelphia Museum of Art, 1973.

Leeper, Jill. "Crossing Musical Borders: The Soundtrack for *Touch of Evil*." *Soundtrack Available: Essays on Film and Popular Music*. Ed. Pamela Robertson Wojcik and Arthur Knight. Durham: Duke UP, 2001. 226–43.

Levering, Ralph B. *The Cold War: A Post–Cold War History*. Arlington Heights, IL: Harlan Davidson, 1994.

Lhamon, W. T. *Deliberate Speed: The Origins of a Cultural Style in the American 1950s*. New pref. Cambridge, MA: Harvard UP, 2002.

Lifton, Betty Jean. *Return to Hiroshima*. New York: Atheneum, 1970.

Lifton, Robert Jay, and Richard Falk. *Indefensible Weapons: The Political and Psychological Case against Nuclearism*. New York: Basic, 1982.

Lipsitz, George. "The Possessive Investment in Whiteness: Racialized Social Democracy and the 'White' Problem in American Studies." *American Quarterly* 4.3 (September 1995): 369–87.

Maher, Paul, Jr. *Kerouac: The Definitive Biography*. Lanham, MD: Taylor Trade, 2004.

Masco, Joseph. *The Nuclear Borderlands: The Manhattan Project in Post–Cold War New Mexico*. Princeton: Princeton UP, 2006.

Matovich, Richard M. *A Concordance to the Collected Poems of Sylvia Plath*. New York: Garland, 1986.

May, Elaine Tyler. *Homeward Bound: American Families in the Cold War Era*. New York: Basic, 1988.

McDonnell, Brian. "Film Noir Style." *Encyclopedia of Film Noir*. Ed. Geoff Mayer and Brian McDonnell. Westport, CT: Greenwood, 2007. 70–81.

McNally, Dennis. *Desolate Angel: Jack Kerouac, the Beat Generation, and America*. New York: Random, 1979.

Meacham, Rebecca. "'The Sun's Children': Shadow Work in the Poetry of LeRoi Jones / Imamu Amiri Baraka." *Post-Jungian Criticism: Theory and Practice*. Ed. James S. Baumlin, Tita French Baumlin, and George H. Jensen. Albany: State U of New York P, 2004. 199–221.

Meatyard, Ralph Eugene. "My Aims." *Ralph Eugene Meatyard*. By Guy Davenport. New York: International Center for Photography, Steidl, 2004. 33–35.

Melville, Herman. "Benito Cereno." *Selected Tales and Poems by Herman Melville*. Ed. Richard Chase. Fort Worth: Harcourt, 1950. 3–91.

Merrill, Thomas F. *Allen Ginsberg*. New York: Twayne, 1969.

Meyerowitz, Joanne, ed. *Not June Cleaver: Women and Gender in Postwar America, 1945–1960*. Philadelphia: Temple UP, 1994.

Mills, C. Wright. *White Collar: The American Middle Classes*. Oxford: Oxford UP, 2002.

Miyao, Daisuke. *The Aesthetic of Shadow: Lighting and Japanese Cinema*. Durham: Duke UP, 2013.

Moore, Alan, and Dave Gibbons. *Watchmen*. 1986. London: Titan, 2007.

Morrison, Toni. *Playing in the Dark: Whiteness and the Literary Imagination*. New York: Vintage, 1992.

Mortenson, Erik. *Capturing the Beat Moment: Cultural Politics and the Poetics of Presence*. Carbondale: Southern Illinois UP, 2010.

Nadel, Alan. *Containment Culture: American Narrative, Postmodernism, and the Atomic Age*. Durham: Duke UP, 1995.

Naremore, James. *The Magic World of Orson Welles*. Dallas: Southern Methodist UP, 1989.

———. *More Than Night: Film Noir in Its Contexts*. Berkeley: U of California P, 1998.

Nelson, Deborah. *Pursuing Privacy in Cold War America*. New York: Columbia UP, 2002.

Neusüss, Floris M., and Renate Heyne. "Rayographs." *Man Ray: Photography and Its Double*. Ed. Emmanuelle de l'Ecotais and Alain Sayag. Corte Madera, CA: Gingko, 1998. 186–206.

Nicosia, Gerald. *Memory Babe: A Critical Biography of Jack Kerouac*. New York: Grove, 1983.

The Night of the Hunter. Dir. Charles Laughton. 1955. MGM Home Entertainment, 2002. DVD.

Noll, Richard. *The Jung Cult: Origins of a Charismatic Movement*. Princeton: Princeton UP, 1994.

Oakes, Guy. *The Imaginary War: Civil Defense and American Cold War Culture*. Oxford: Oxford UP, 1994.

Our Moral Defenses. US Department of Defense, Armed Forces International Films. Ca. 1951. 16-millimeter black-and-white print. Fort Devens Collection, Harvard Film Archive, Harvard Library.

Papageorge, Tod. *Walker Evans and Robert Frank: An Essay on Influence.* New Haven, CT: Yale University Art Gallery, 1981.

Paton, Fiona. "Beyond Bakhtin: Towards a Cultural Stylistics." *College English* 63 (November 2000): 166–94.

———. "Reconceiving Kerouac: Why We Should Teach *Doctor Sax.*" *The Beat Generation: Critical Essays.* Ed. Kostas Myrsiades. New York: Peter Lang, 2002. 121–53.

Pavitt, Jane. "The Bomb in the Brain." *Cold War Modern: Design 1945–1970.* Ed. David Crowley and Jane Pavitt. London: V and A, 2008. 101–21.

Peel, Robin. *Writing Back: Sylvia Plath and Cold War Politics.* Madison, NJ: Fairleigh Dickinson UP, 2002.

Phillips, Sandra S. "William Klein's New York." *Life Is Good and Good for You in New York.* By William Klein. San Francisco: San Francisco Museum of Art, 1995. 3–26.

Place, Janey and Lowell Peterson. "Some Visual Motifs of Film Noir." 1974. *Film Noir Reader.* Ed. Alain Silver and James Ursini. New York: Limelight, 1998. 65–76.

Plath, Sylvia. *The Bell Jar.* 1963. London: Faber and Faber, 1988.

———. *The Collected Poems.* Ed. Ted Hughes. Cutchogue, NY: Buccaneer, 1981.

———. *Johnny Panic and the Bible of Dreams: Short Stories, Prose and Diary Excerpts.* New York: Harper, 1979.

———. *The Journals of Sylvia Plath.* Foreword by Ted Hughes. New York: Dial, 1982.

Plato. *The Republic.* Trans. G. M. A. Grube. Indianapolis: Hackett, 1992.

Pliny the Elder. *Natural History: A Selection.* Trans. John F. Healy. New York: Penguin, 1991.

Porfirio, Robert G. "No Way Out: Existential Motifs in the Film Noir." *Perspectives on Film Noir.* Ed. R. Barton Palmer. New York: Simon Schuster Macmillan, 1996. 115–28.

Prelude to War. Dir. Frank Capra. 1942. Echo Bridge Home Entertainment, 2001. DVD.

Presnell, Don, and Marty McGee. *A Critical History of Television's "The Twilight Zone," 1959–1964.* Jefferson, NC: McFarland, 1998.

Return to the Source: Philosophy and "The Matrix." Dir. Josh Oreck. Warner Brothers Entertainment, 2004. DVD.

Rhem, James. "Behind the Billboard or Lucybelle Unmasked." Preface. *The Family Album of Lucybelle Crater and Other Figurative Photographs.* By Ralph Eugene Meatyard. New York: D.A.P. / Distributed Art Publishers, 2002.

Ribuffo, Leo P. "Will the Sixties Never End? Or Perhaps at Least the Thirties? Or Maybe Even the Progressive Era? Contrarian Thoughts on Change and Continuity in American Political Culture at the Turn of the Millennium." *Rethinking Cold War Culture.* Ed. Peter J. Kuznick and James Gilbert. Washington: Smithsonian Institution, 2001. 201–23.

Riesman, David, Nathan Glazer, Reuel Denney. *The Lonely Crowd, Revised Edition: A Study of the Changing American Character.* New Haven: Yale UP, 2001.

Roach, Ronald R. "Archetypal Metaphor and *The Shadow* Radio Drama." *Popular Culture Review* 10 (August 1999): 101–9.

Robinson, Paul. *Freud and His Critics.* Berkeley: U of California P, 1993.

Rose, Jacqueline. *The Haunting of Sylvia Plath.* London: Virago, 1991.

Royle, Nicholas. *The Uncanny.* Manchester: Manchester UP, 2003.

Salvesen, Britt. "Harry Callahan: The Photographer at Work." *Harry Callahan: The Photographer at Work.* By Salvesen. Tucson: Center for Creative Photography, University of Arizona, 2006. 13–50.

Sandeen, Eric. *Picturing an Exhibition: "The Family of Man" and 1950s America.* Albuquerque: U of New Mexico P, 1995.

Sander, Gordon F. *Serling: The Rise and Twilight of Television's Last Angry Man.* New York: Dutton, 1992.

Savoy, Eric. Introduction. *American Gothic: New Interventions in a National Narrative.* Ed. Robert K. Martin and Eric Savoy. Iowa City: U of Iowa P, 1998. vii–xii.

———. "The Rise of American Gothic." *The Cambridge Companion to Gothic Fiction.* Ed. Jerrold E. Hogle. Cambridge: Cambridge UP, 2002. 167–88.

Schaefer, William. "Shadow Photographs, Ruins, and Shanghai's Projected Past." *PMLA* 122.1 (2007): 124–34.

Schrader, Paul. "Notes on *Film Noir.*" *Film Noir Reader.* Ed. Alain Silver and James Ursini. New York: Limelight, 2000. 53–63.

Schumacher, Michael. *Dharma Lion: A Critical Biography of Allen Ginsberg.* New York: St. Martin's, 1992.

The Shadow: A Detective Magazine 1.2 (1931). New York: Street and Smith Publications.

The Shadow Magazine. 13.1 (1935). New York: Street and Smith Publications.

The Shadow: Radio's Greatest Man of Mystery. CD collection. Cedar Knolls, NJ: Radio Spirits, 2006.

Sherry, Michael S. *In the Shadow of War: The United States since the 1930s.* New Haven: Yale UP, 1995.

Silver, Alain. "*Kiss Me Deadly*: Evidence of a Style." *Film Noir Reader*. Ed. Alain Silver and James Ursini. New York: Limelight, 2000. 209–35.

Sirridge, Mary. "The Treachery of the Commonplace." *Philosophy in "The Twilight Zone."* Ed. Noel Carroll and Lester H. Hunt. Chichester, UK: Blackwell, 2009. 58–76.

Slemmons, Rod. *Like a One-Eyed Cat: Photographs by Lee Friedlander, 1956–1987*. New York: Abrams, 1989.

Smith, Henry Holmes. "Across the Atlantic and Out of the Woods: Moholy-Nagy's Contribution to Photography in the United States." *Photographs of Moholy-Nagy: From the Collection of William Larson*. Ed. Leland D. Rice and David W. Steadman. Claremont, CA: Galleries of Pomona College. 13–18.

Smith, Robert C. *The Wounded Jung*. Evanston, IL: Northwestern UP, 1996.

Sollors, Werner. *Amiri Baraka / LeRoi Jones: The Quest for a "Populist Modernism."* New York: Columbia UP, 1978.

Sorensen, Roy. *Seeing Dark Things: The Philosophy of Shadows*. New York: Oxford UP, 2008.

Spicer, Andrew. *Film Noir*. Harlow, UK: Longman/Pearson Educational, 2002.

Steichen, Edward. Introduction. *The Family of Man*. Exhibition catalog. New York: Museum of Modern Art, 1986.

Steinbauer-Grötsch, Barbara. *Die lange Nacht der Schatten: Film noir und Filmexil*. Berlin: Bertz, 1997.

Stephenson, Gregory. *The Daybreak Boys: Essays on the Literature of the Beat Generation*. Carbondale: Southern Illinois UP, 1990.

Stevenson, Anne. *Bitter Fame: A Life of Sylvia Plath; The Celebrated and Controversial Biography of the Legendary Poet*. Boston: Houghton Mifflin, 1998.

Stoichita, Victor I. *A Short History of the Shadow*. London: Reaktion, 1999.

Stoichita, Victor I., et al. *La Sombra*. Exhibition catalog. Madrid: Fundacion Caja Madrid, 2009.

Storr, Robert. *Gerhard Richter: Doubt and Belief in Painting*. New York: Museum of Modern Art, 2003.

Strangeways, Al. *Sylvia Plath: The Shaping of Shadows*. London: Associated University Presses, 1998.

Stubbs, John. "The Evolution of Orson Welles's *Touch of Evil* from Novel to Film." *Cinema Journal* 24.2 (Winter 1985): 19–39.

Szarkowski, John. Foreword. *Harry Callahan: The Photographer at Work*. By Britt Salvesen. Tucson: Center for Creative Photography, University of Arizona, 2006. 13–50.

———. *Mirrors and Windows: American Photography since 1960*. New York: Museum of Modern Art, 1978. 11–26.

Takata, Ken. "Towards an Elegance of Movement—Walker Evans and Robert Frank Revisited." *Journal of American Culture* 12.1 (1989): 55–64.

Tanizaki, Junichirō. *In Praise of Shadows.* Trans. Thomas J. Harper. London: Vintage, 1991.

Tannenbaum, Barbara. "Fiction as a Higher Truth." *Ralph Eugene Meatyard: An American Visionary.* Ed. Tannenbaum. Ohio: Akron Art Museum, 1991. 13–52.

Taylor, Eugene. *Shadow Culture: Psychology and Spirituality in America.* Washington: Counterpoint, 1999.

Telotte, J. P. "In the Cinematic Zone of *The Twilight Zone.*" *Science Fiction Film and Television* 3.1 (2010): 1–17.

Theado, Matt. *Understanding Jack Kerouac.* Columbia: U of South Carolina P, 2000.

Titus, A. Costandina. "The Mushroom Cloud as Kitsch." *Atomic Culture: How We Learned to Stop Worrying and Love the Bomb.* Ed. Scott C. Zeman and Michael A. Amundson. Boulder: UP of Colorado, 2004. 101–24.

Tollin, Anthony. "Spotlight on *The Shadow.*" *Two Classic Adventures of "The Shadow."* Encinitas, CA: Nostalgia Ventures, 2006. 4–5.

Touch of Evil. Dir. Orson Welles. 1958. Universal Studios, 1986; 1998 restoration released 2000. DVD.

Trigilio, Tony. *Allen Ginsberg's Buddhist Poetics.* Carbondale: Southern Illinois UP, 2007.

Tuttle, William M., Jr. "America's Children in an Era of War, Hot and Cold: The Holocaust, the Bomb, and Child Rearing in the 1940s." *Rethinking Cold War Culture.* Ed. Peter J. Kuznick and James Gilbert. Washington: Smithsonian Institution, 2001. 14–34.

The Twilight Zone: The Complete Definitive Collection. Image Entertainment, 2006. DVD.

Tytell, John. *Naked Angels: The Lives and Literature of the Beat Generation.* New York: McGraw-Hill, 1976.

Venuti, Lawrence. "Rod Serling, Television Censorship, *The Twilight Zone.*" *Western Humanities Review* 35 (Winter 1981): 354–66.

Vernet, Marc. "Film Noir on the Edge of Doom." *Shades of Noir: A Reader.* Ed. Joan Copjec. London: Verso, 1993. 1–31.

Vettel-Becker, Patricia. *Shooting from the Hip: Photography, Masculinity, and Postwar America.* Minneapolis: U of Minnesota P, 2005.

Walker, Hamza. "Cut It Out 1997." *Witness to Her Art.* Ed. Rhea Anastas with Michael Brenson. New York: Center for Curatorial Studies, Bard College, 2006. 280–82.

Walker, Michael. Introduction. *The Book of Film Noir.* Ed. Ian Cameron. New York: Continuum, 1992. 8–38.

Wallace, David Foster. *Infinite Jest*. 1996. New York: Back Bay, 2006.

Wartenberg, Thomas E. "Blending Fiction and Reality: 'The Odyssey of Flight 33.'" *Philosophy in "The Twilight Zone."* Ed. Noel Carroll and Lester H. Hunt. Chichester, UK: Blackwell, 2009. 123–35.

Watts, Jerry Gafio. *Amiri Baraka: The Politics and Art of a Black Intellectual*. New York: New York UP, 2001.

Weber, Samuel. "The Sideshow, or: Remarks on a Canny Moment." *Modern Language Notes* 88 (1973): 1102–33.

Weinreich, Regina. *The Spontaneous Poetics of Jack Kerouac: A Study of the Fiction*. Carbondale: Southern Illinois UP, 1987.

Westerbeck, Colin, and Joel Meyerowitz. *Bystander: A History of Street Photography*. Boston: Bulfinch, 1994.

Whitfield, Stephen J. *The Culture of the Cold War*. Baltimore: Johns Hopkins UP, 1991.

———. "Still the Best Catch There Is: Joseph Heller's *Catch-22*." *Rethinking Cold War Culture*. Ed. Peter J. Kuznick and James Gilbert. Washington: Smithsonian Institutional, 2001. 175–200.

Whyte, William H. *The Organizational Man*. Philadelphia: U of Pennsylvania P, 2002.

Williams-Forson, Psyche A. *Building Houses Out of Chicken Legs: Black Women, Food, and Power*. Chapel Hill: U of North Carolina P, 2006.

Wilson, Sloan. *The Man in the Gray Flannel Suit*. Cambridge, MA: Da Capo, 2002.

Worland, Rick. "Sign-Posts Up Ahead: *The Twilight Zone*, *The Outer Limits*, and TV Political Fantasy 1959–65." *Science Fiction Studies* 23.1 (March 1996): 103–22.

Young, Cynthia. "Interview with Guy Davenport." *Ralph Eugene Meatyard*. By Guy Davenport. New York: International Center for Photography, Steidl, 2004. 21–31.

———. Introduction. *Ralph Eugene Meatyard*. By Guy Davenport. New York: International Center for Photography, Steidl, 2004. 8–13.

Zicree, Marc Scott. *The "Twilight Zone" Companion*. Beverly Hills: Silman-James, 1989.

INDEX

ERIK MORTENSON is an assistant professor in the Department of English and Comparative Literature at Koç University in Istanbul, Turkey. His first book, *Capturing the Beat Moment: Cultural Politics and the Poetics of Presence*, was selected as a *Choice* Outstanding Academic Title.